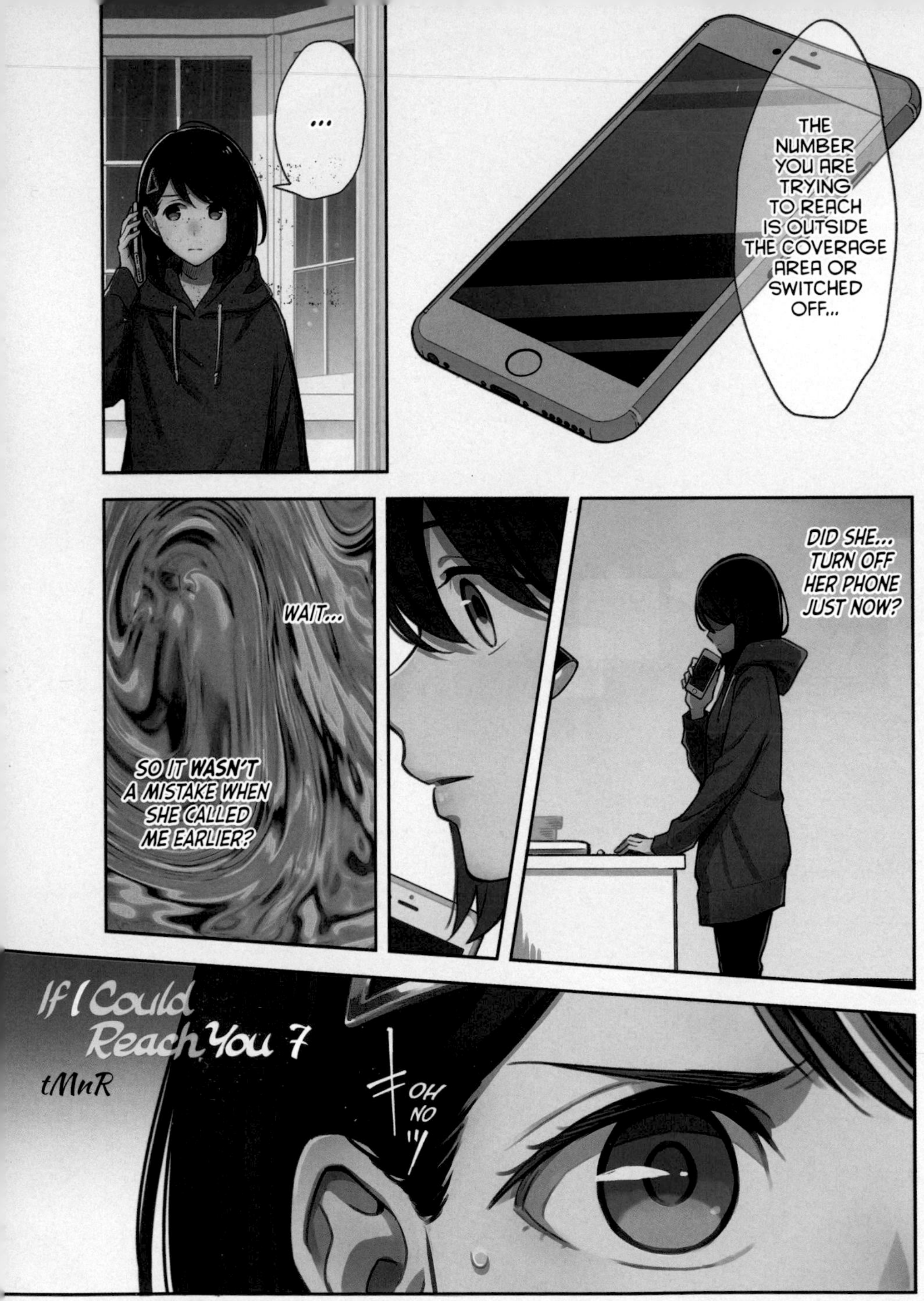
THE NUMBER YOU ARE TRYING TO REACH IS OUTSIDE THE COVERAGE AREA OR SWITCHED OFF...
...
DID SHE... TURN OFF HER PHONE JUST NOW?
WAIT...
SO IT WASN'T A MISTAKE WHEN SHE CALLED ME EARLIER?
OH NO
If I Could Reach You 7
tMnR

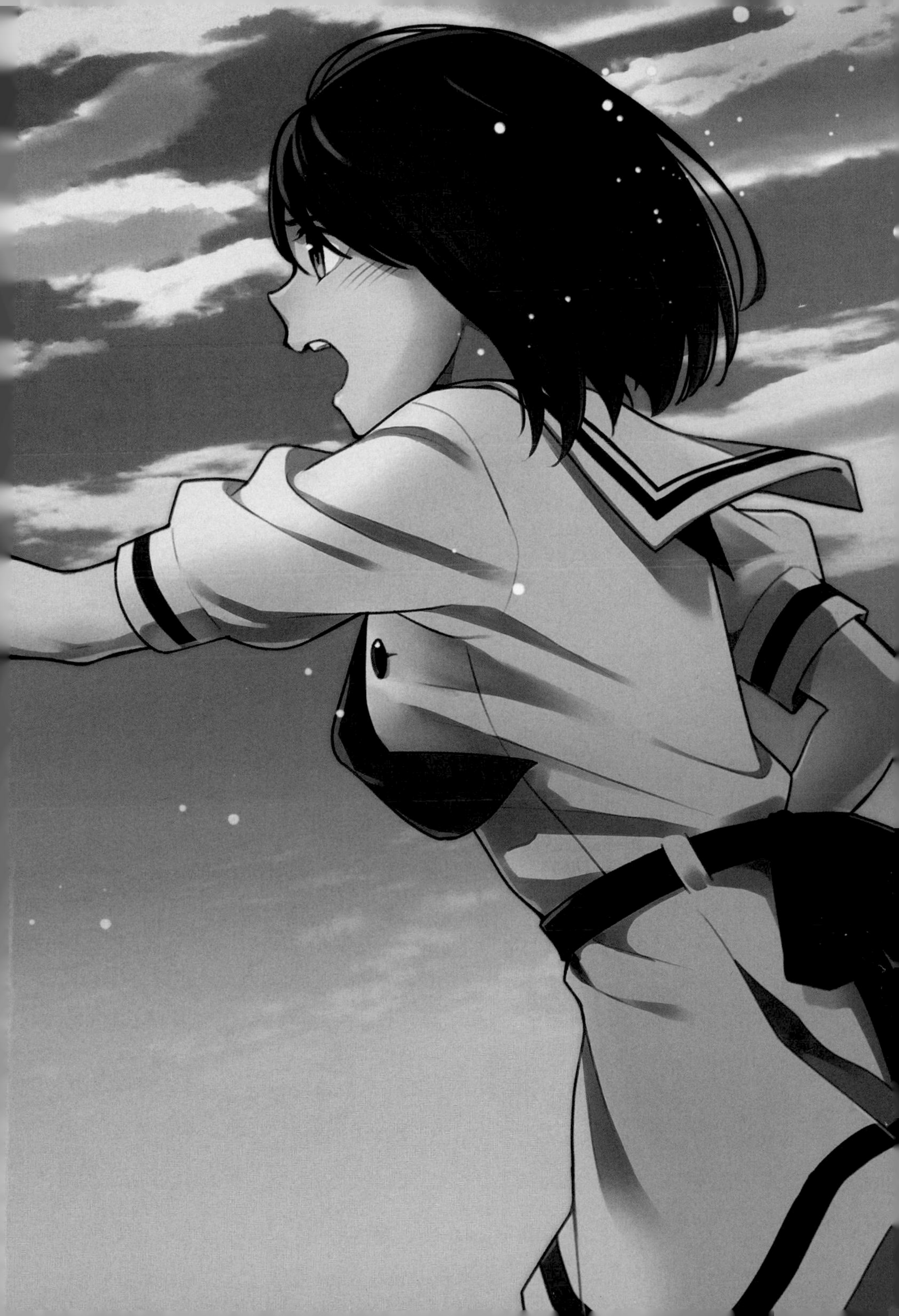

Chapter 31

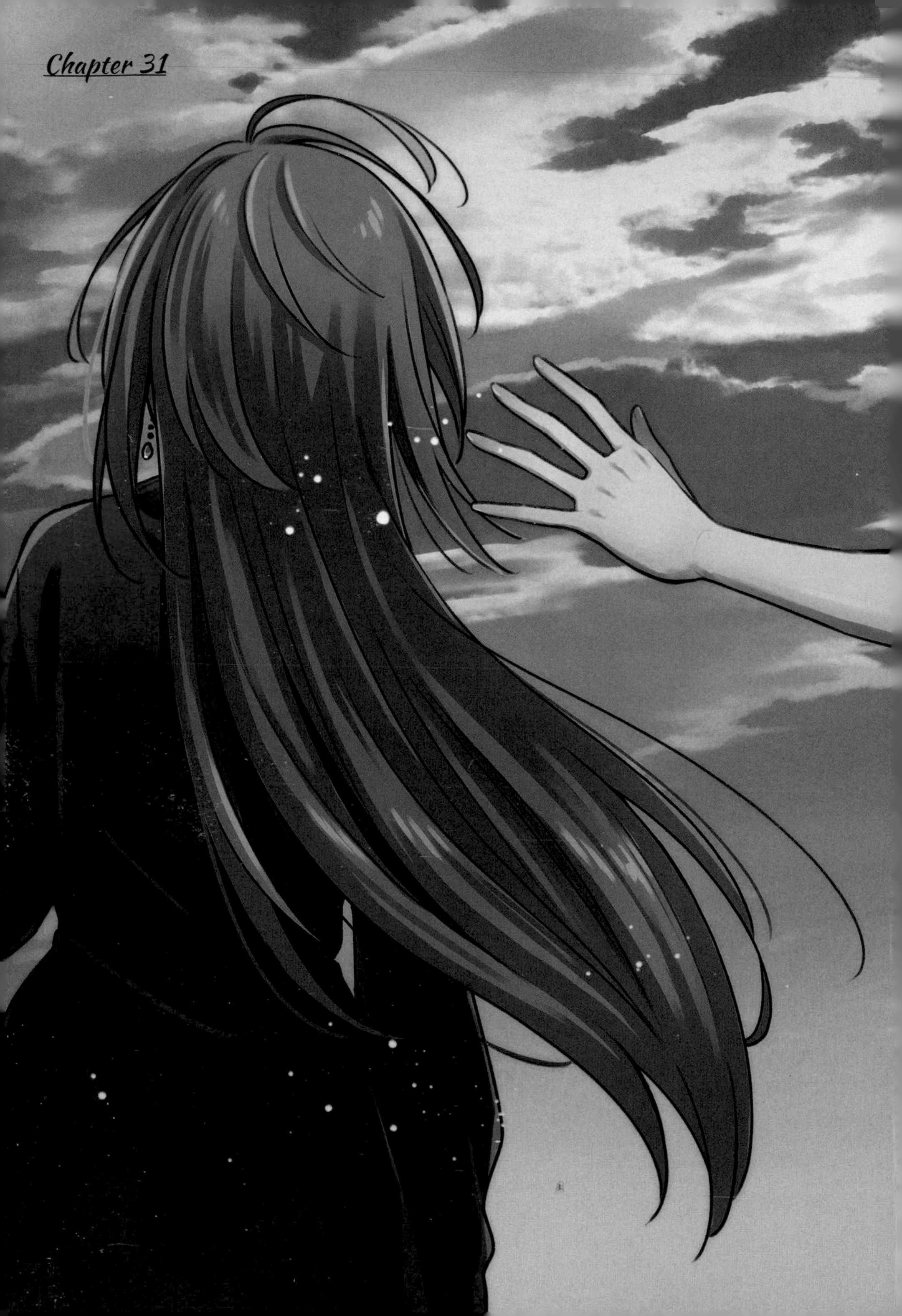

If I Could Reach You

7

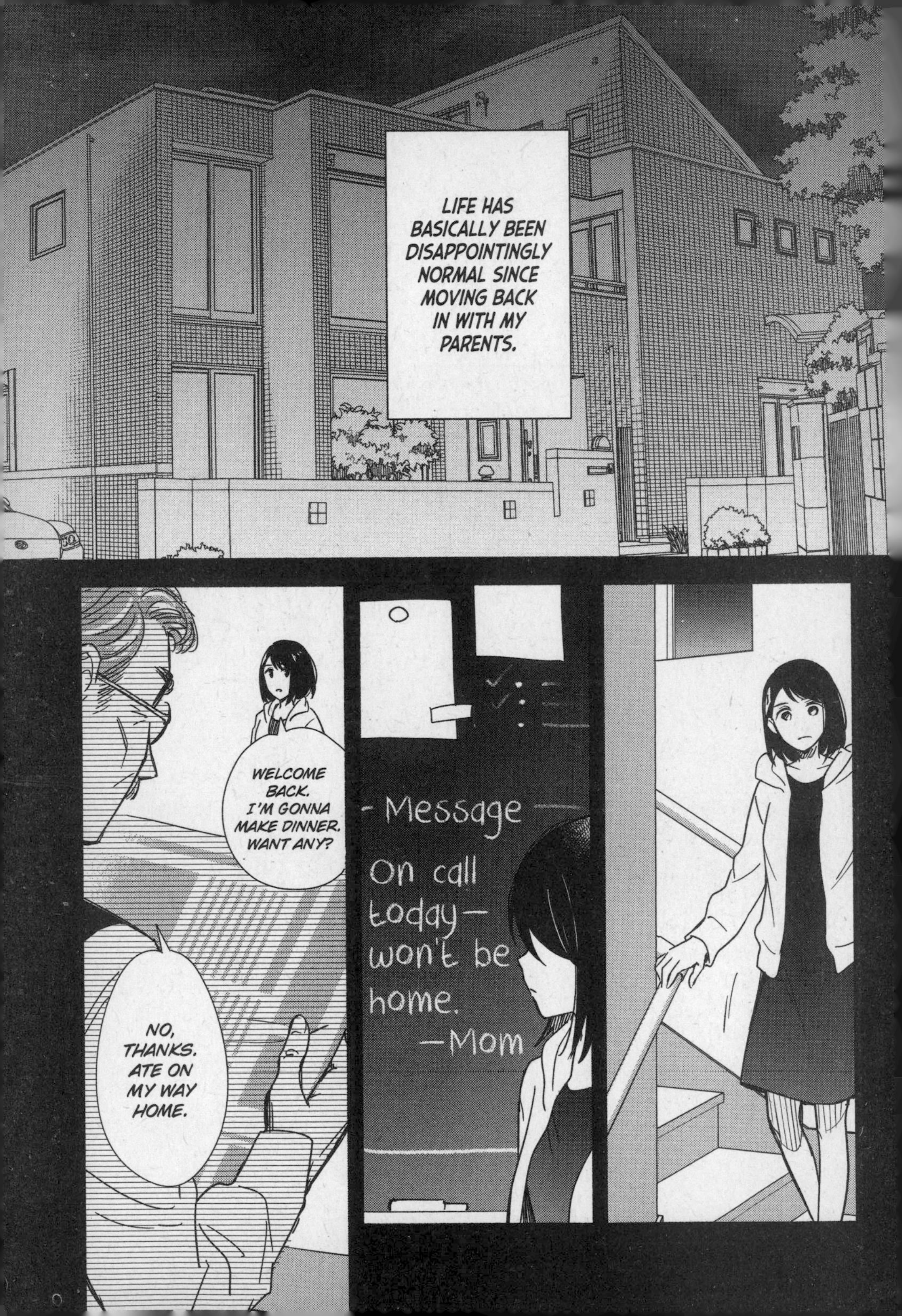
LIFE HAS BASICALLY BEEN DISAPPOINTINGLY NORMAL SINCE MOVING BACK IN WITH MY PARENTS.
Message
On call today— won't be home. —Mom
WELCOME BACK. I'M GONNA MAKE DINNER. WANT ANY?
NO, THANKS. ATE ON MY WAY HOME.

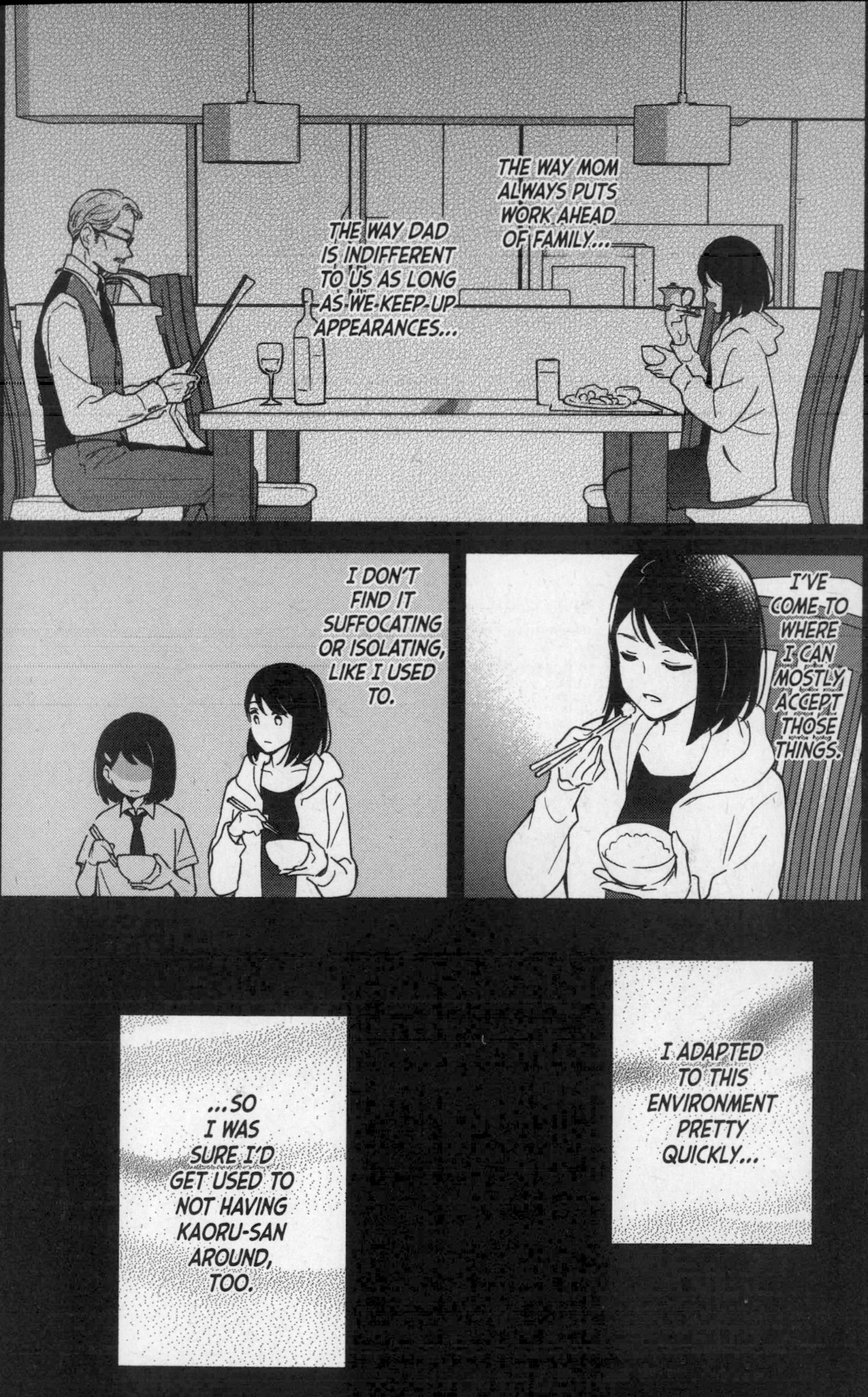
THE WAY MOM ALWAYS PUTS WORK AHEAD OF FAMILY...
THE WAY DAD IS INDIFFERENT TO US AS LONG AS WE KEEP UP APPEARANCES...
I'VE COME TO WHERE I CAN MOSTLY ACCEPT THOSE THINGS.
I DON'T FIND IT SUFFOCATING OR ISOLATING, LIKE I USED TO.
I ADAPTED TO THIS ENVIRONMENT PRETTY QUICKLY...
...SO I WAS SURE I'D GET USED TO NOT HAVING KAORU-SAN AROUND, TOO.

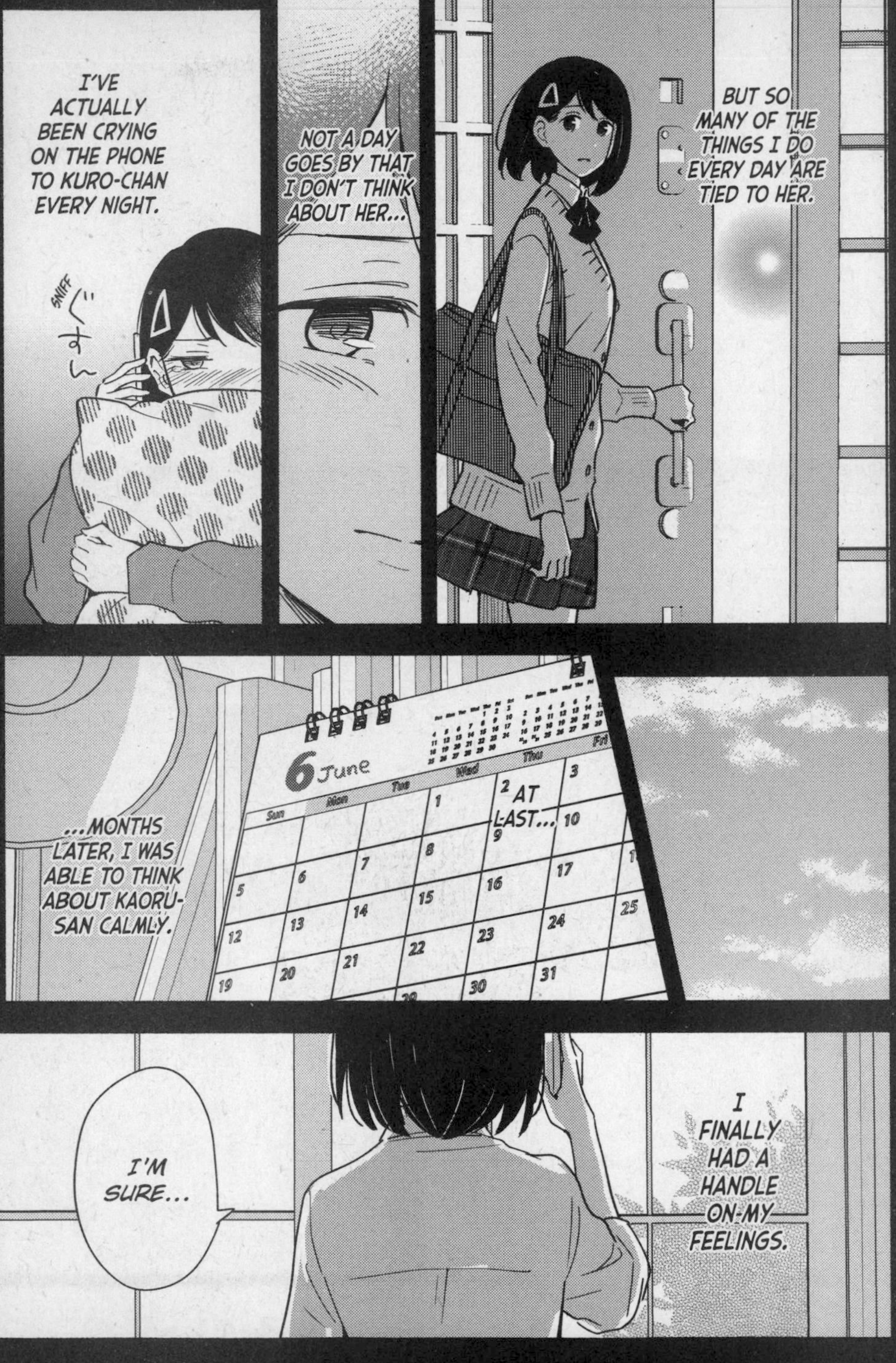
BUT SO MANY OF THE THINGS I DO EVERY DAY ARE TIED TO HER.
NOT A DAY GOES BY THAT I DON'T THINK ABOUT HER...
I'VE ACTUALLY BEEN CRYING ON THE PHONE TO KURO-CHAN EVERY NIGHT.
SNIFF
ぐすん
6 June
AT LAST...
...MONTHS LATER, I WAS ABLE TO THINK ABOUT KAORU-SAN CALMLY.
I FINALLY HAD A HANDLE ON MY FEELINGS.
I'M SURE...

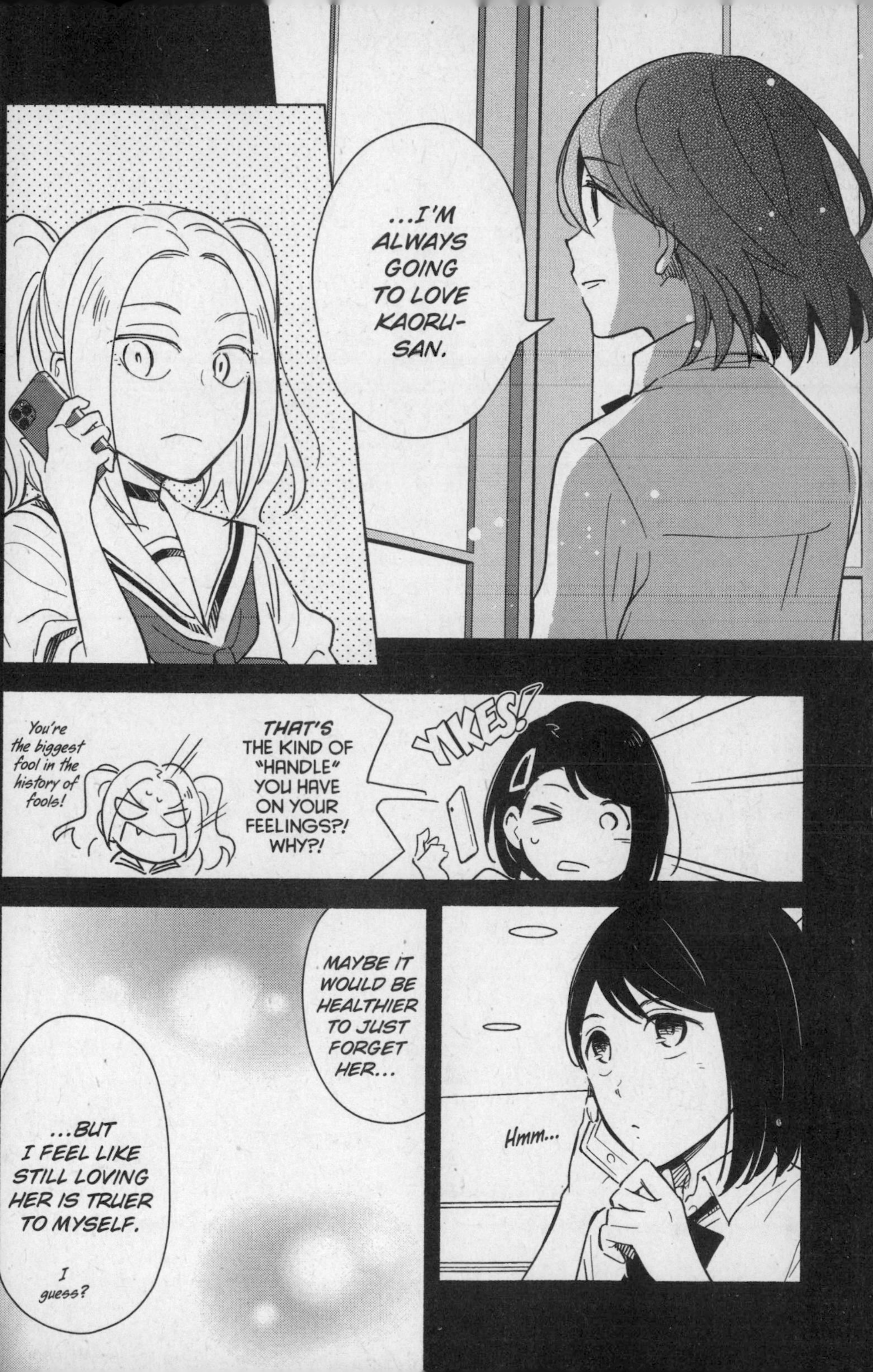
...I'M ALWAYS GOING TO LOVE KAORU-SAN.
YIKES!
THAT'S THE KIND OF "HANDLE" YOU HAVE ON YOUR FEELINGS?! WHY?!
You're the biggest fool in the history of fools!
MAYBE IT WOULD BE HEALTHIER TO JUST FORGET HER...
Hmm...
...BUT I FEEL LIKE STILL LOVING HER IS TRUER TO MYSELF.
I guess?

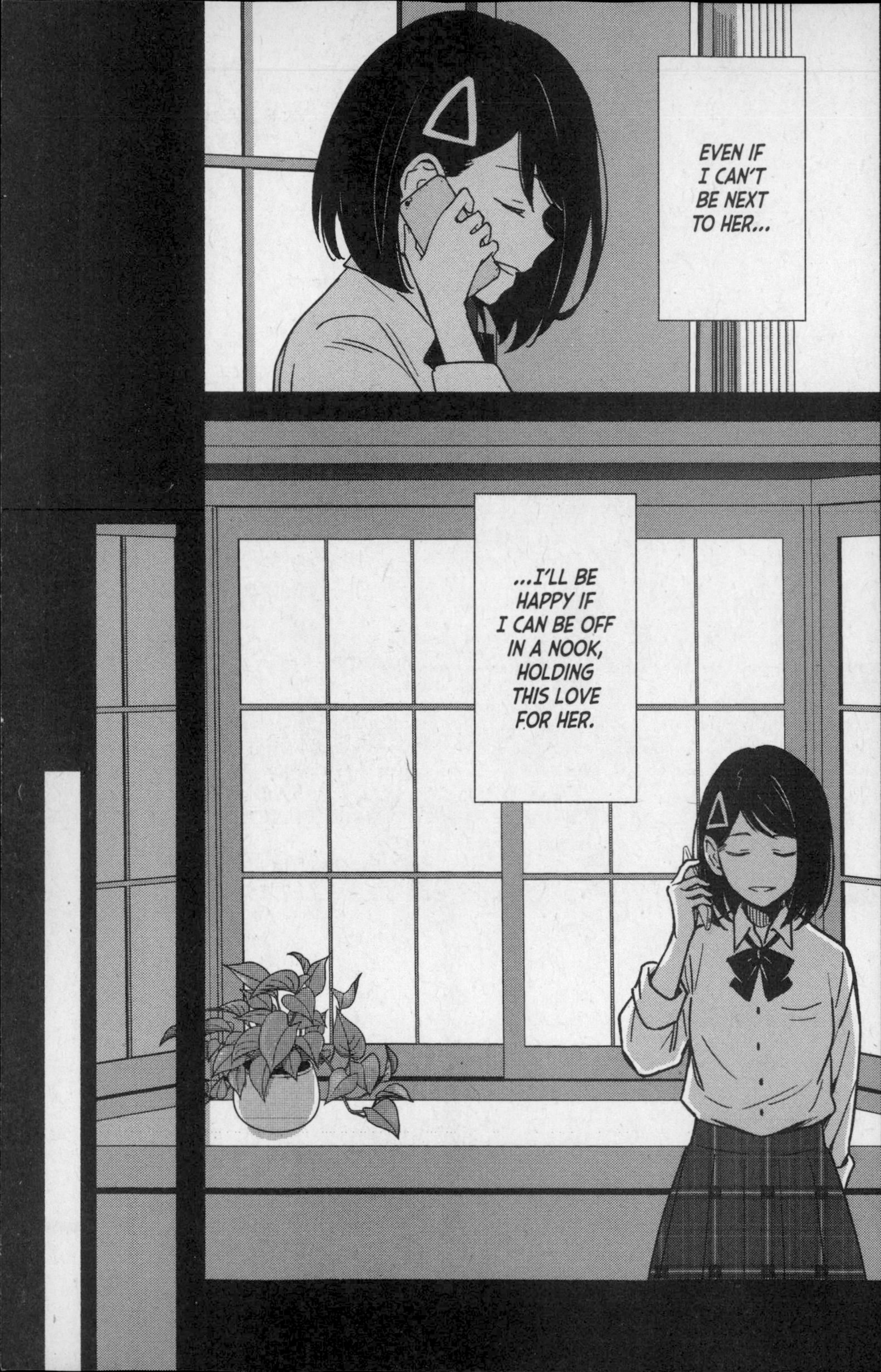
EVEN IF I CAN'T BE NEXT TO HER...
...I'LL BE HAPPY IF I CAN BE OFF IN A NOOK, HOLDING THIS LOVE FOR HER.

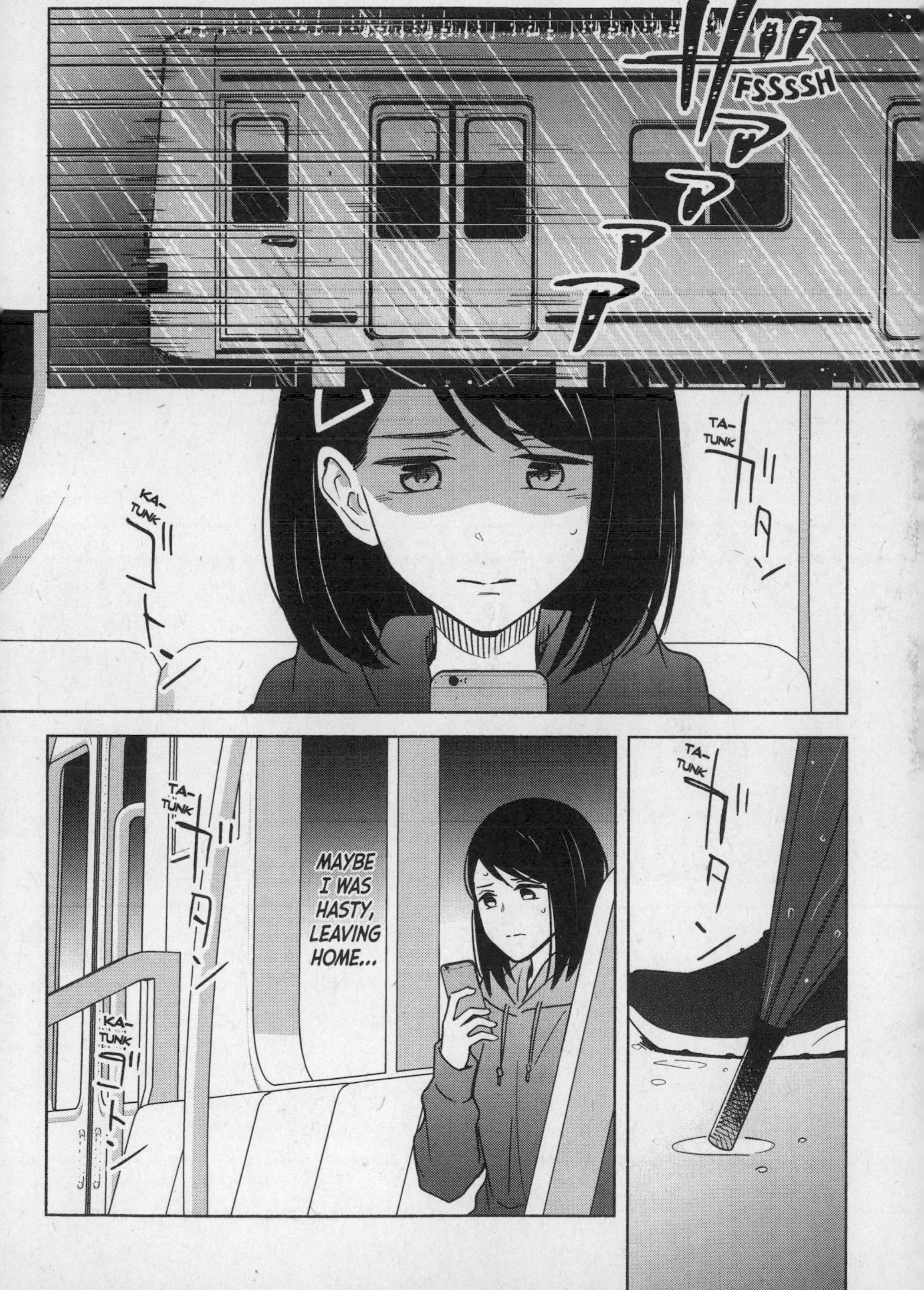
FSSSSH
TA-TUNK
KA-TUNK
TA-TUNK
TA-TUNK
MAYBE I WAS HASTY, LEAVING HOME...
KA-TUNK

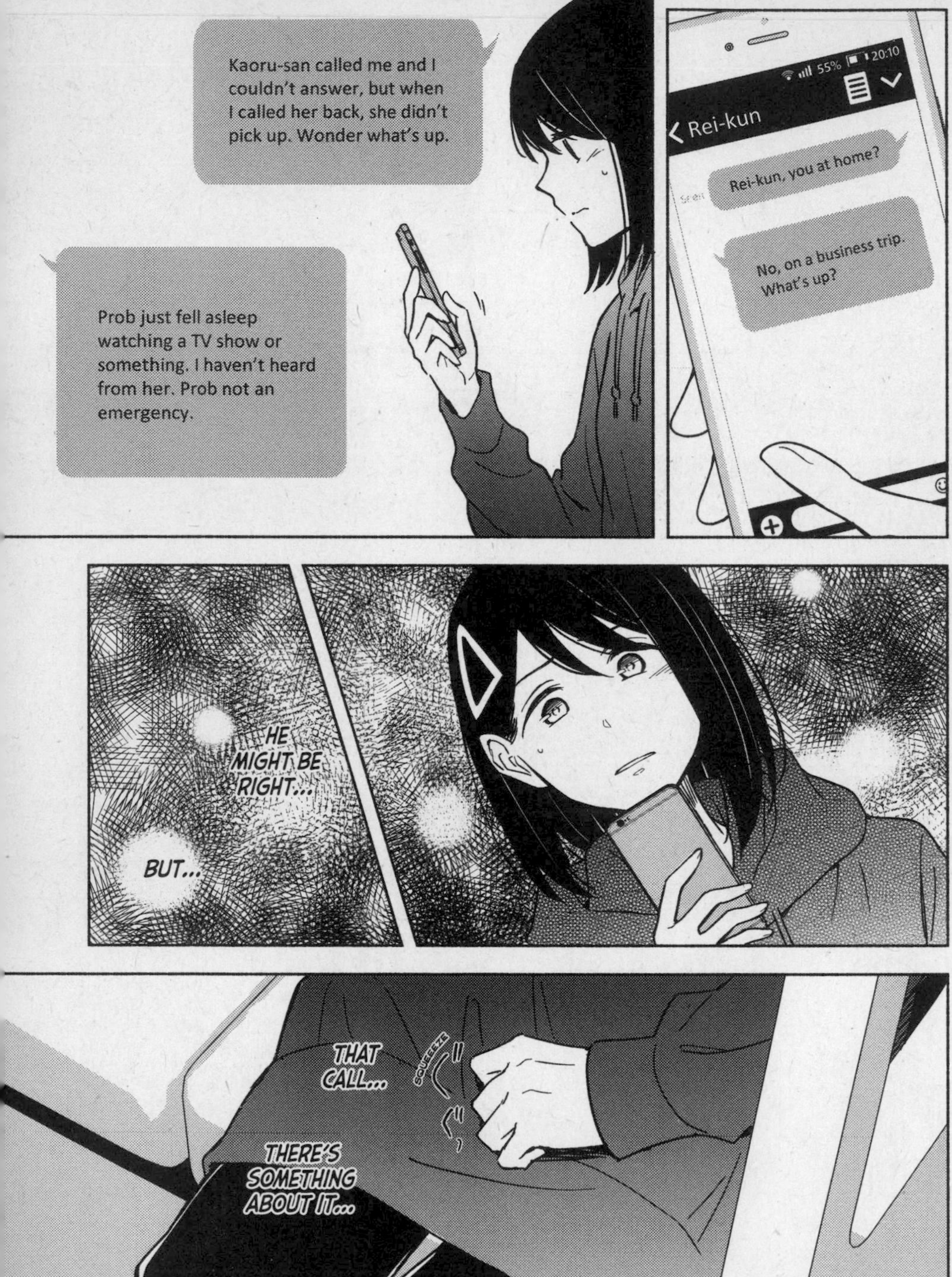
Rei-kun
Rei-kun, you at home?
No, on a business trip. What's up?
Kaoru-san called me and I couldn't answer, but when I called her back, she didn't pick up. Wonder what's up.
Prob just fell asleep watching a TV show or something. I haven't heard from her. Prob not an emergency.
HE MIGHT BE RIGHT...
BUT...
THAT CALL...
SQUEEEZE
THERE'S SOMETHING ABOUT IT...

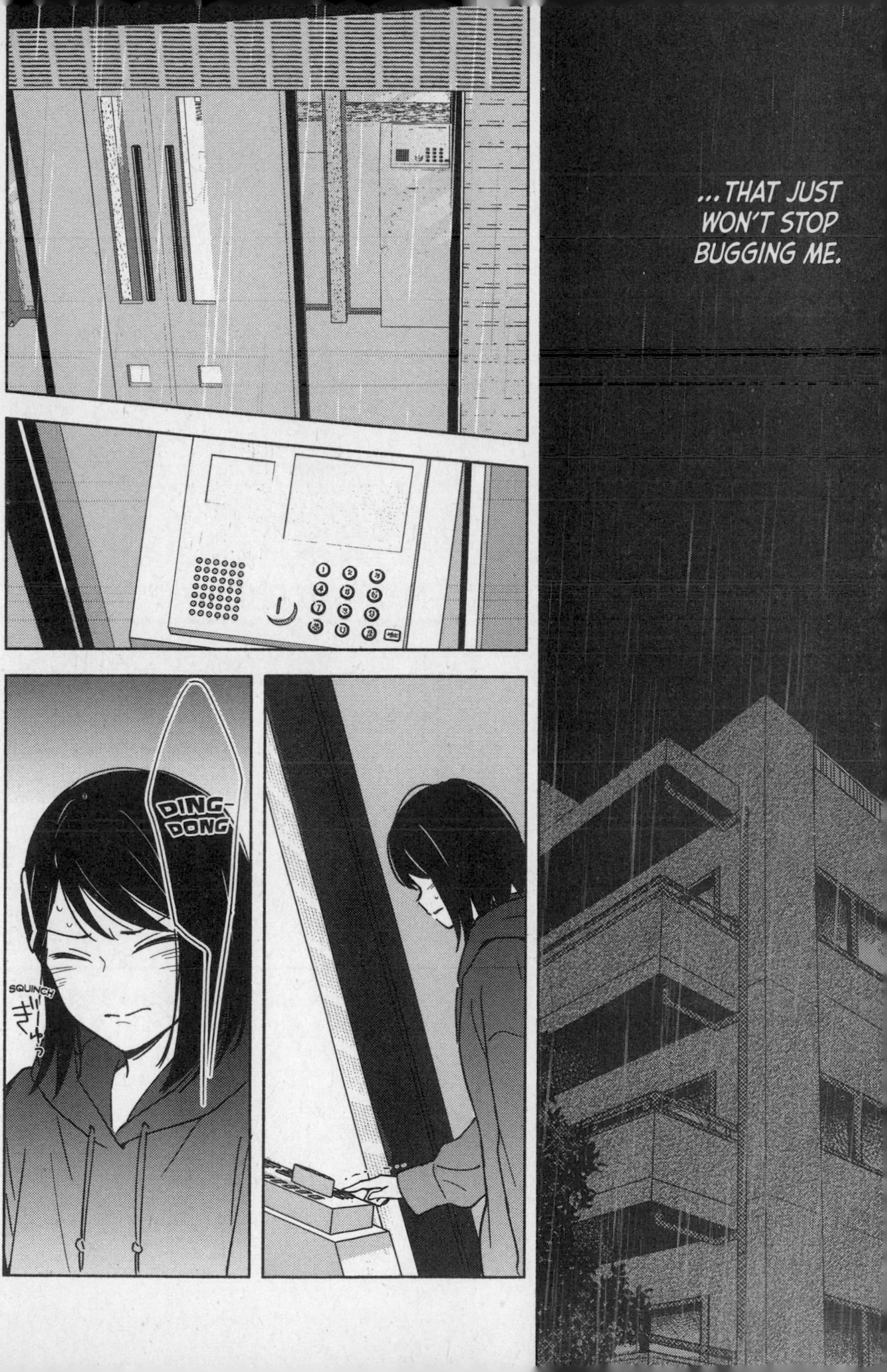
...THAT JUST WON'T STOP BUGGING ME.
DING-DONG
SQUINCH

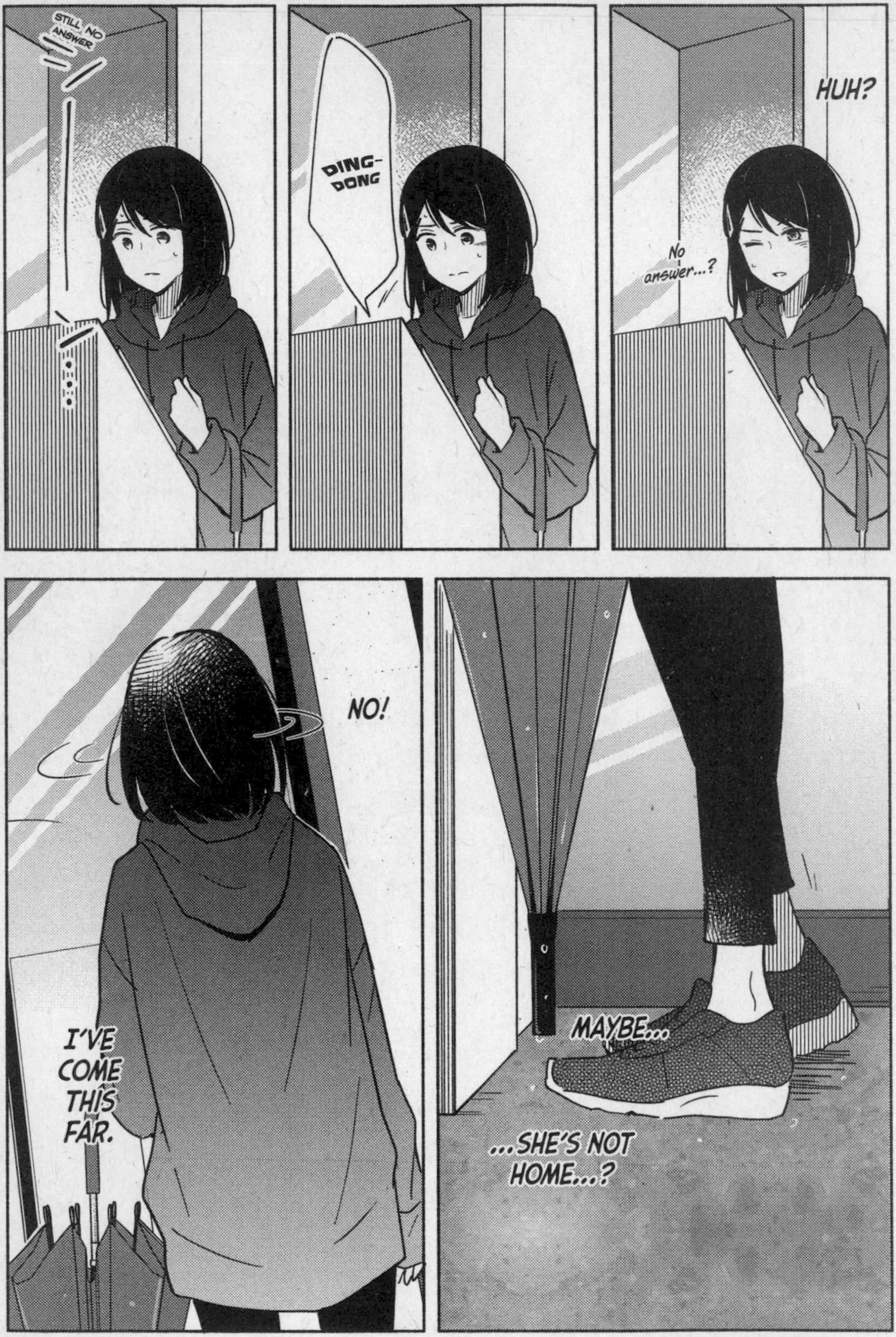
HUH?
No answer...?
DING-DONG
STILL NO ANSWER
MAYBE...
...SHE'S NOT HOME...?
NO!
I'VE COME THIS FAR.

I CAN'T STOP NOW.

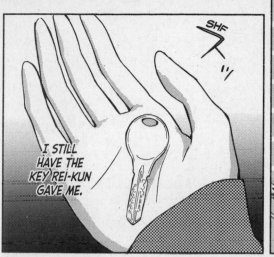

SHF

I STILL HAVE THE KEY REI-KUN GAVE ME.

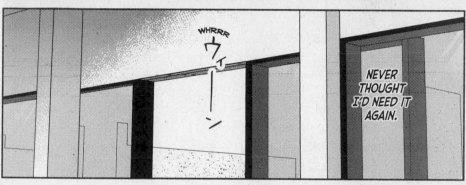

WHRRR

NEVER THOUGHT I'D NEED IT AGAIN.

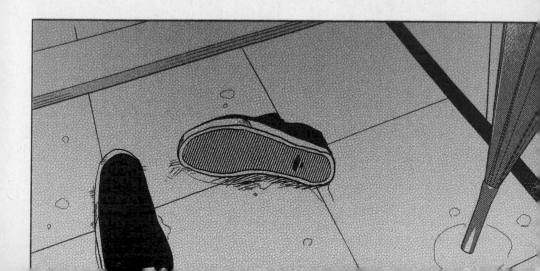

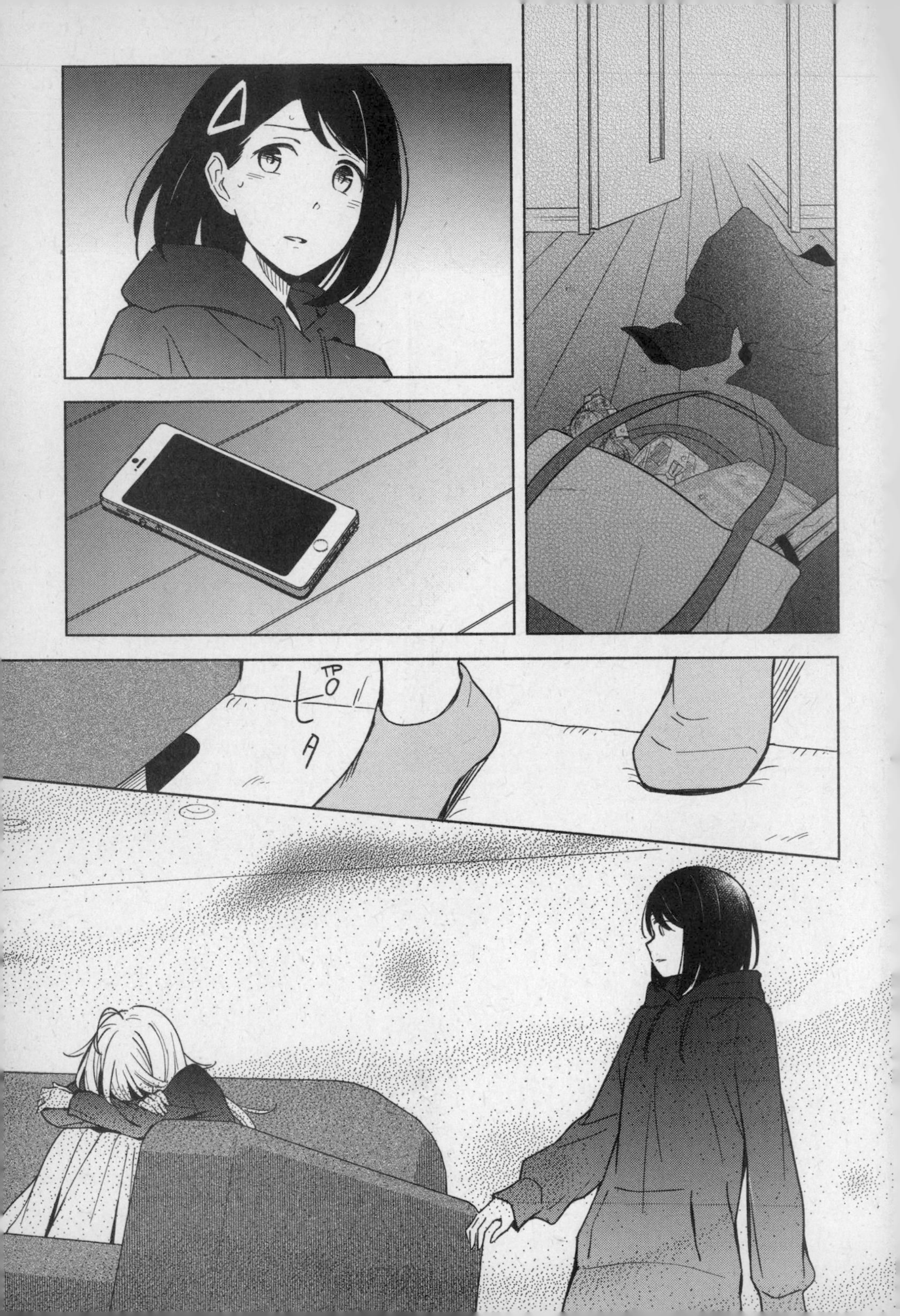
TP

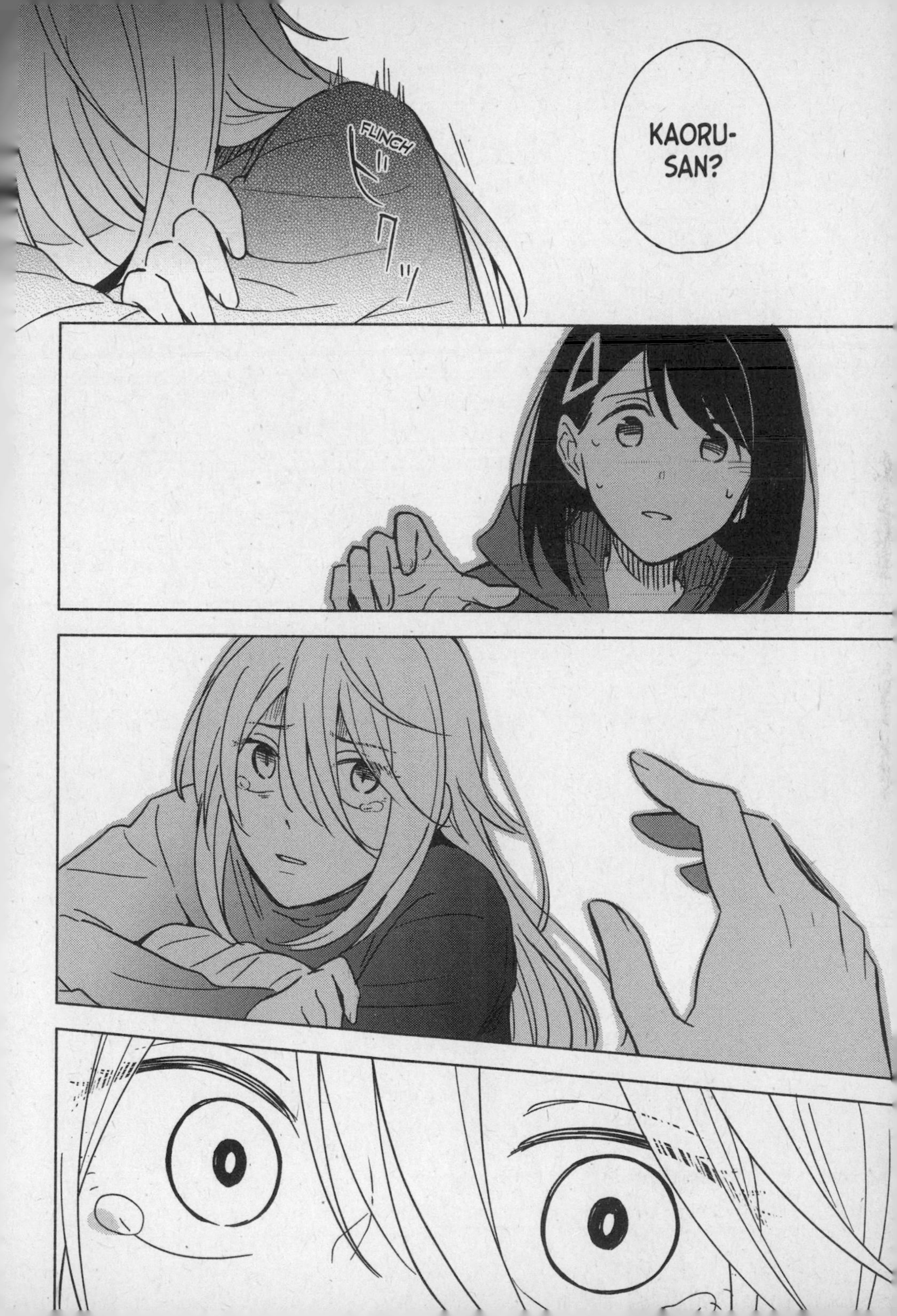
KAORU-SAN?
FLINCH

U...
UTA...
CH—

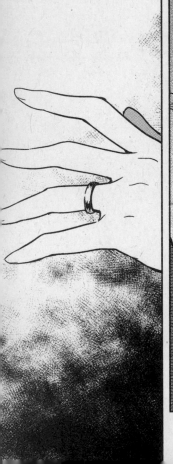

Um...

TH—

THAT
CALL
EARLIER...
ARE
YOU—

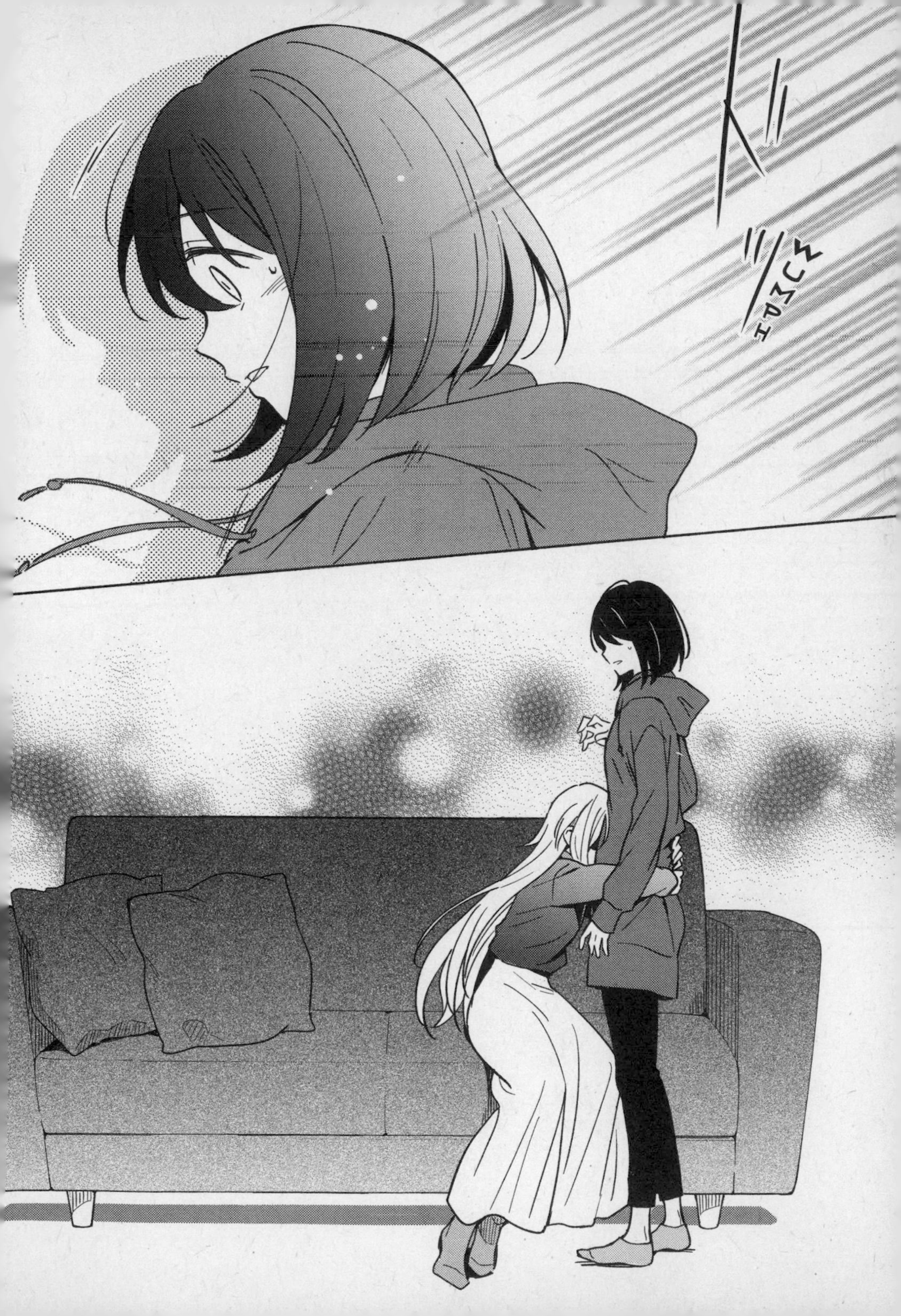
WUMPH

If I Could
Reach You

If I Could Reach You

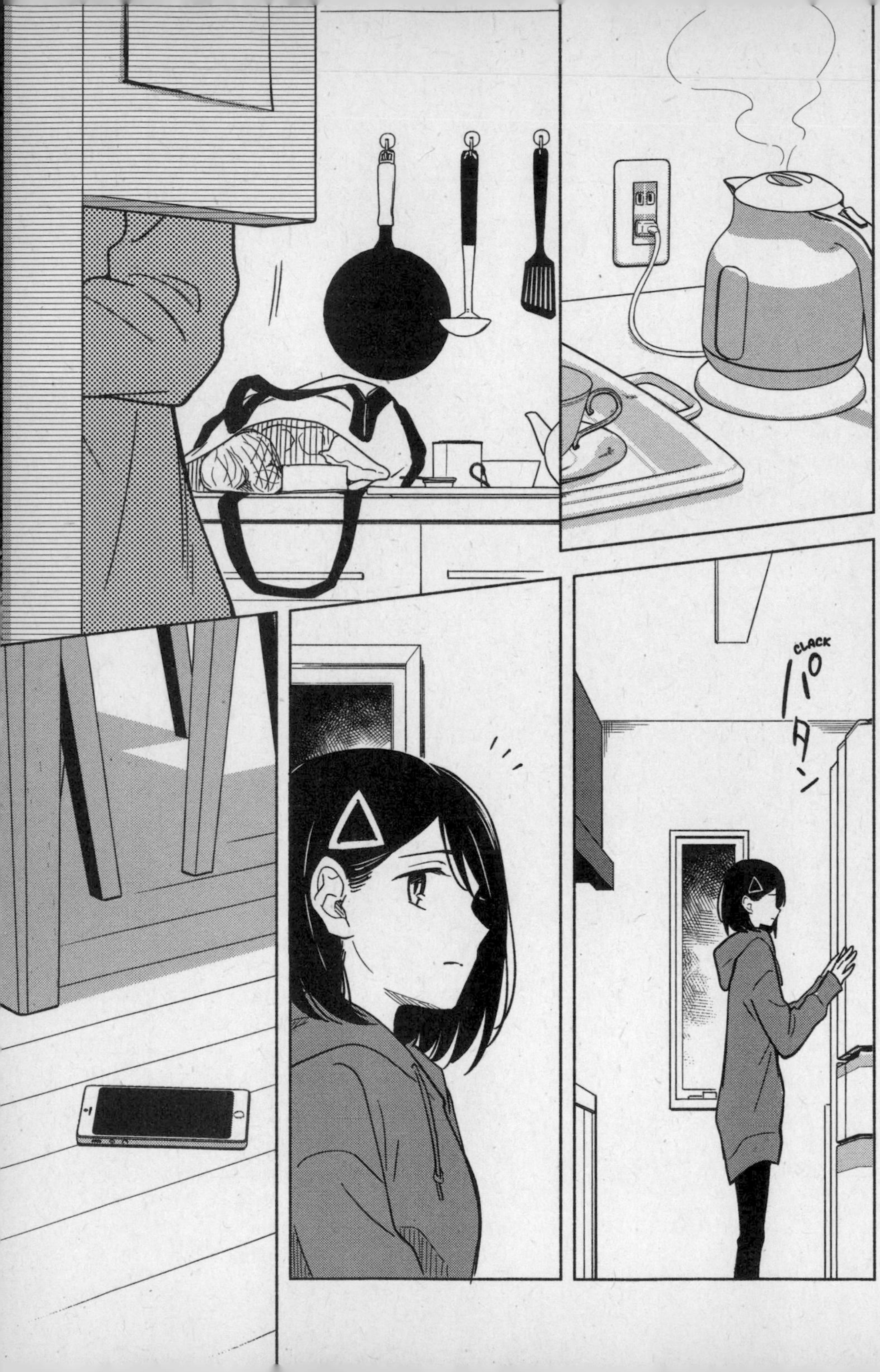
CLACK

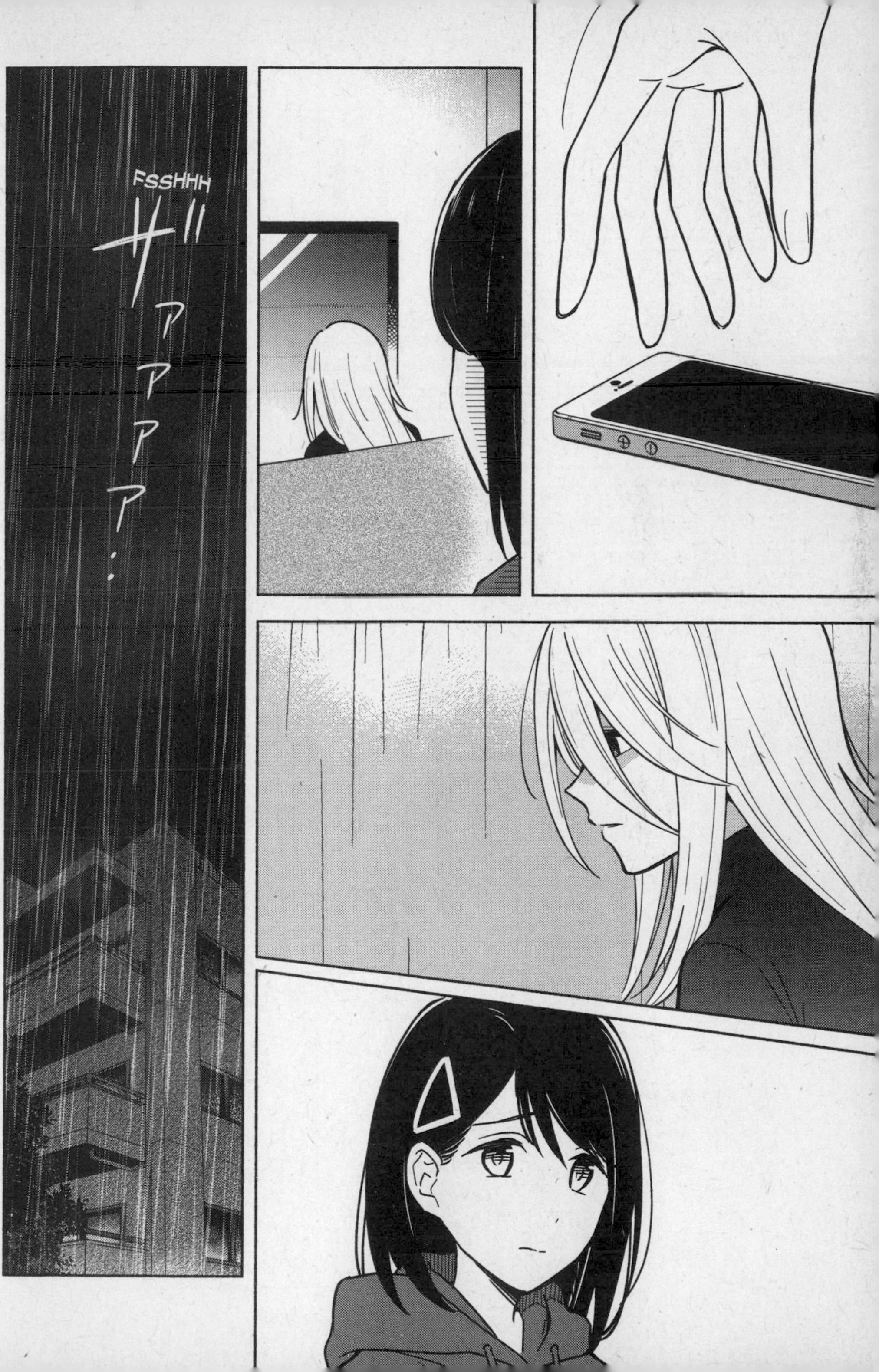
FSSHHH
ザァァァァ…

Chapter 32

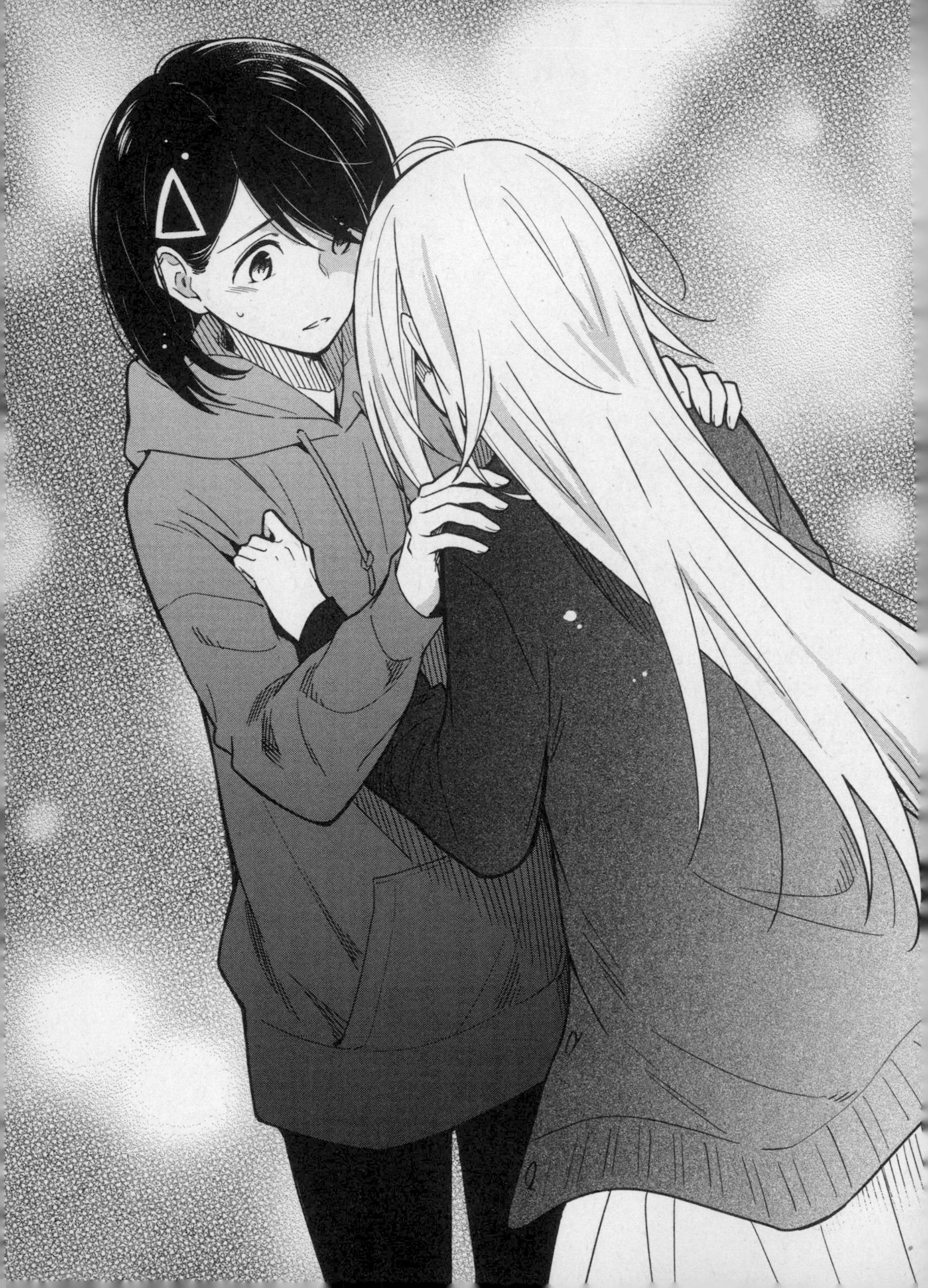

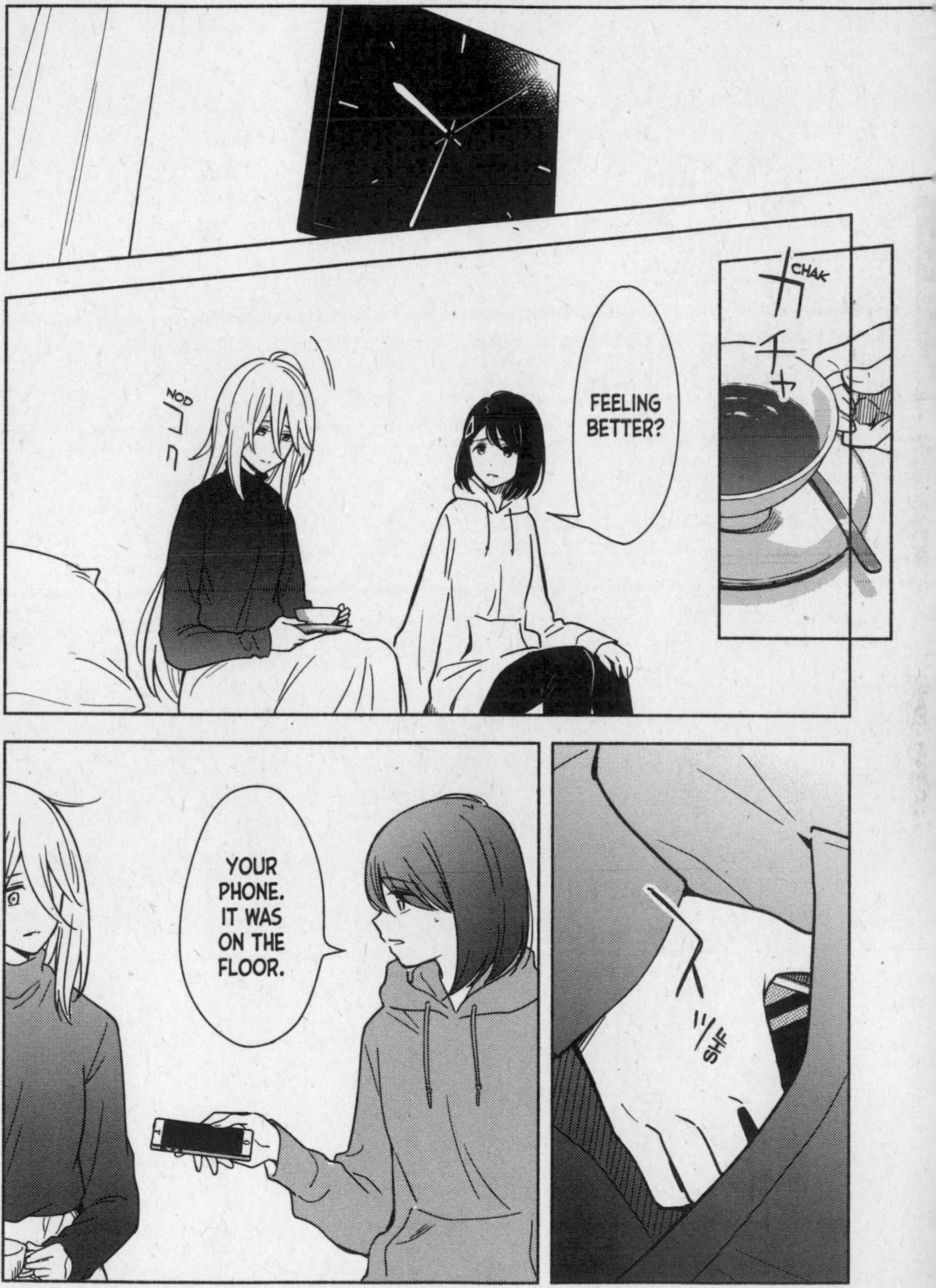
CHAK
カチャ
FEELING BETTER?
NOD
コク
SHF
YOUR PHONE. IT WAS ON THE FLOOR.

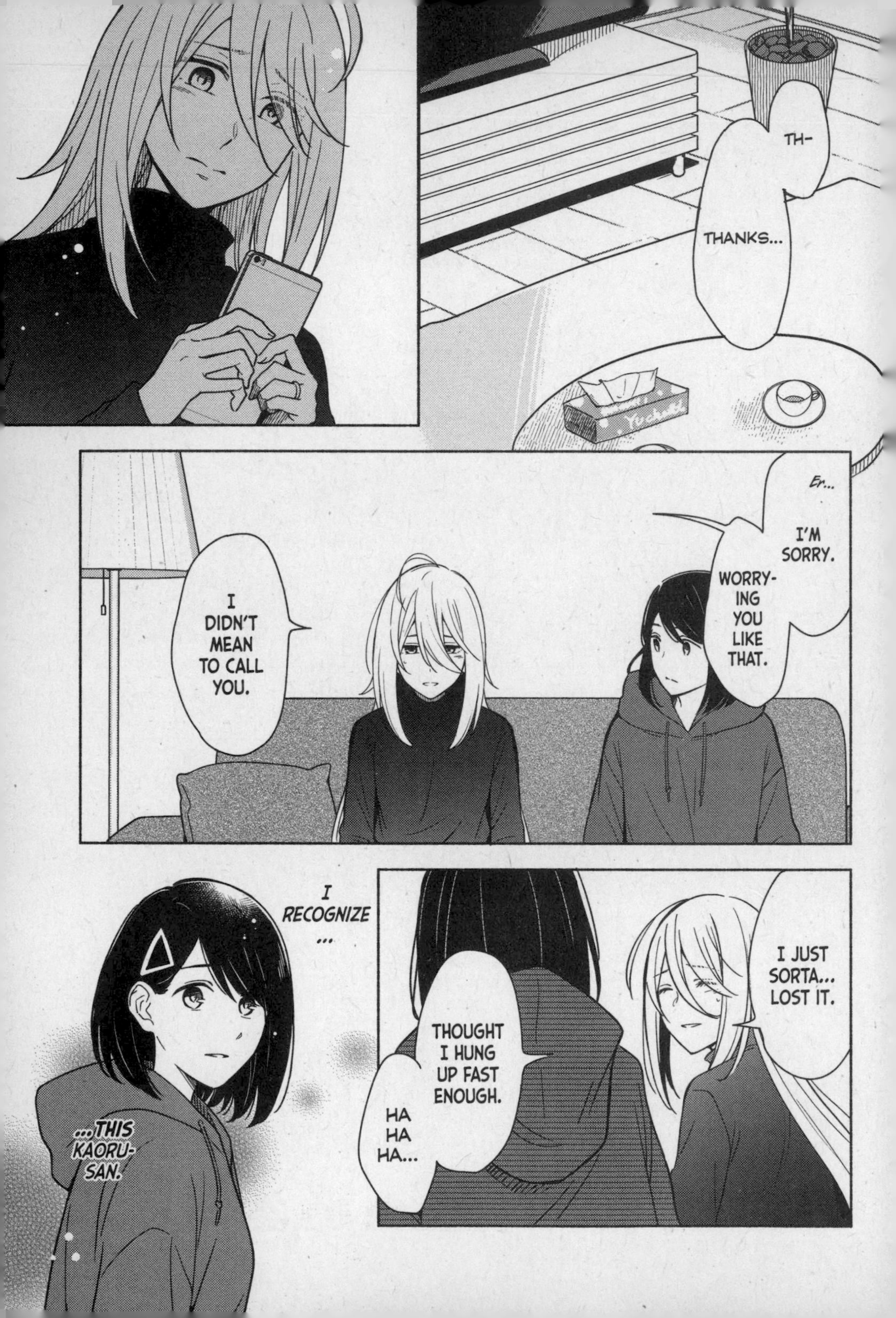
TH-
THANKS...
Er...
I'M SORRY.
WORRYING YOU LIKE THAT.
I DIDN'T MEAN TO CALL YOU.
I JUST SORTA... LOST IT.
THOUGHT I HUNG UP FAST ENOUGH.
HA HA HA...
I RECOGNIZE ...
...THIS KAORU-SAN.

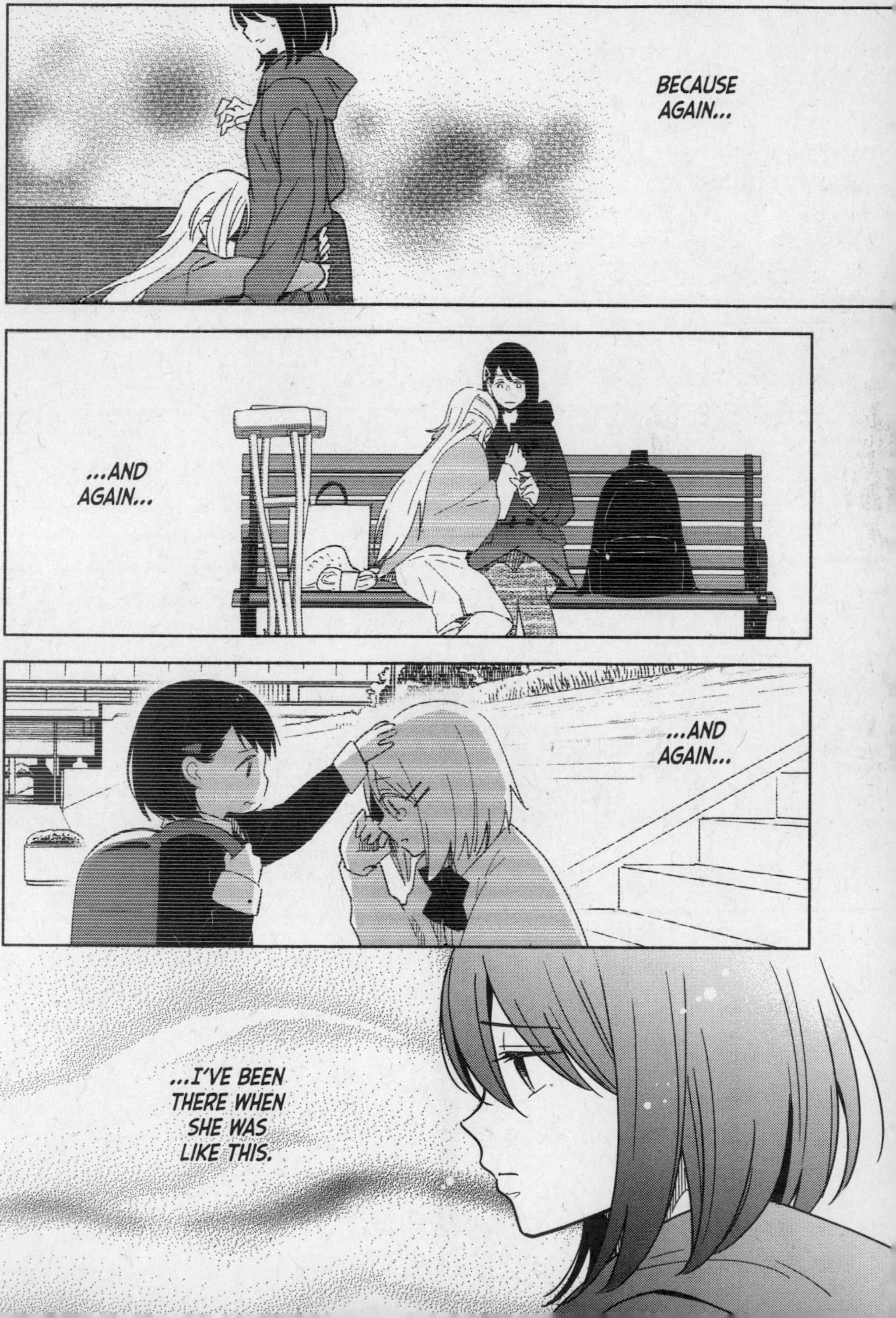
BECAUSE AGAIN...
...AND AGAIN...
...AND AGAIN...
...I'VE BEEN THERE WHEN SHE WAS LIKE THIS.

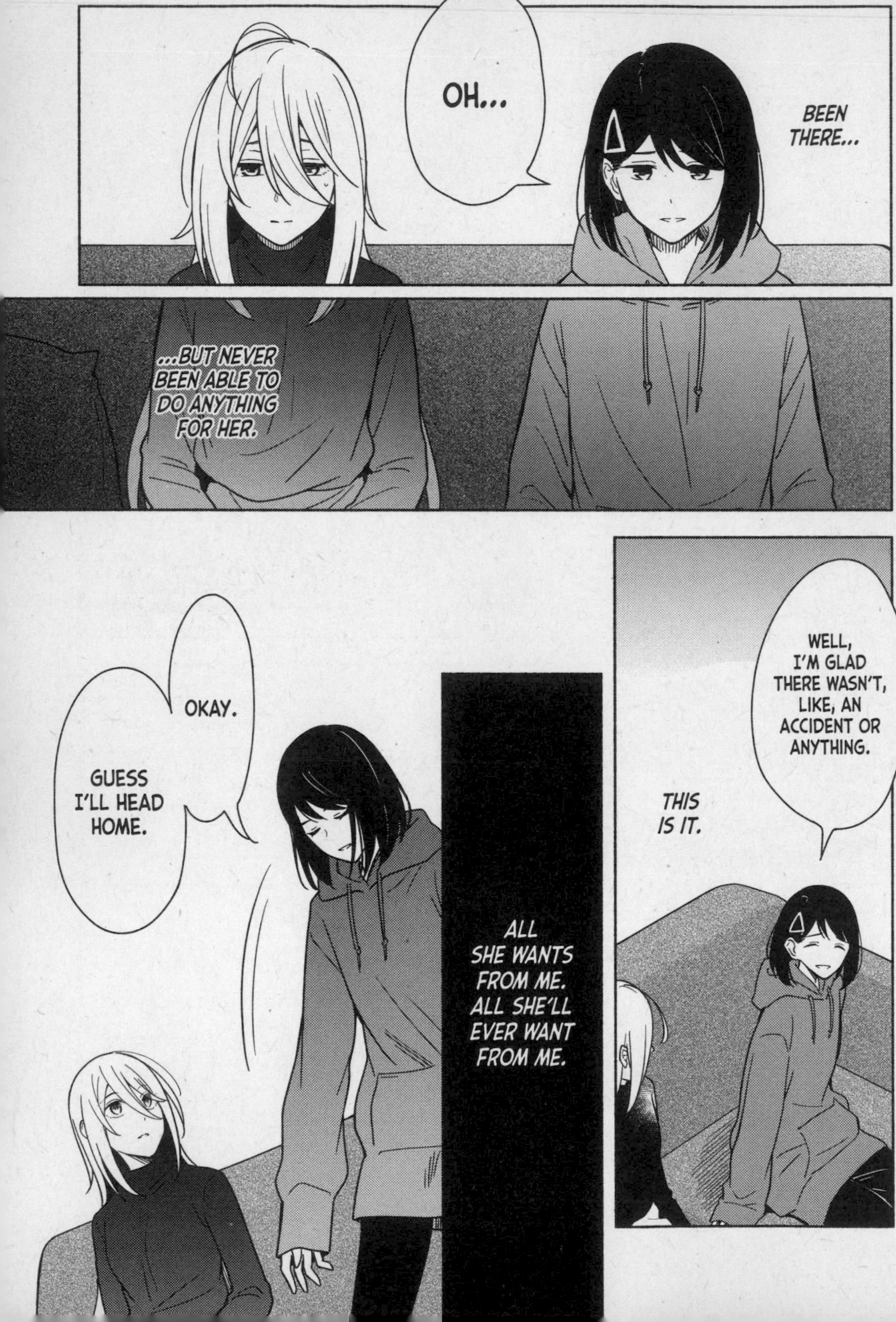
OH...
BEEN THERE...
...BUT NEVER BEEN ABLE TO DO ANYTHING FOR HER.
WELL, I'M GLAD THERE WASN'T, LIKE, AN ACCIDENT OR ANYTHING.
THIS IS IT.
ALL SHE WANTS FROM ME. ALL SHE'LL EVER WANT FROM ME.
OKAY.
GUESS I'LL HEAD HOME.

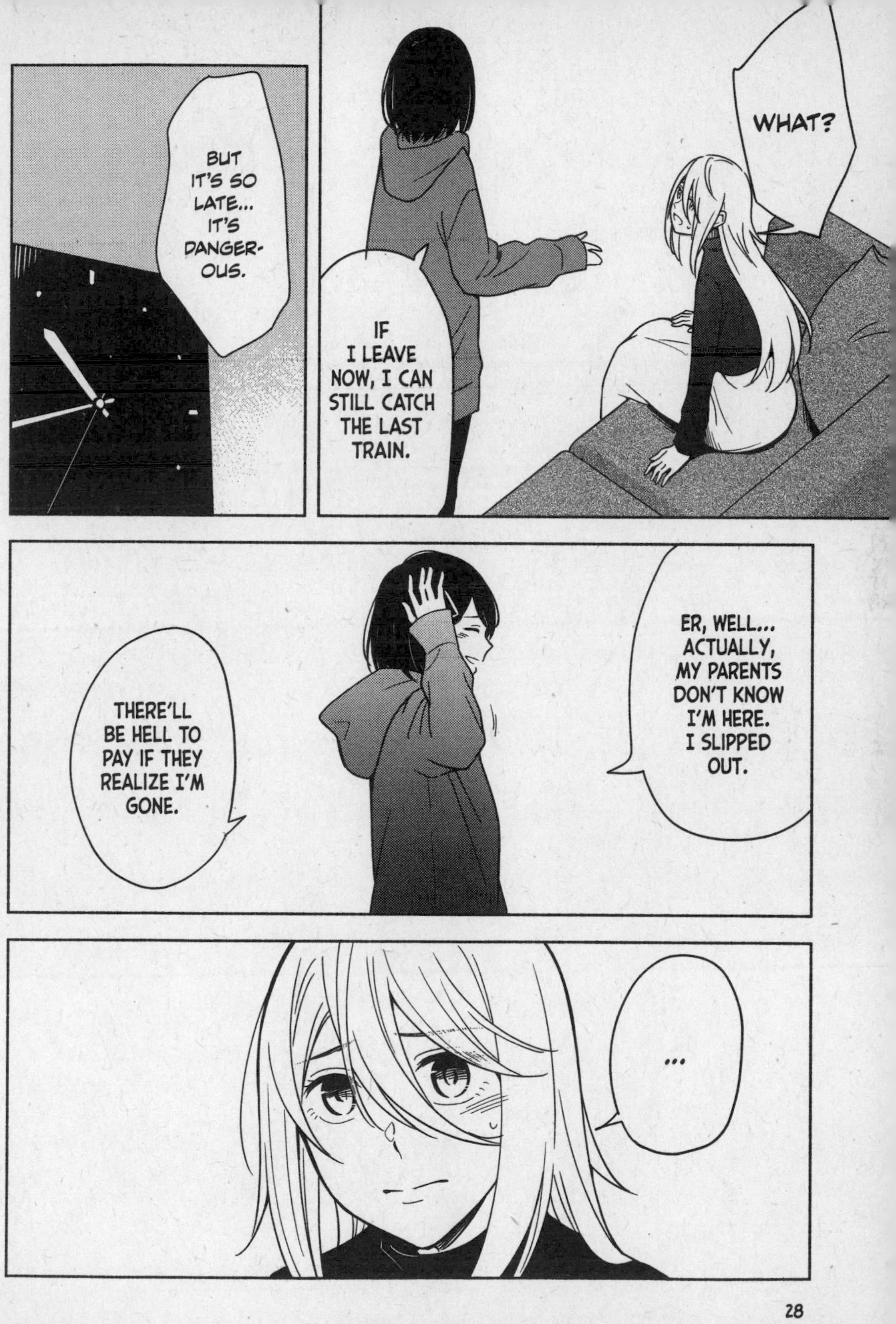
IF I LEAVE NOW, I CAN STILL CATCH THE LAST TRAIN.
WHAT?
BUT IT'S SO LATE... IT'S DANGER-OUS.
ER, WELL... ACTUALLY, MY PARENTS DON'T KNOW I'M HERE. I SLIPPED OUT.
THERE'LL BE HELL TO PAY IF THEY REALIZE I'M GONE.
...

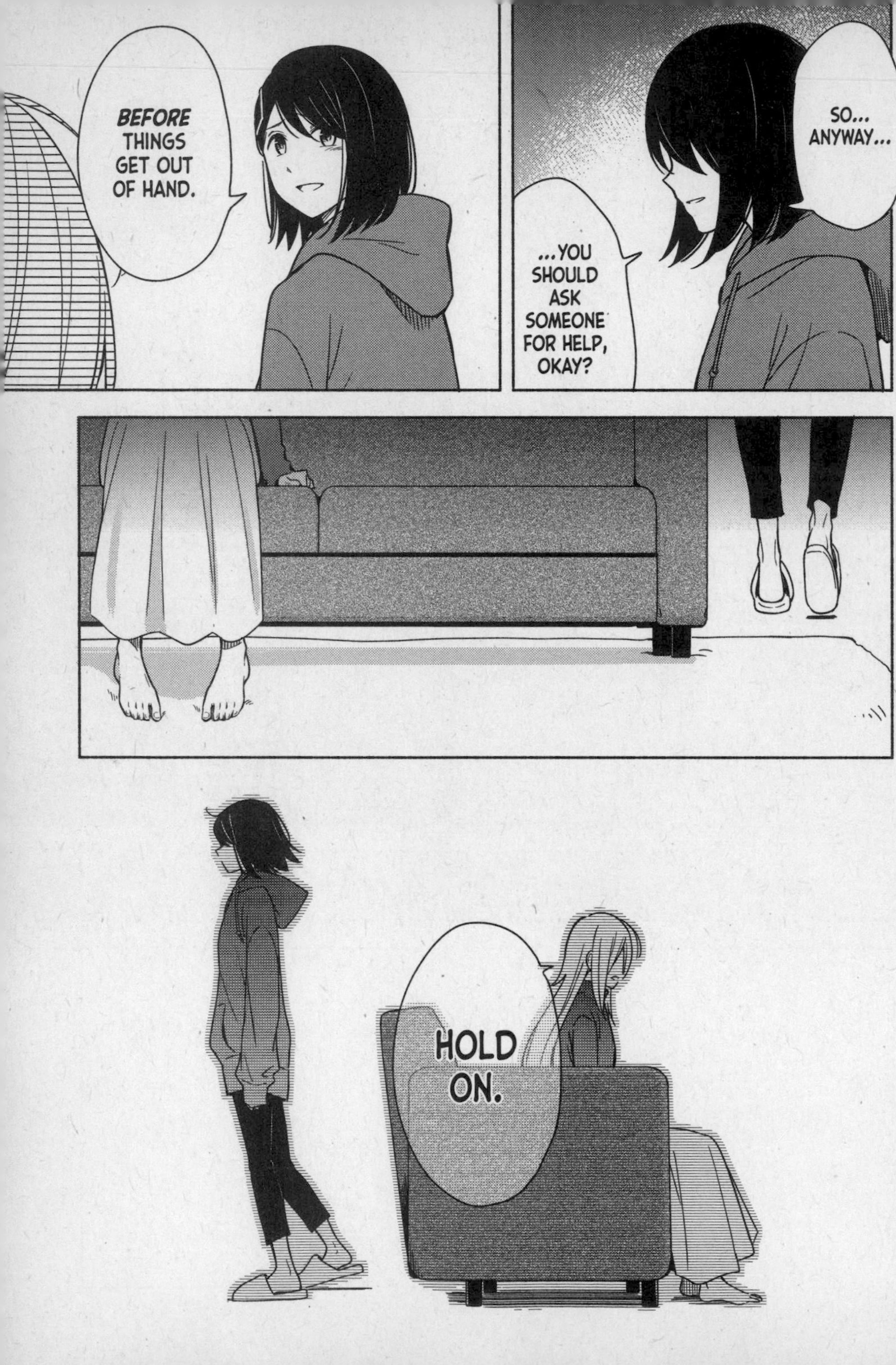
SO... ANYWAY...
...YOU SHOULD ASK SOMEONE FOR HELP, OKAY?
BEFORE THINGS GET OUT OF HAND.
HOLD ON.

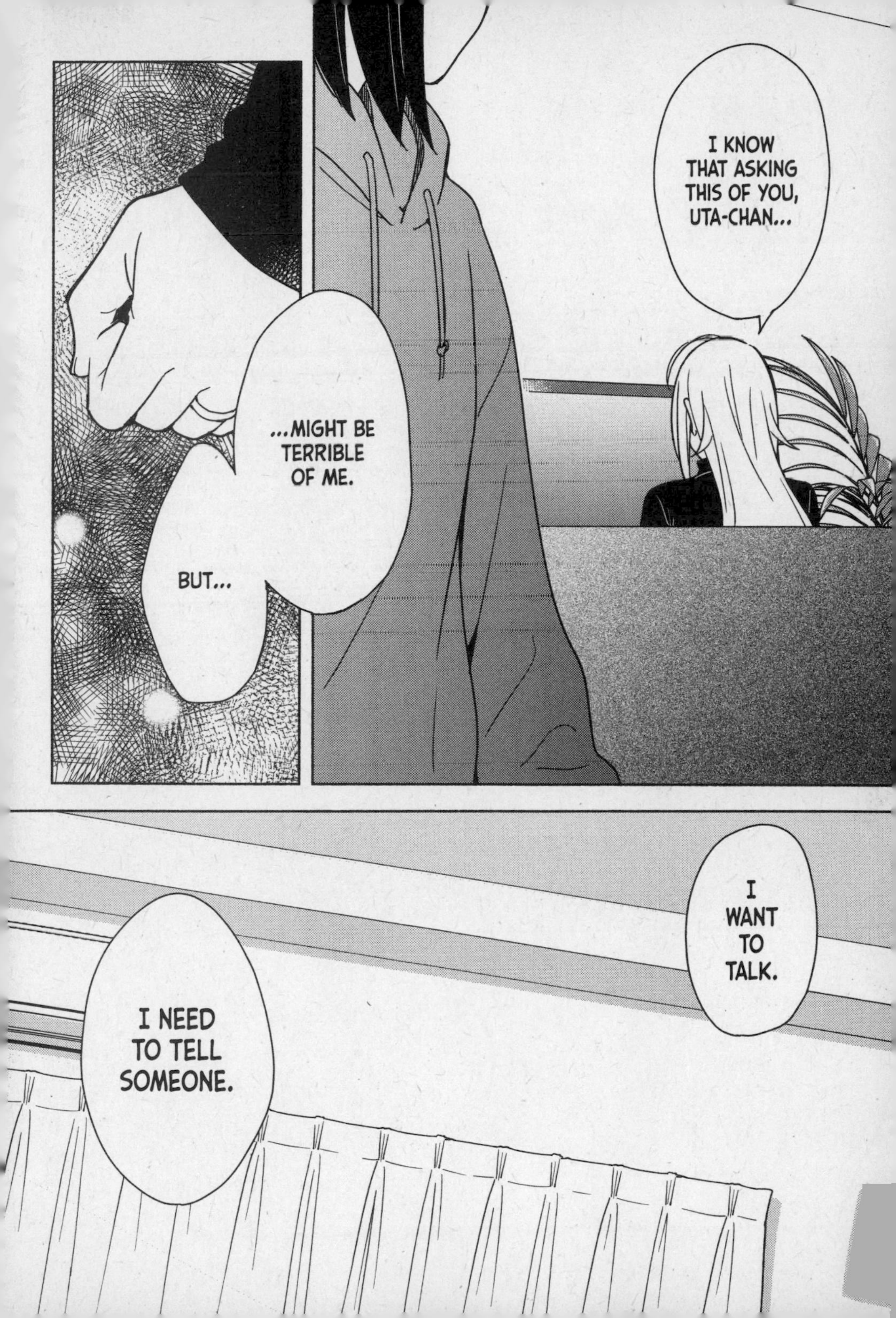
I KNOW THAT ASKING THIS OF YOU, UTA-CHAN...
...MIGHT BE TERRIBLE OF ME.
BUT...
I WANT TO TALK.
I NEED TO TELL SOMEONE.

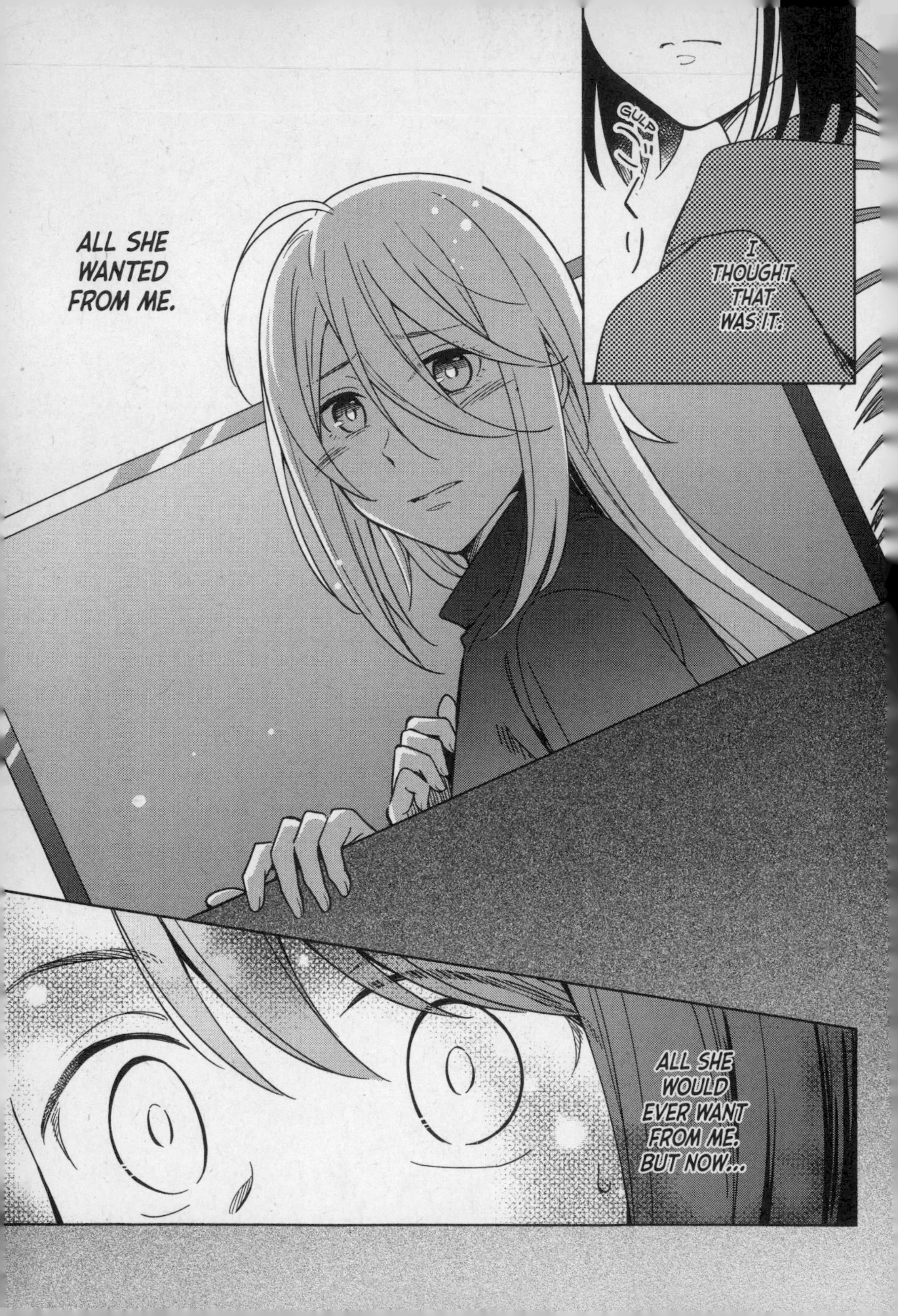
GULP
I THOUGHT THAT WAS IT.
ALL SHE WANTED FROM ME.
ALL SHE WOULD EVER WANT FROM ME. BUT NOW...

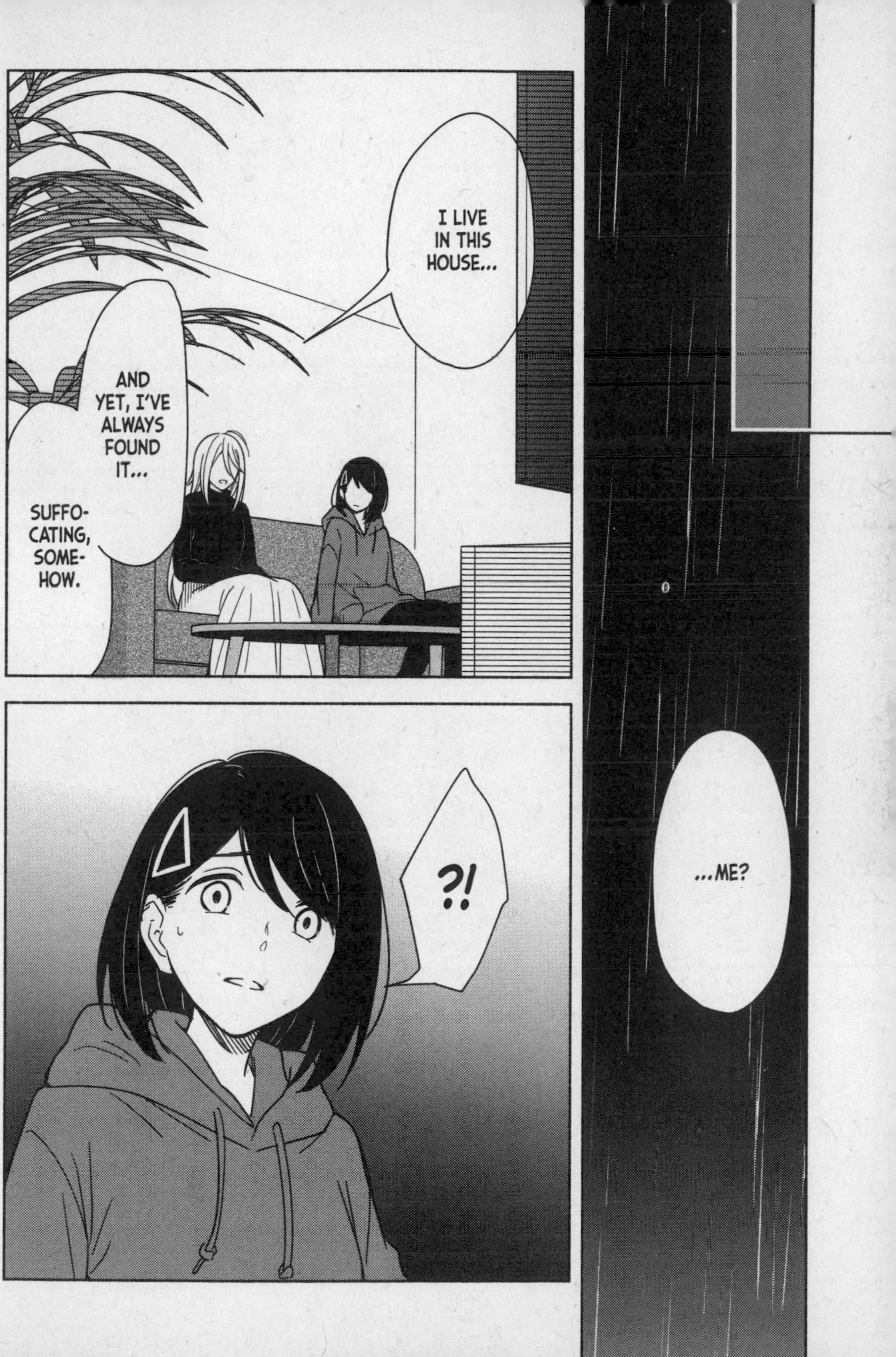
...ME?
I LIVE IN THIS HOUSE...
AND YET, I'VE ALWAYS FOUND IT...
SUFFOCATING, SOMEHOW.
?!

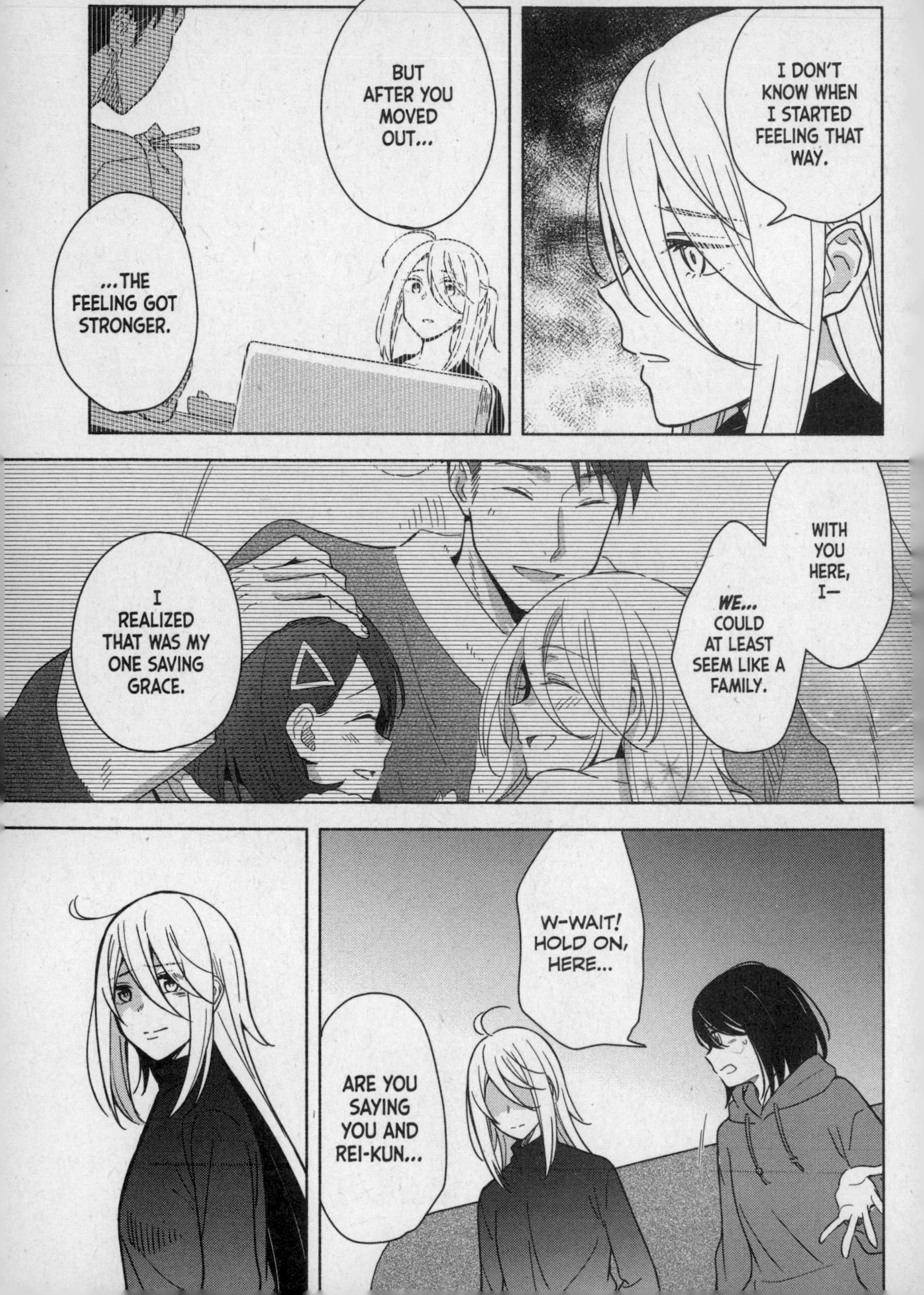
I DON'T KNOW WHEN I STARTED FEELING THAT WAY.
BUT AFTER YOU MOVED OUT...
...THE FEELING GOT STRONGER.
WITH YOU HERE, I—
WE... COULD AT LEAST SEEM LIKE A FAMILY.
I REALIZED THAT WAS MY ONE SAVING GRACE.
W-WAIT! HOLD ON, HERE...
ARE YOU SAYING YOU AND REI-KUN...

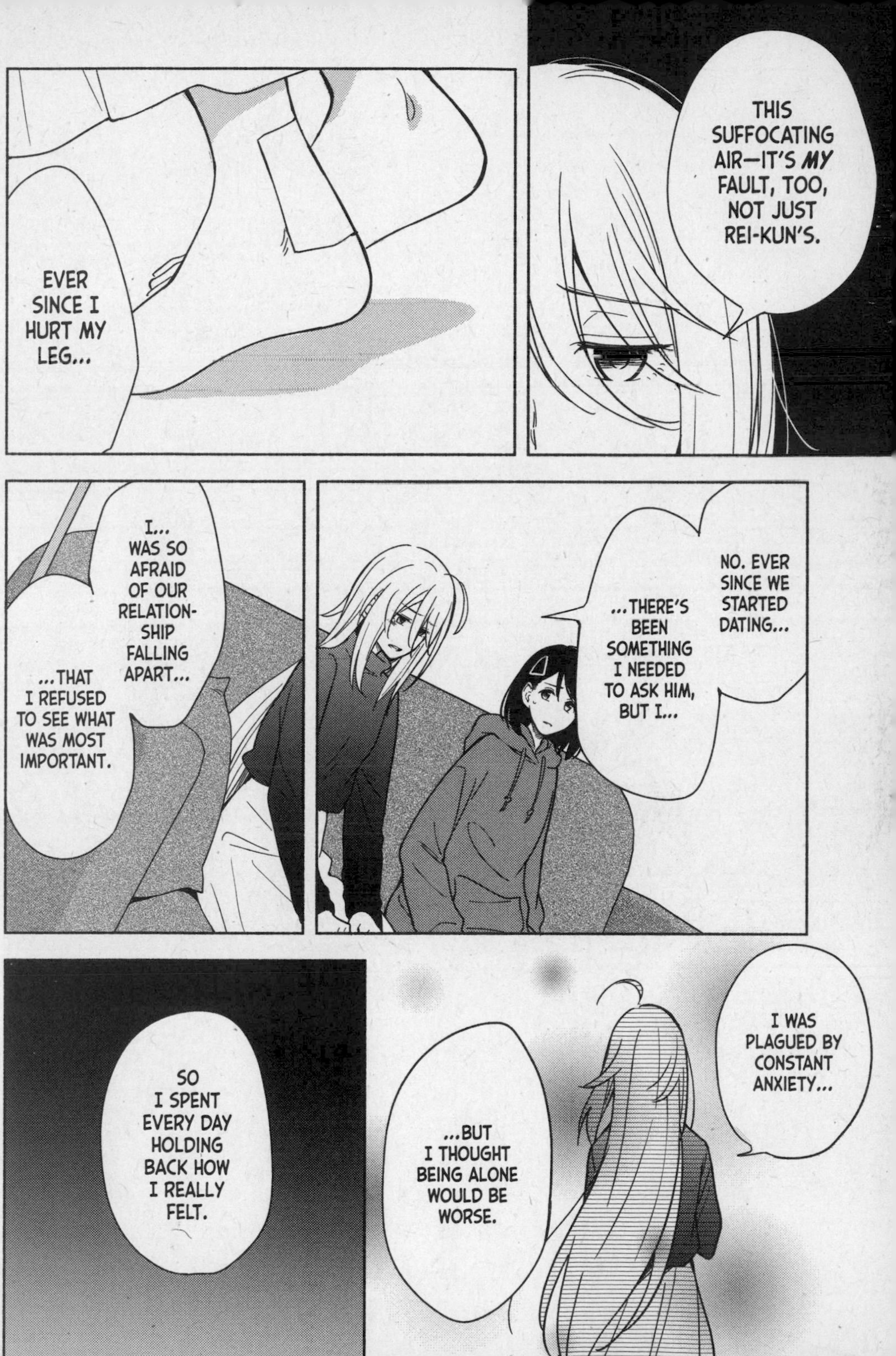
THIS SUFFOCATING AIR—IT'S *MY* FAULT, TOO, NOT JUST REI-KUN'S.
EVER SINCE I HURT MY LEG...
NO. EVER SINCE WE STARTED DATING...
...THERE'S BEEN SOMETHING I NEEDED TO ASK HIM, BUT I...
I... WAS SO AFRAID OF OUR RELATION-SHIP FALLING APART...
...THAT I REFUSED TO SEE WHAT WAS MOST IMPORTANT.
I WAS PLAGUED BY CONSTANT ANXIETY...
...BUT I THOUGHT BEING ALONE WOULD BE WORSE.
SO I SPENT EVERY DAY HOLDING BACK HOW I REALLY FELT.

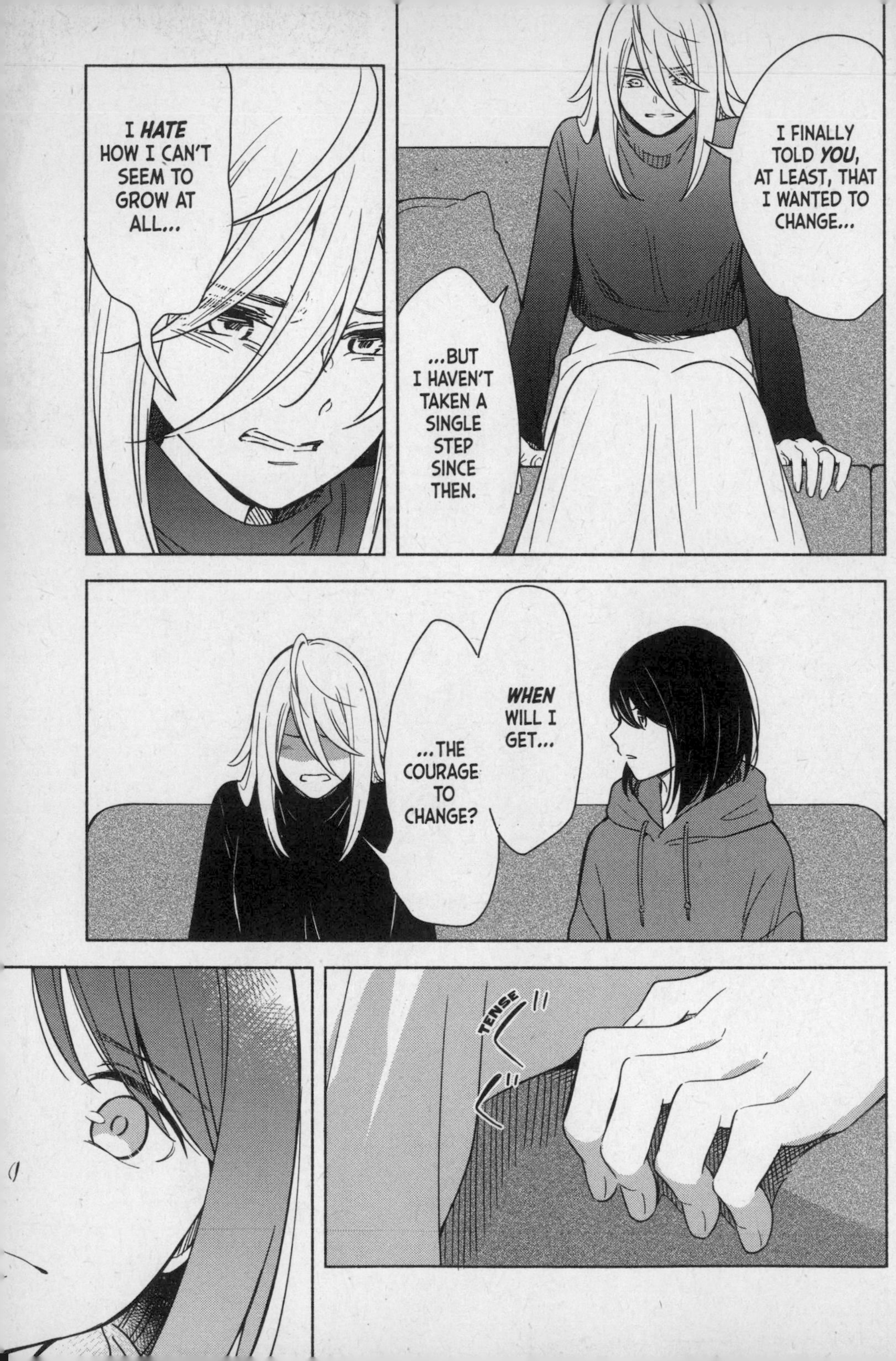
I FINALLY TOLD *YOU*, AT LEAST, THAT I WANTED TO CHANGE...
...BUT I HAVEN'T TAKEN A SINGLE STEP SINCE THEN.
I *HATE* HOW I CAN'T SEEM TO GROW AT ALL...
WHEN WILL I GET...
...THE COURAGE TO CHANGE?
TENSE

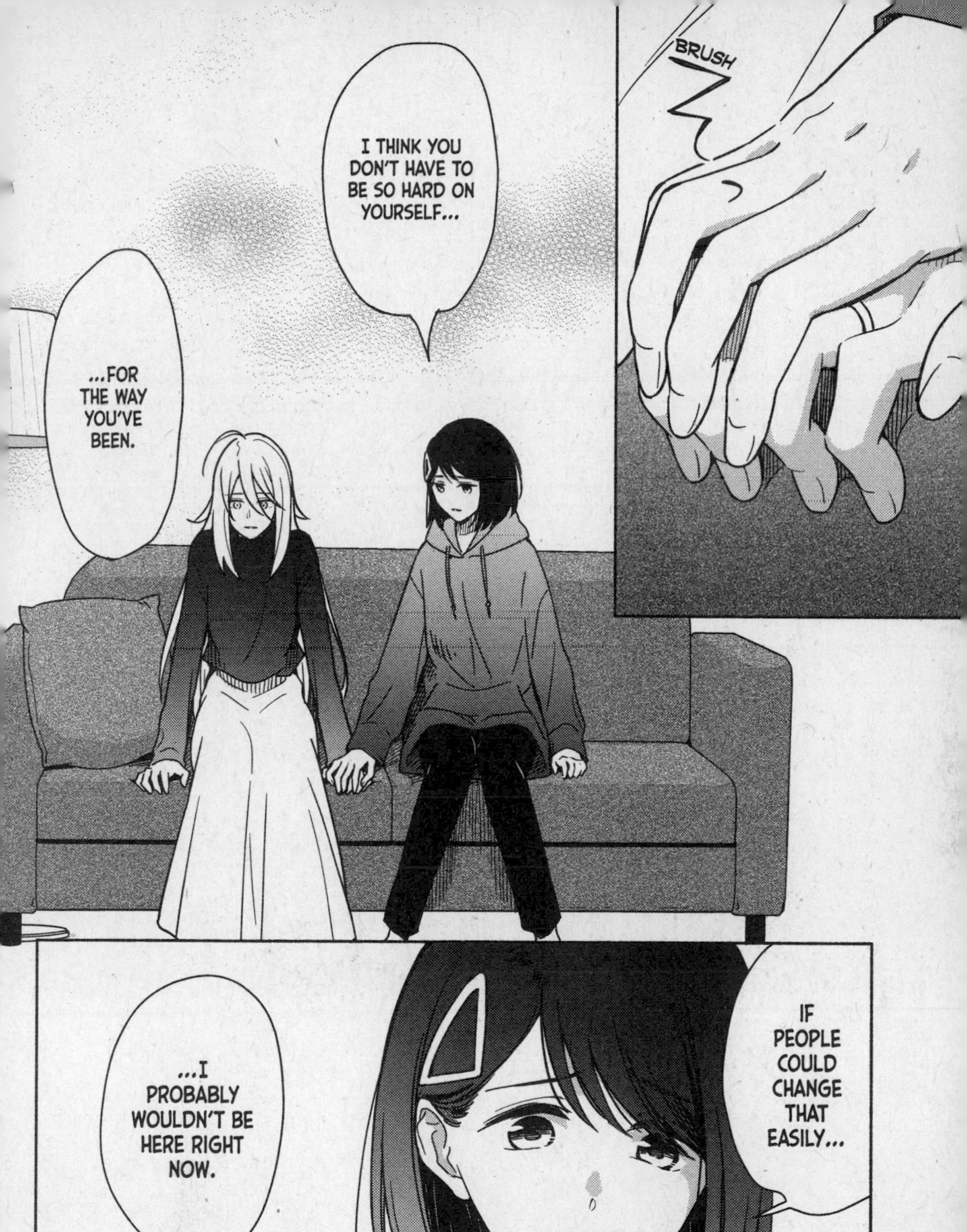
BRUSH
I THINK YOU DON'T HAVE TO BE SO HARD ON YOURSELF...
...FOR THE WAY YOU'VE BEEN.
IF PEOPLE COULD CHANGE THAT EASILY...
...I PROBABLY WOULDN'T BE HERE RIGHT NOW.

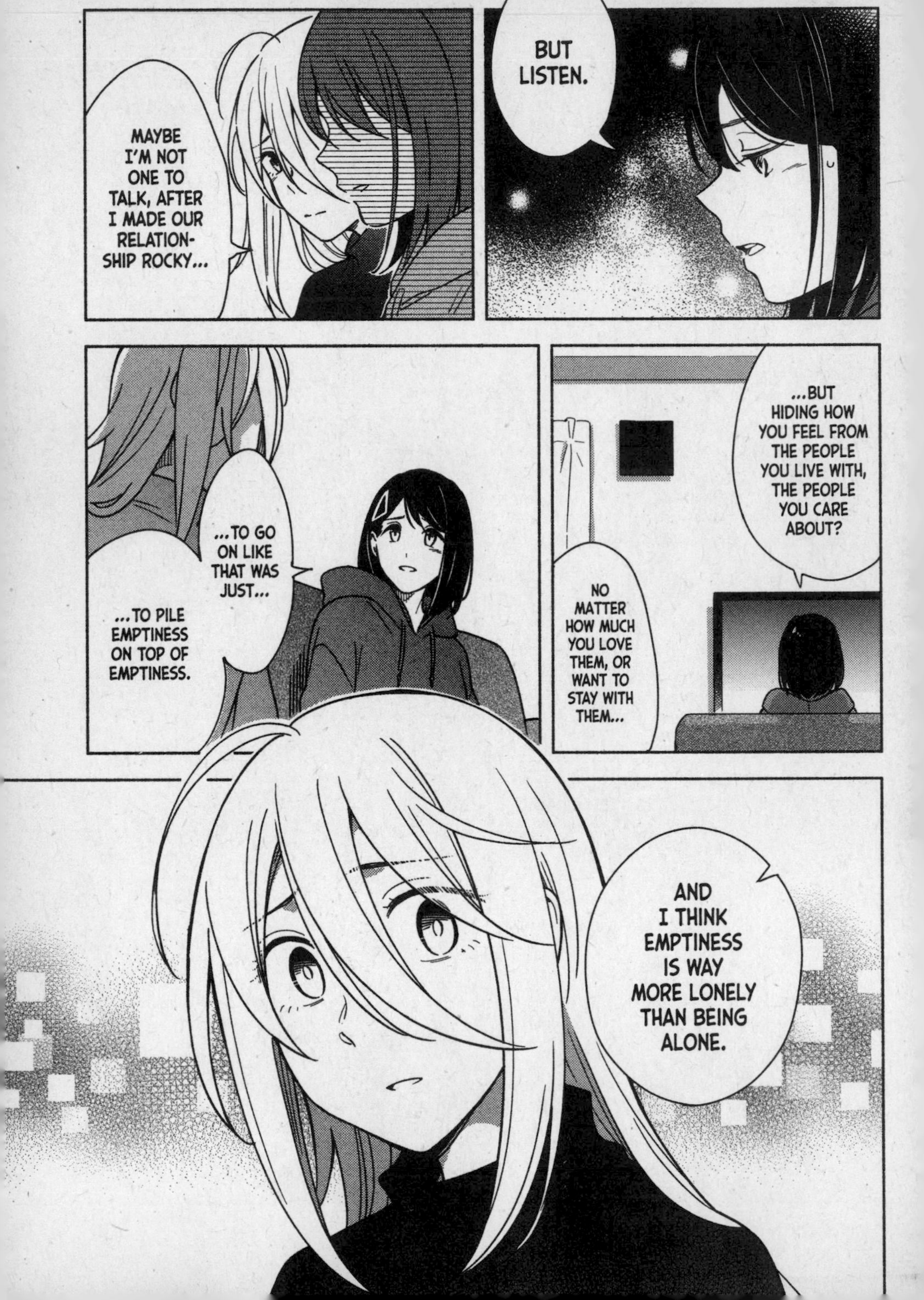
BUT LISTEN.
MAYBE I'M NOT ONE TO TALK, AFTER I MADE OUR RELATIONSHIP ROCKY...
...BUT HIDING HOW YOU FEEL FROM THE PEOPLE YOU LIVE WITH, THE PEOPLE YOU CARE ABOUT?
NO MATTER HOW MUCH YOU LOVE THEM, OR WANT TO STAY WITH THEM...
...TO GO ON LIKE THAT WAS JUST...
...TO PILE EMPTINESS ON TOP OF EMPTINESS.
AND I THINK EMPTINESS IS WAY MORE LONELY THAN BEING ALONE.

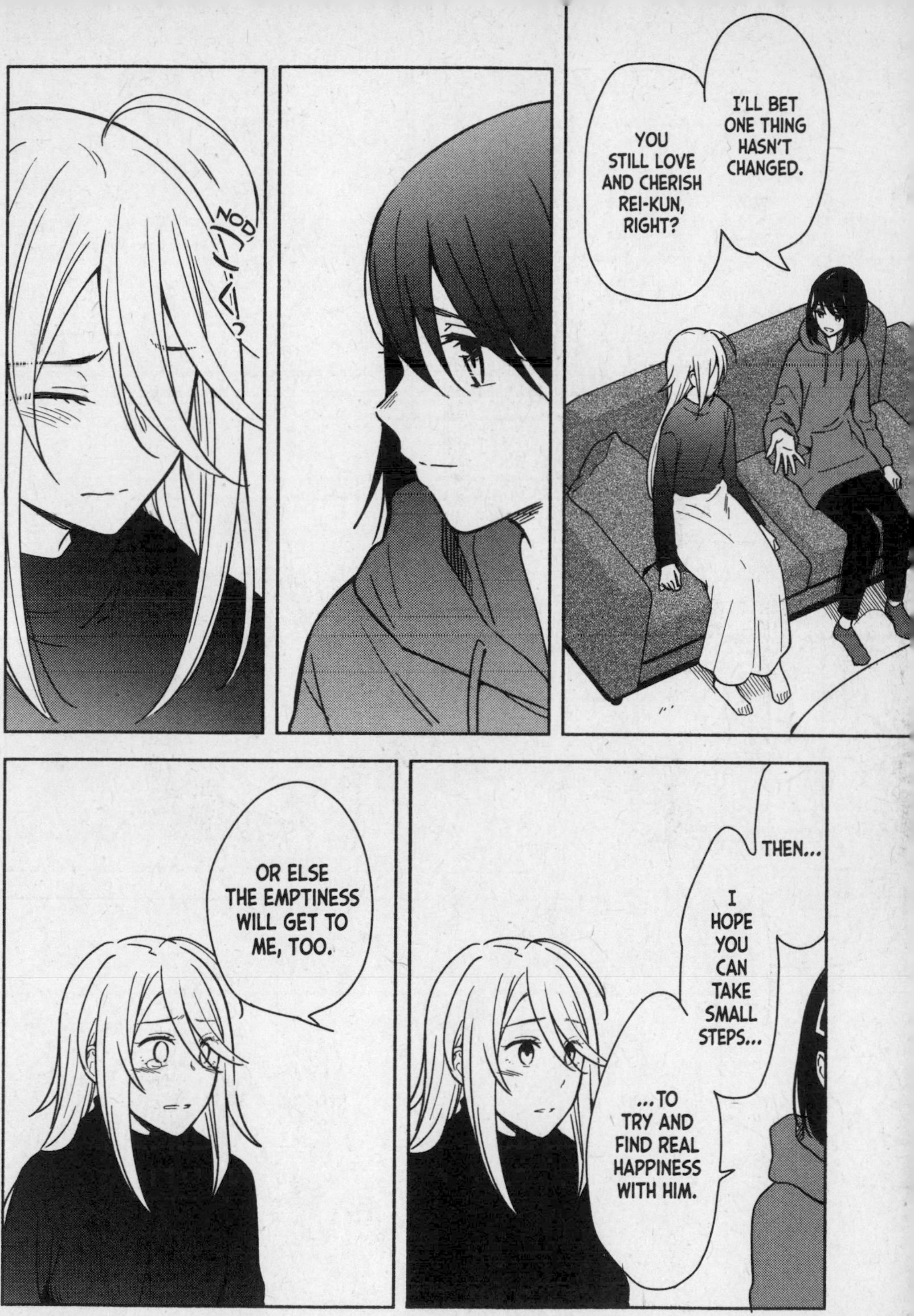
I'LL BET ONE THING HASN'T CHANGED.
YOU STILL LOVE AND CHERISH REI-KUN, RIGHT?
NOD
THEN...
I HOPE YOU CAN TAKE SMALL STEPS...
...TO TRY AND FIND REAL HAPPINESS WITH HIM.
OR ELSE THE EMPTINESS WILL GET TO ME, TOO.

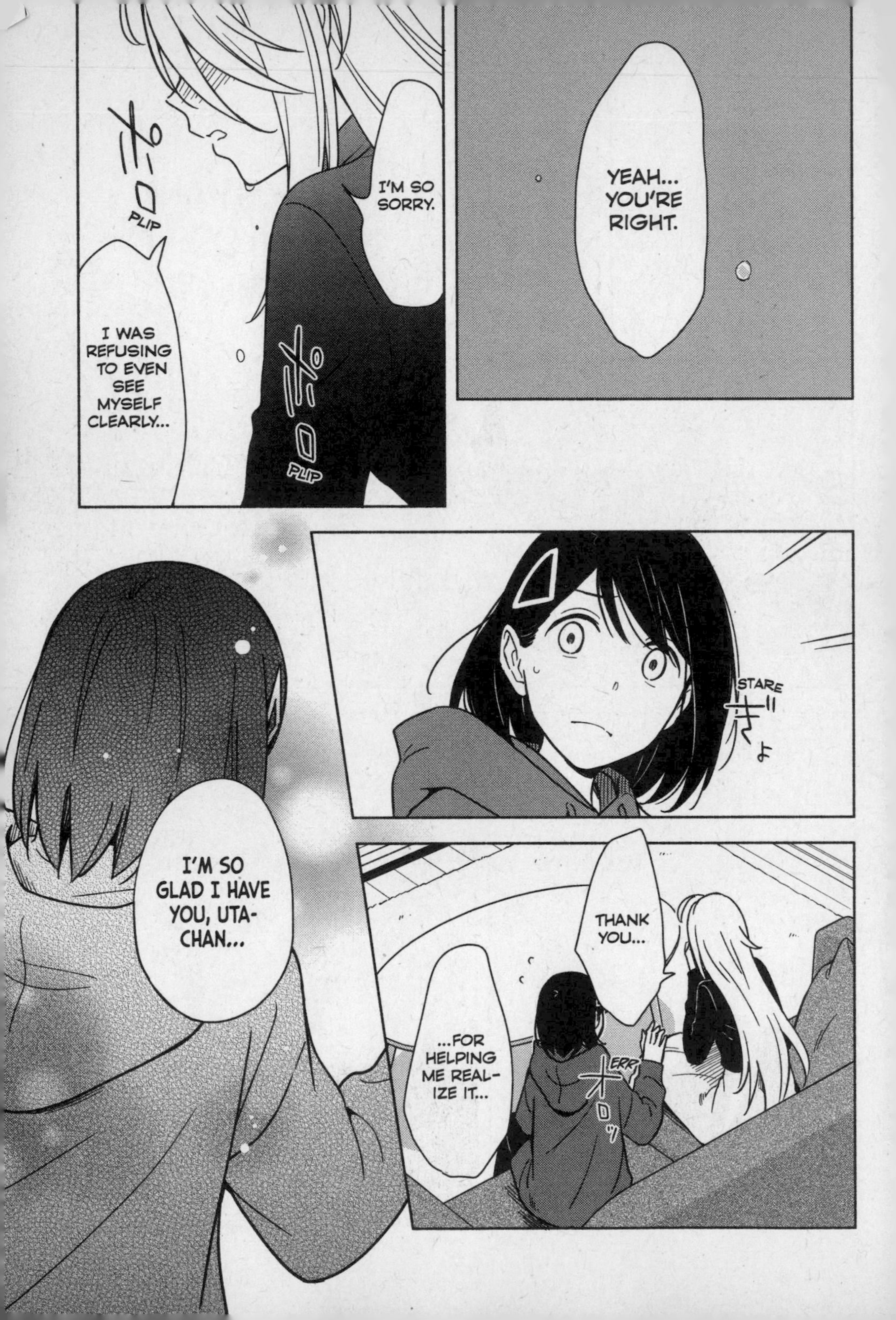
YEAH... YOU'RE RIGHT.
I'M SO SORRY.
PLIP
I WAS REFUSING TO EVEN SEE MYSELF CLEARLY...
PLIP
STARE
THANK YOU...
...FOR HELPING ME REALIZE IT...
ERR
I'M SO GLAD I HAVE YOU, UTA-CHAN...

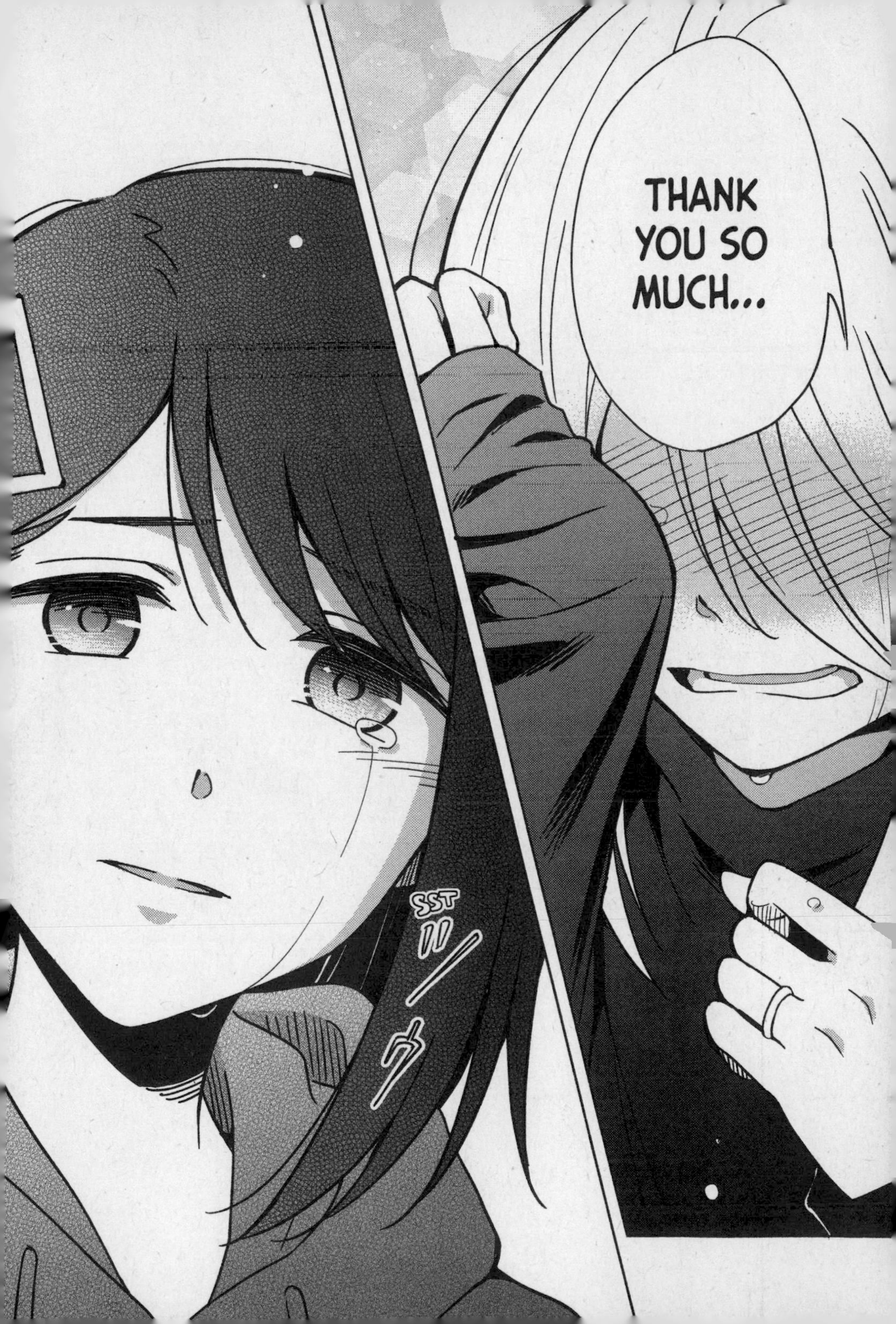
THANK YOU SO MUCH...
SST

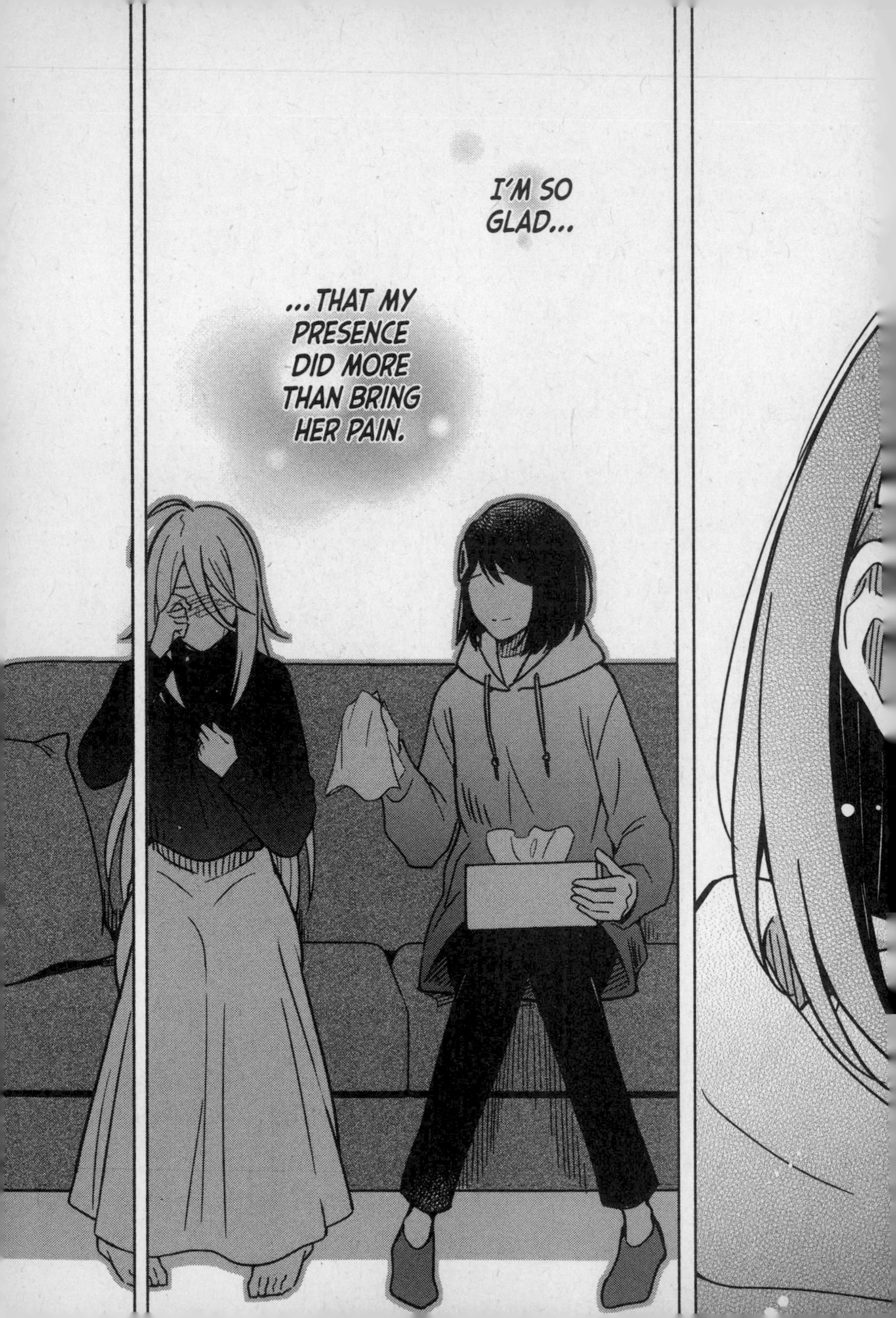
I'M SO GLAD...
...THAT MY PRESENCE DID MORE THAN BRING HER PAIN.

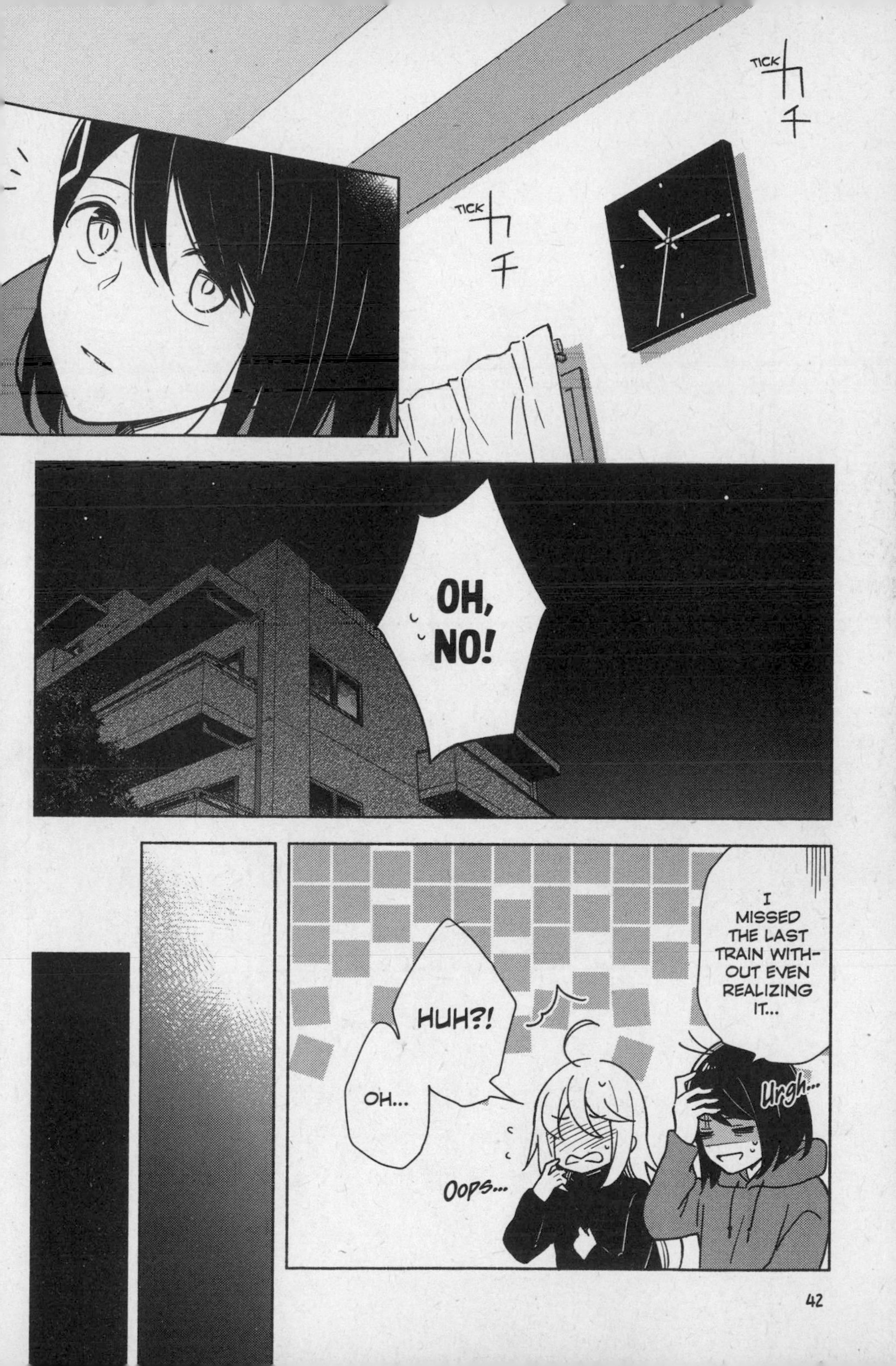
TICK
カチ
TICK
カチ
OH, NO!
I MISSED THE LAST TRAIN WITH-OUT EVEN REALIZING IT...
Urgh...
HUH?!
OH...
Oops...

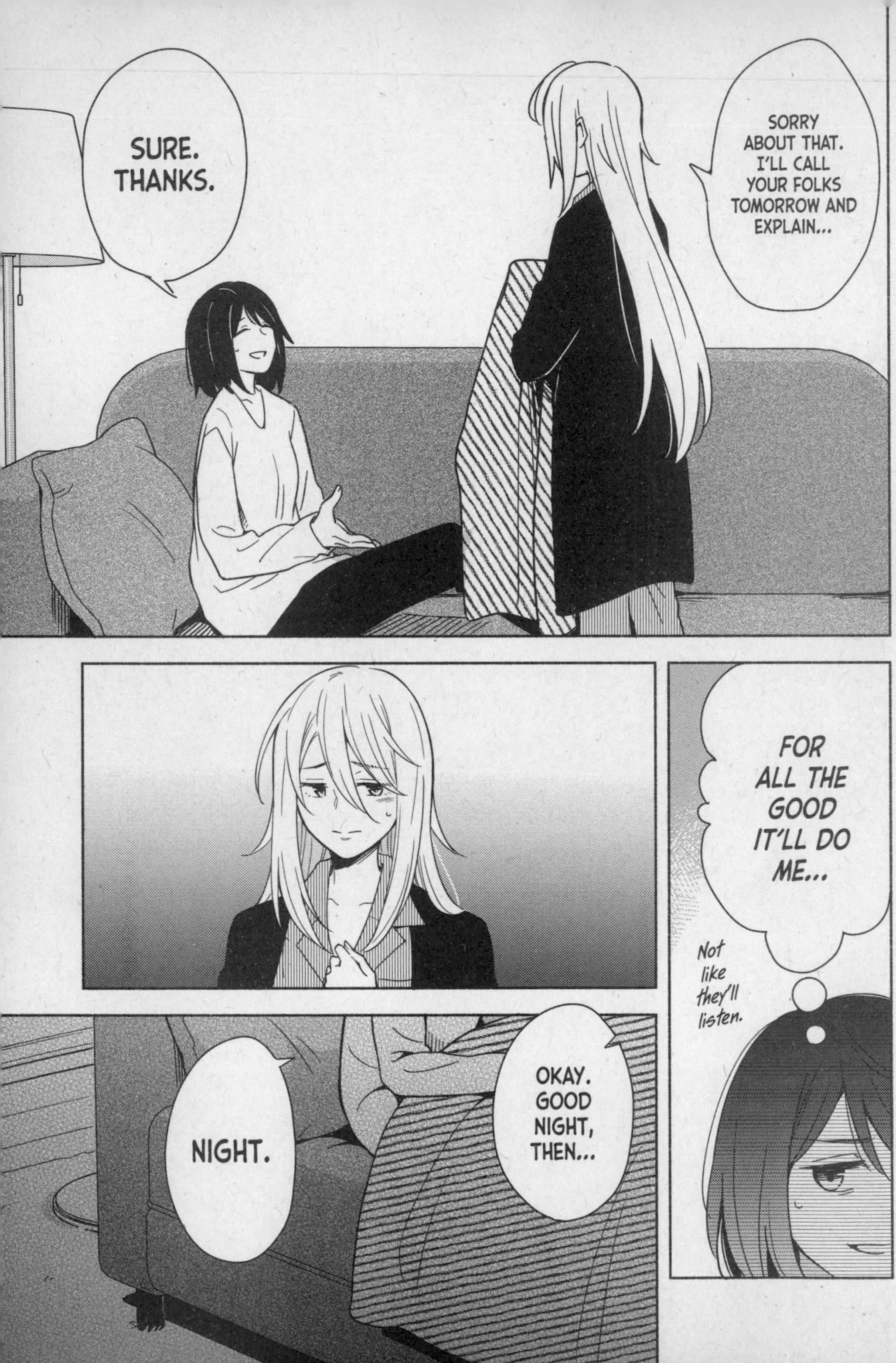
SORRY ABOUT THAT. I'LL CALL YOUR FOLKS TOMORROW AND EXPLAIN...
SURE. THANKS.
FOR ALL THE GOOD IT'LL DO ME...
Not like they'll listen.
OKAY. GOOD NIGHT, THEN...
NIGHT.

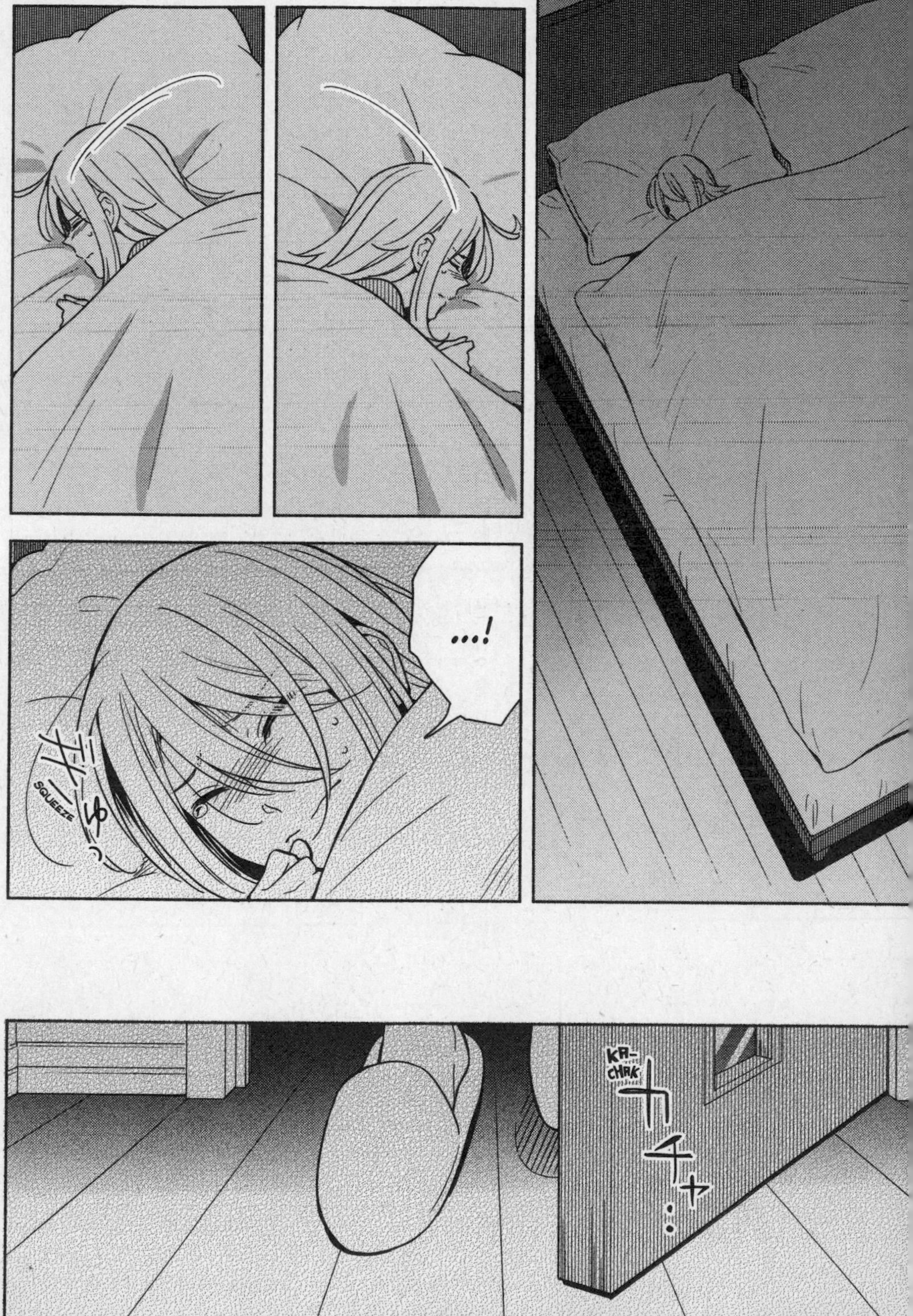
...!
SQUEEZE
KA-CHAK

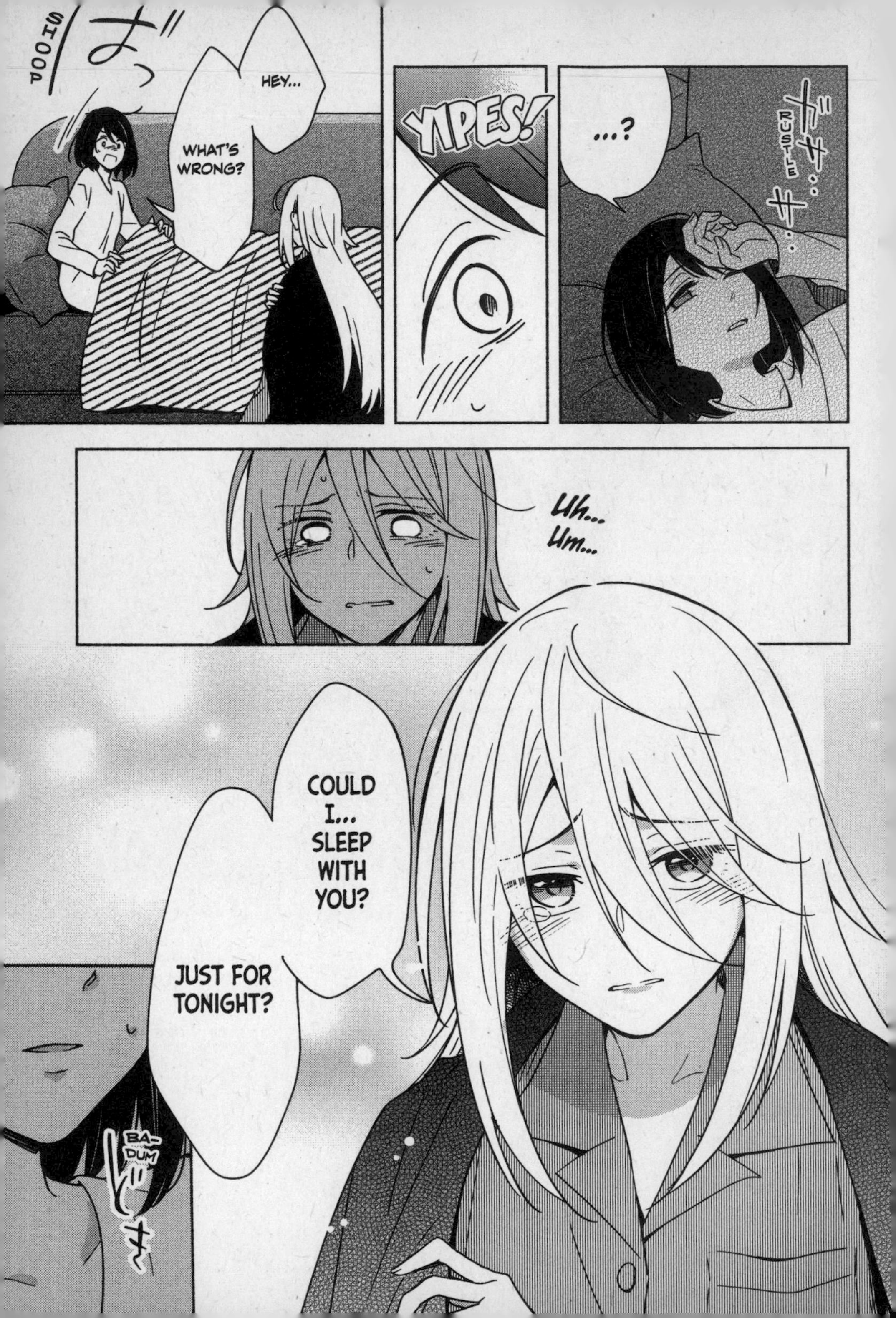
RUSTLE
...?
YIPES!
SHOOP
HEY...
WHAT'S WRONG?
Uh... Um...
COULD I... SLEEP WITH YOU?
JUST FOR TONIGHT?
BA-DUM

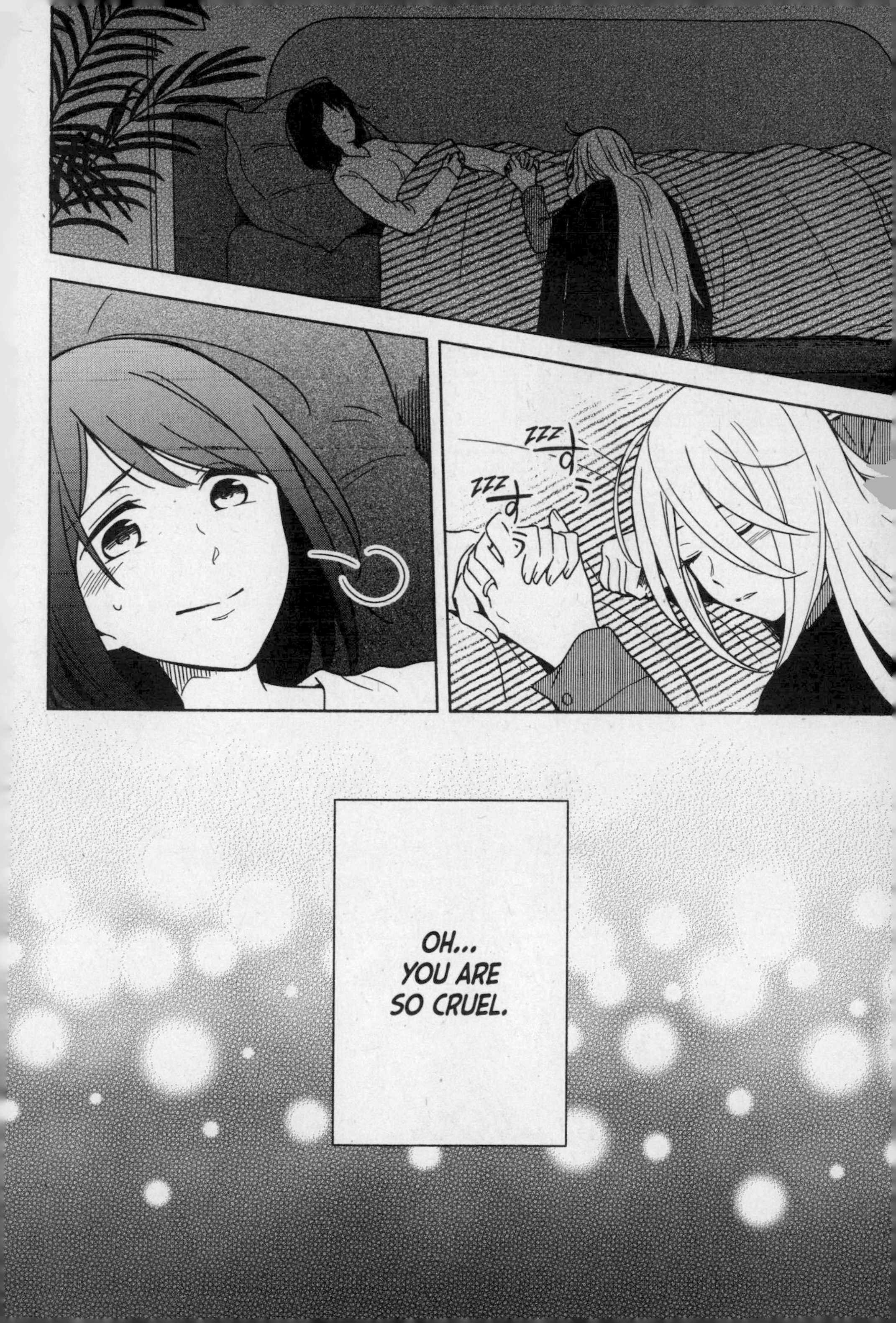
ZZZ
ZZZ
OH... YOU ARE SO CRUEL.

If I Could
Reach You

If I Could
Reach You

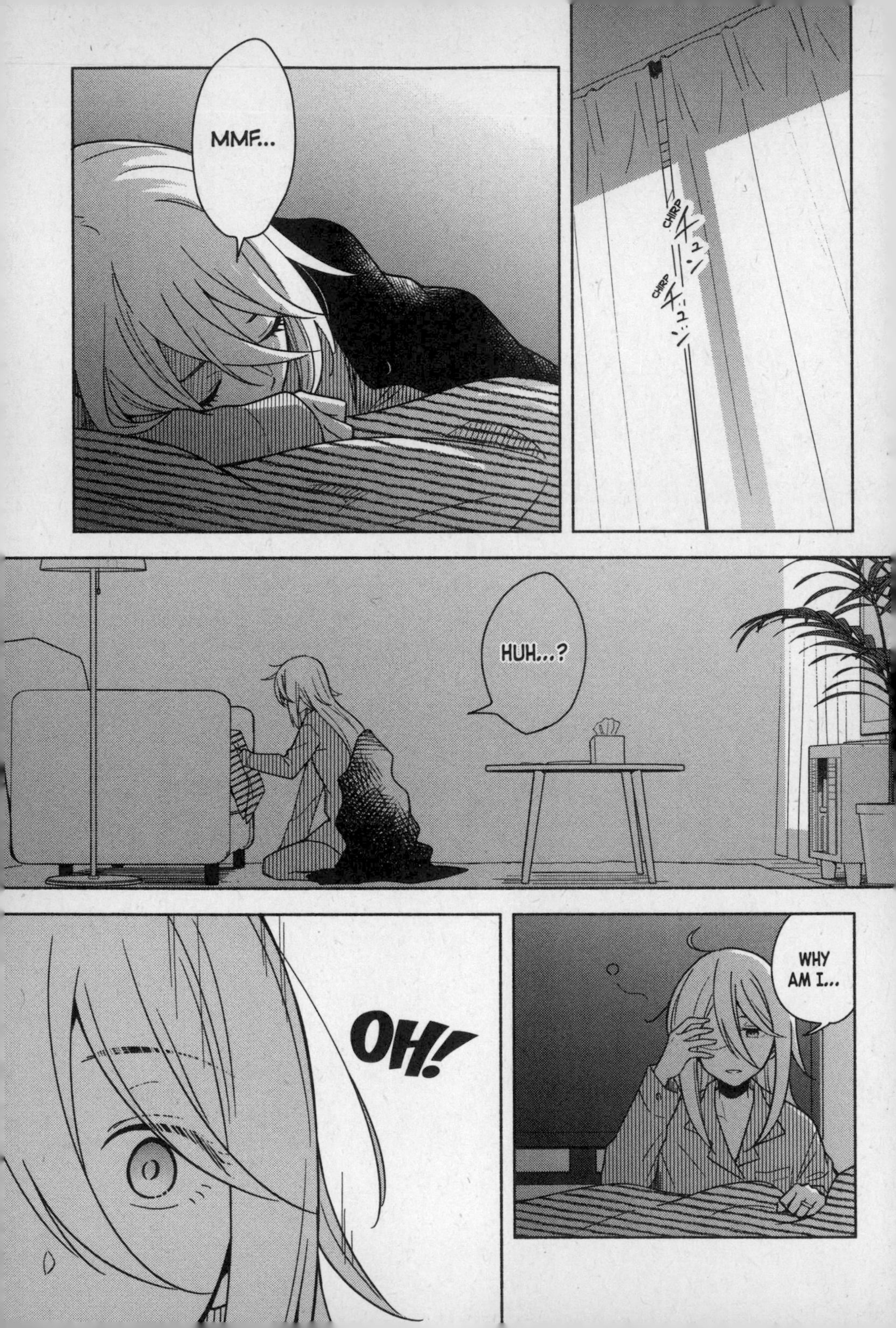
CHIRP
CHIRP
MMF...
HUH...?
WHY AM I...
OH!

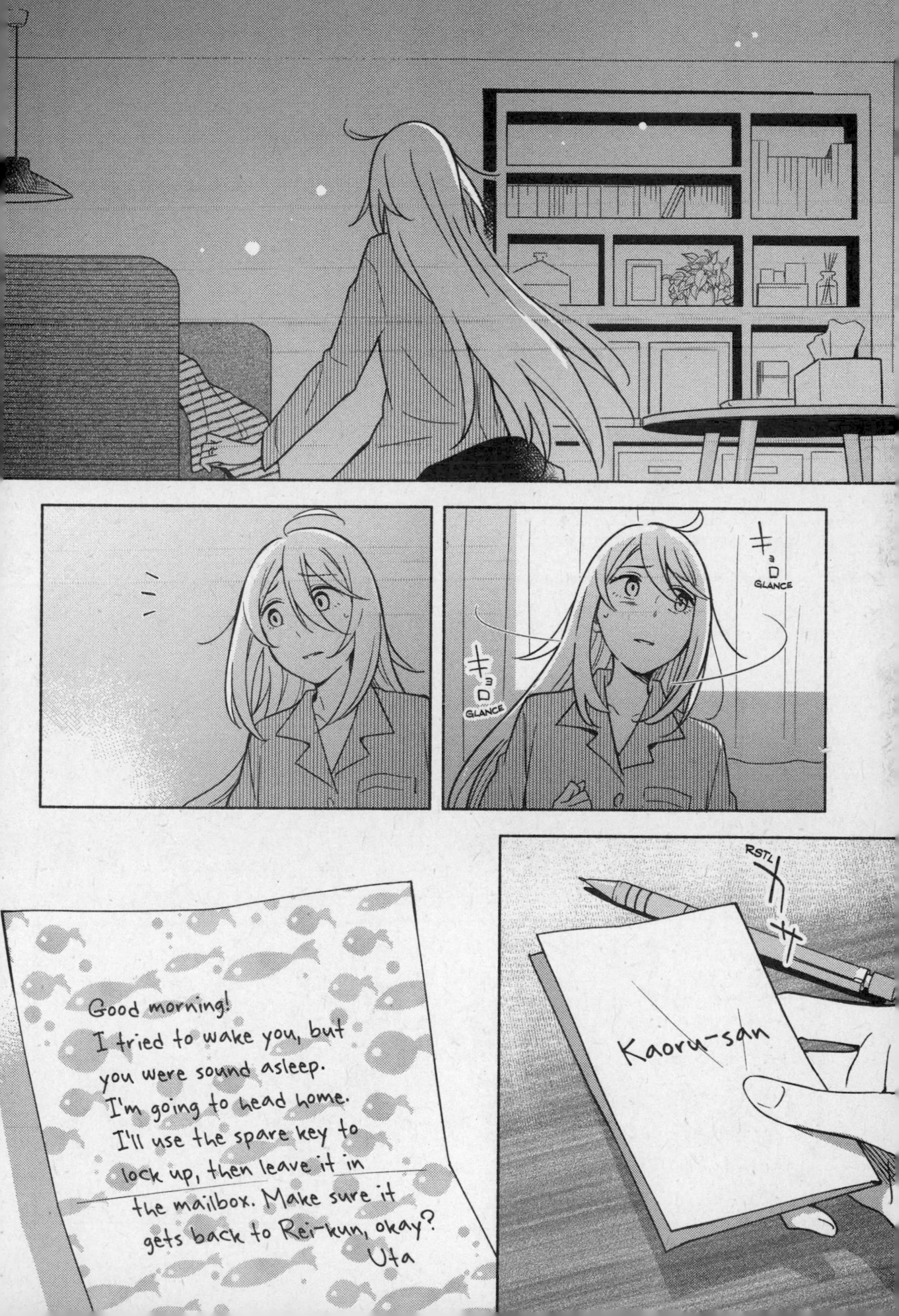
GLANCE
GLANCE
RSTL
Kaoru-san
Good morning!
I tried to wake you, but
you were sound asleep.
I'm going to head home.
I'll use the spare key to
lock up, then leave it in
the mailbox. Make sure it
gets back to Rei-kun, okay?
Uta

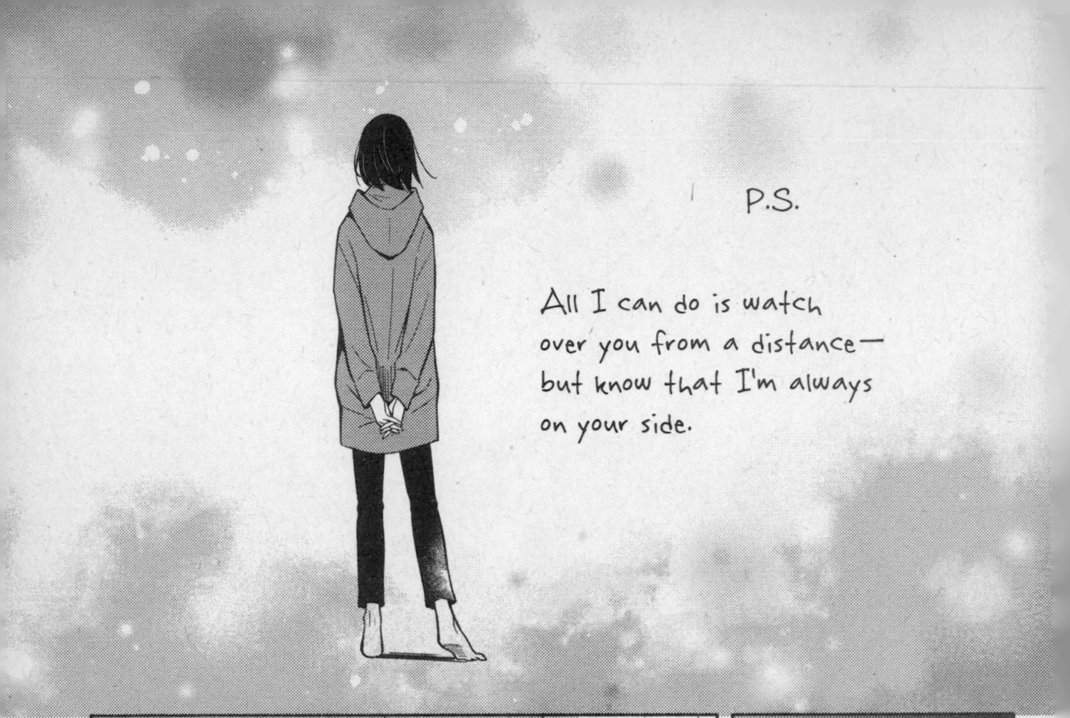
P.S.
All I can do is watch over you from a distance—but know that I'm always on your side.

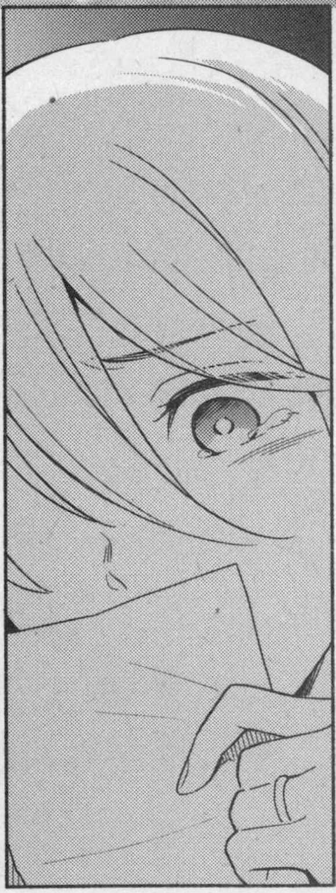

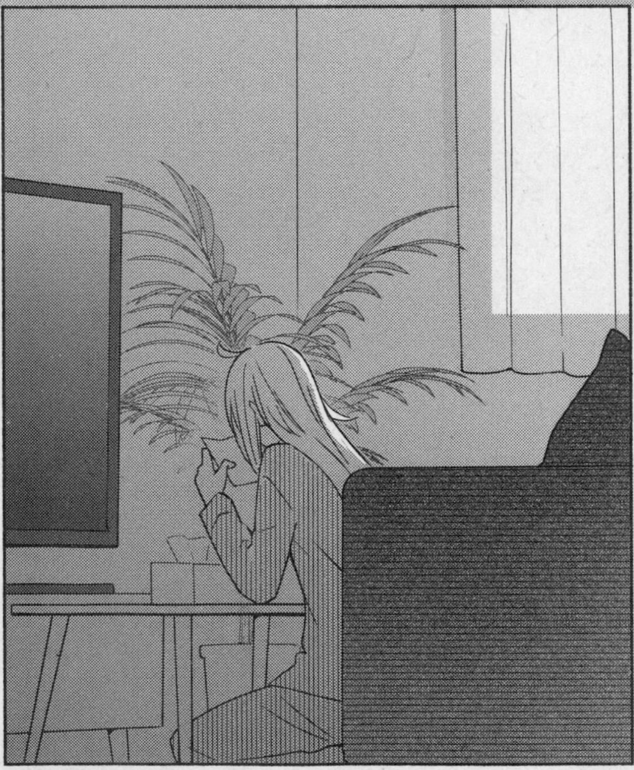

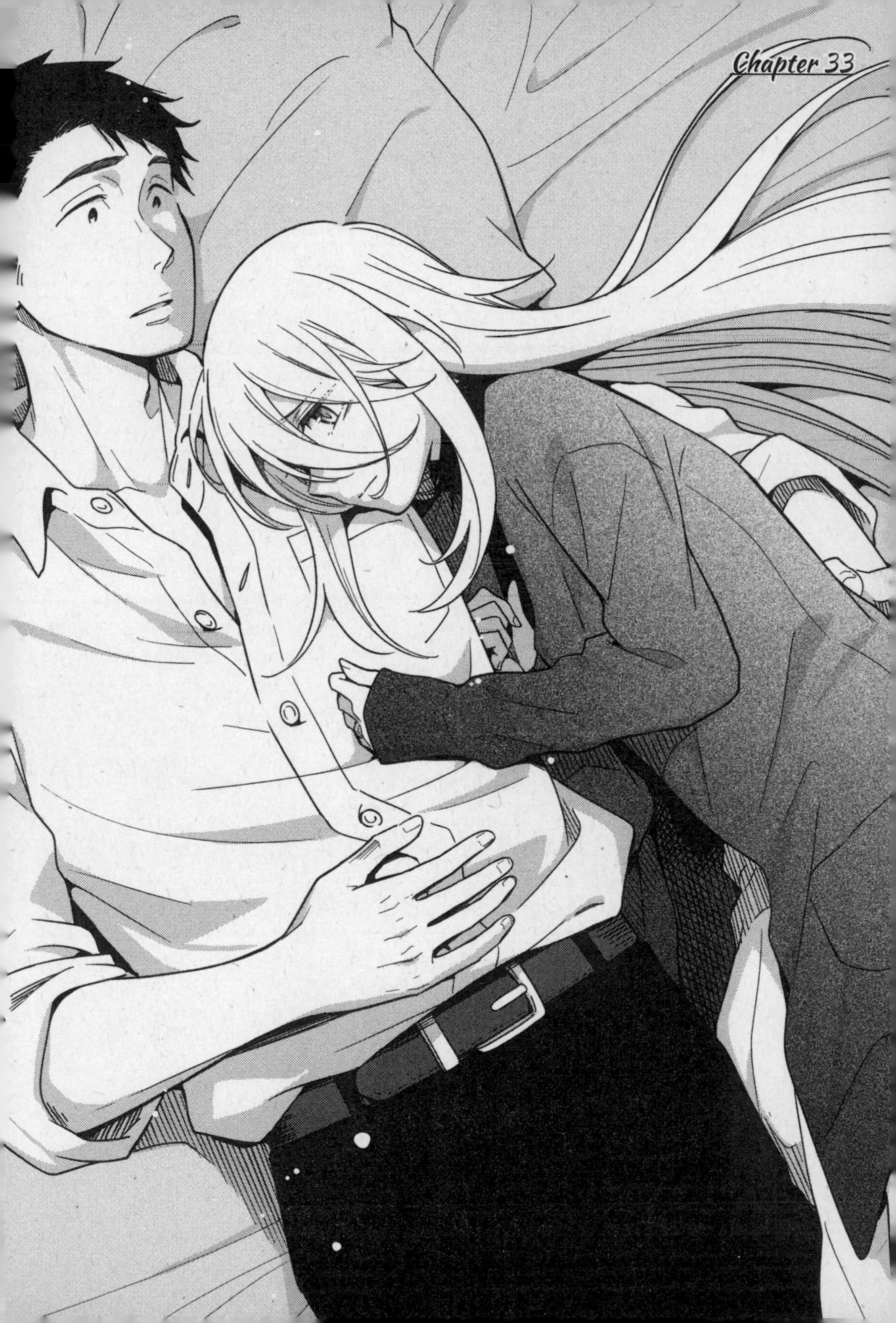
Chapter 33

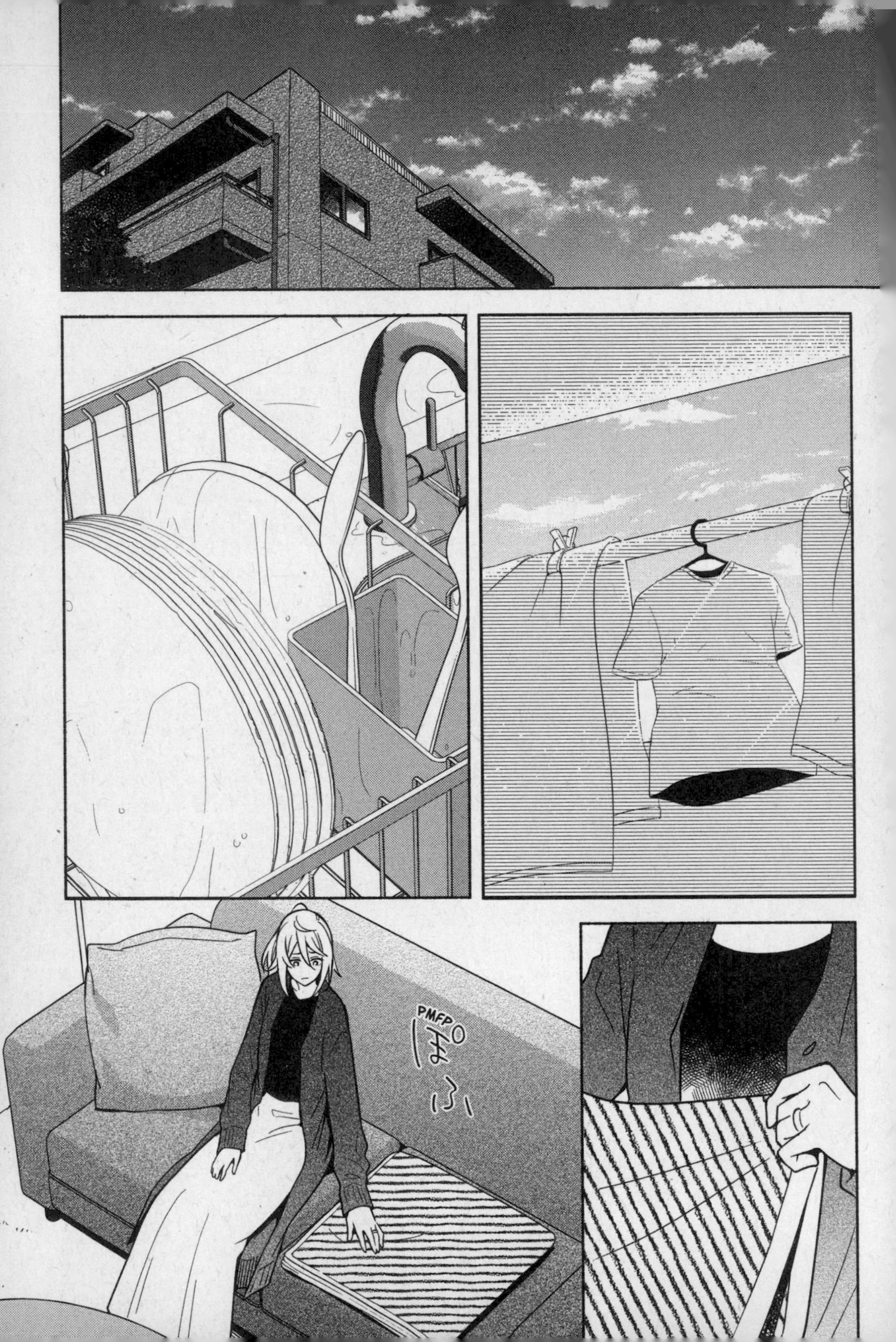
PMFP
ぽふ

WHAT AM I DOING?

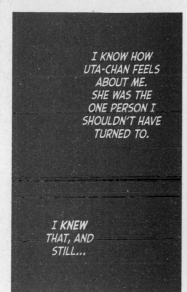

I KNOW HOW UTA-CHAN FEELS ABOUT ME. SHE WAS THE ONE PERSON I SHOULDN'T HAVE TURNED TO.

I KNEW THAT, AND STILL...

SHAKE

Oh...

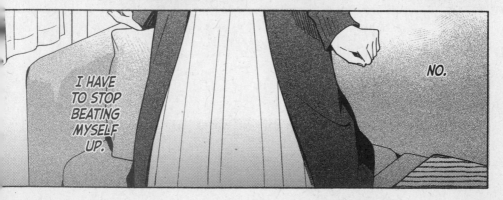

I HAVE TO STOP BEATING MYSELF UP.

NO.

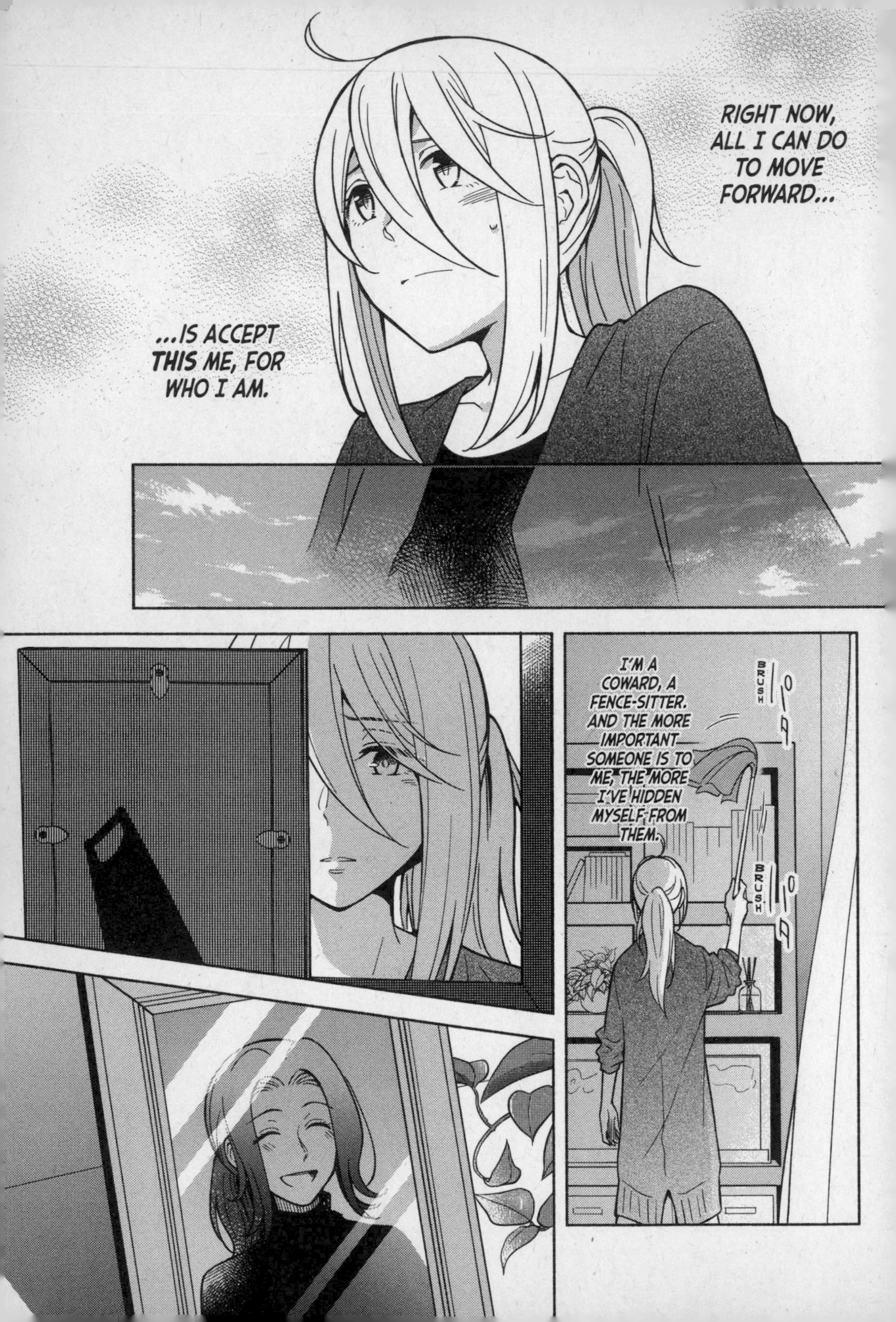
RIGHT NOW, ALL I CAN DO TO MOVE FORWARD...
...IS ACCEPT THIS ME, FOR WHO I AM.
BRUSH
BRUSH
I'M A COWARD, A FENCE-SITTER. AND THE MORE IMPORTANT SOMEONE IS TO ME, THE MORE I'VE HIDDEN MYSELF FROM THEM.

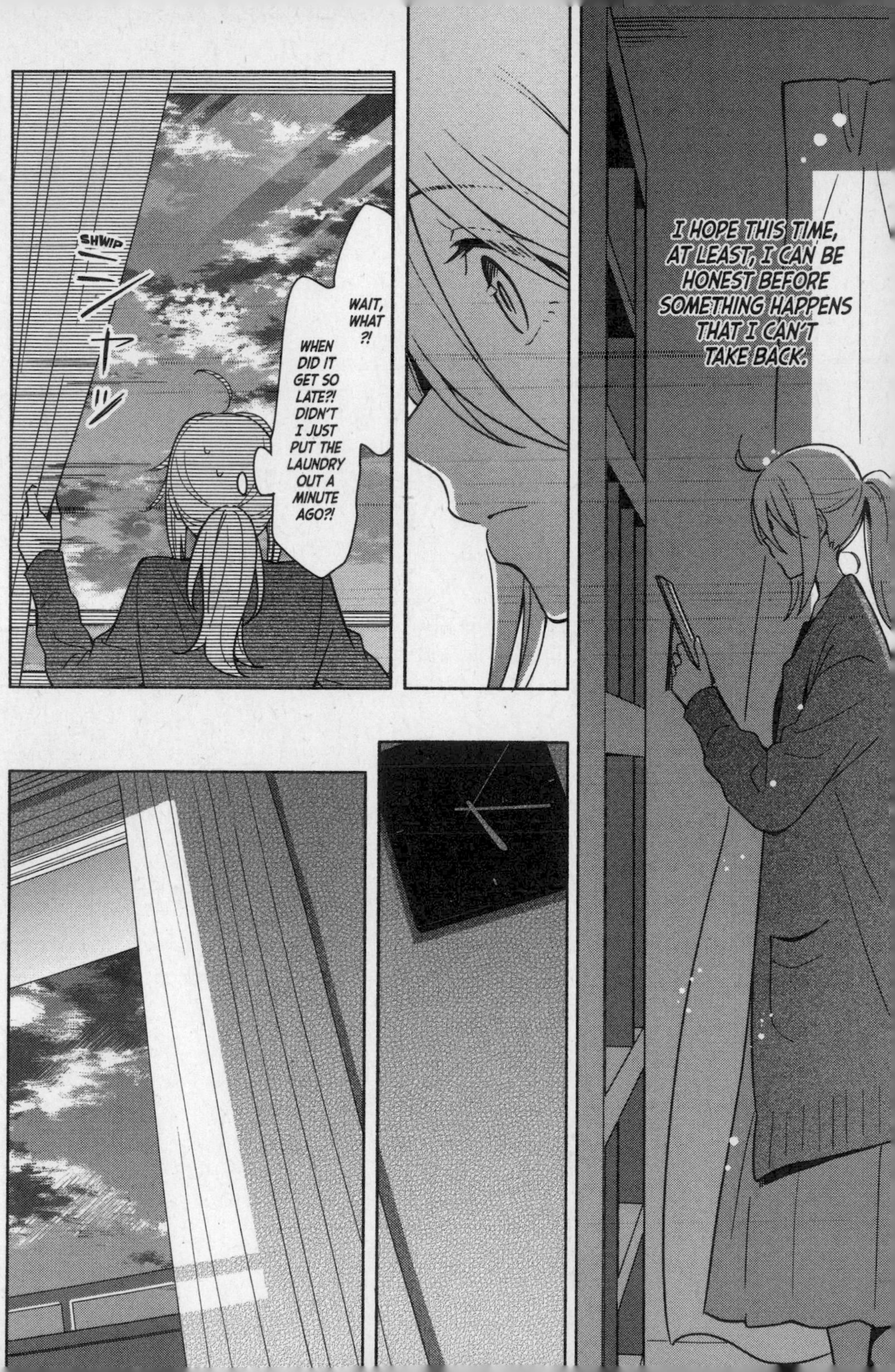
I HOPE THIS TIME, AT LEAST, I CAN BE HONEST BEFORE SOMETHING HAPPENS THAT I CAN'T TAKE BACK.
WAIT, WHAT?!
WHEN DID IT GET SO LATE?! DIDN'T I JUST PUT THE LAUNDRY OUT A MINUTE AGO?!
SHWIP

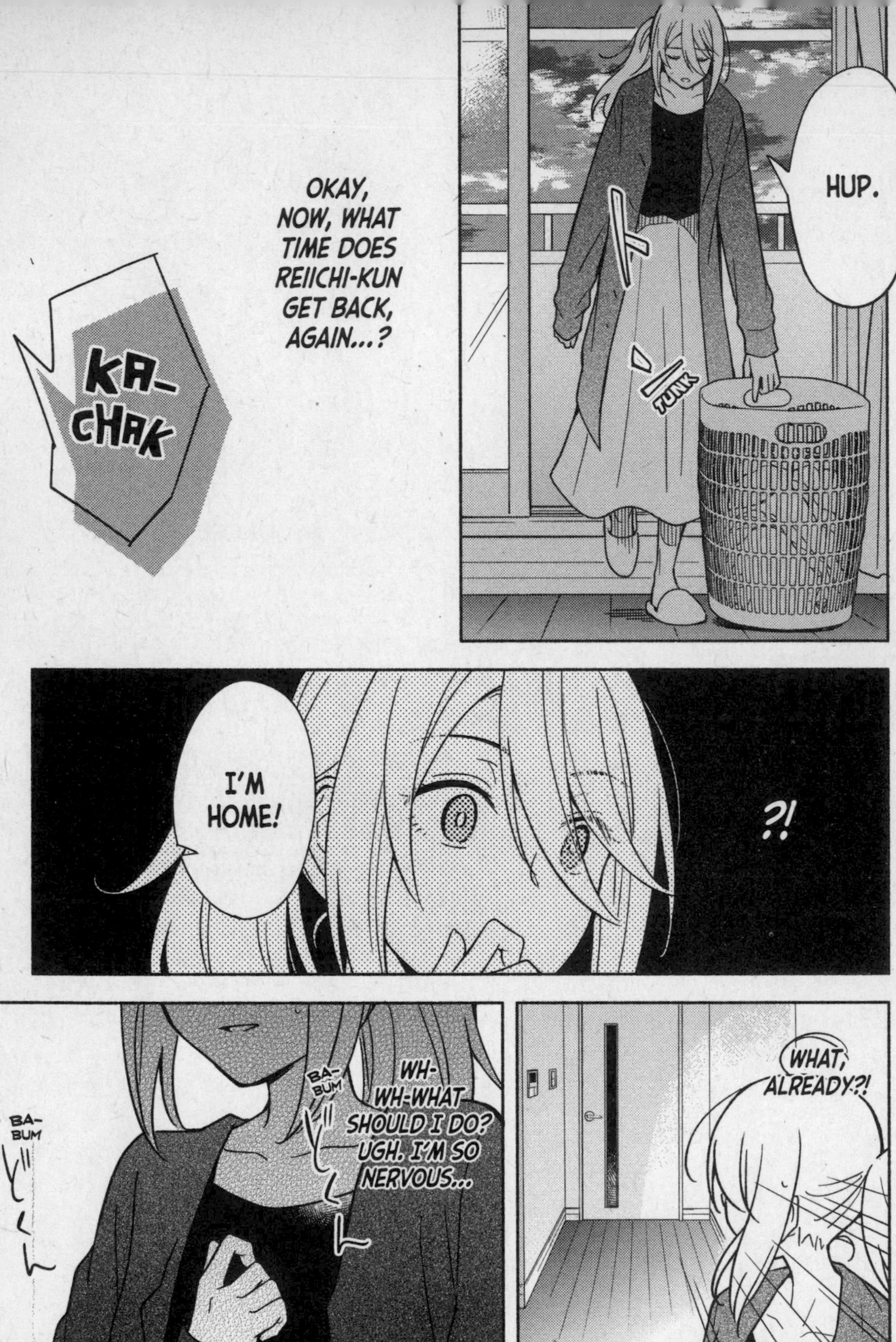
HUP.
TUNK
OKAY, NOW, WHAT TIME DOES REIICHI-KUN GET BACK, AGAIN...?
KA-CHAK
I'M HOME!
?!
WHAT, ALREADY?!
WH-WH-WHAT SHOULD I DO? UGH. I'M SO NERVOUS...
BA-BUM
BA-BUM

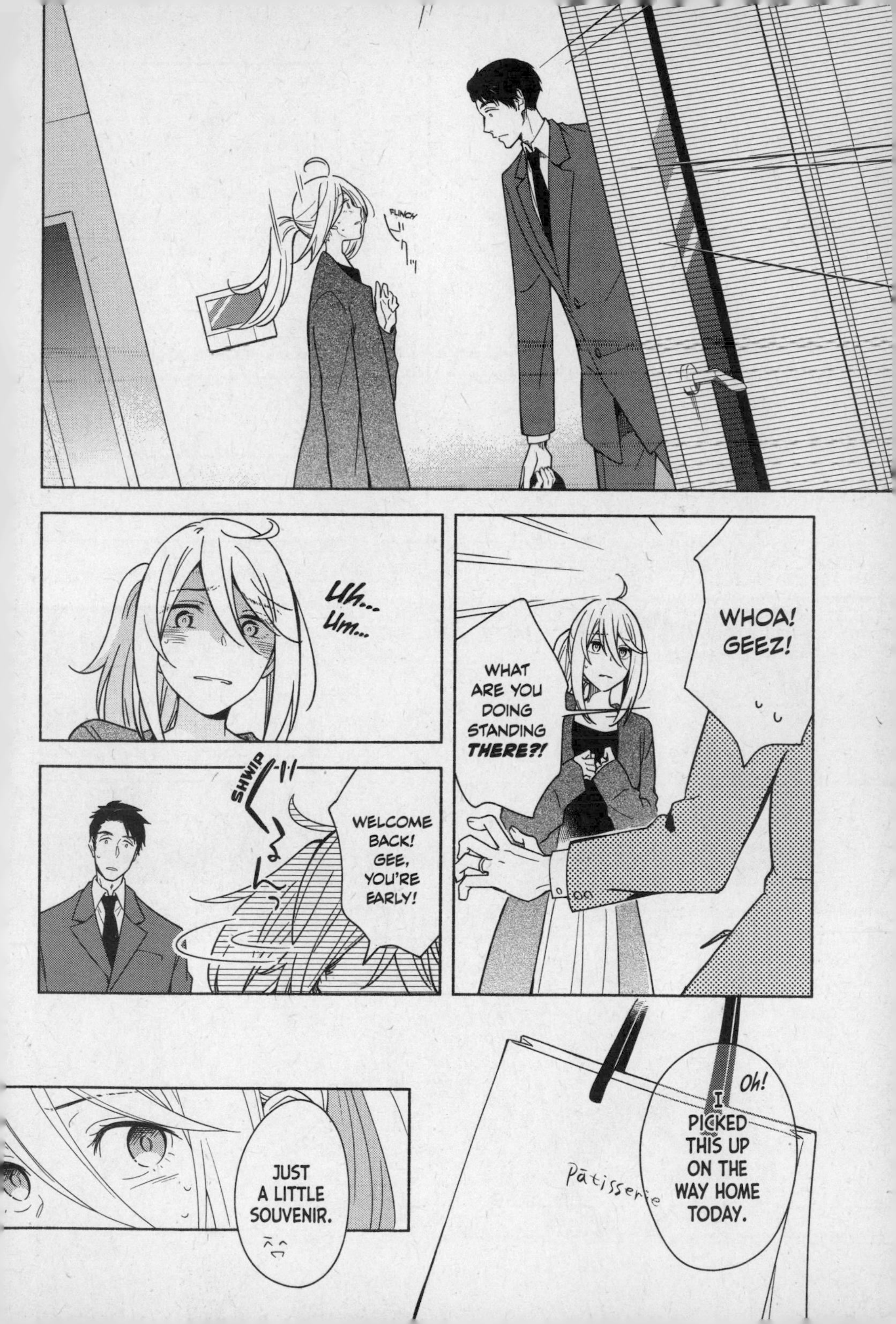
FLINCH
WHOA! GEEZ!
WHAT ARE YOU DOING STANDING THERE?!
Uh... Um...
SHWIP
WELCOME BACK! GEE, YOU'RE EARLY!
Oh!
I PICKED THIS UP ON THE WAY HOME TODAY.
Pâtisserie
JUST A LITTLE SOUVENIR.

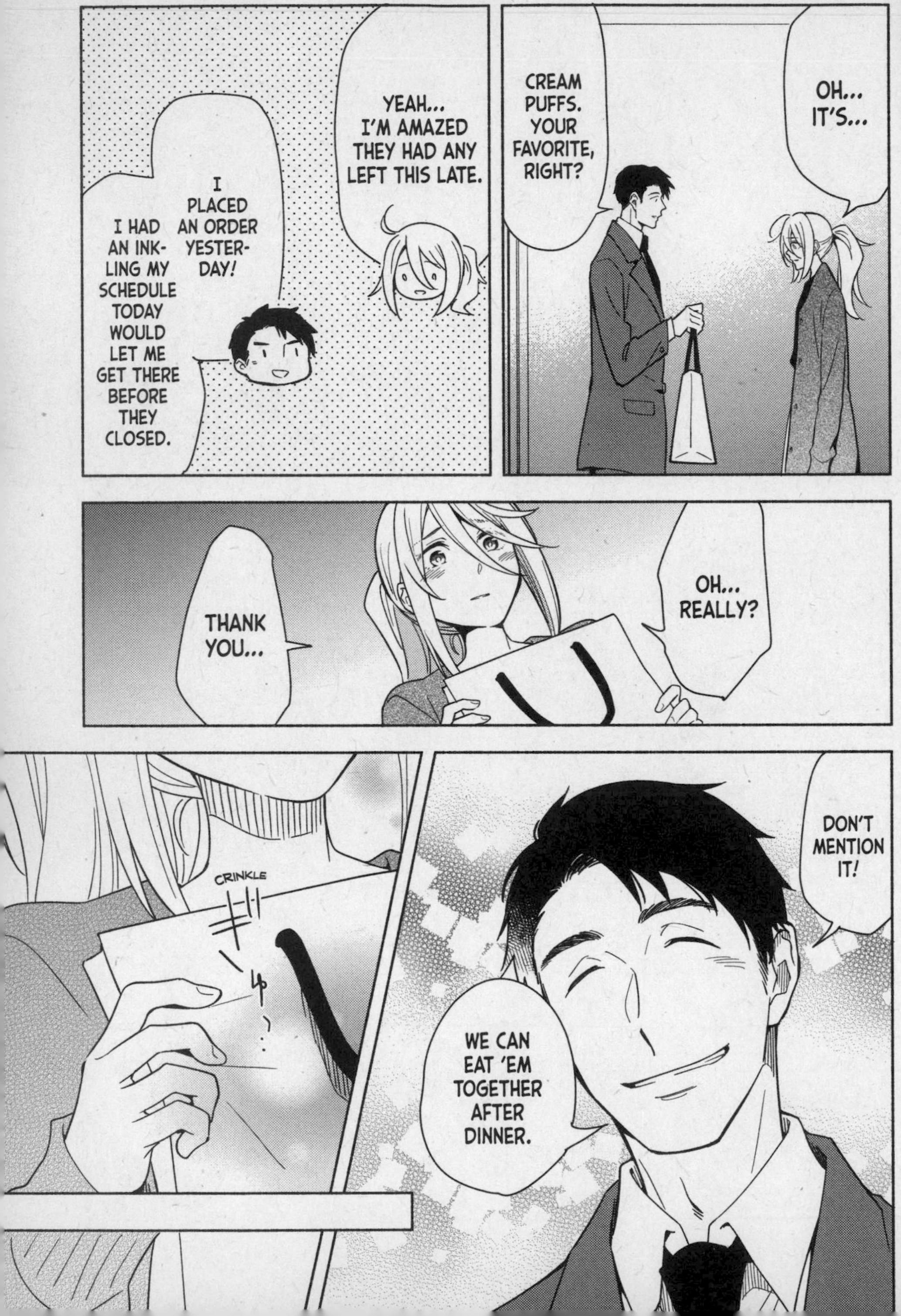
OH... IT'S...
CREAM PUFFS. YOUR FAVORITE, RIGHT?
YEAH... I'M AMAZED THEY HAD ANY LEFT THIS LATE.
I PLACED AN ORDER YESTERDAY!
I HAD AN INKLING MY SCHEDULE TODAY WOULD LET ME GET THERE BEFORE THEY CLOSED.
OH... REALLY?
THANK YOU...
DON'T MENTION IT!
WE CAN EAT 'EM TOGETHER AFTER DINNER.
CRINKLE

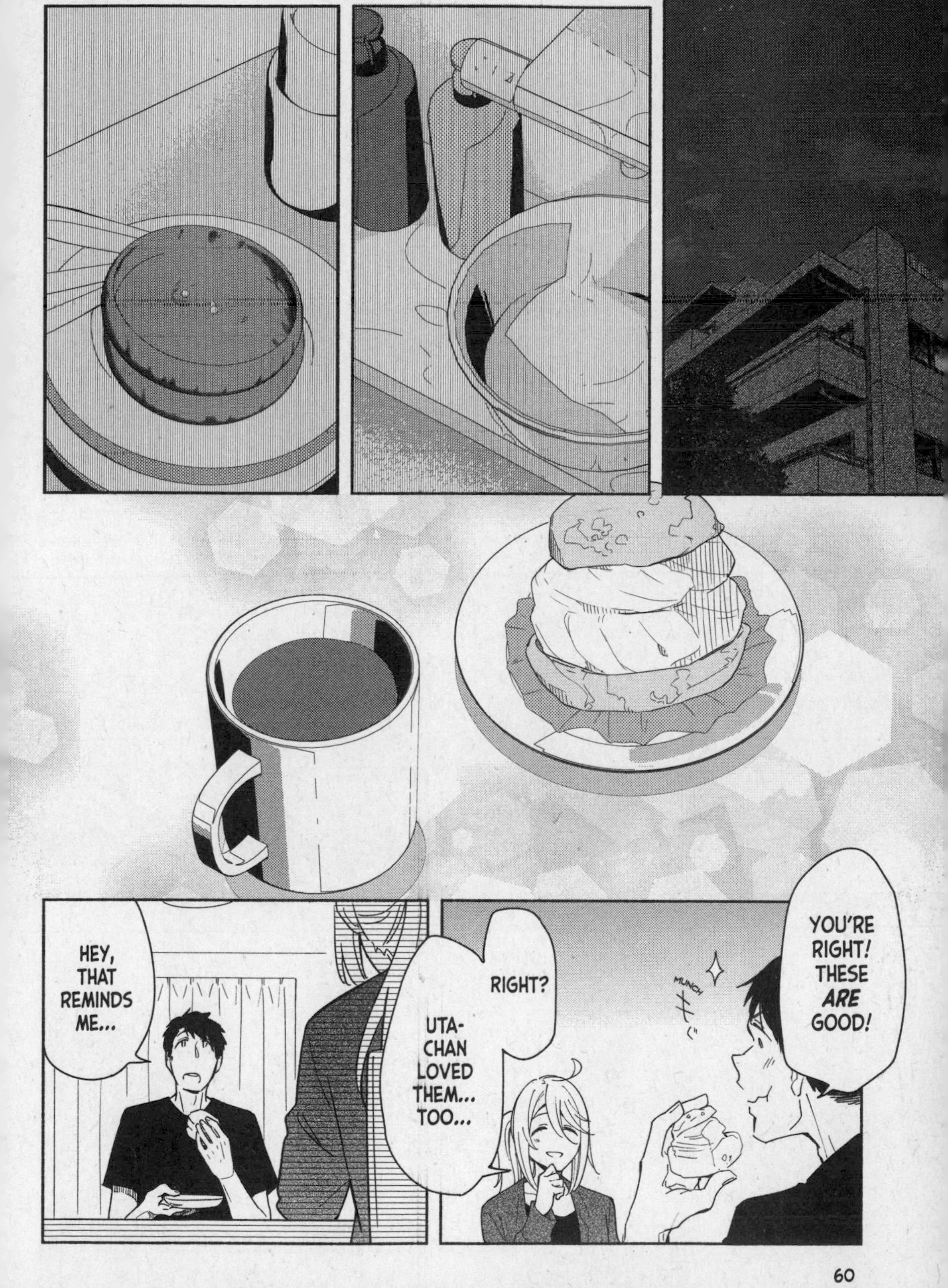
YOU'RE RIGHT! THESE *ARE* GOOD!
MUNCH
RIGHT?
UTA-CHAN LOVED THEM... TOO...
HEY, THAT REMINDS ME...

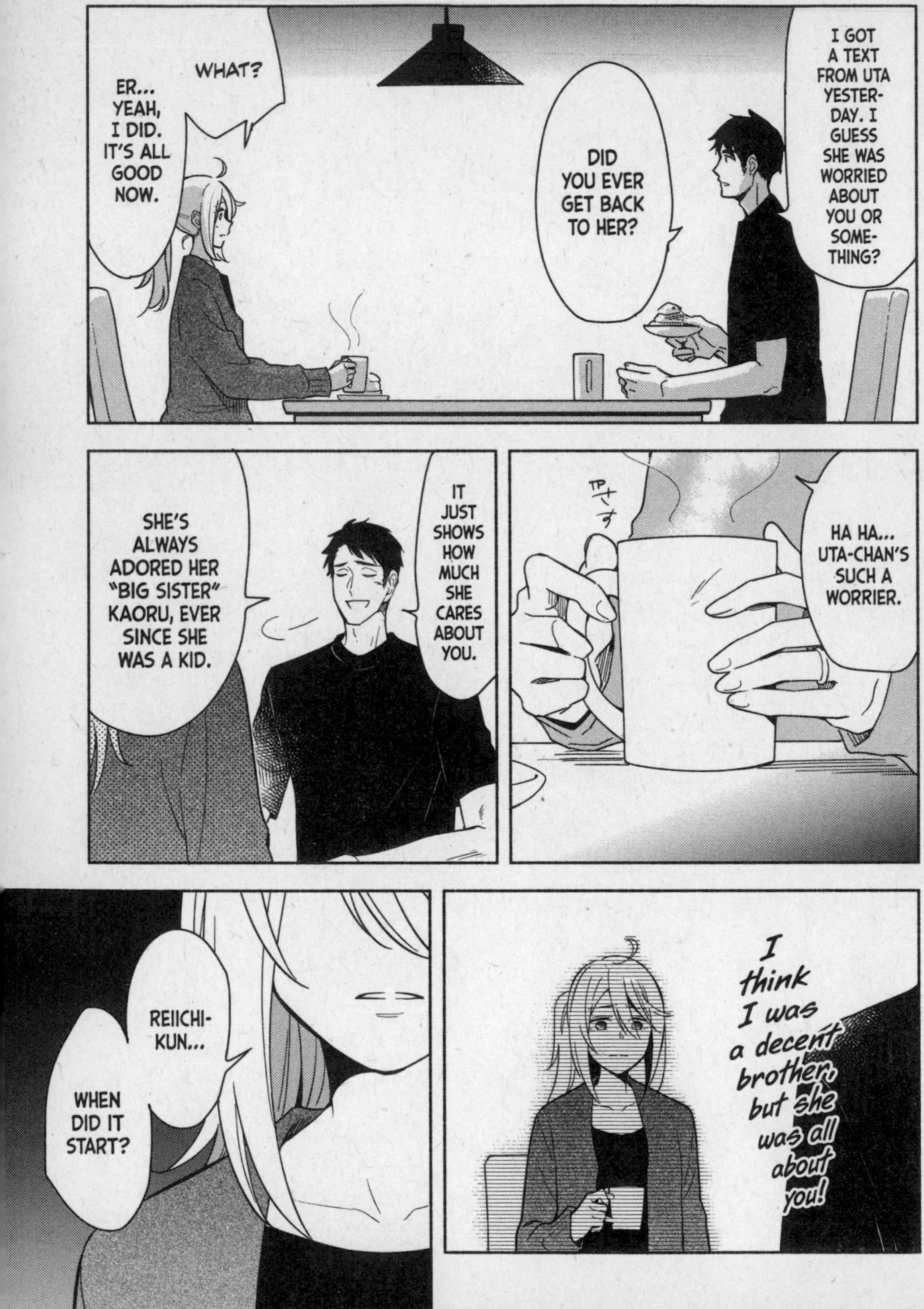
I GOT A TEXT FROM UTA YESTERDAY. I GUESS SHE WAS WORRIED ABOUT YOU OR SOMETHING?
DID YOU EVER GET BACK TO HER?
WHAT?
ER... YEAH, I DID. IT'S ALL GOOD NOW.
HA HA... UTA-CHAN'S SUCH A WORRIER.
IT JUST SHOWS HOW MUCH SHE CARES ABOUT YOU.
SHE'S ALWAYS ADORED HER "BIG SISTER" KAORU, EVER SINCE SHE WAS A KID.
I think I was a decent brother, but she was all about you!
REIICHI-KUN...
WHEN DID IT START?

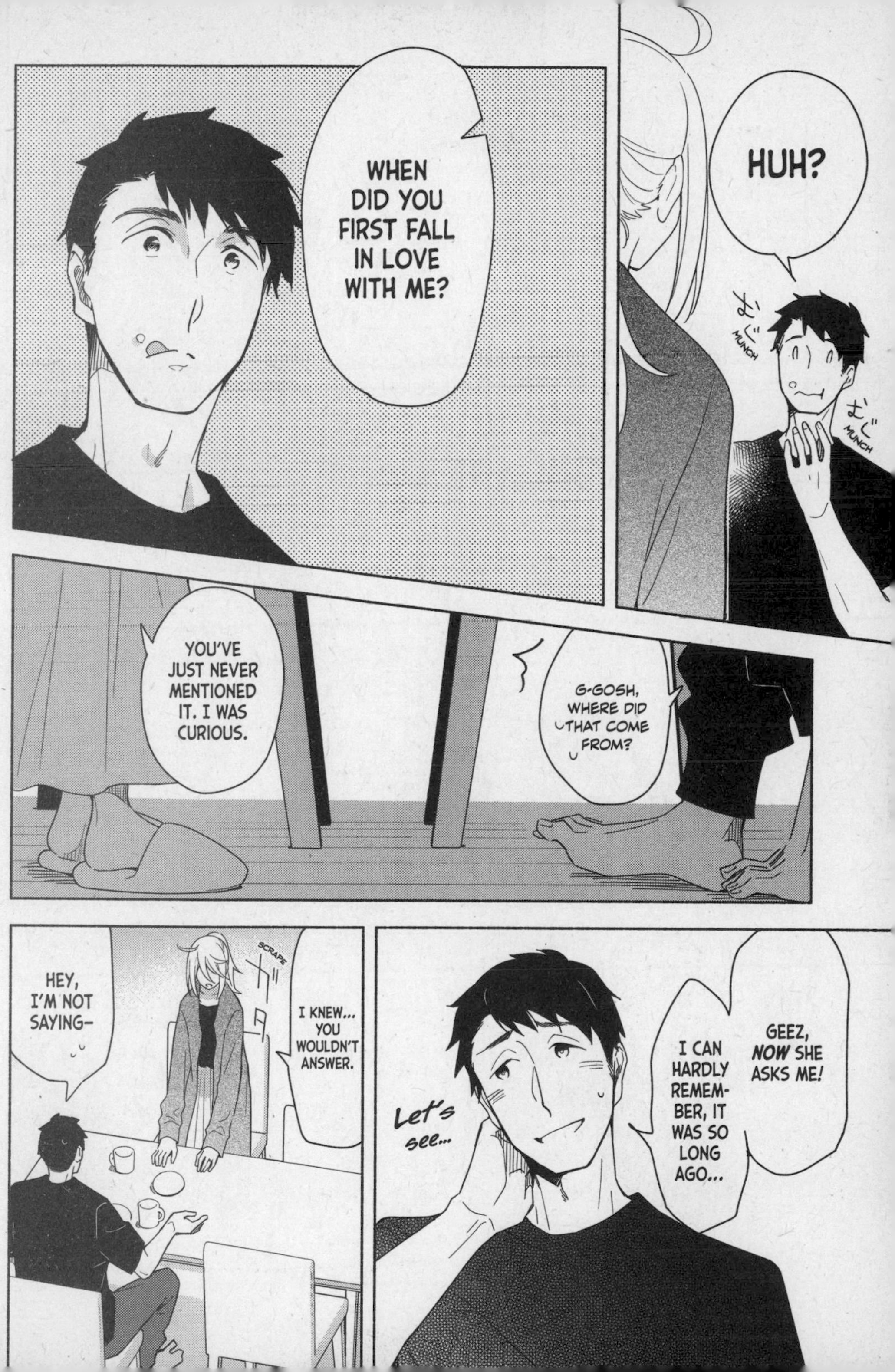
HUH?
むぐ MUNCH
むぐ MUNCH
WHEN DID YOU FIRST FALL IN LOVE WITH ME?
G-GOSH, WHERE DID THAT COME FROM?
YOU'VE JUST NEVER MENTIONED IT. I WAS CURIOUS.
GEEZ, *NOW* SHE ASKS ME!
I CAN HARDLY REMEM-BER, IT WAS SO LONG AGO...
Let's see...
I KNEW... YOU WOULDN'T ANSWER.
SCRAPE
HEY, I'M NOT SAYING-

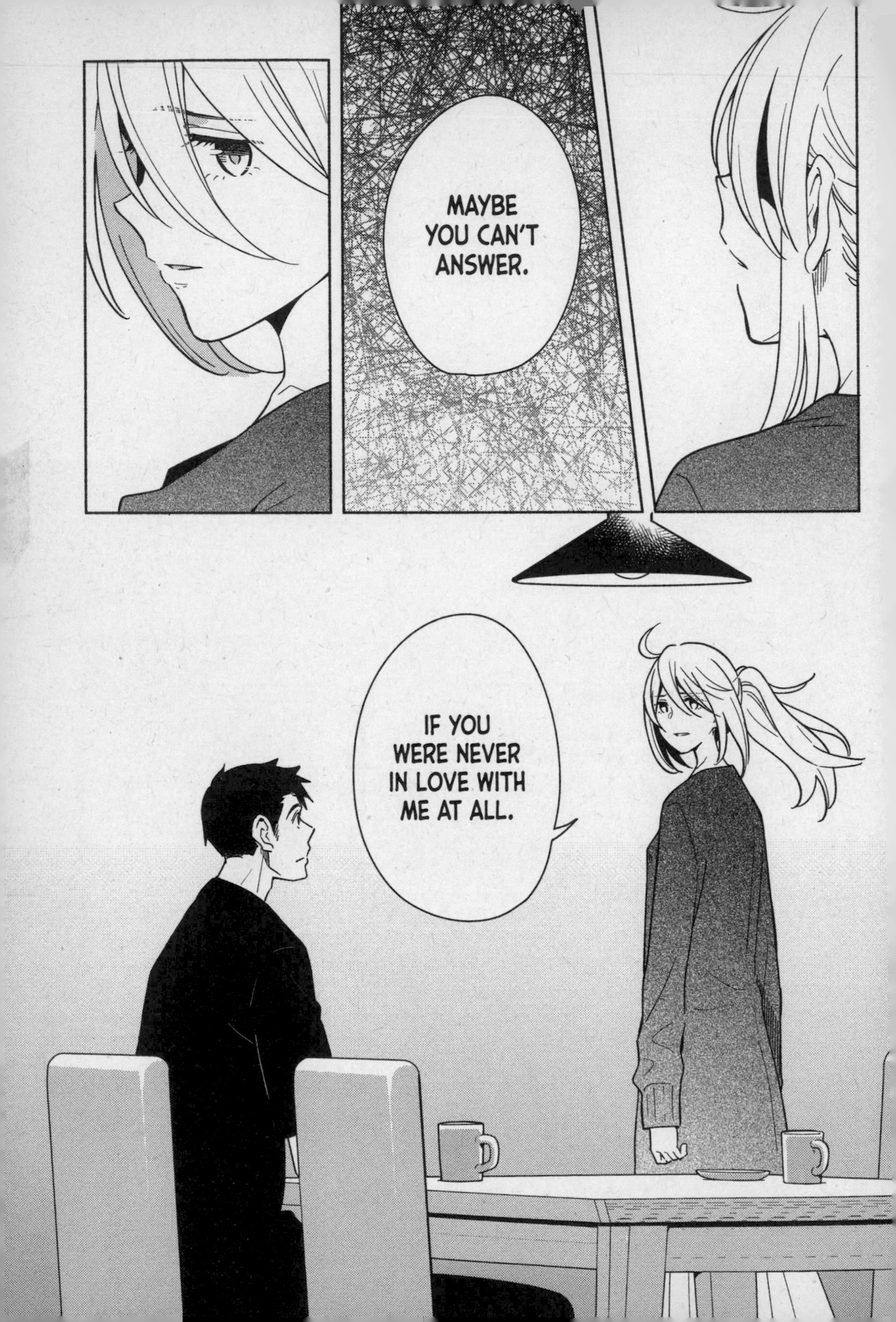
MAYBE YOU CAN'T ANSWER.
IF YOU WERE NEVER IN LOVE WITH ME AT ALL.

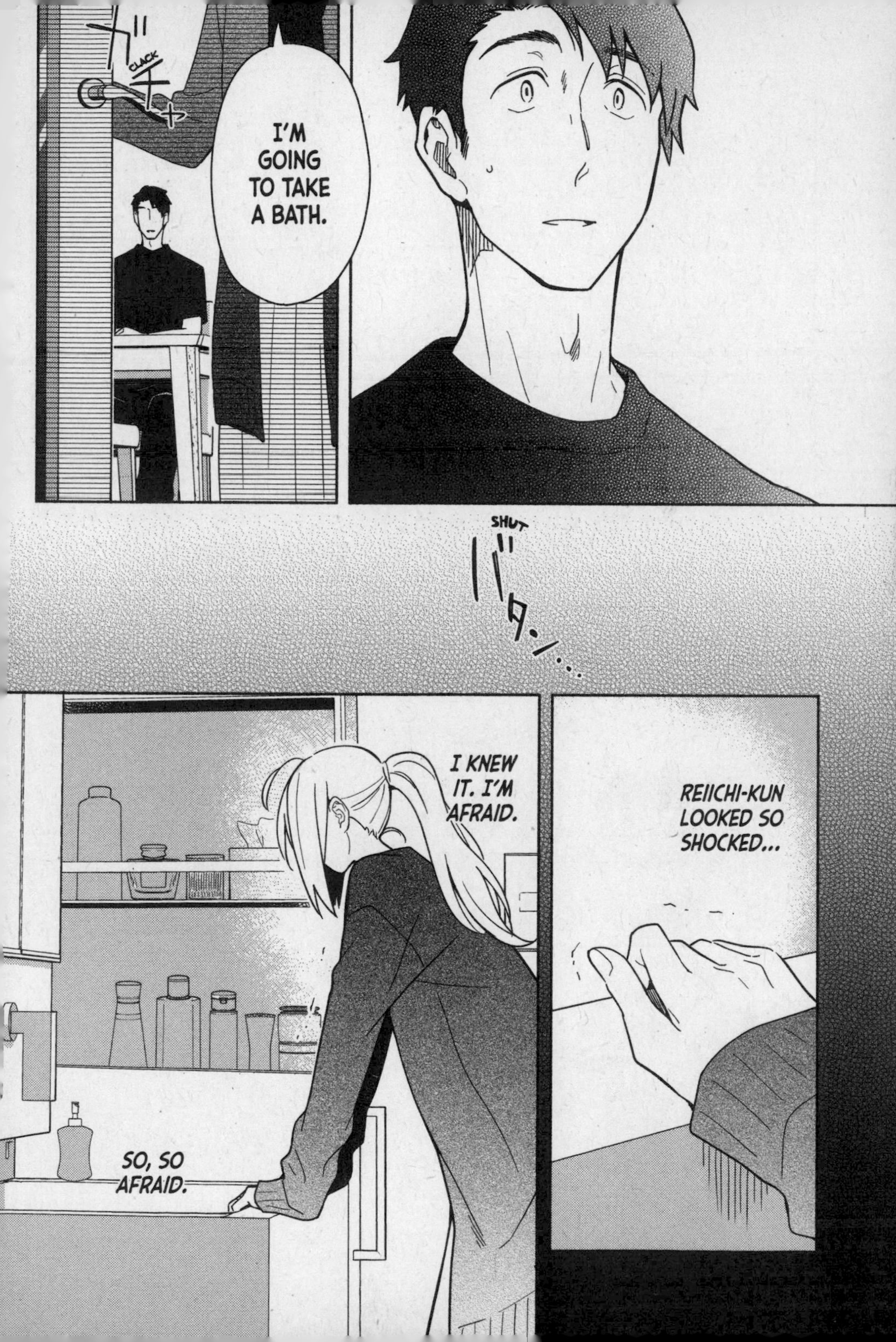
CLACK
I'M GOING TO TAKE A BATH.
SHUT
REIICHI-KUN LOOKED SO SHOCKED...
I KNEW IT. I'M AFRAID.
SO, SO AFRAID.

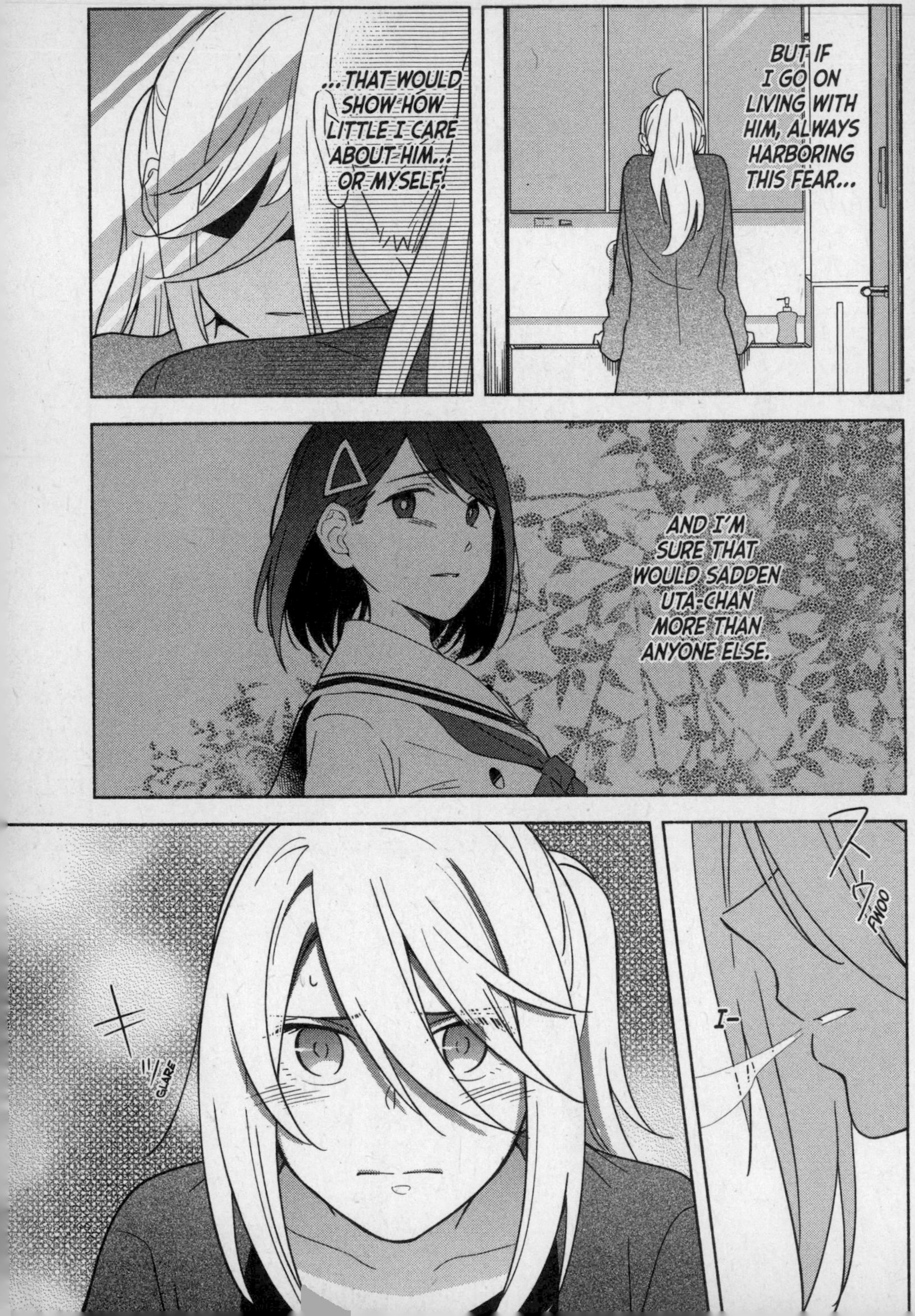

BUT IF I GO ON LIVING WITH HIM, ALWAYS HARBORING THIS FEAR...
...THAT WOULD SHOW HOW LITTLE I CARE ABOUT HIM... OR MYSELF.
AND I'M SURE THAT WOULD SADDEN UTA-CHAN MORE THAN ANYONE ELSE.
FWOO
I—
GLARE

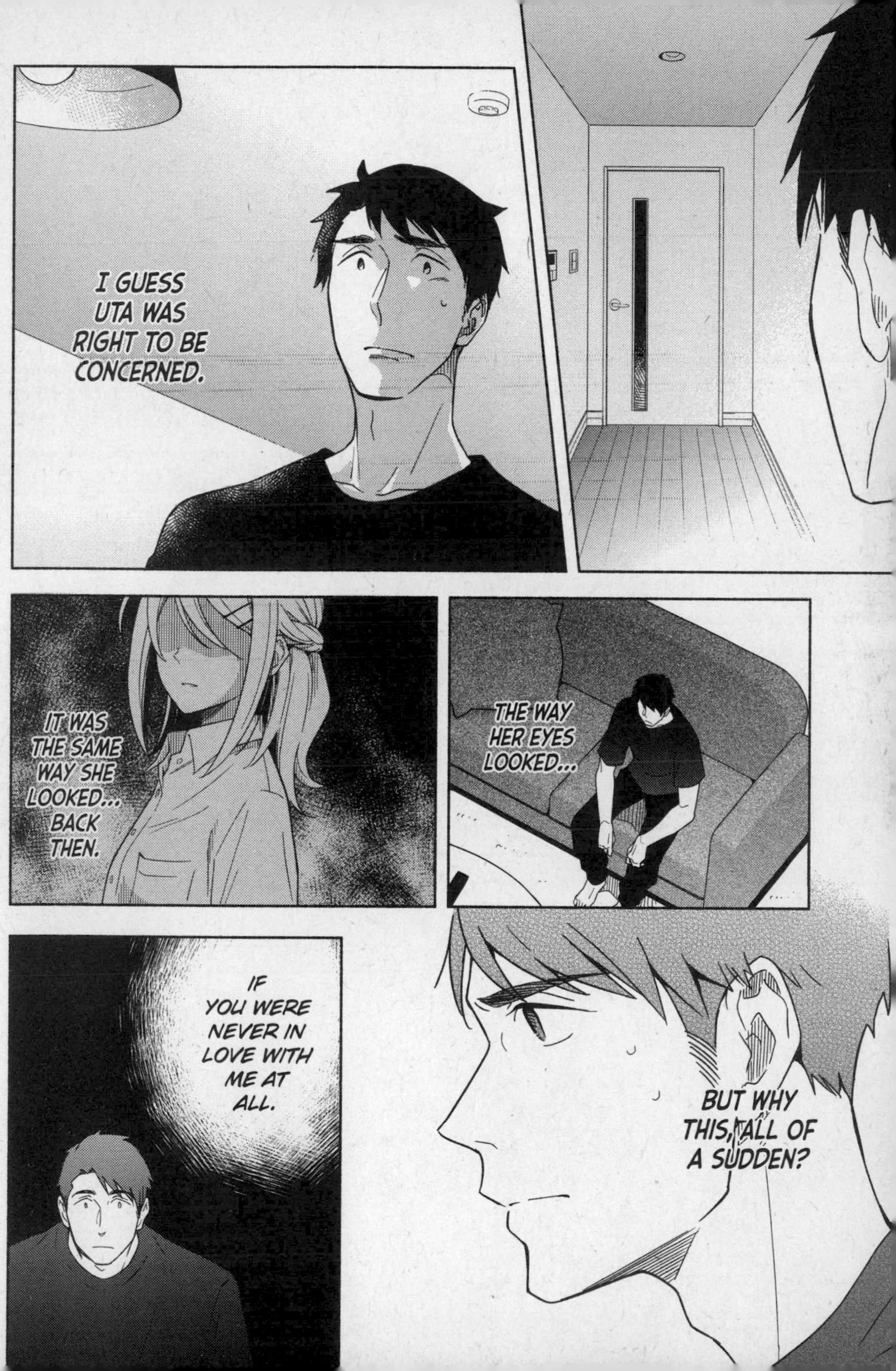
I GUESS UTA WAS RIGHT TO BE CONCERNED.
THE WAY HER EYES LOOKED...
IT WAS THE SAME WAY SHE LOOKED... BACK THEN.
BUT WHY THIS, ALL OF A SUDDEN?
IF YOU WERE NEVER IN LOVE WITH ME AT ALL.

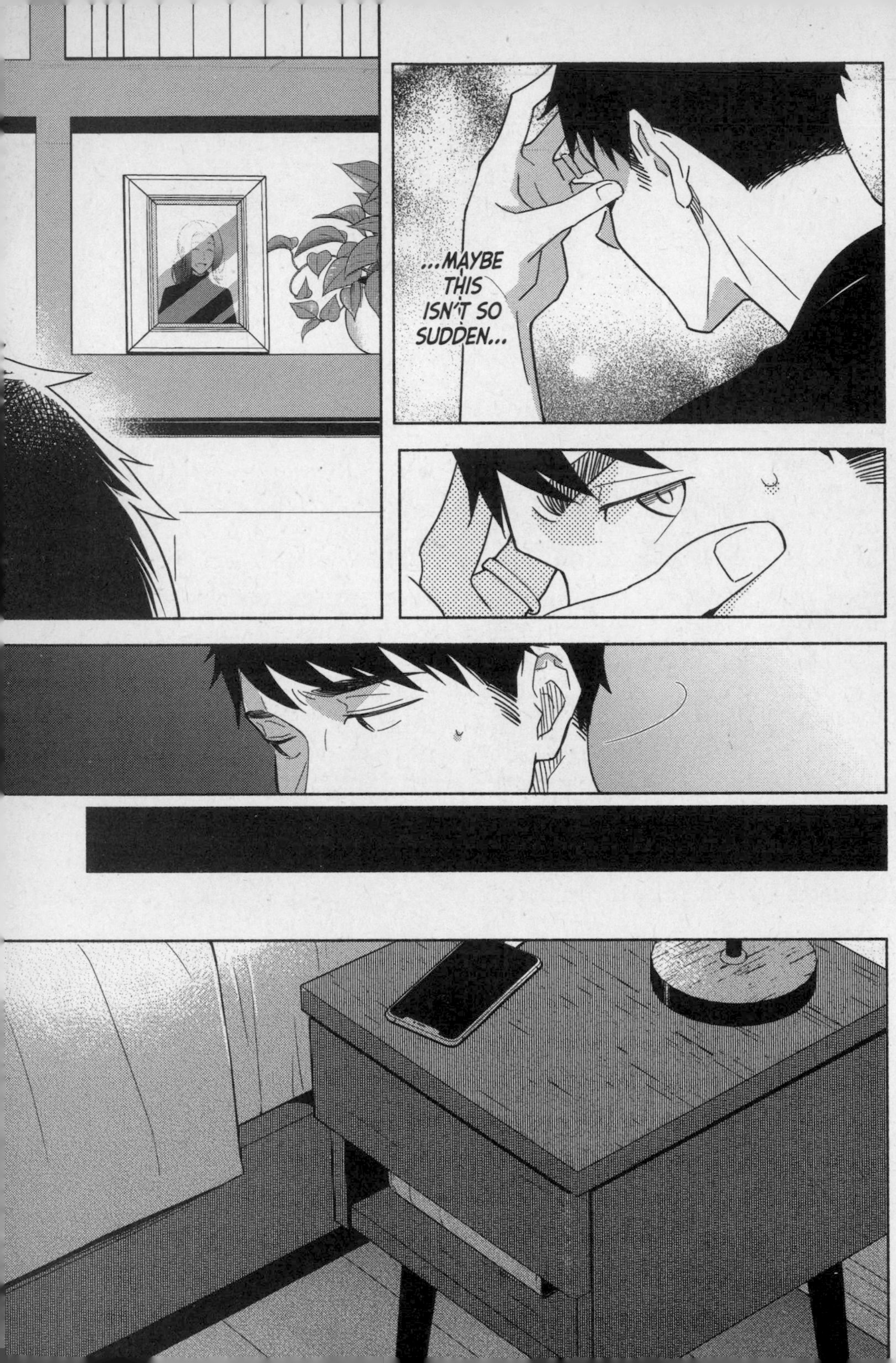
...MAYBE THIS ISN'T SO SUDDEN...

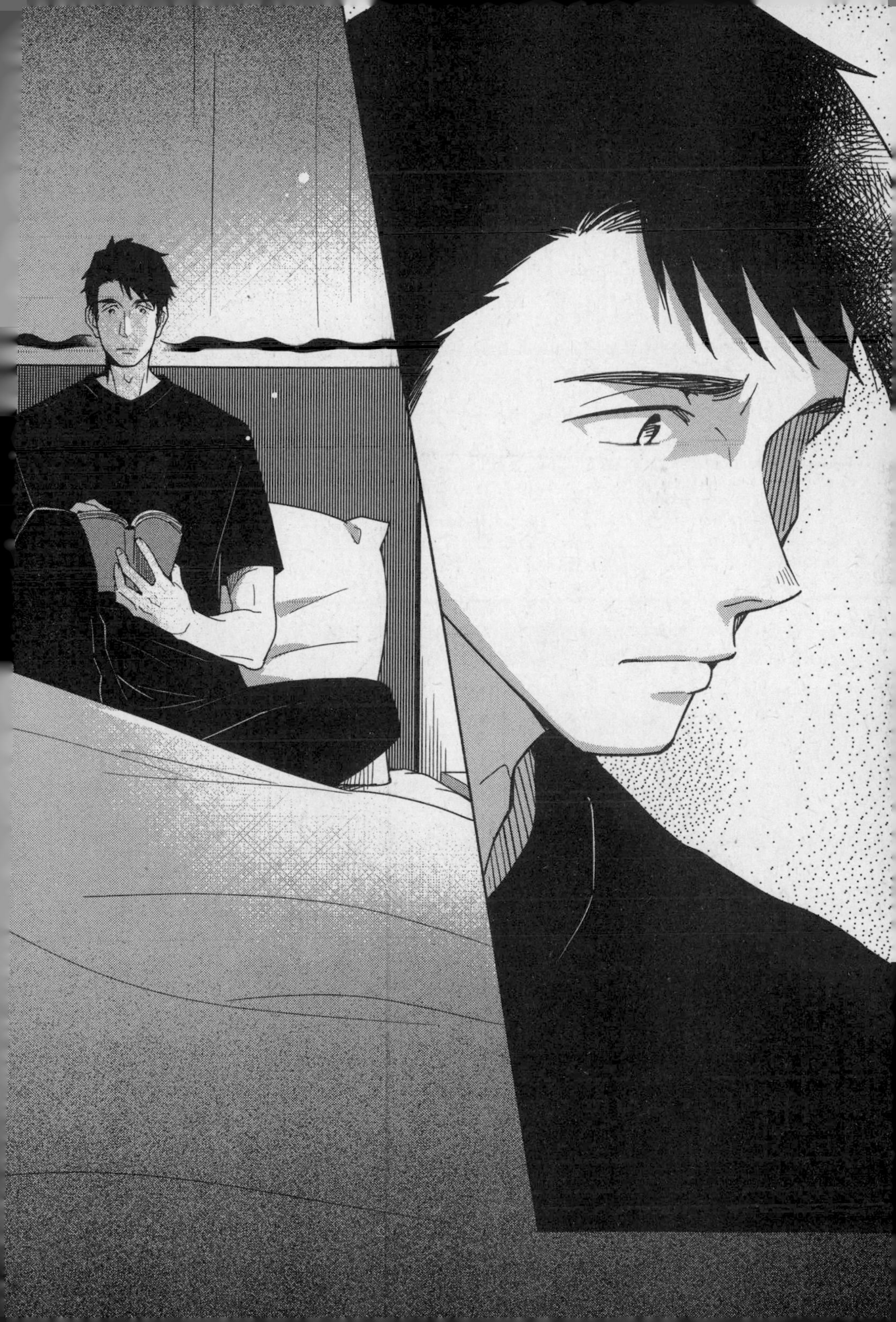

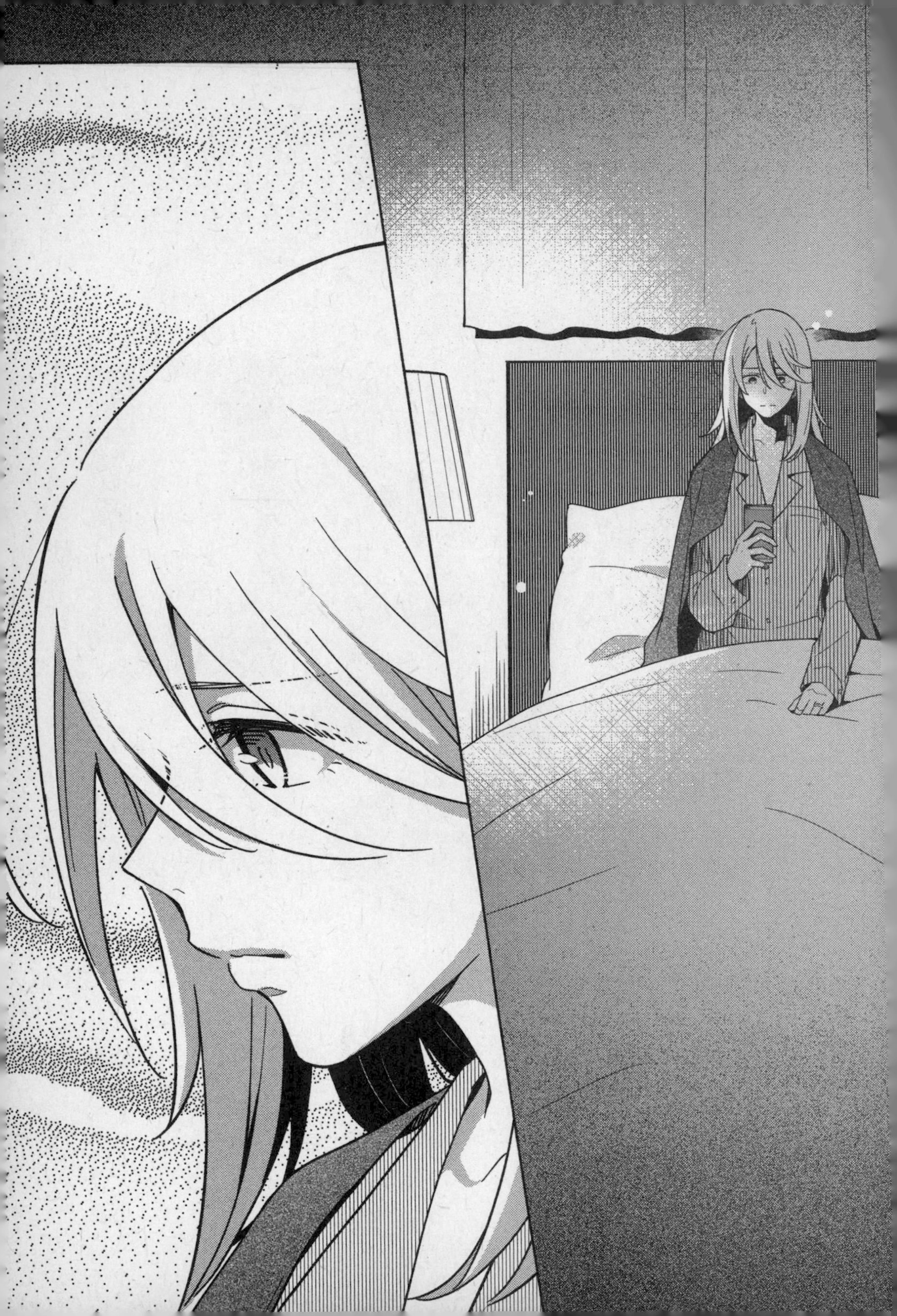

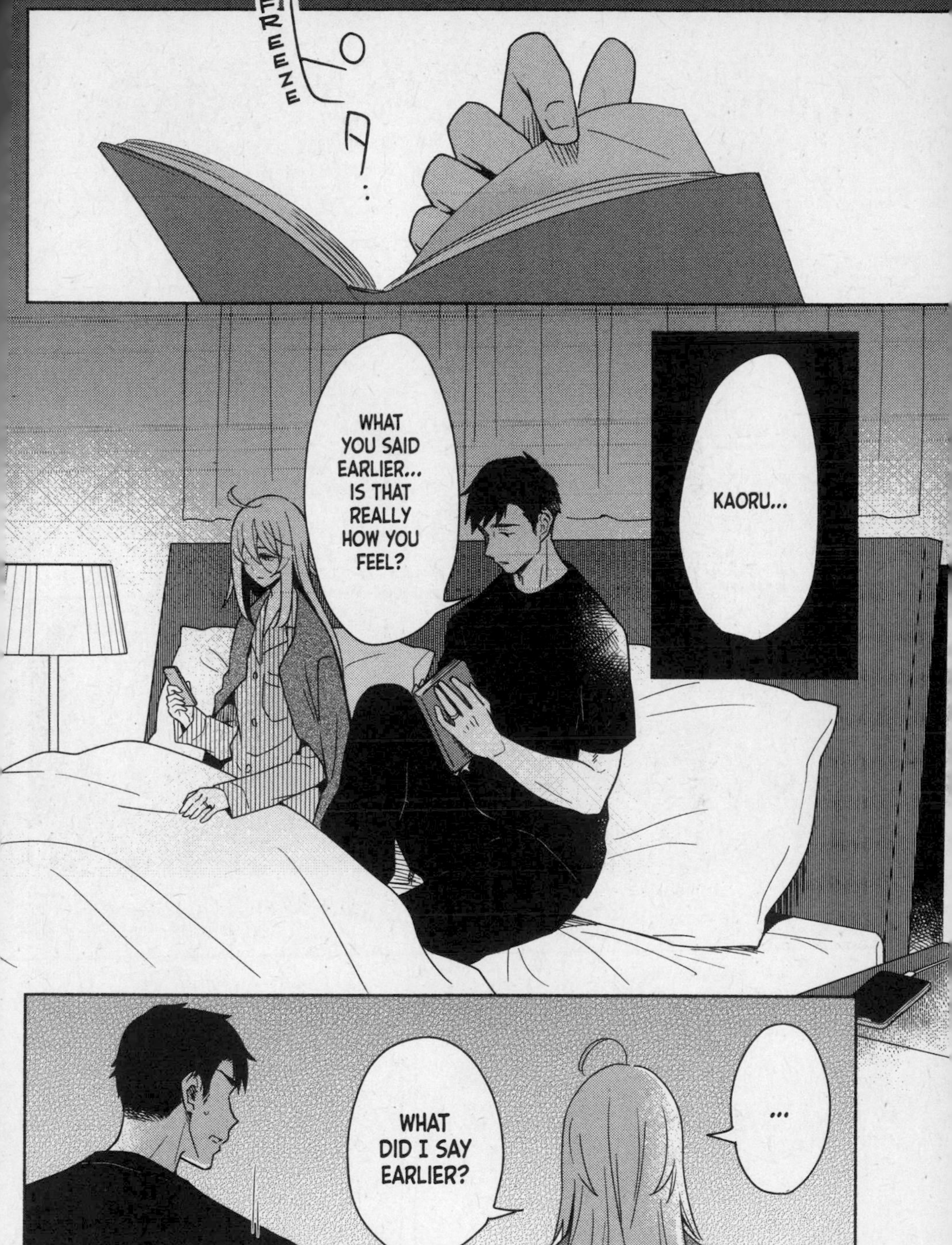
FREEZE
KAORU...
WHAT YOU SAID EARLIER... IS THAT REALLY HOW YOU FEEL?
...
WHAT DID I SAY EARLIER?

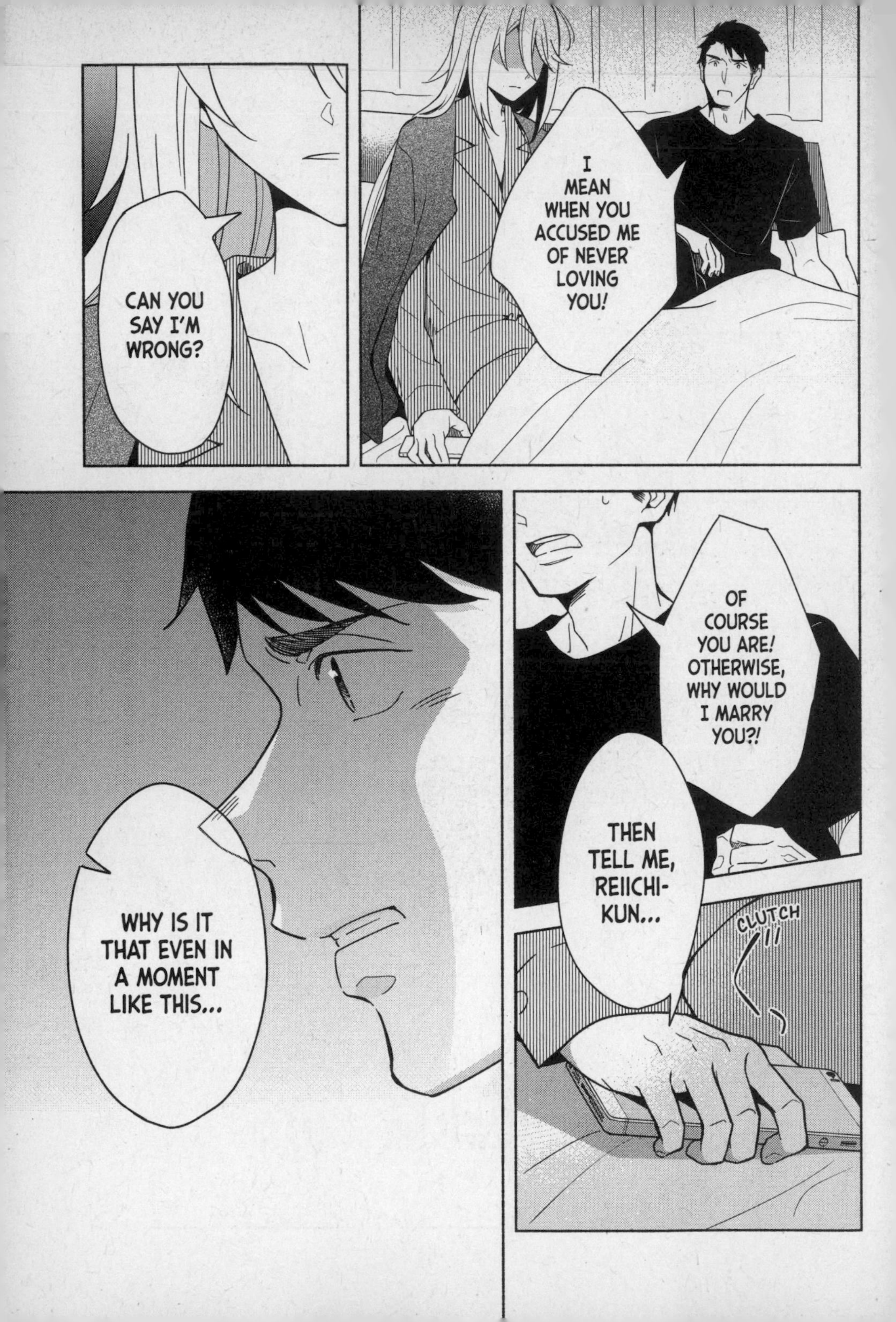
I MEAN WHEN YOU ACCUSED ME OF NEVER LOVING YOU!
CAN YOU SAY I'M WRONG?
OF COURSE YOU ARE! OTHERWISE, WHY WOULD I MARRY YOU?!
THEN TELL ME, REIICHI-KUN...
CLUTCH
WHY IS IT THAT EVEN IN A MOMENT LIKE THIS...

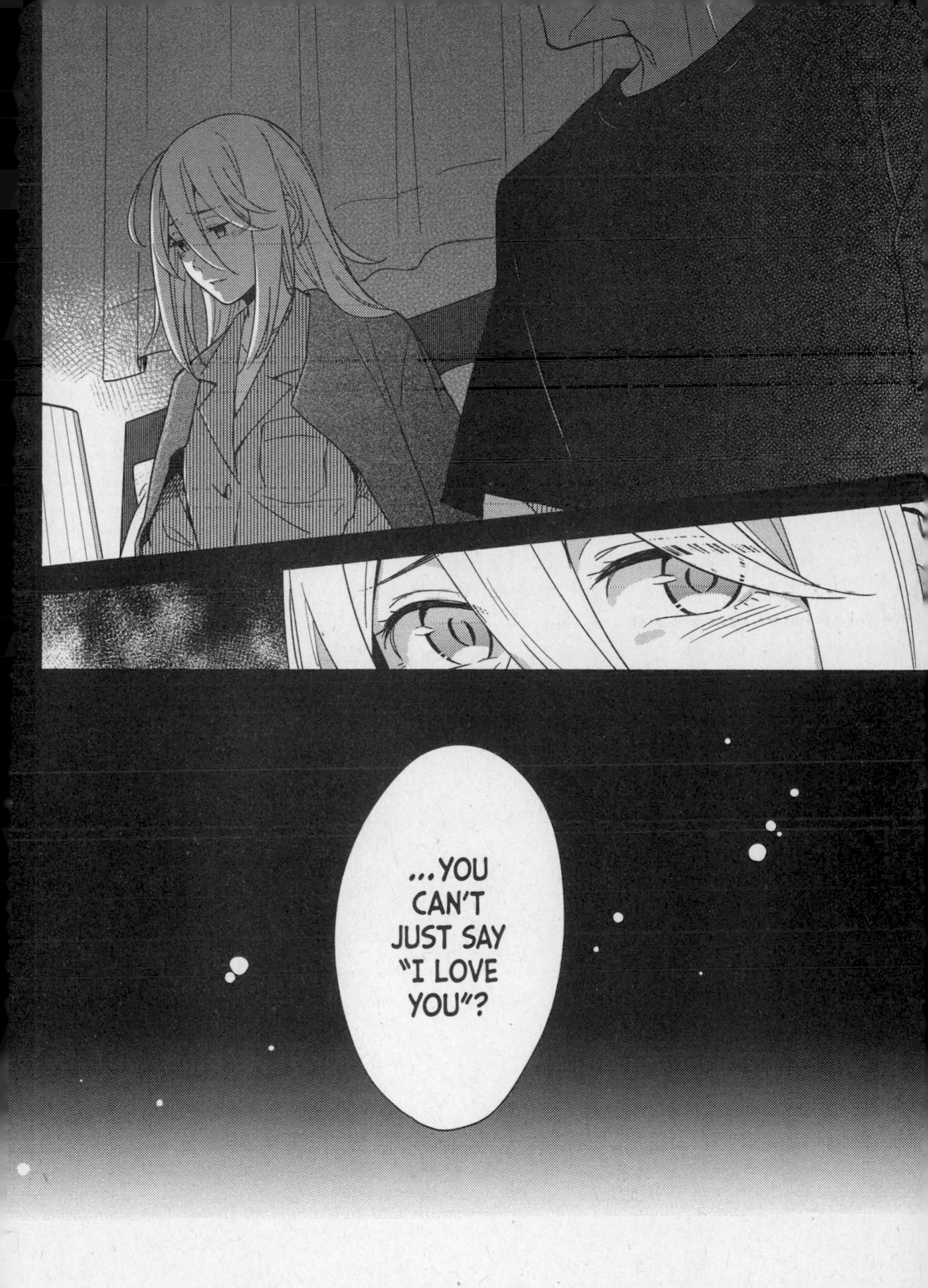
...YOU CAN'T JUST SAY "I LOVE YOU"?

If I Could
Reach You

If I Could
Reach You

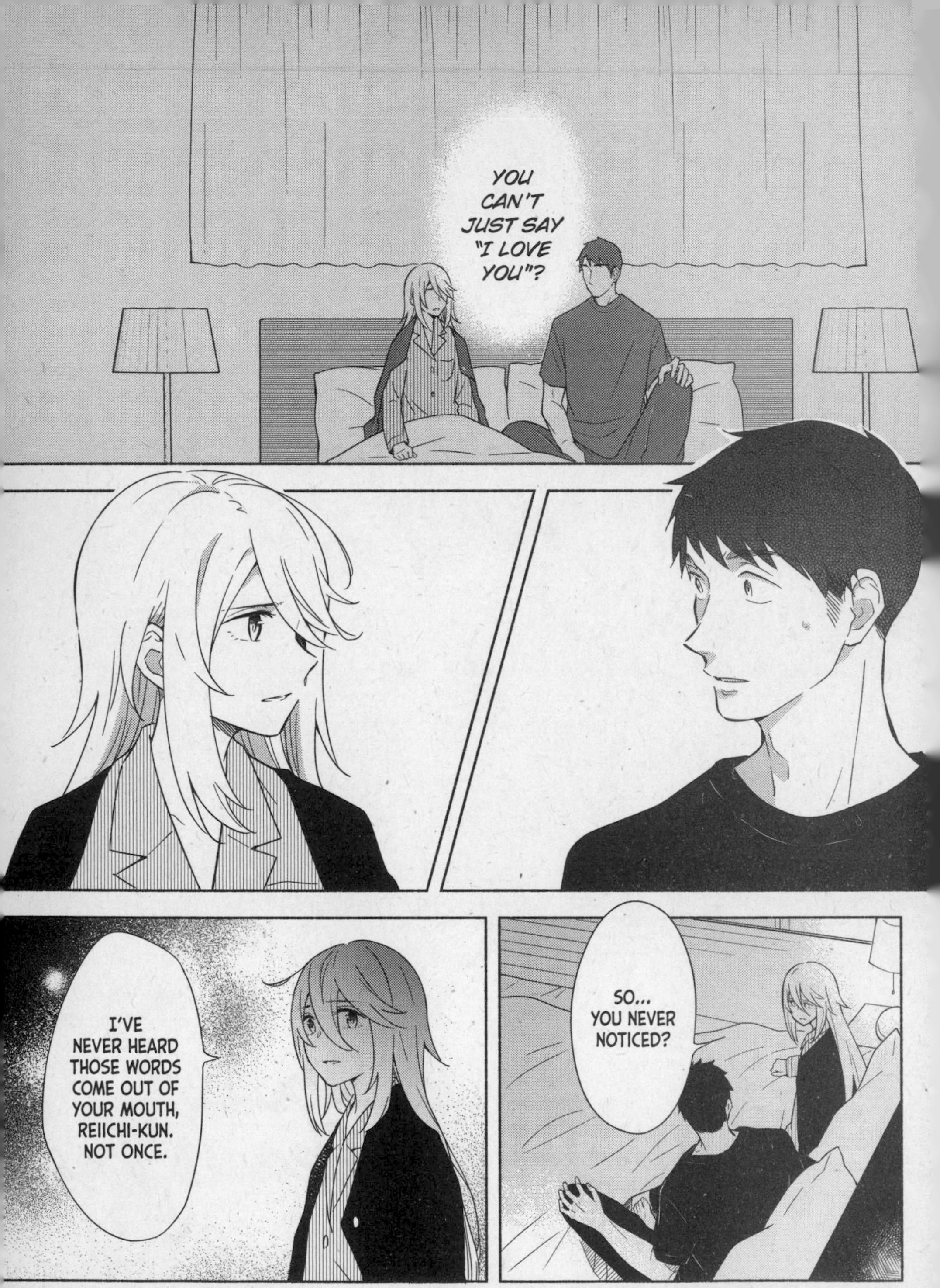
YOU CAN'T JUST SAY "I LOVE YOU"?
SO... YOU NEVER NOTICED?
I'VE NEVER HEARD THOSE WORDS COME OUT OF YOUR MOUTH, REIICHI-KUN. NOT ONCE.

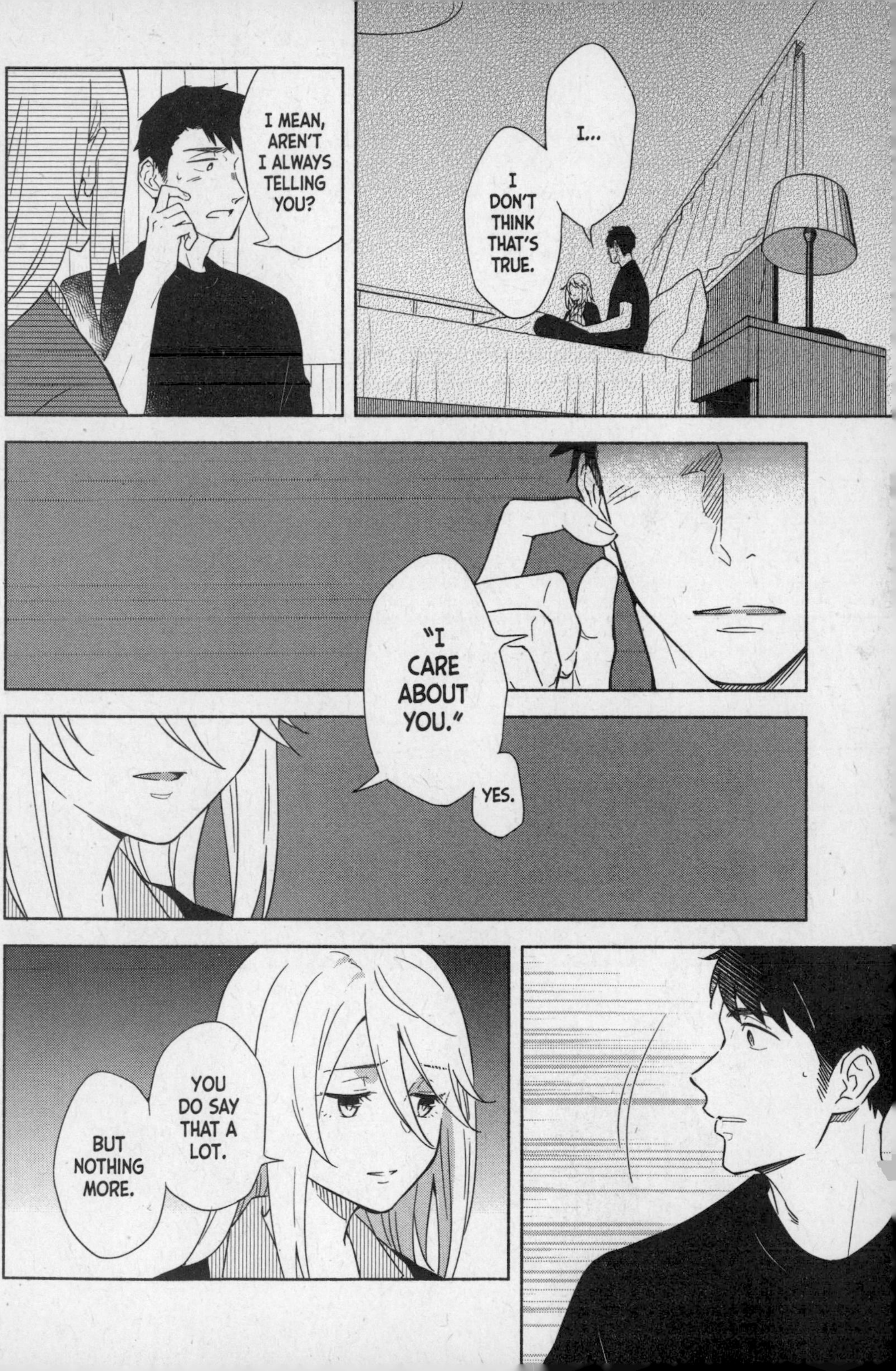
I...
I DON'T THINK THAT'S TRUE.
I MEAN, AREN'T I ALWAYS TELLING YOU?
"I CARE ABOUT YOU."
YES.
YOU DO SAY THAT A LOT.
BUT NOTHING MORE.

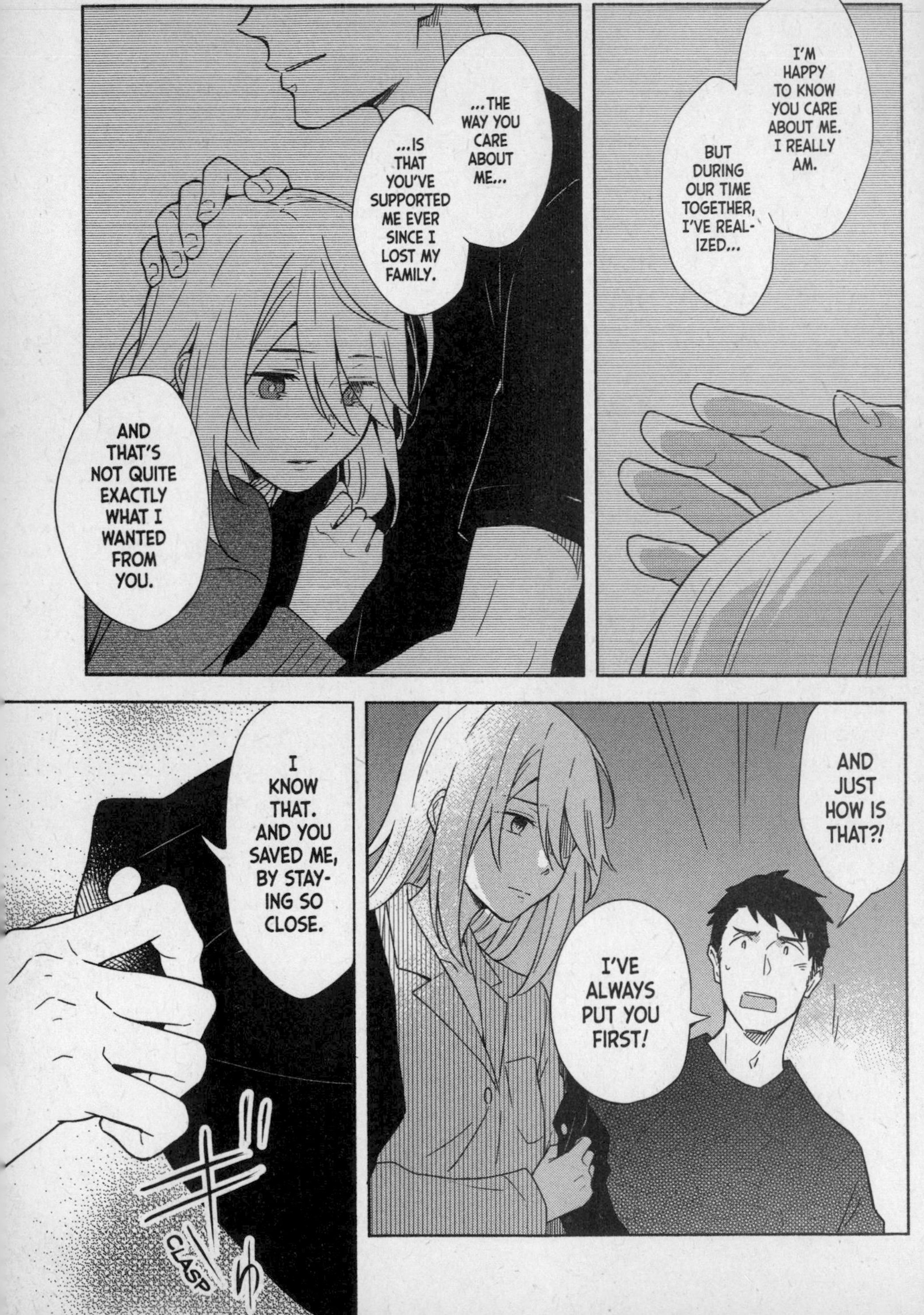
I'M HAPPY TO KNOW YOU CARE ABOUT ME. I REALLY AM.
BUT DURING OUR TIME TOGETHER, I'VE REAL-IZED...
...THE WAY YOU CARE ABOUT ME...
...IS THAT YOU'VE SUPPORTED ME EVER SINCE I LOST MY FAMILY.
AND THAT'S NOT QUITE EXACTLY WHAT I WANTED FROM YOU.
AND JUST HOW IS THAT?!
I'VE ALWAYS PUT YOU FIRST!
I KNOW THAT. AND YOU SAVED ME, BY STAY-ING SO CLOSE.
CLASP

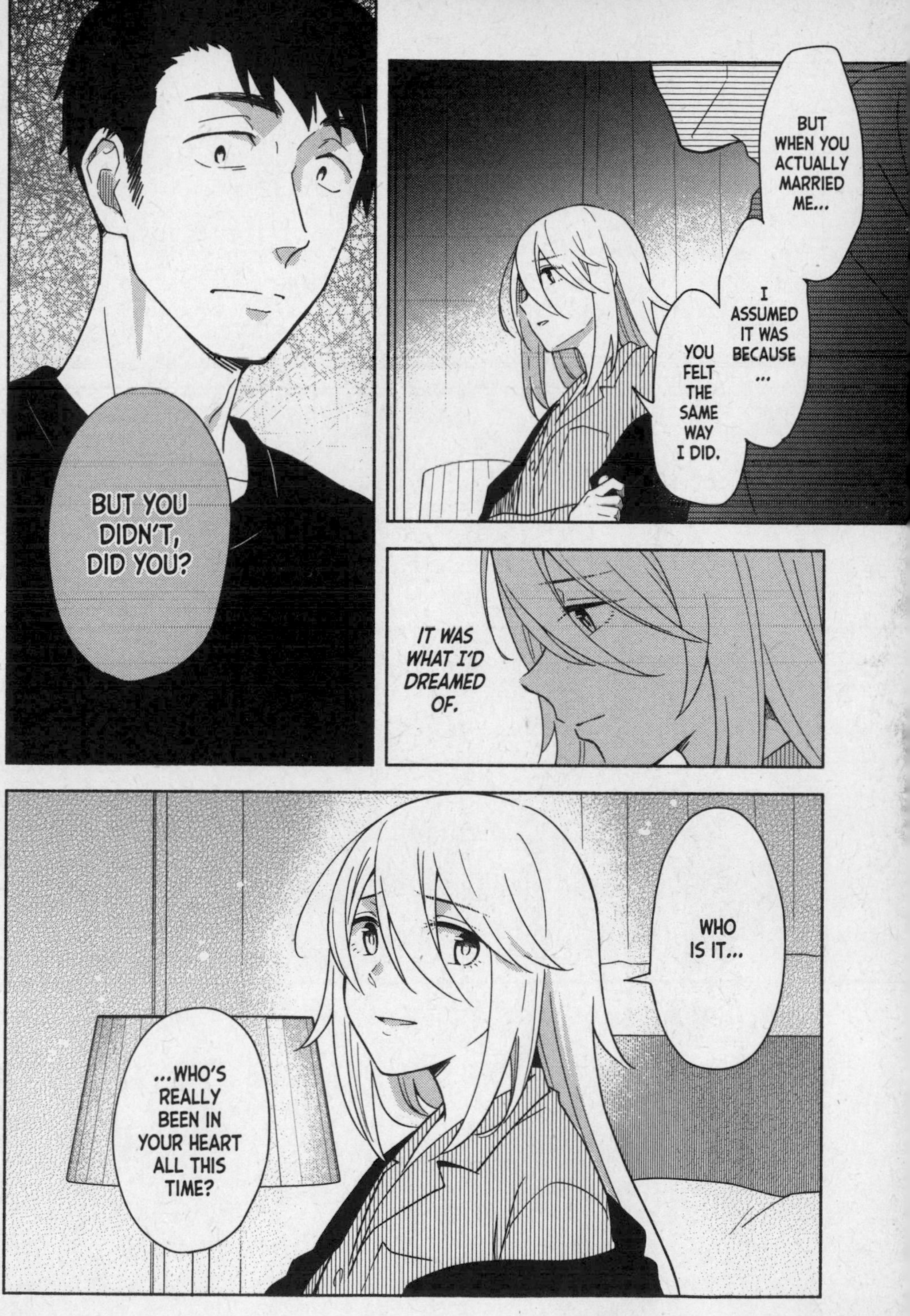
BUT WHEN YOU ACTUALLY MARRIED ME...
I ASSUMED IT WAS BECAUSE...
YOU FELT THE SAME WAY I DID.
IT WAS WHAT I'D DREAMED OF.
BUT YOU DIDN'T, DID YOU?
WHO IS IT...
...WHO'S REALLY BEEN IN YOUR HEART ALL THIS TIME?

Chapter 34

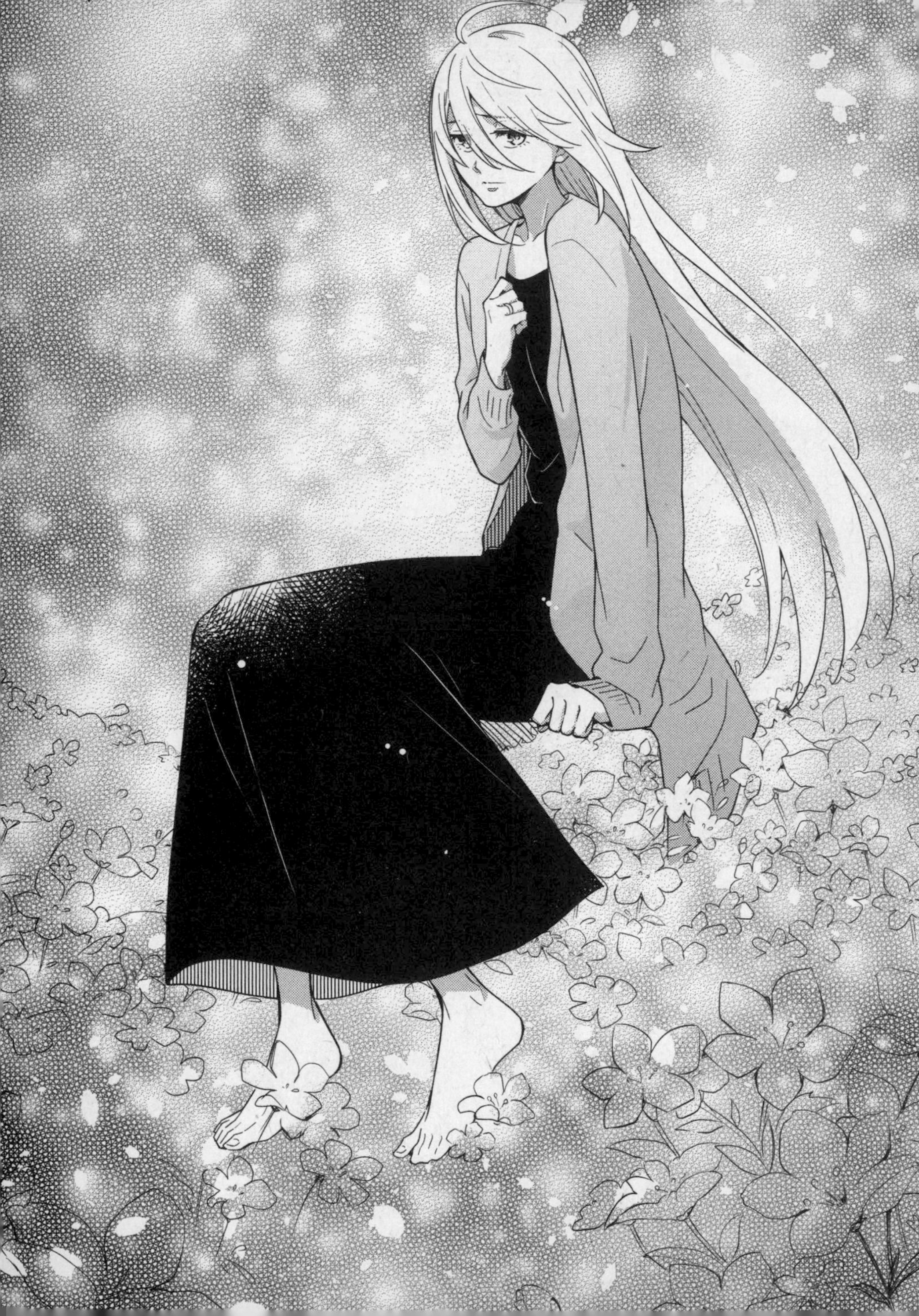

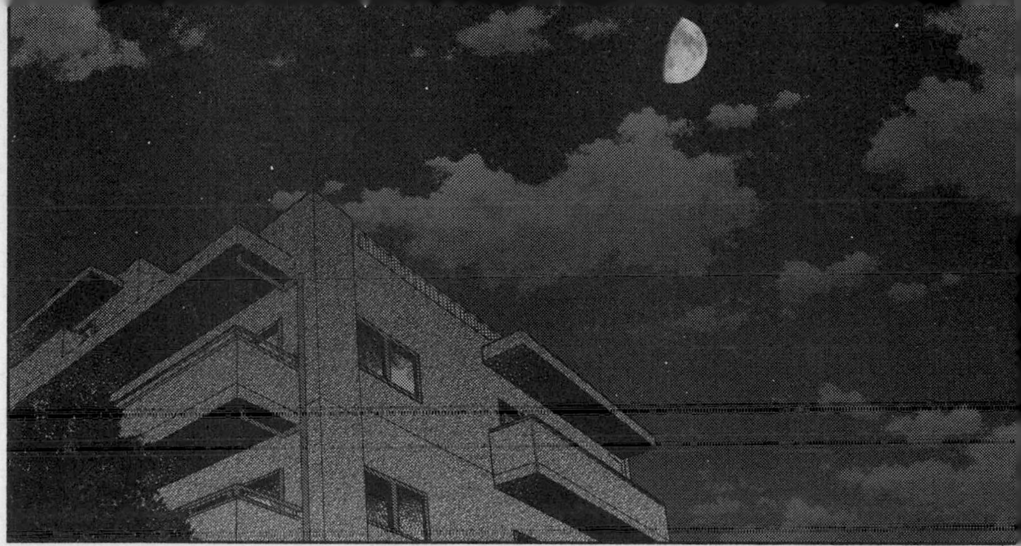

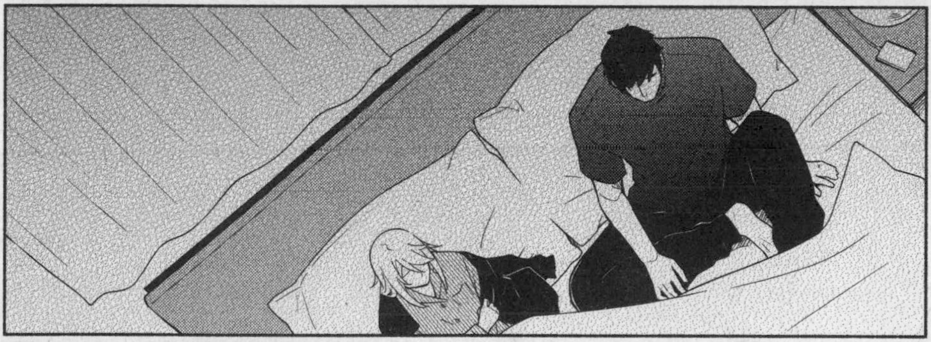

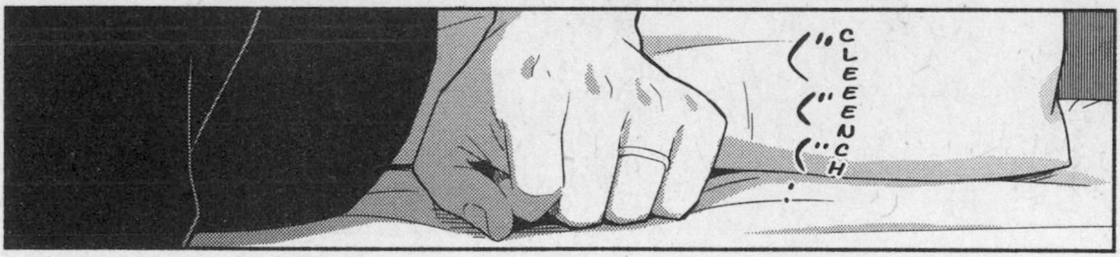
CLEEENCH

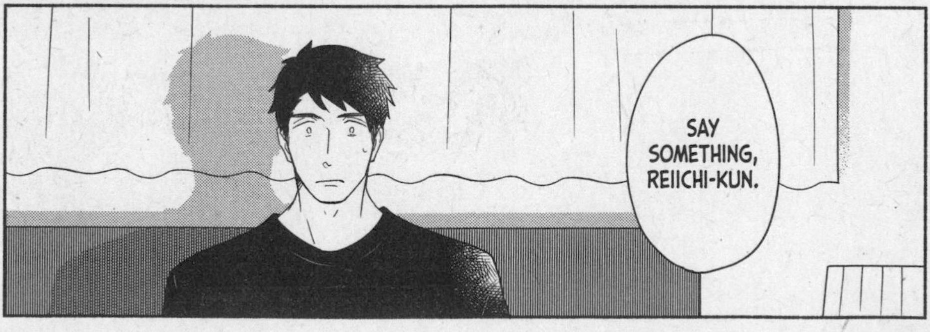
SAY SOMETHING, REIICHI-KUN.

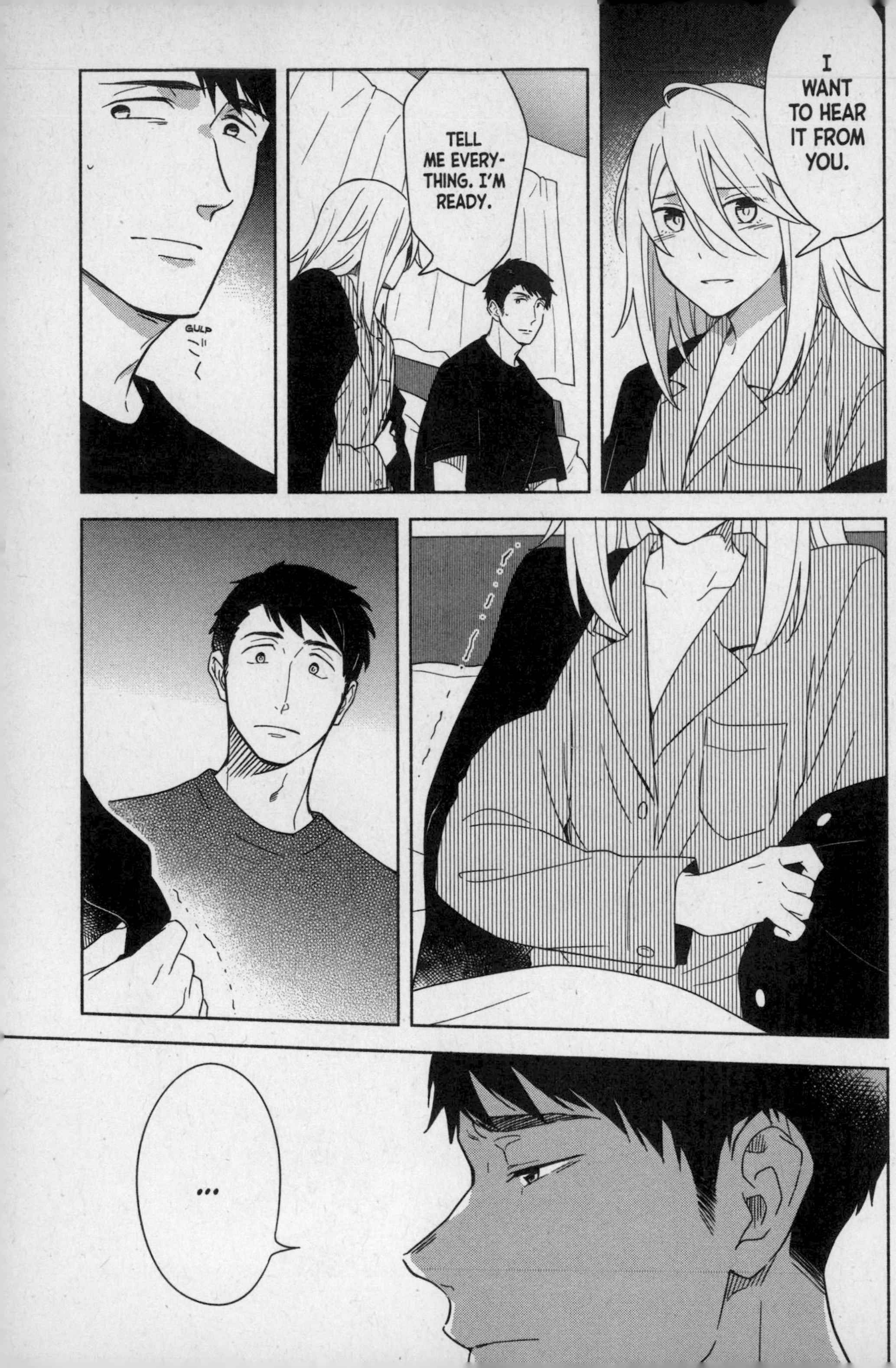
I WANT TO HEAR IT FROM YOU.
TELL ME EVERY-THING. I'M READY.
GULP
...

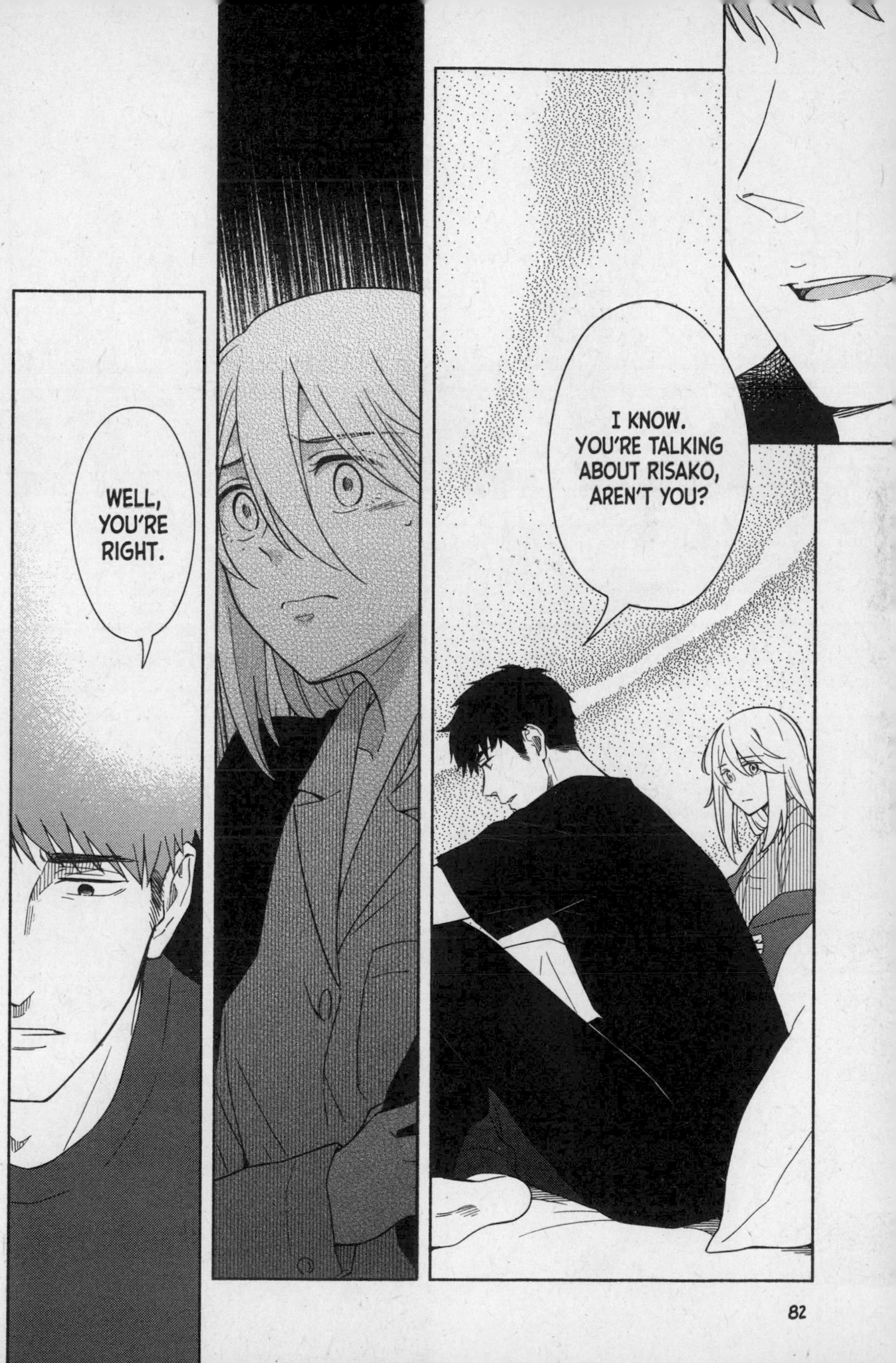
I KNOW. YOU'RE TALKING ABOUT RISAKO, AREN'T YOU?
WELL, YOU'RE RIGHT.

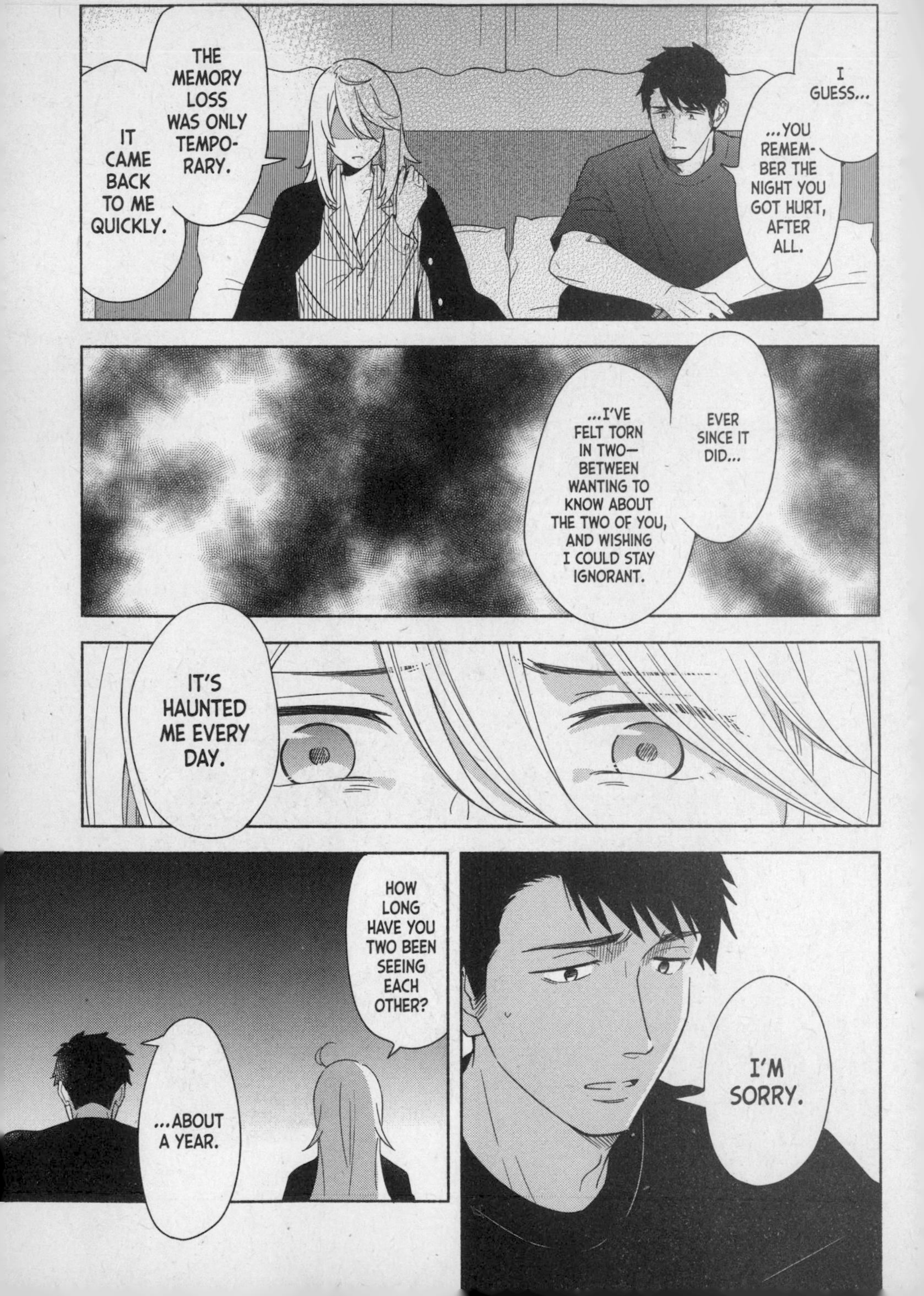
I GUESS...
...YOU REMEMBER THE NIGHT YOU GOT HURT, AFTER ALL.
THE MEMORY LOSS WAS ONLY TEMPORARY.
IT CAME BACK TO ME QUICKLY.
EVER SINCE IT DID...
...I'VE FELT TORN IN TWO—BETWEEN WANTING TO KNOW ABOUT THE TWO OF YOU, AND WISHING I COULD STAY IGNORANT.
IT'S HAUNTED ME EVERY DAY.
I'M SORRY.
HOW LONG HAVE YOU TWO BEEN SEEING EACH OTHER?
...ABOUT A YEAR.

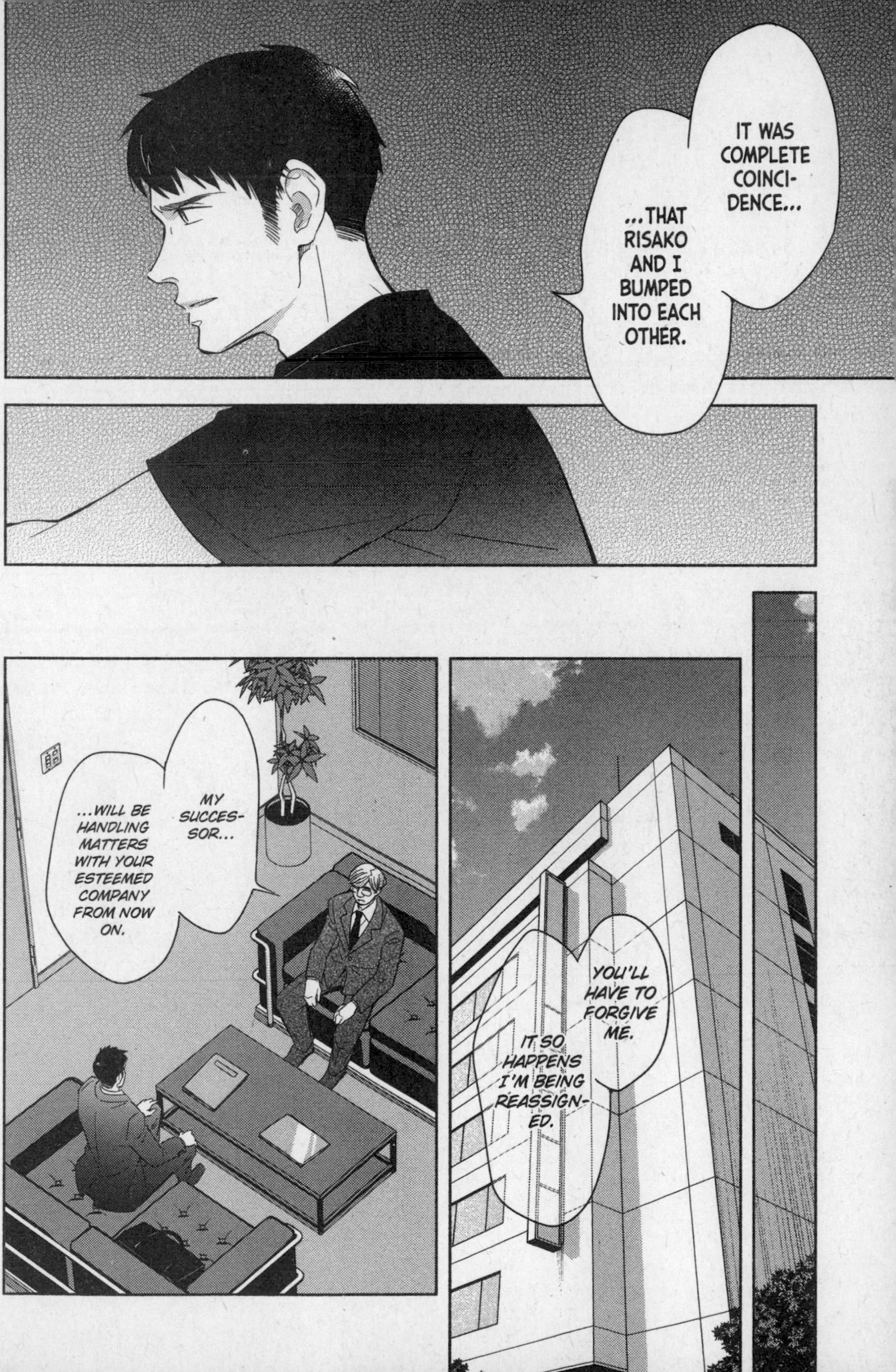
IT WAS COMPLETE COINCIDENCE...
...THAT RISAKO AND I BUMPED INTO EACH OTHER.
YOU'LL HAVE TO FORGIVE ME.
IT SO HAPPENS I'M BEING REASSIGNED.
MY SUCCESSOR...
...WILL BE HANDLING MATTERS WITH YOUR ESTEEMED COMPANY FROM NOW ON.

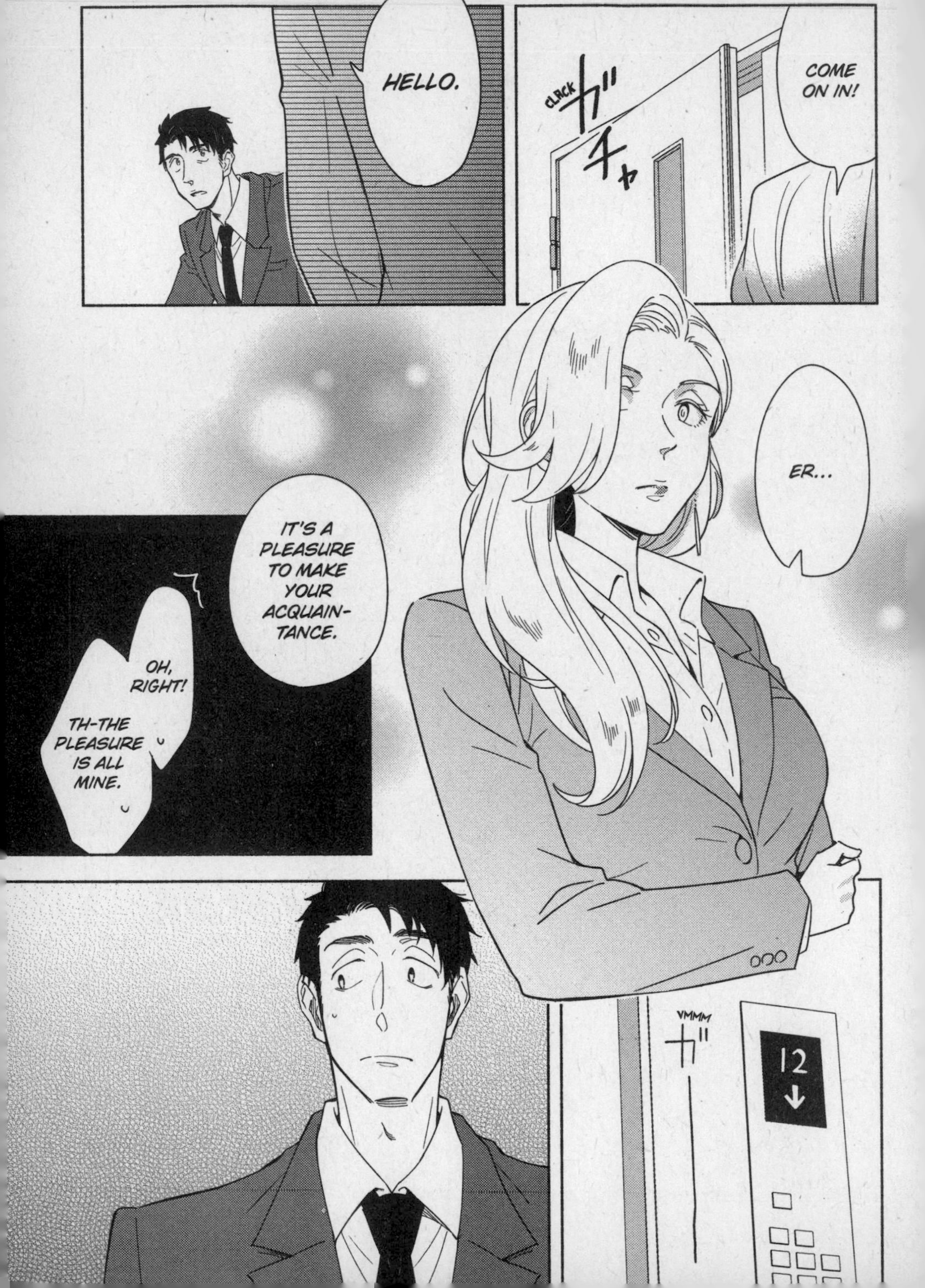
CLACK
ガチャ
COME ON IN!
HELLO.
ER...
IT'S A PLEASURE TO MAKE YOUR ACQUAINTANCE.
OH, RIGHT!
TH-THE PLEASURE IS ALL MINE.
VMMM
ガ
12

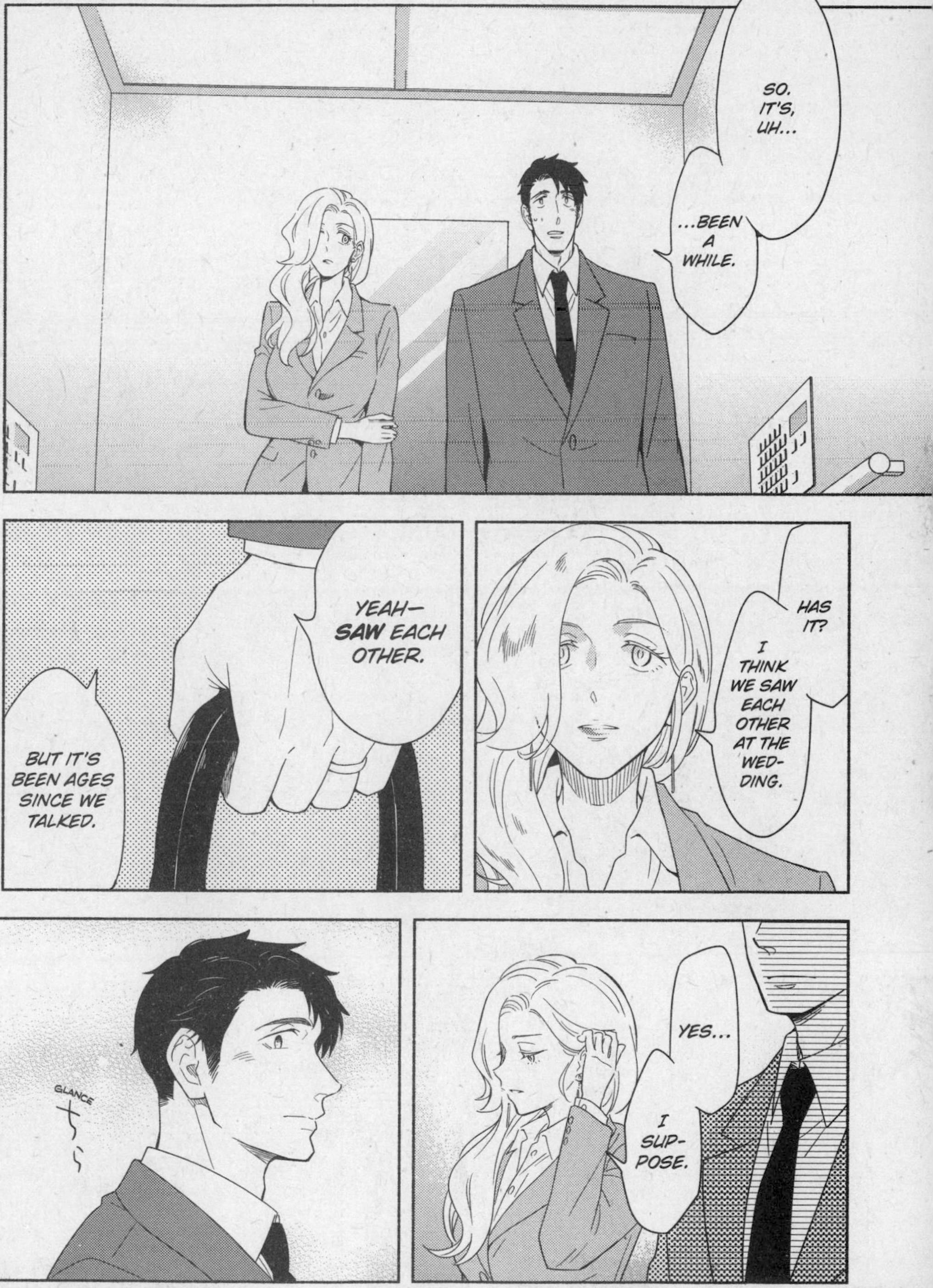
SO. IT'S, UH...
...BEEN A WHILE.
HAS IT?
I THINK WE SAW EACH OTHER AT THE WEDDING.
YEAH— SAW EACH OTHER.
BUT IT'S BEEN AGES SINCE WE TALKED.
YES...
I SUPPOSE.
GLANCE

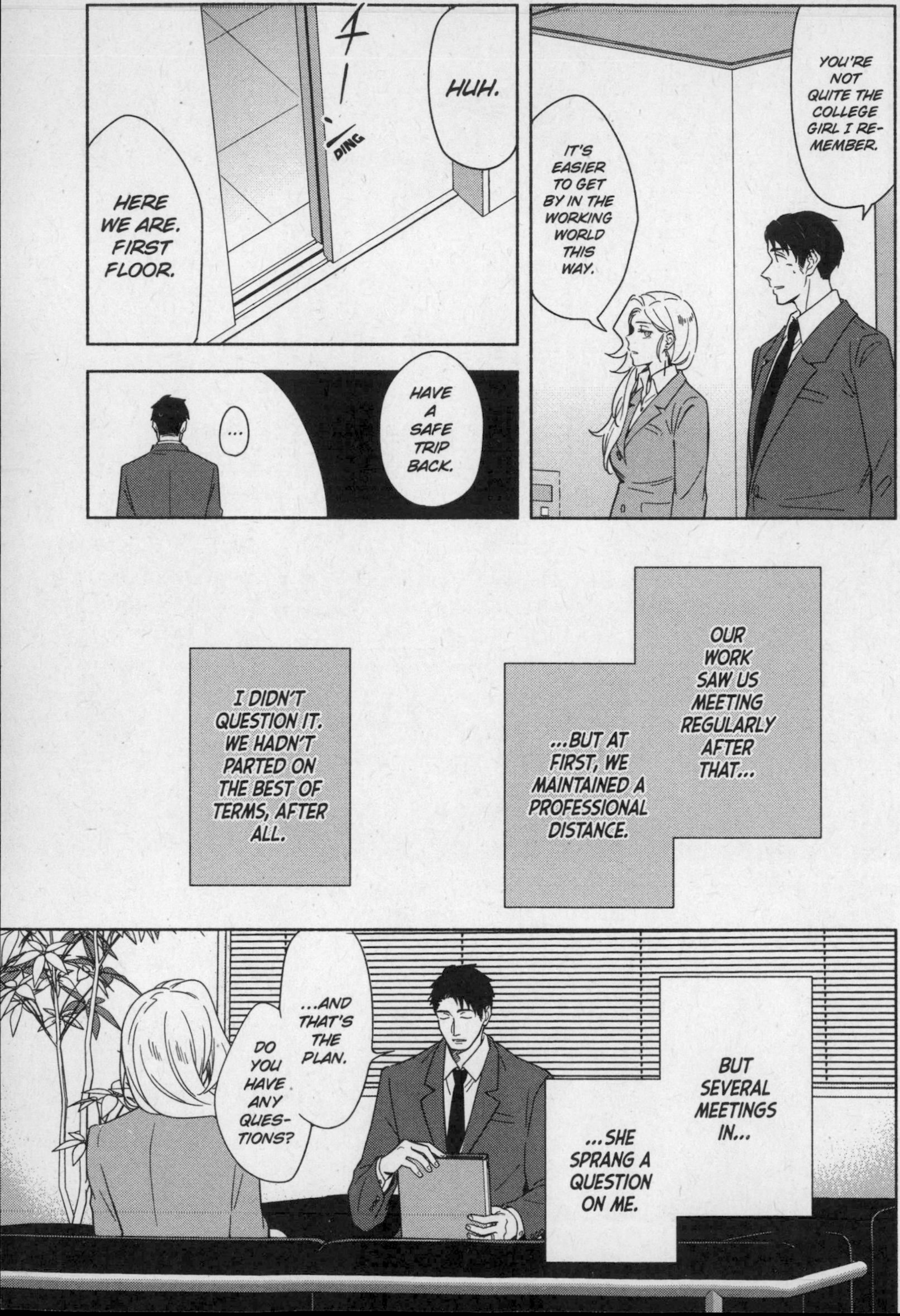
YOU'RE NOT QUITE THE COLLEGE GIRL I REMEMBER.
IT'S EASIER TO GET BY IN THE WORKING WORLD THIS WAY.
HUH.
DING
HERE WE ARE. FIRST FLOOR.
HAVE A SAFE TRIP BACK.
...
OUR WORK SAW US MEETING REGULARLY AFTER THAT...
...BUT AT FIRST, WE MAINTAINED A PROFESSIONAL DISTANCE.
I DIDN'T QUESTION IT. WE HADN'T PARTED ON THE BEST OF TERMS, AFTER ALL.
BUT SEVERAL MEETINGS IN...
...SHE SPRANG A QUESTION ON ME.
...AND THAT'S THE PLAN.
DO YOU HAVE ANY QUES-TIONS?

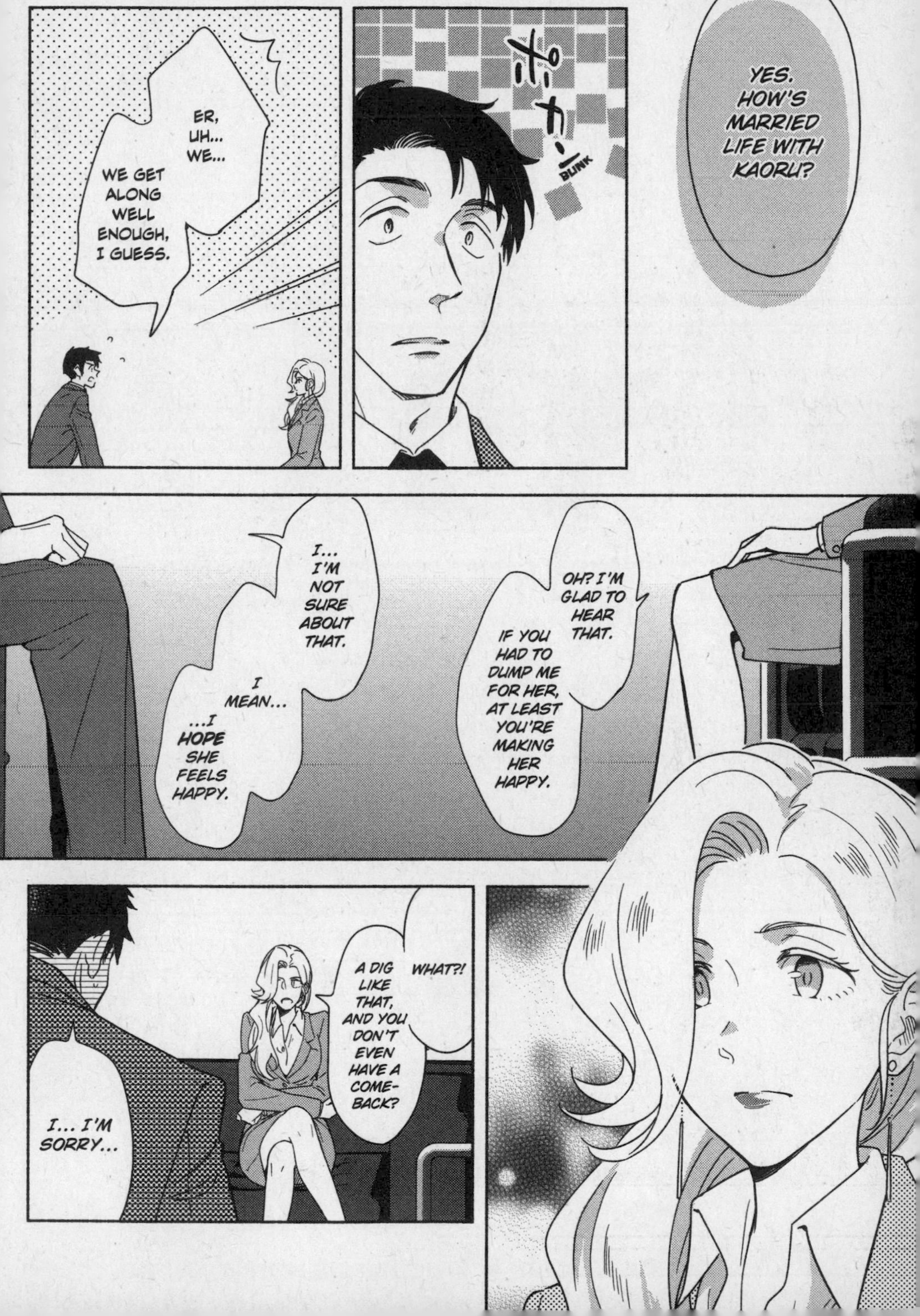
YES. HOW'S MARRIED LIFE WITH KAORU?
BLINK
ER, UH... WE...
WE GET ALONG WELL ENOUGH, I GUESS.
OH? I'M GLAD TO HEAR THAT.
IF YOU HAD TO DUMP ME FOR HER, AT LEAST YOU'RE MAKING HER HAPPY.
I... I'M NOT SURE ABOUT THAT.
I MEAN...
...I **HOPE** SHE FEELS HAPPY.
WHAT?!
A DIG LIKE THAT, AND YOU DON'T EVEN HAVE A COME-BACK?
I... I'M SORRY...

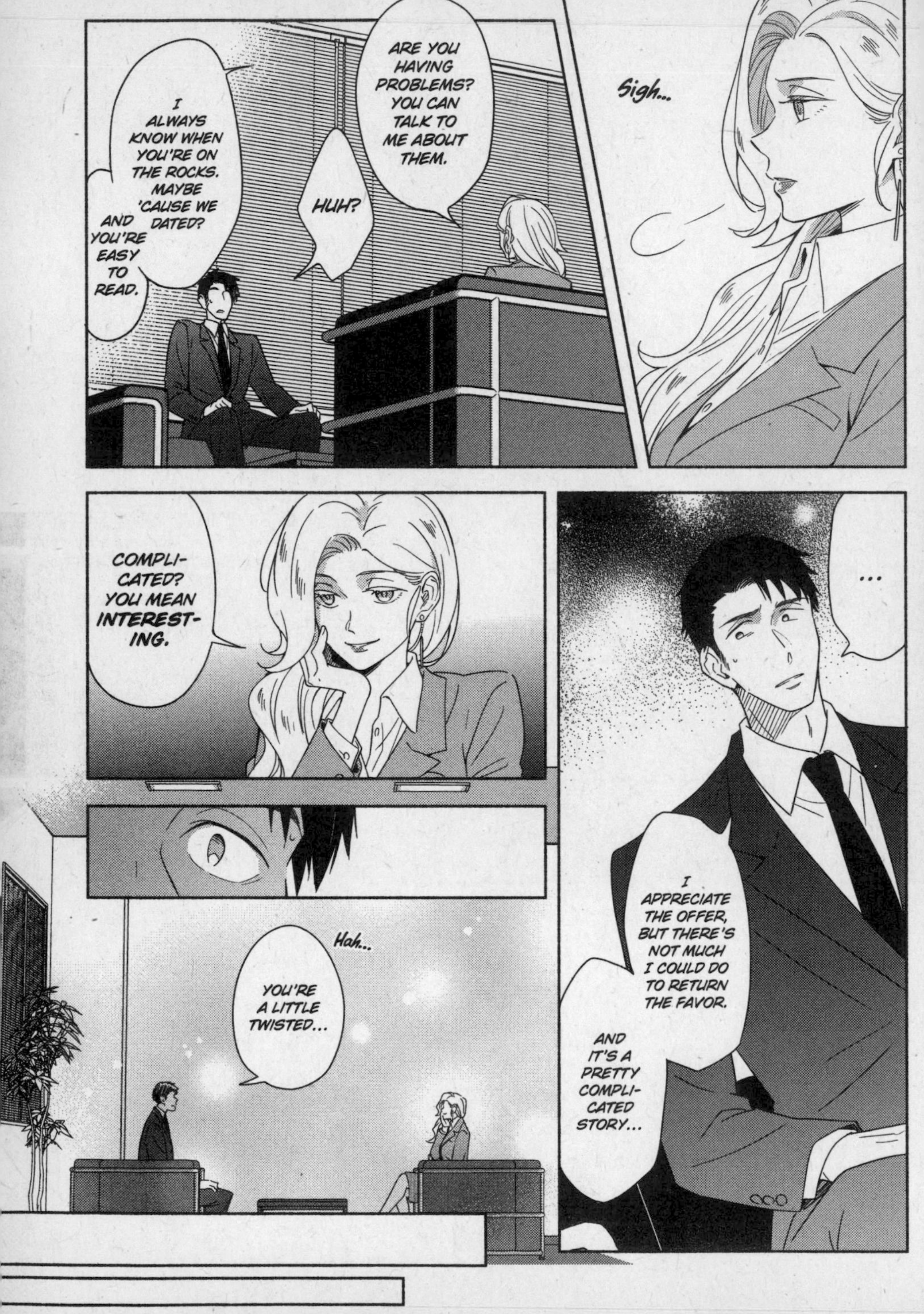
Sigh...
ARE YOU HAVING PROBLEMS? YOU CAN TALK TO ME ABOUT THEM.
HUH?
I ALWAYS KNOW WHEN YOU'RE ON THE ROCKS. MAYBE 'CAUSE WE DATED?
AND YOU'RE EASY TO READ.
...
I APPRECIATE THE OFFER, BUT THERE'S NOT MUCH I COULD DO TO RETURN THE FAVOR.
AND IT'S A PRETTY COMPLICATED STORY...
COMPLICATED? YOU MEAN INTERESTING.
Hah...
YOU'RE A LITTLE TWISTED...

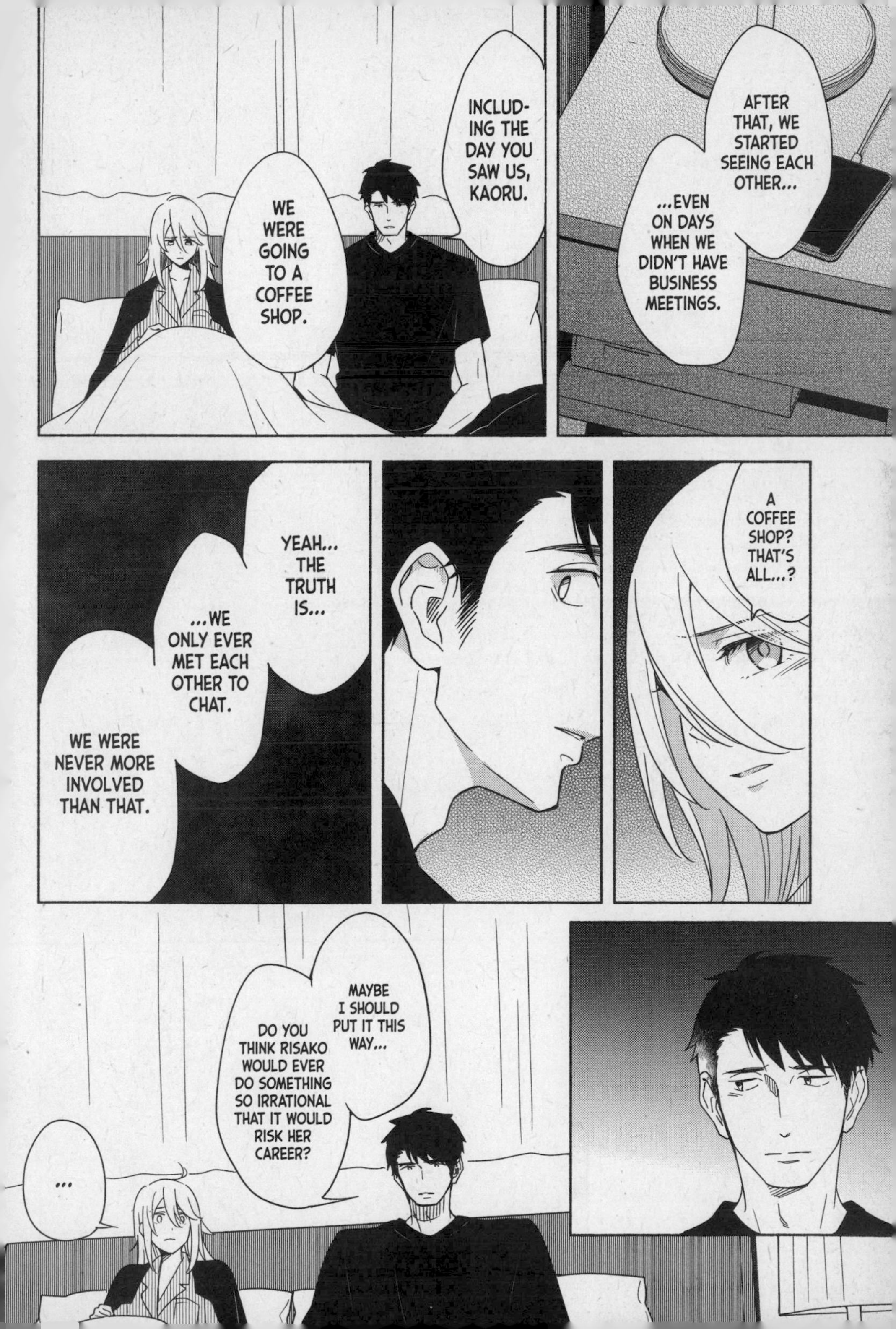
AFTER THAT, WE STARTED SEEING EACH OTHER...
...EVEN ON DAYS WHEN WE DIDN'T HAVE BUSINESS MEETINGS.
INCLUD-ING THE DAY YOU SAW US, KAORU.
WE WERE GOING TO A COFFEE SHOP.
A COFFEE SHOP? THAT'S ALL...?
YEAH... THE TRUTH IS...
...WE ONLY EVER MET EACH OTHER TO CHAT.
WE WERE NEVER MORE INVOLVED THAN THAT.
MAYBE I SHOULD PUT IT THIS WAY...
DO YOU THINK RISAKO WOULD EVER DO SOMETHING SO IRRATIONAL THAT IT WOULD RISK HER CAREER?
...

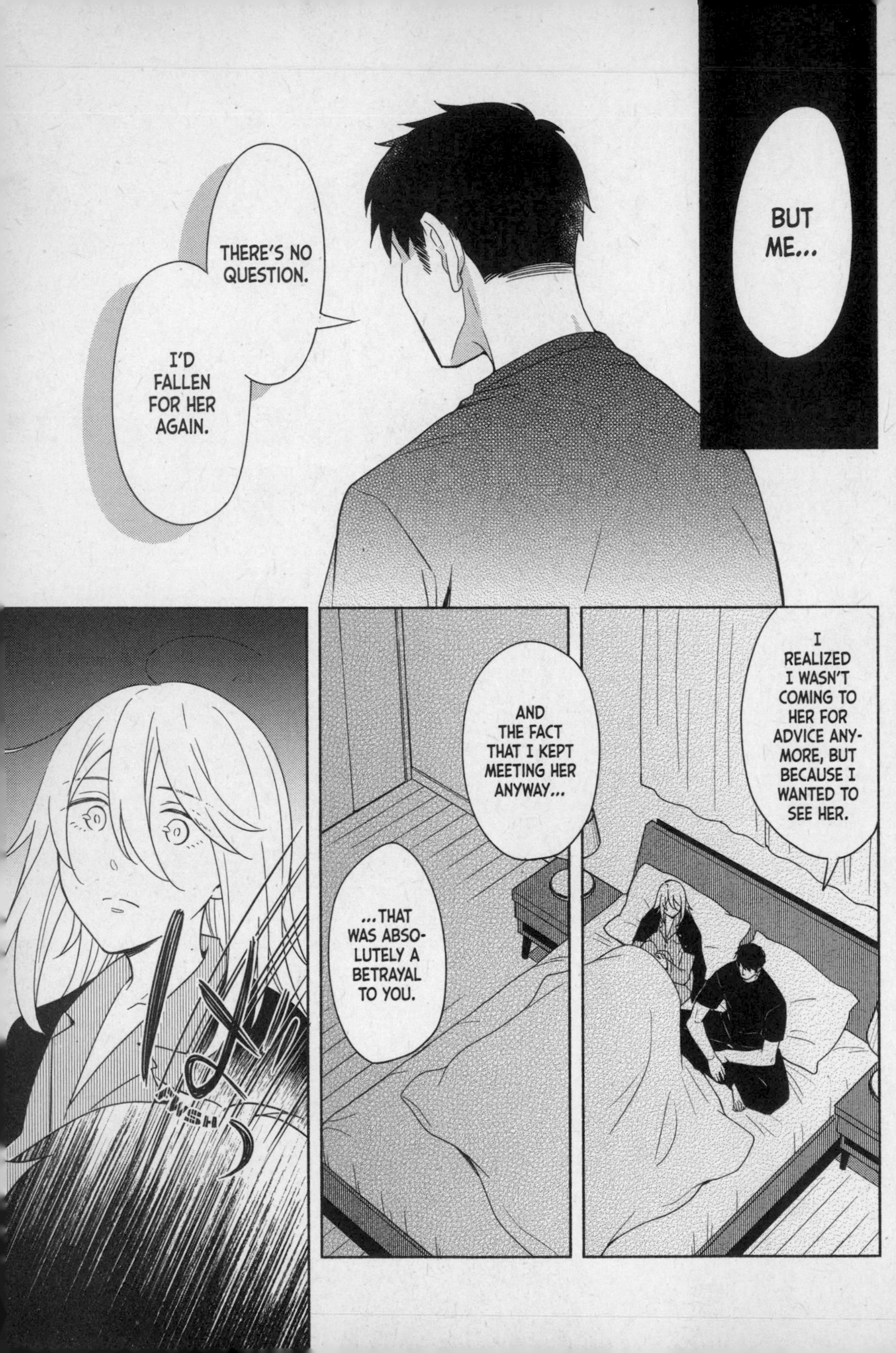
BUT ME...
THERE'S NO QUESTION.
I'D FALLEN FOR HER AGAIN.
I REALIZED I WASN'T COMING TO HER FOR ADVICE ANY-MORE, BUT BECAUSE I WANTED TO SEE HER.
AND THE FACT THAT I KEPT MEETING HER ANYWAY...
...THAT WAS ABSO-LUTELY A BETRAYAL TO YOU.

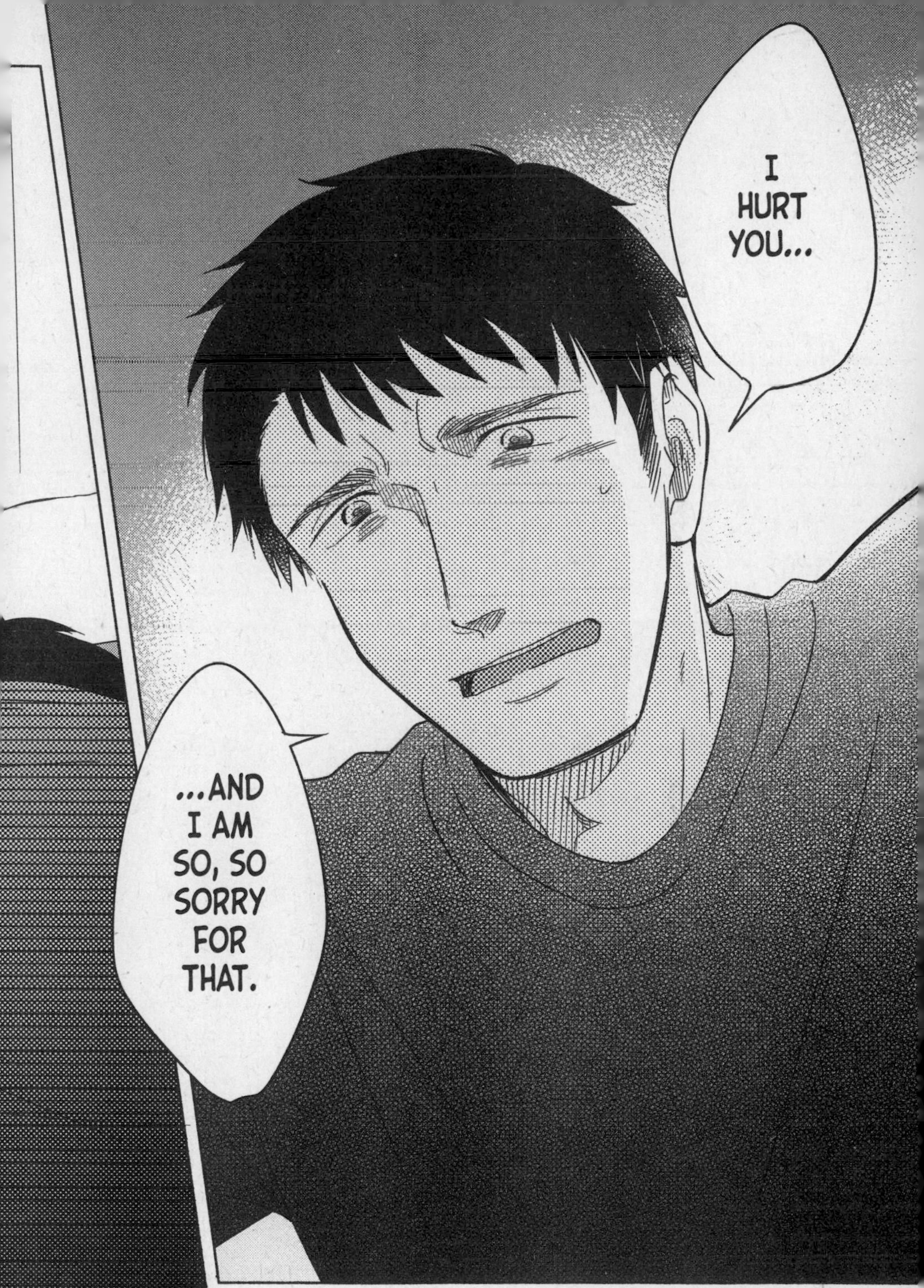
I HURT YOU...
...AND I AM SO, SO SORRY FOR THAT.

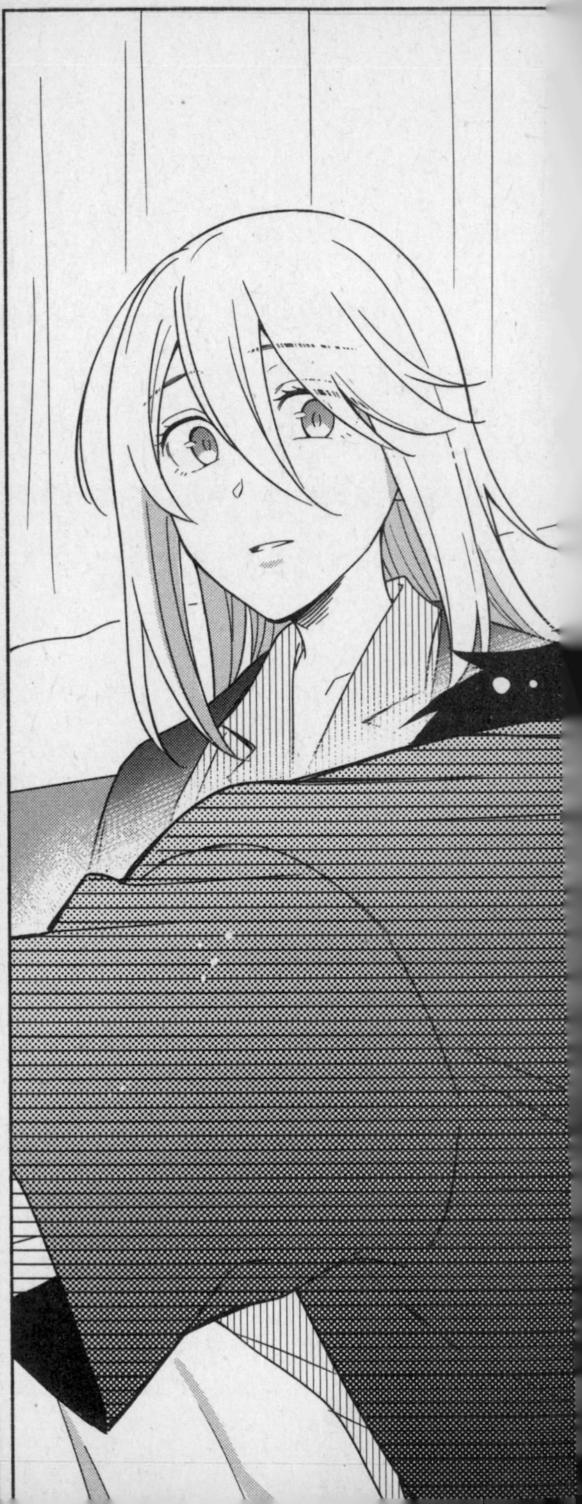

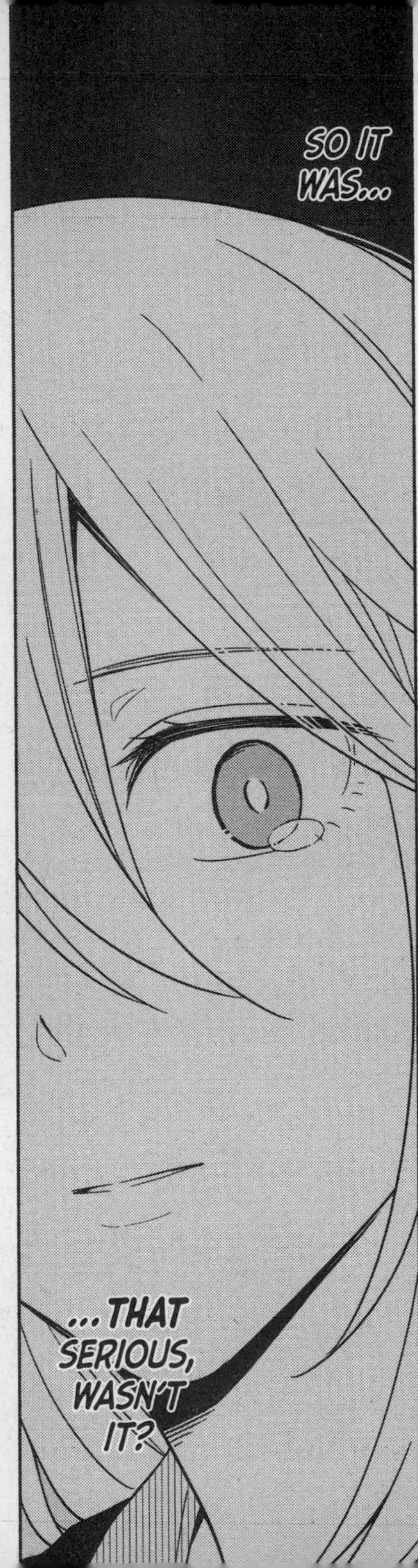
SO IT WAS...
...THAT SERIOUS, WASN'T IT?

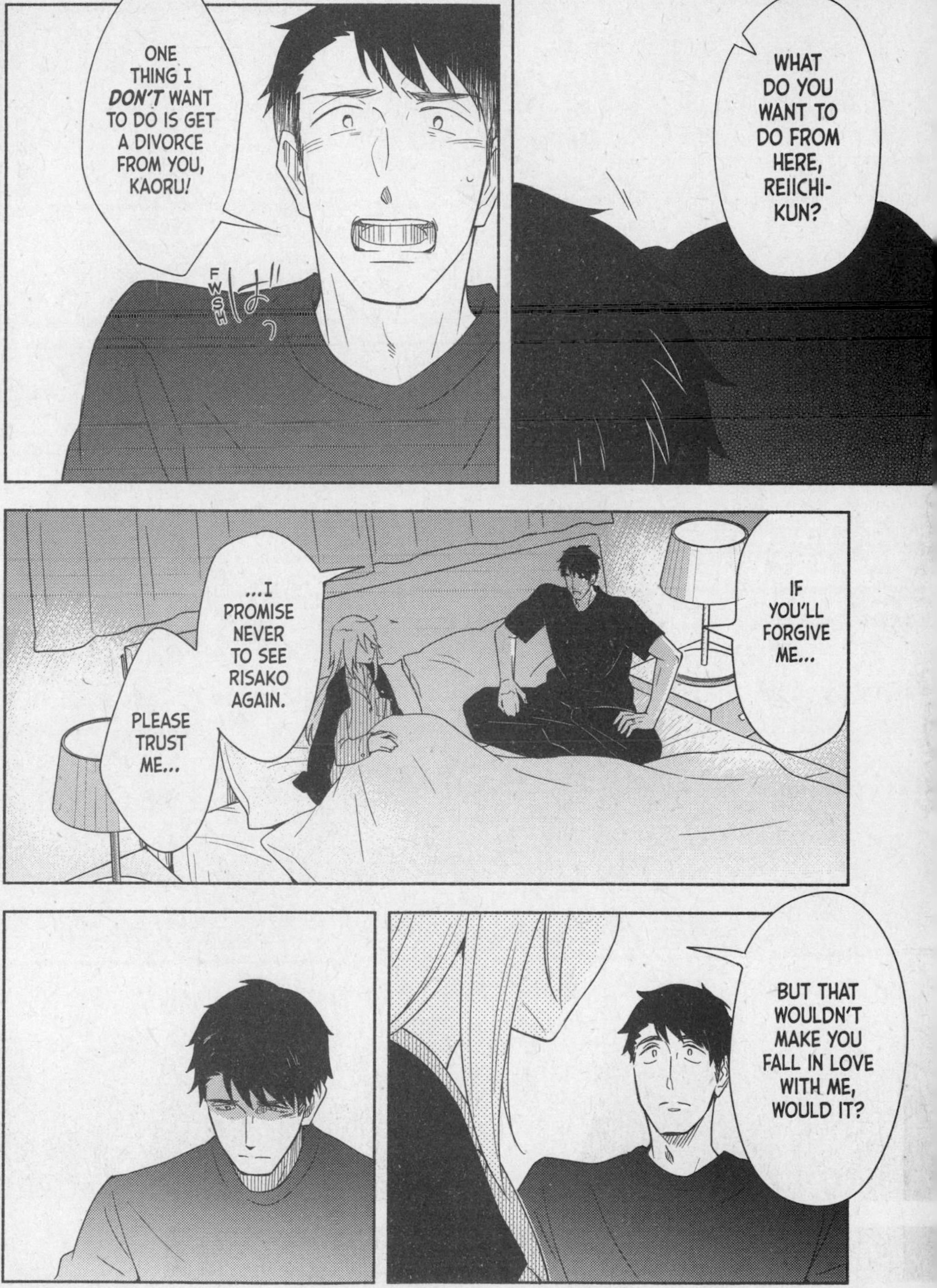
WHAT DO YOU WANT TO DO FROM HERE, REIICHI-KUN?
ONE THING I DON'T WANT TO DO IS GET A DIVORCE FROM YOU, KAORU!
FWSH
IF YOU'LL FORGIVE ME...
...I PROMISE NEVER TO SEE RISAKO AGAIN.
PLEASE TRUST ME...
BUT THAT WOULDN'T MAKE YOU FALL IN LOVE WITH ME, WOULD IT?

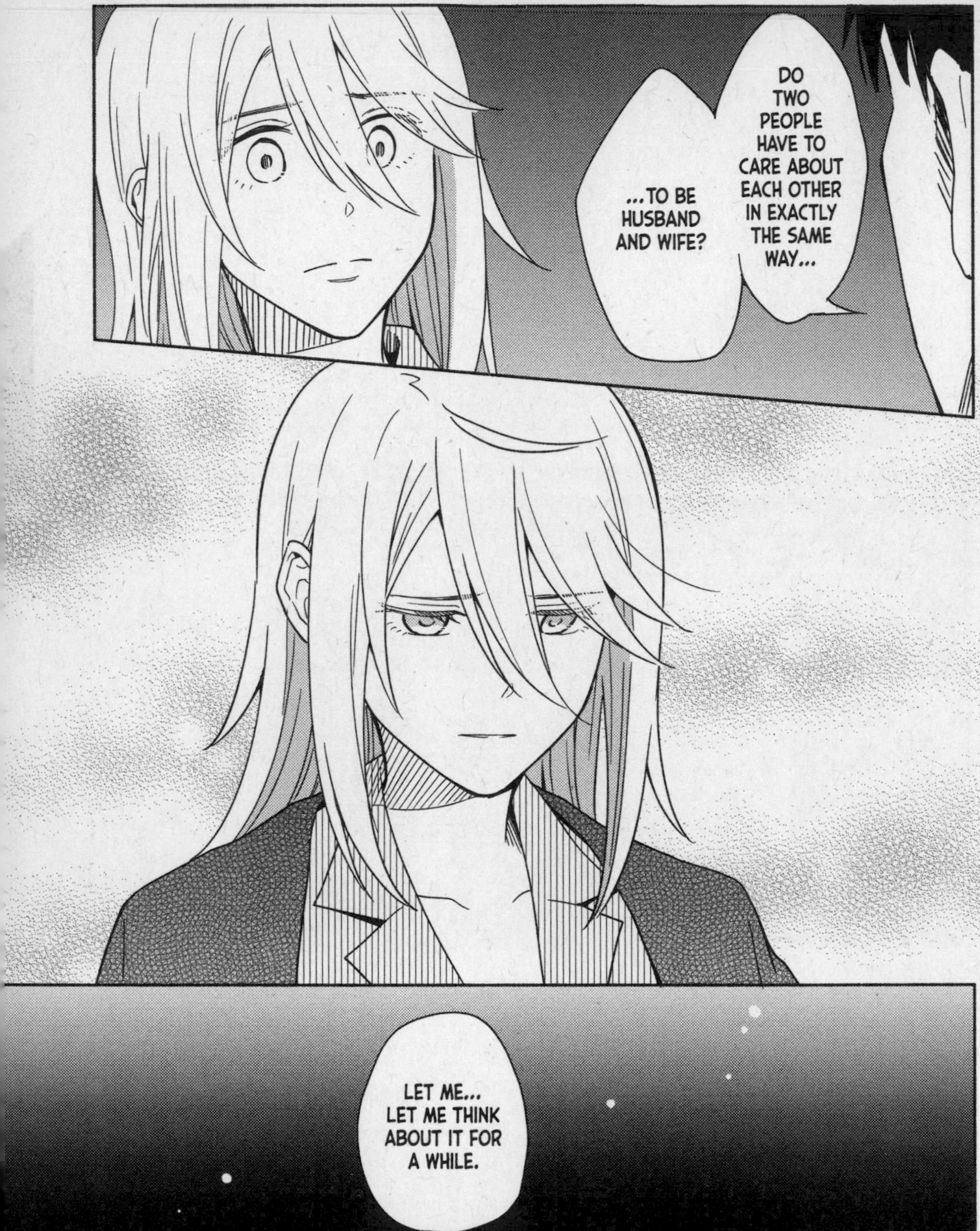
DO TWO PEOPLE HAVE TO CARE ABOUT EACH OTHER IN EXACTLY THE SAME WAY...
...TO BE HUSBAND AND WIFE?
LET ME... LET ME THINK ABOUT IT FOR A WHILE.

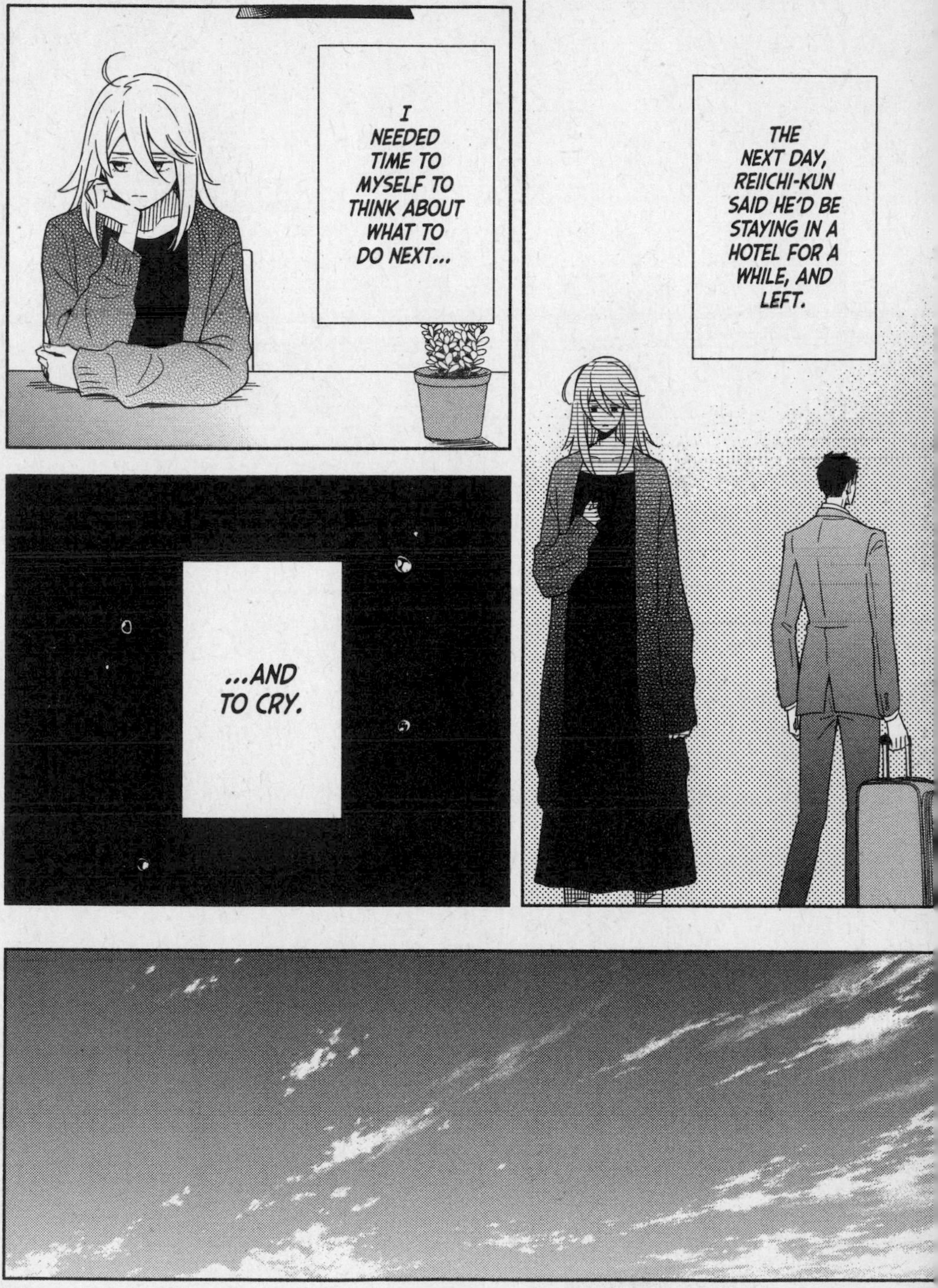
THE NEXT DAY, REIICHI-KUN SAID HE'D BE STAYING IN A HOTEL FOR A WHILE, AND LEFT.
I NEEDED TIME TO MYSELF TO THINK ABOUT WHAT TO DO NEXT...
...AND TO CRY.

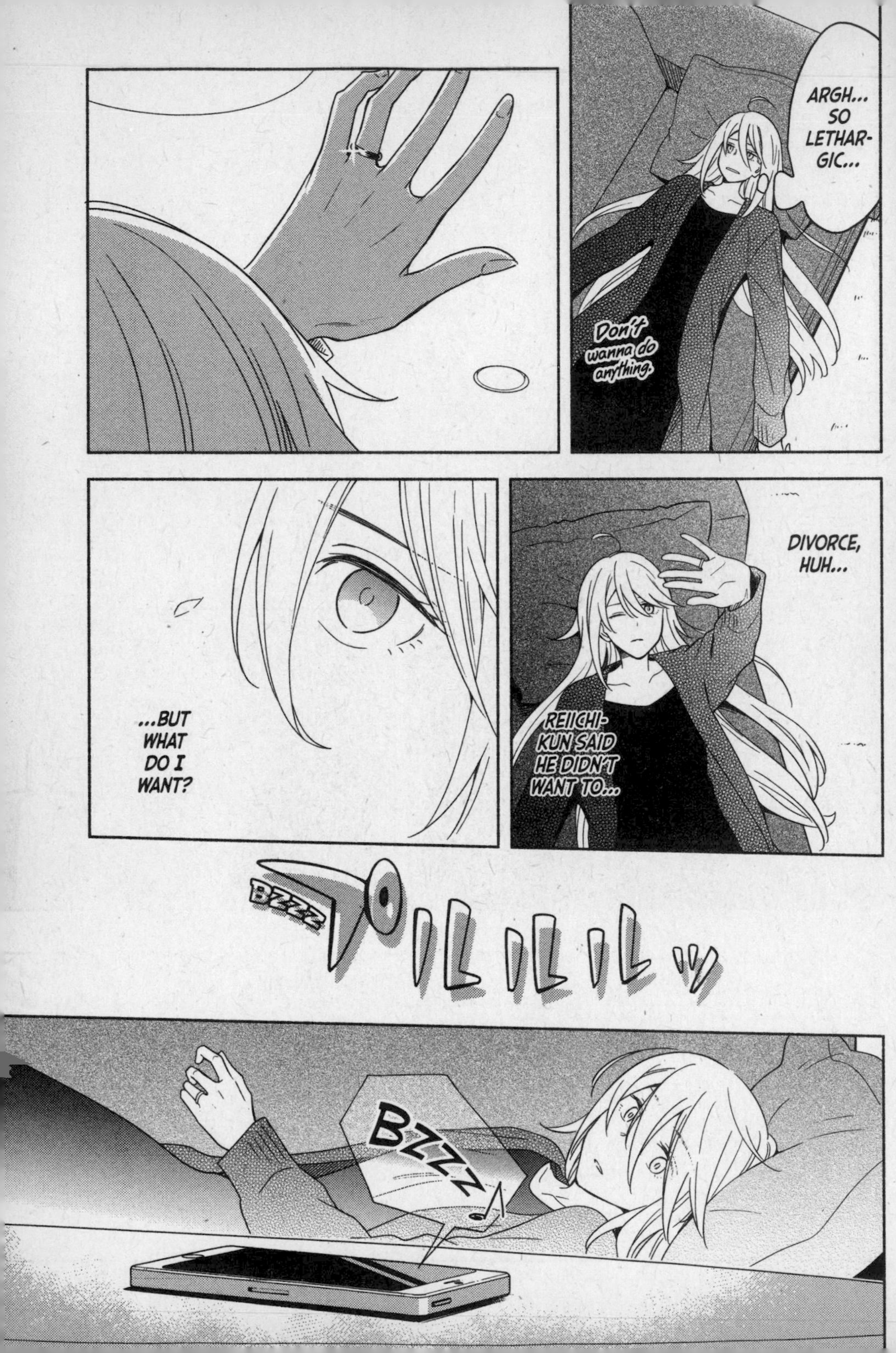
ARGH... SO LETHARGIC...
Don't wanna do anything.
DIVORCE, HUH...
REIICHI-KUN SAID HE DIDN'T WANT TO...
...BUT WHAT DO I WANT?
BZZZ
BZZZ

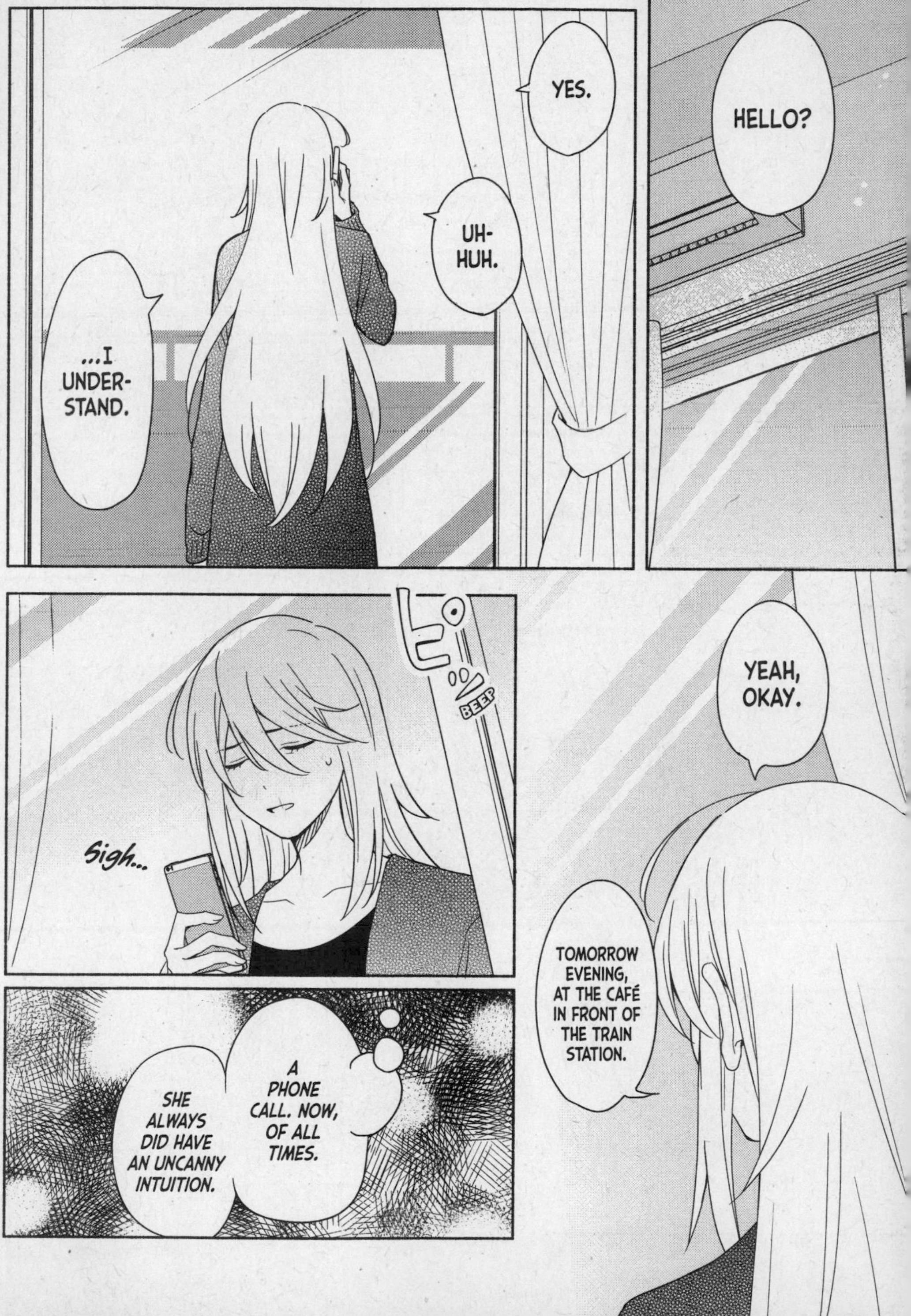
HELLO?
YES.
UH-HUH.
...I UNDER-STAND.
YEAH, OKAY.
TOMORROW EVENING, AT THE CAFÉ IN FRONT OF THE TRAIN STATION.
BEEP
Sigh...
A PHONE CALL. NOW, OF ALL TIMES.
SHE ALWAYS DID HAVE AN UNCANNY INTUITION.

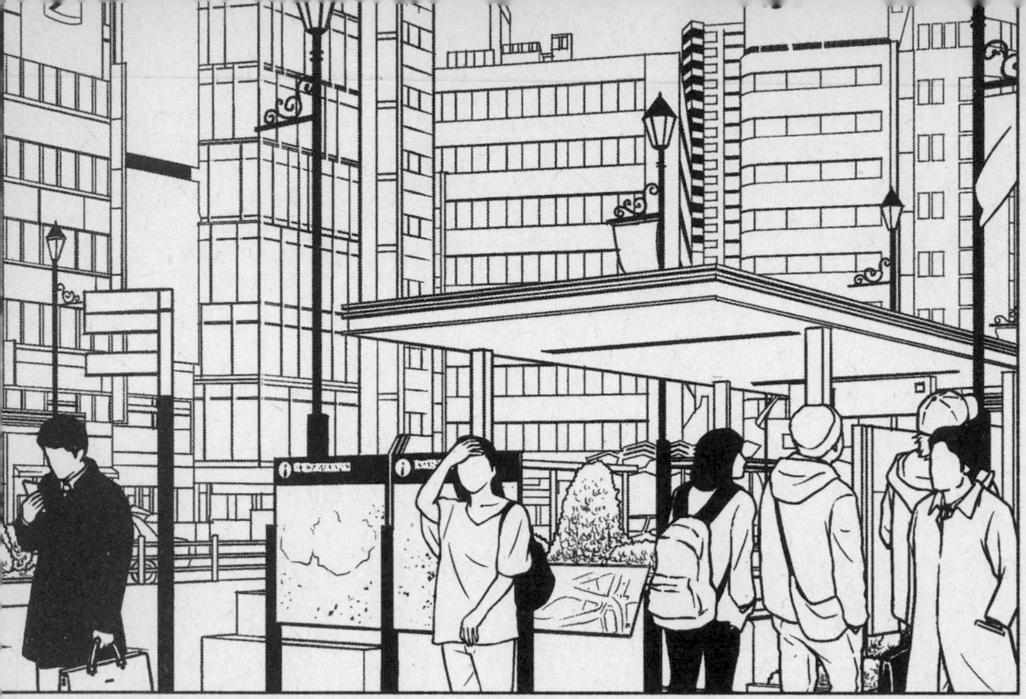

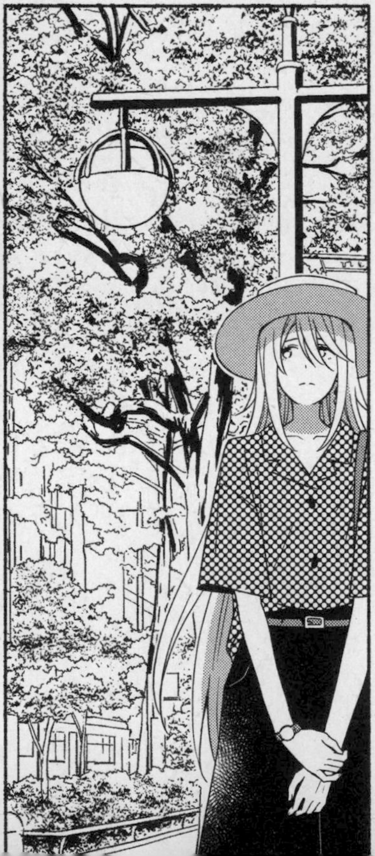

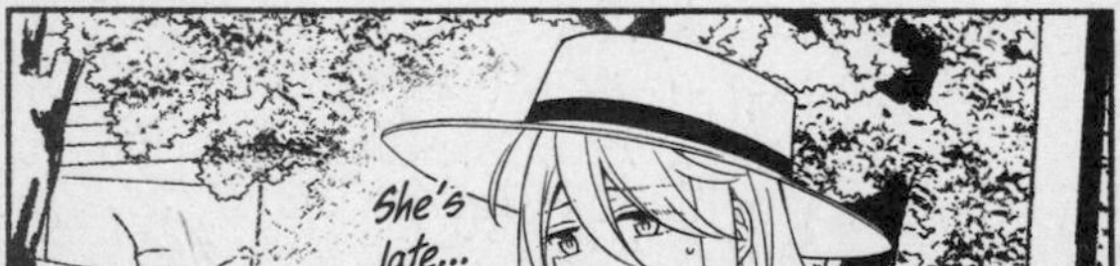
She's late...

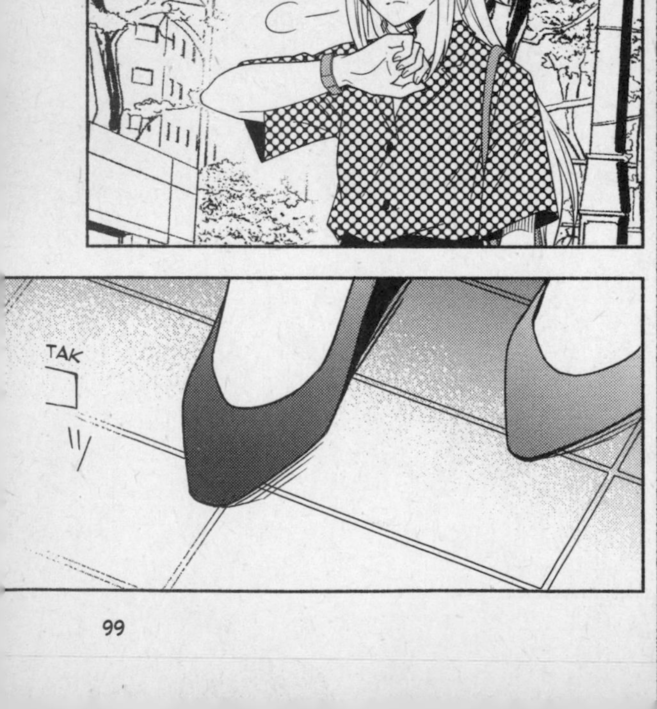
TAK

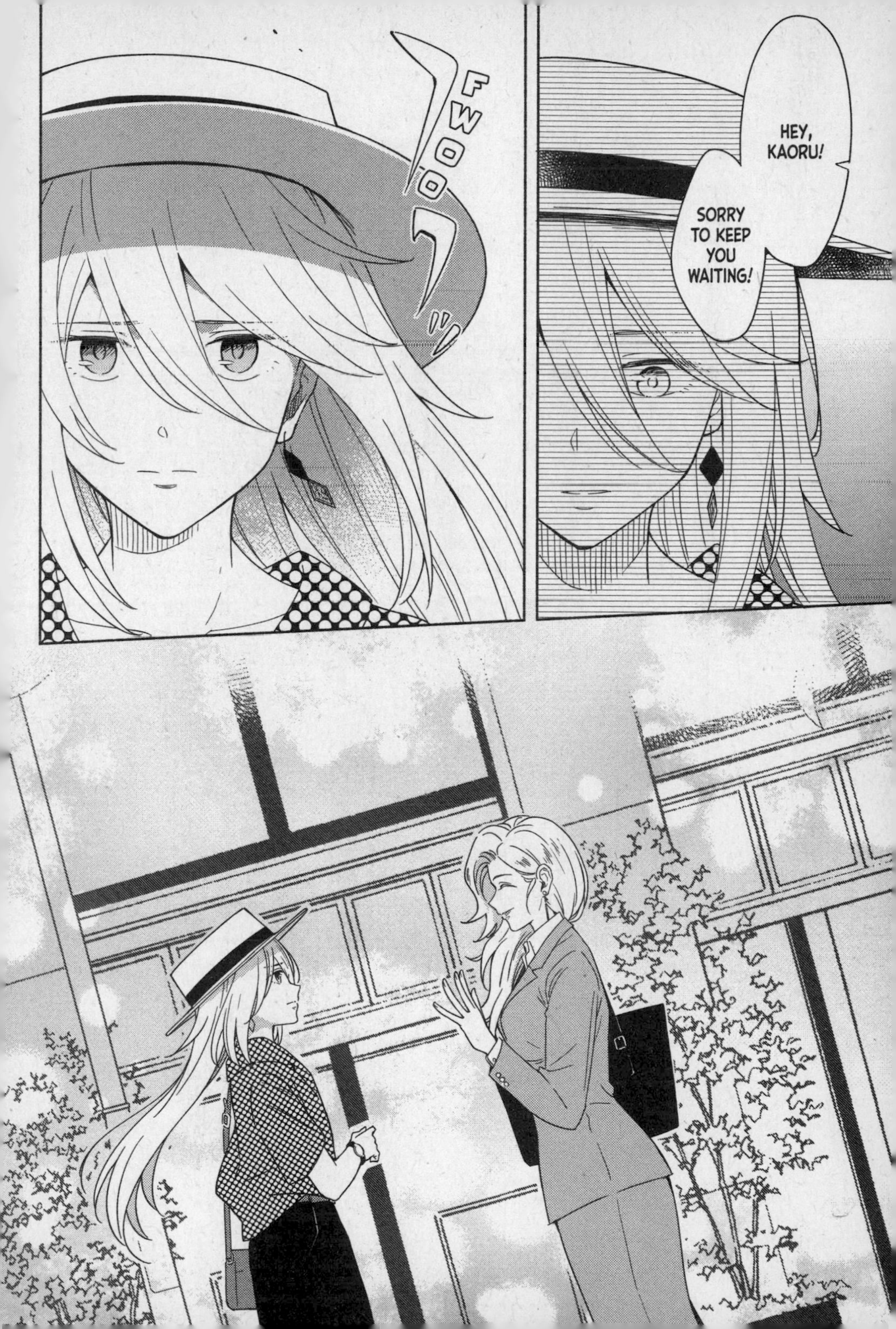
HEY, KAORU!
SORRY TO KEEP YOU WAITING!
FWOO

If I Could
Reach You

If I Could
Reach You

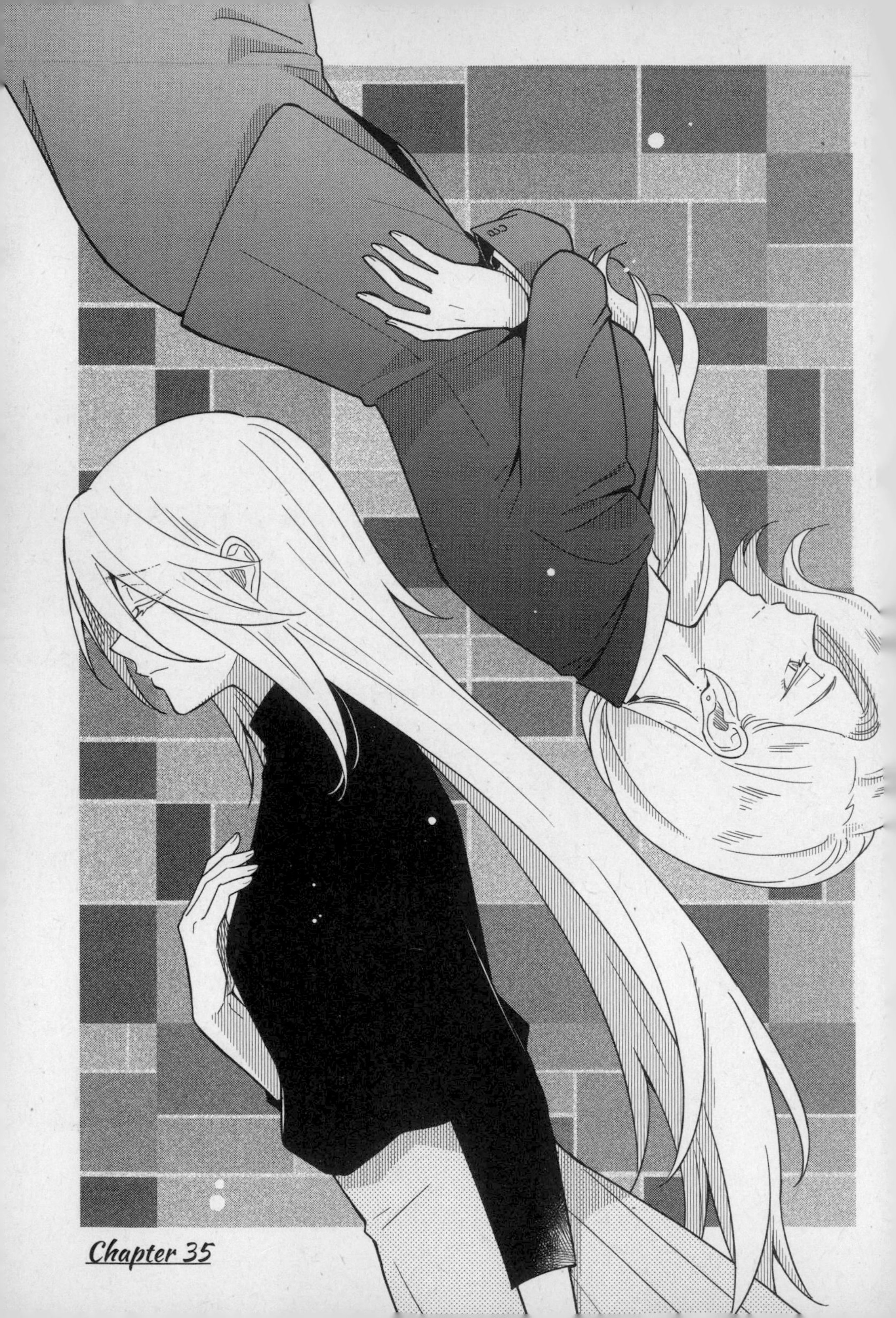

Chapter 35

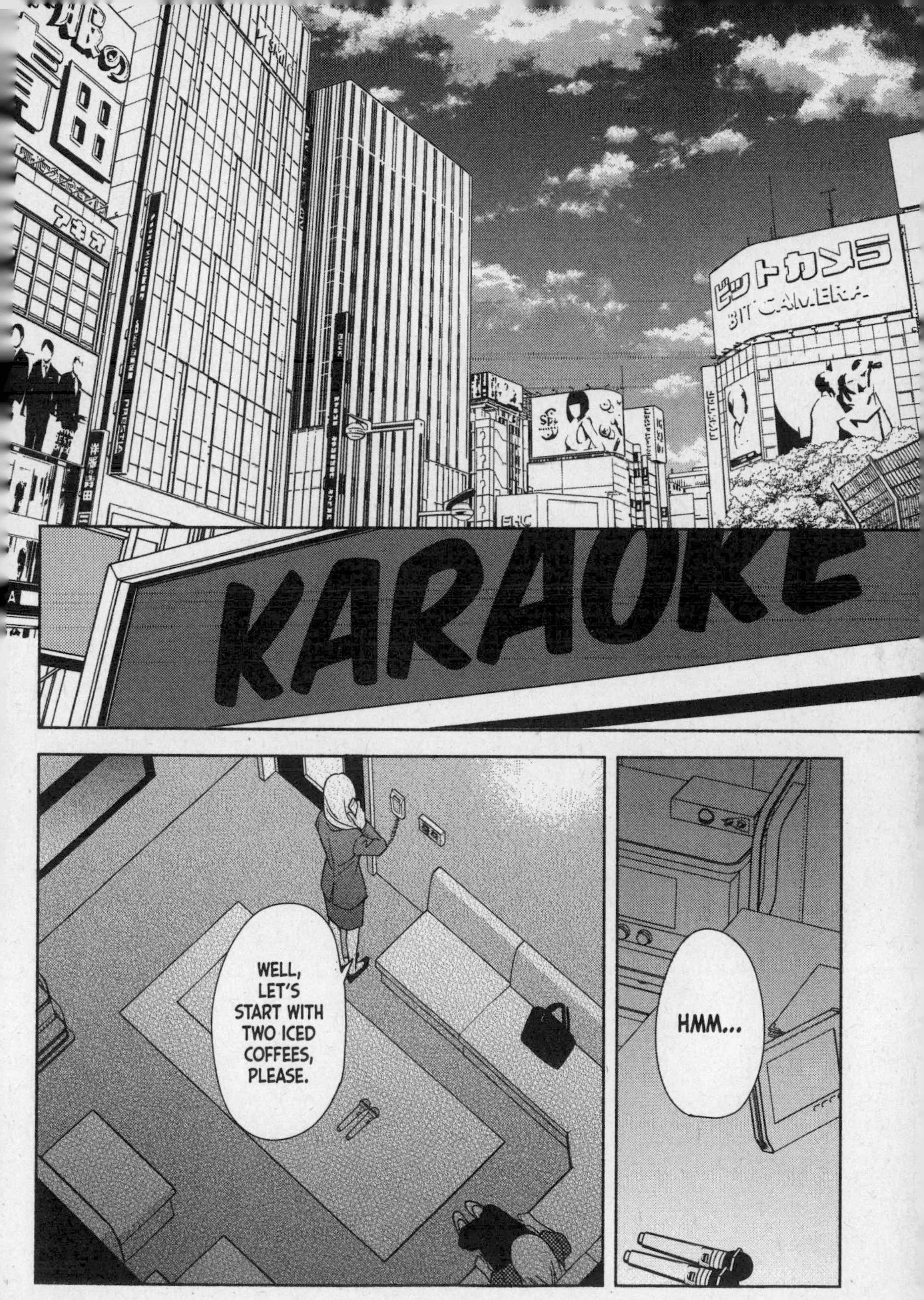
ビットカメラ
BIT CAMERA
KARAOKE
HMM...
WELL, LET'S START WITH TWO ICED COFFEES, PLEASE.

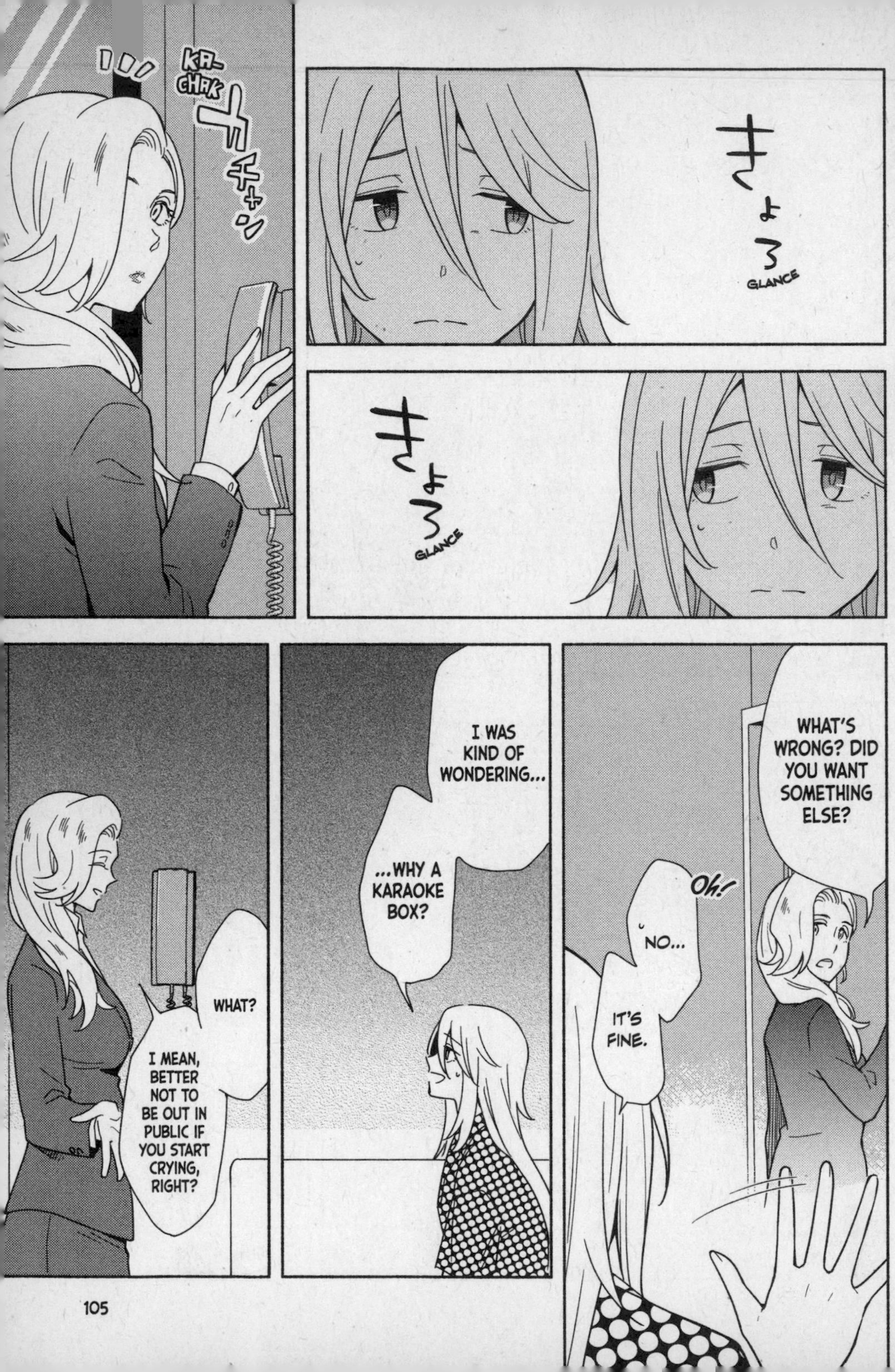
きょろ
GLANCE
きょろ
GLANCE
KA-CHAK
ガチャッ
WHAT'S WRONG? DID YOU WANT SOMETHING ELSE?
Oh!
NO...
IT'S FINE.
I WAS KIND OF WONDERING...
...WHY A KARAOKE BOX?
WHAT?
I MEAN, BETTER NOT TO BE OUT IN PUBLIC IF YOU START CRYING, RIGHT?

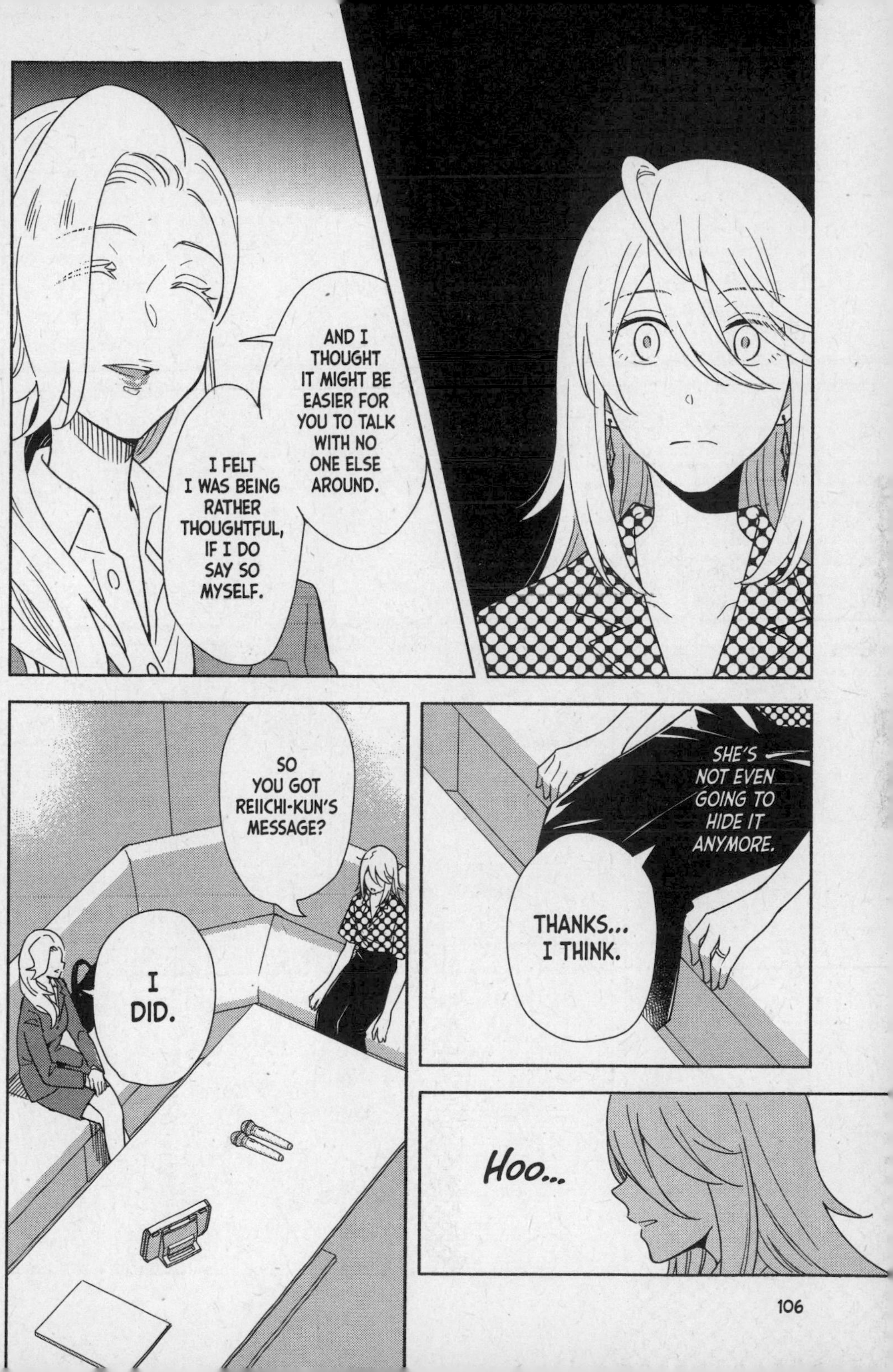
AND I THOUGHT IT MIGHT BE EASIER FOR YOU TO TALK WITH NO ONE ELSE AROUND.
I FELT I WAS BEING RATHER THOUGHTFUL, IF I DO SAY SO MYSELF.
SO YOU GOT REIICHI-KUN'S MESSAGE?
I DID.
SHE'S NOT EVEN GOING TO HIDE IT ANYMORE.
THANKS... I THINK.
Hoo...

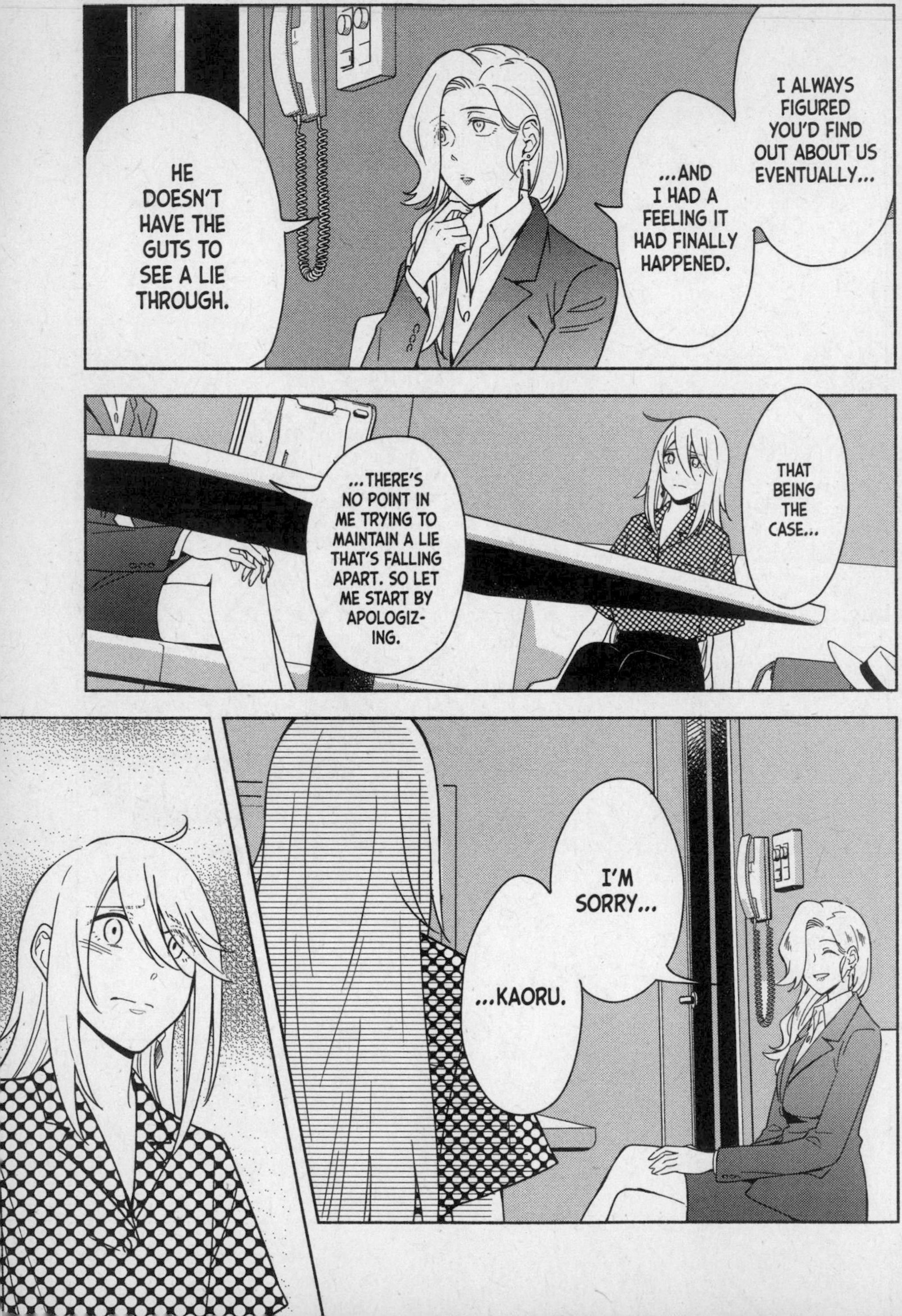
I ALWAYS FIGURED YOU'D FIND OUT ABOUT US EVENTUALLY...
...AND I HAD A FEELING IT HAD FINALLY HAPPENED.
HE DOESN'T HAVE THE GUTS TO SEE A LIE THROUGH.
THAT BEING THE CASE...
...THERE'S NO POINT IN ME TRYING TO MAINTAIN A LIE THAT'S FALLING APART. SO LET ME START BY APOLOGIZ-ING.
I'M SORRY...
...KAORU.

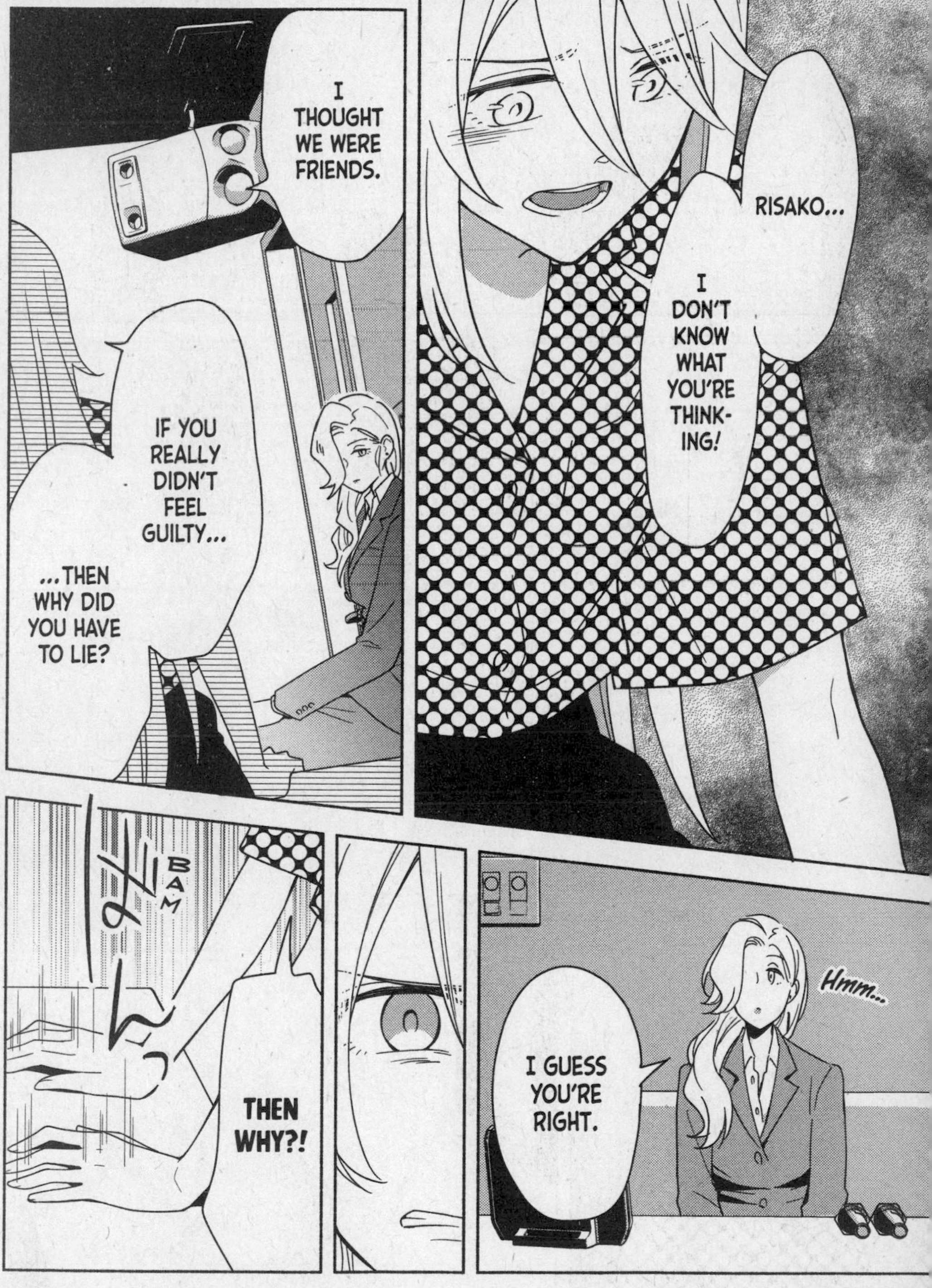
RISAKO...
I DON'T KNOW WHAT YOU'RE THINKING!
I THOUGHT WE WERE FRIENDS.
IF YOU REALLY DIDN'T FEEL GUILTY...
...THEN WHY DID YOU HAVE TO LIE?
Hmm...
I GUESS YOU'RE RIGHT.
THEN WHY?!
BAM

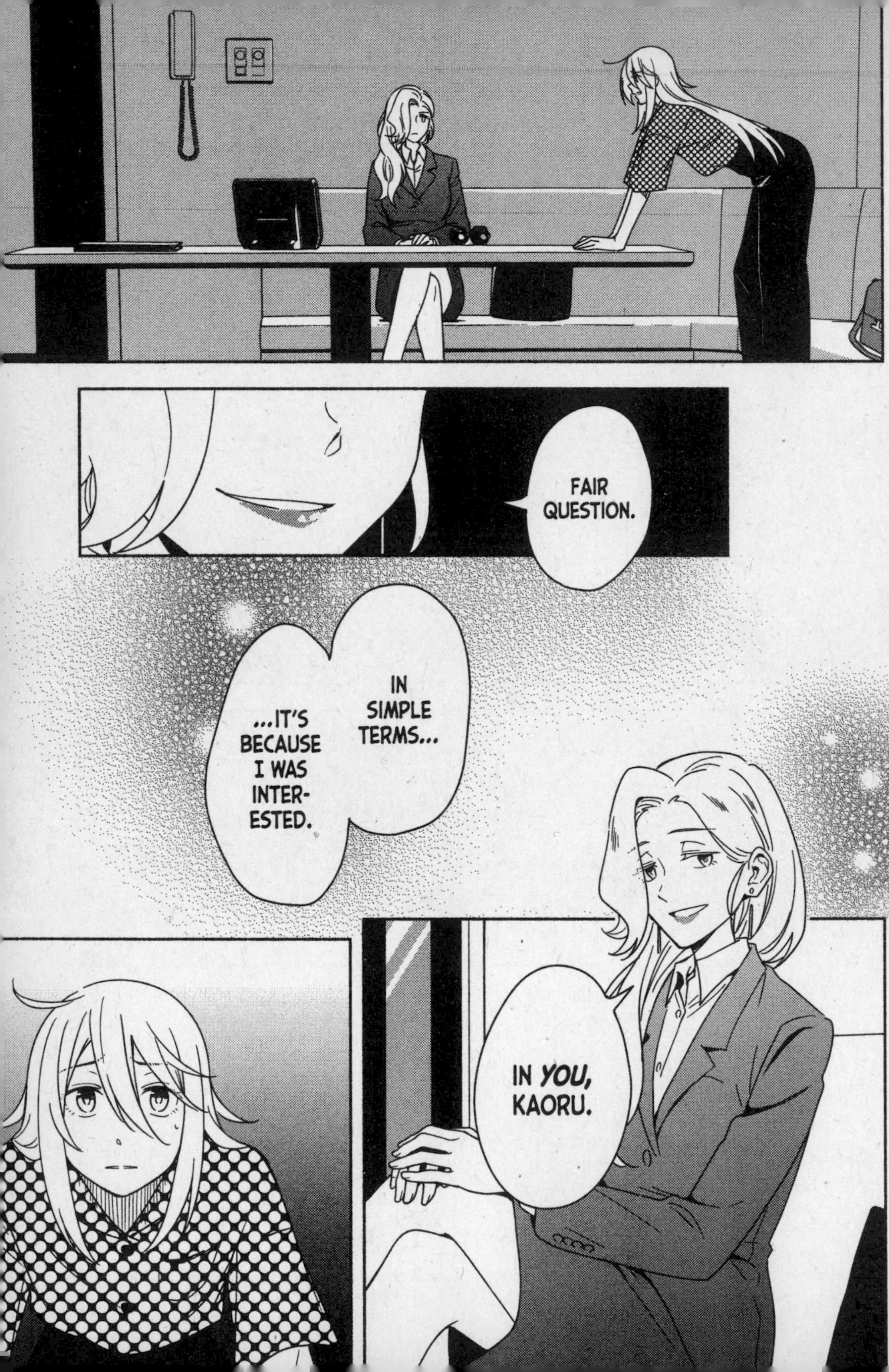
FAIR QUESTION.
IN SIMPLE TERMS...
...IT'S BECAUSE I WAS INTERESTED.
IN *YOU*, KAORU.

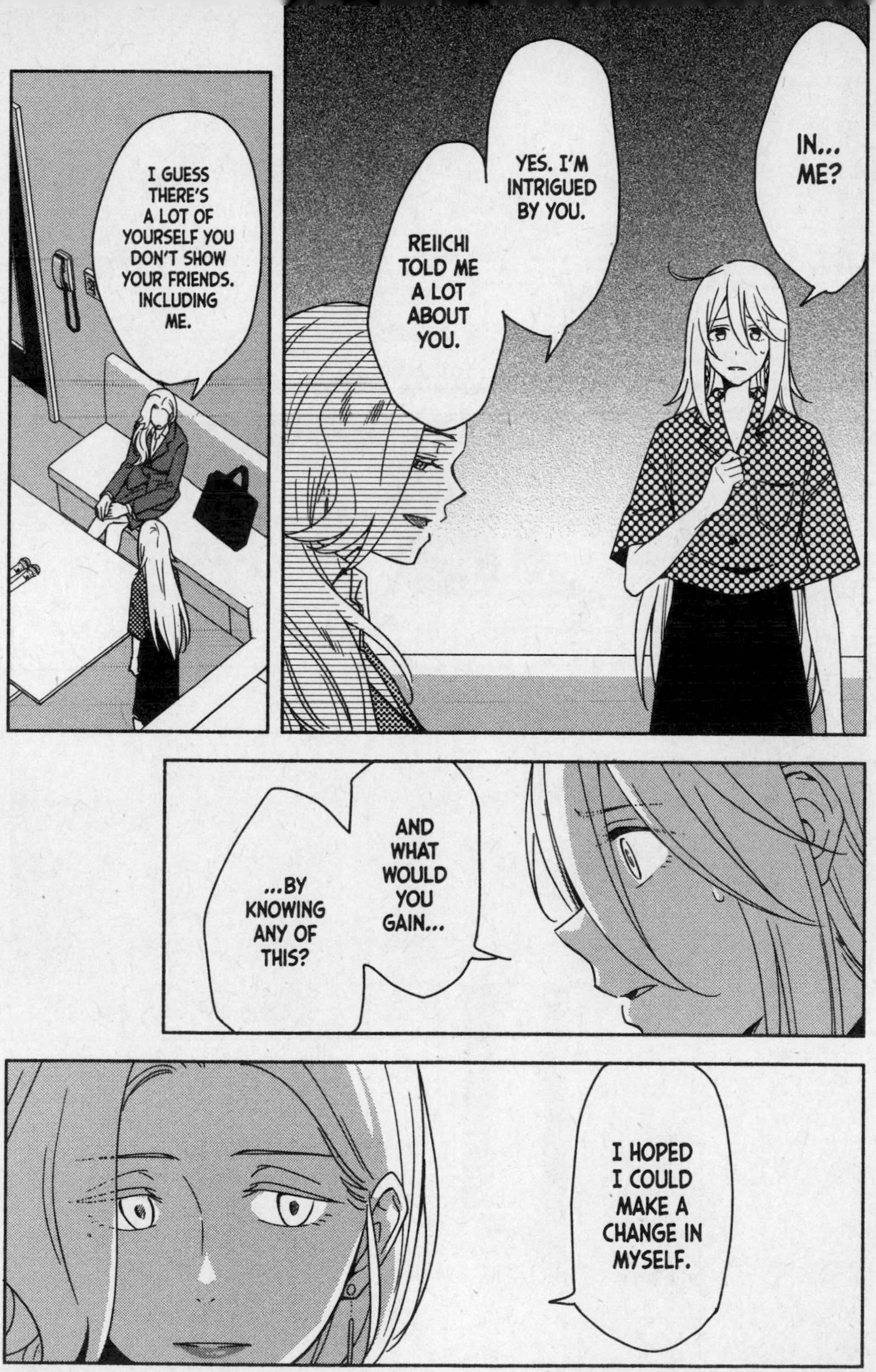
IN... ME?
YES. I'M INTRIGUED BY YOU.
REIICHI TOLD ME A LOT ABOUT YOU.
I GUESS THERE'S A LOT OF YOURSELF YOU DON'T SHOW YOUR FRIENDS. INCLUDING ME.
AND WHAT WOULD YOU GAIN...
...BY KNOWING ANY OF THIS?
I HOPED I COULD MAKE A CHANGE IN MYSELF.

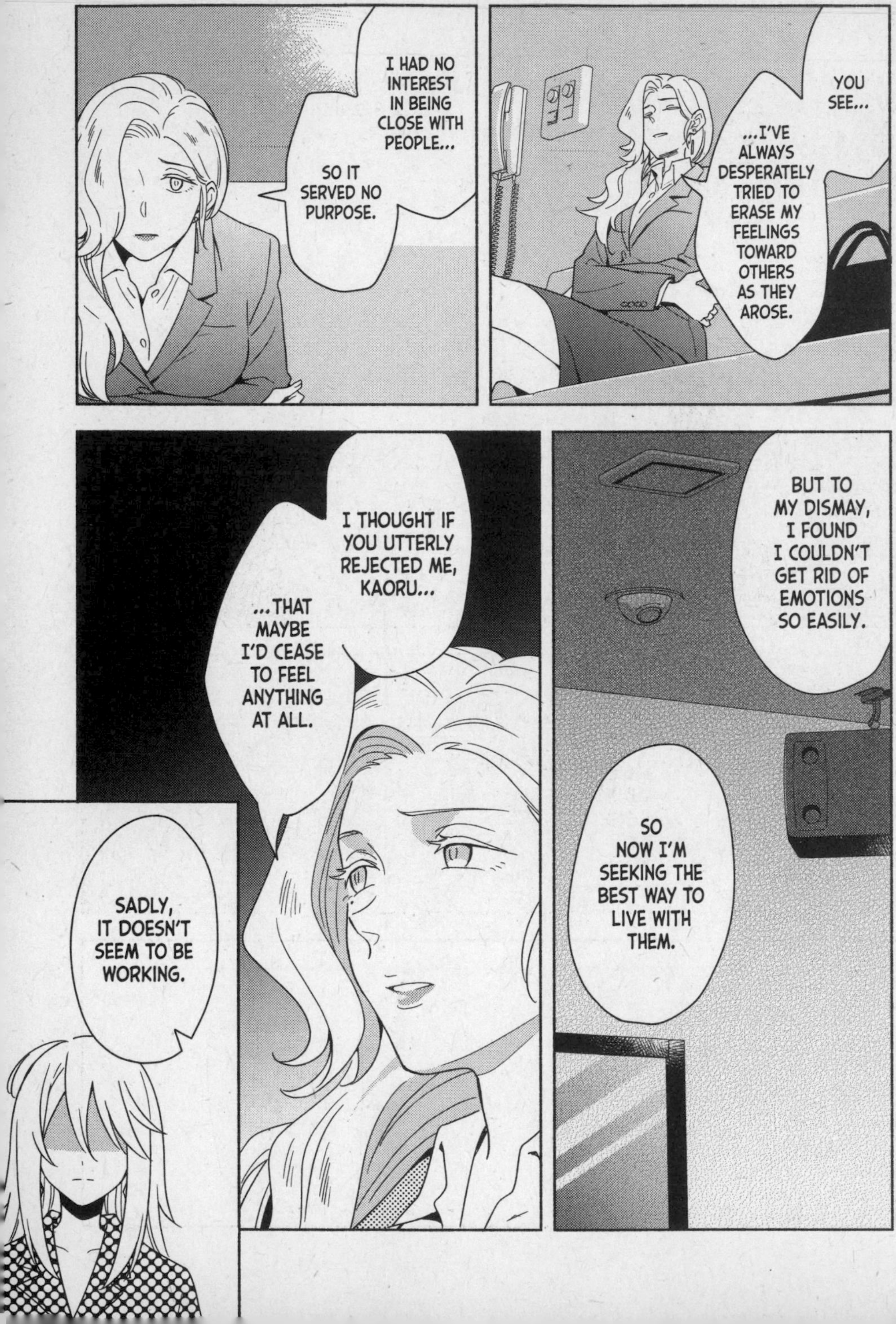
YOU SEE...
...I'VE ALWAYS DESPERATELY TRIED TO ERASE MY FEELINGS TOWARD OTHERS AS THEY AROSE.
I HAD NO INTEREST IN BEING CLOSE WITH PEOPLE...
SO IT SERVED NO PURPOSE.
BUT TO MY DISMAY, I FOUND I COULDN'T GET RID OF EMOTIONS SO EASILY.
SO NOW I'M SEEKING THE BEST WAY TO LIVE WITH THEM.
I THOUGHT IF YOU UTTERLY REJECTED ME, KAORU...
...THAT MAYBE I'D CEASE TO FEEL ANYTHING AT ALL.
SADLY, IT DOESN'T SEEM TO BE WORKING.

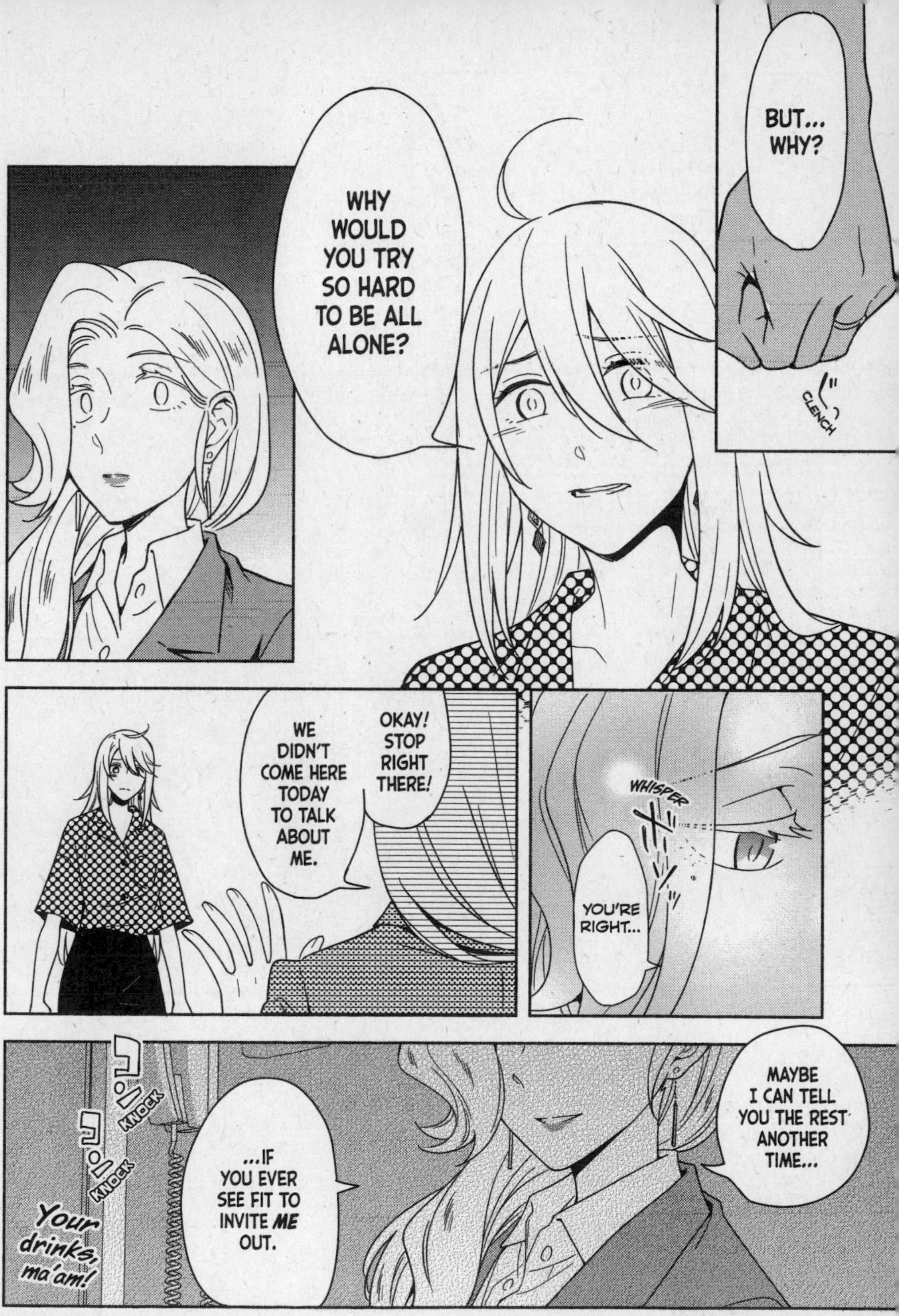
BUT... WHY?
CLENCH
WHY WOULD YOU TRY SO HARD TO BE ALL ALONE?
WHISPER
YOU'RE RIGHT...
OKAY! STOP RIGHT THERE!
WE DIDN'T COME HERE TODAY TO TALK ABOUT ME.
MAYBE I CAN TELL YOU THE REST ANOTHER TIME...
...IF YOU EVER SEE FIT TO INVITE *ME* OUT.
KNOCK
KNOCK
Your drinks, ma'am!

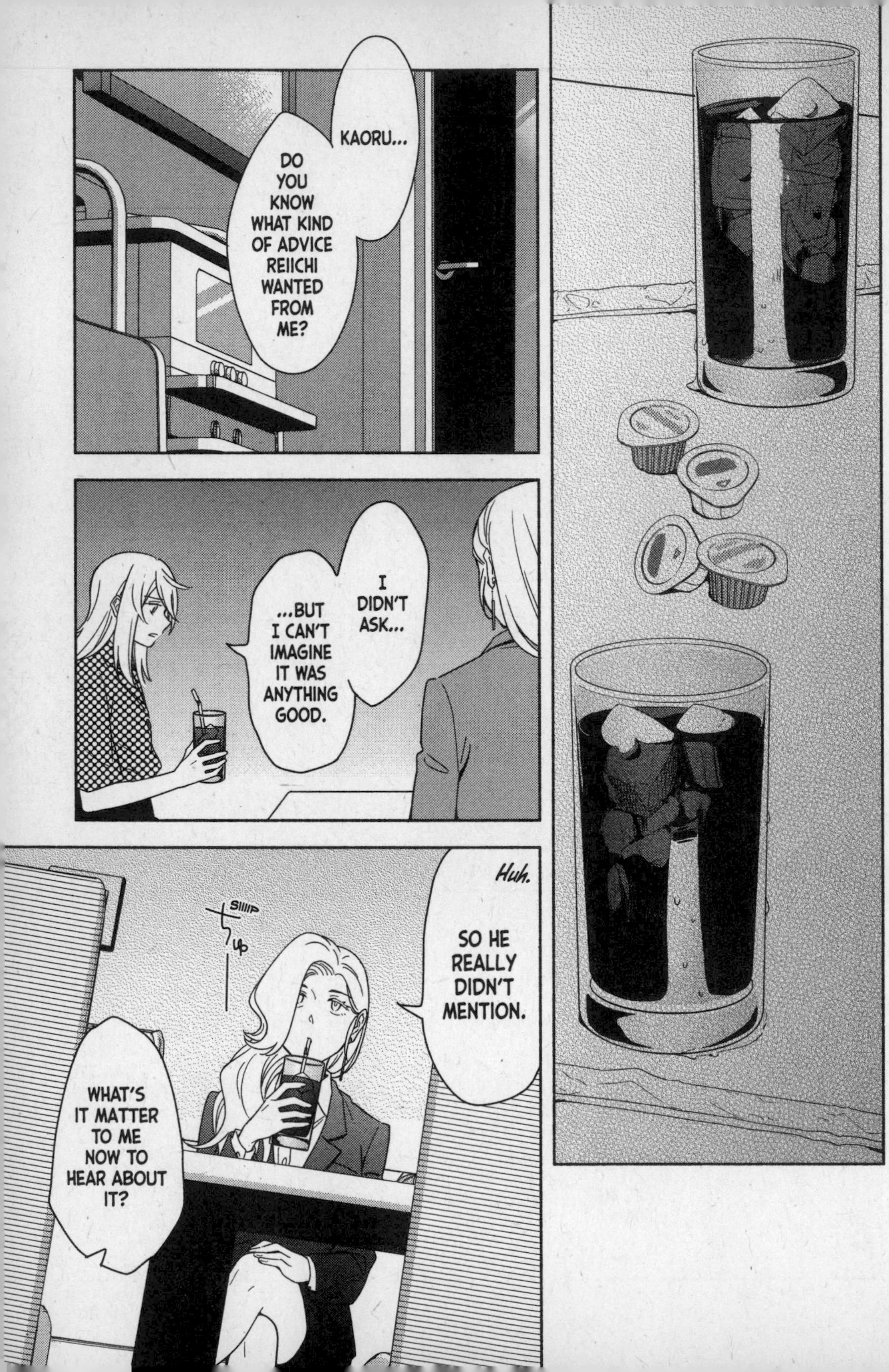
KAORU...
DO YOU KNOW WHAT KIND OF ADVICE REIICHI WANTED FROM ME?
I DIDN'T ASK...
...BUT I CAN'T IMAGINE IT WAS ANYTHING GOOD.
Huh.
SO HE REALLY DIDN'T MENTION.
SIIIP
up
WHAT'S IT MATTER TO ME NOW TO HEAR ABOUT IT?

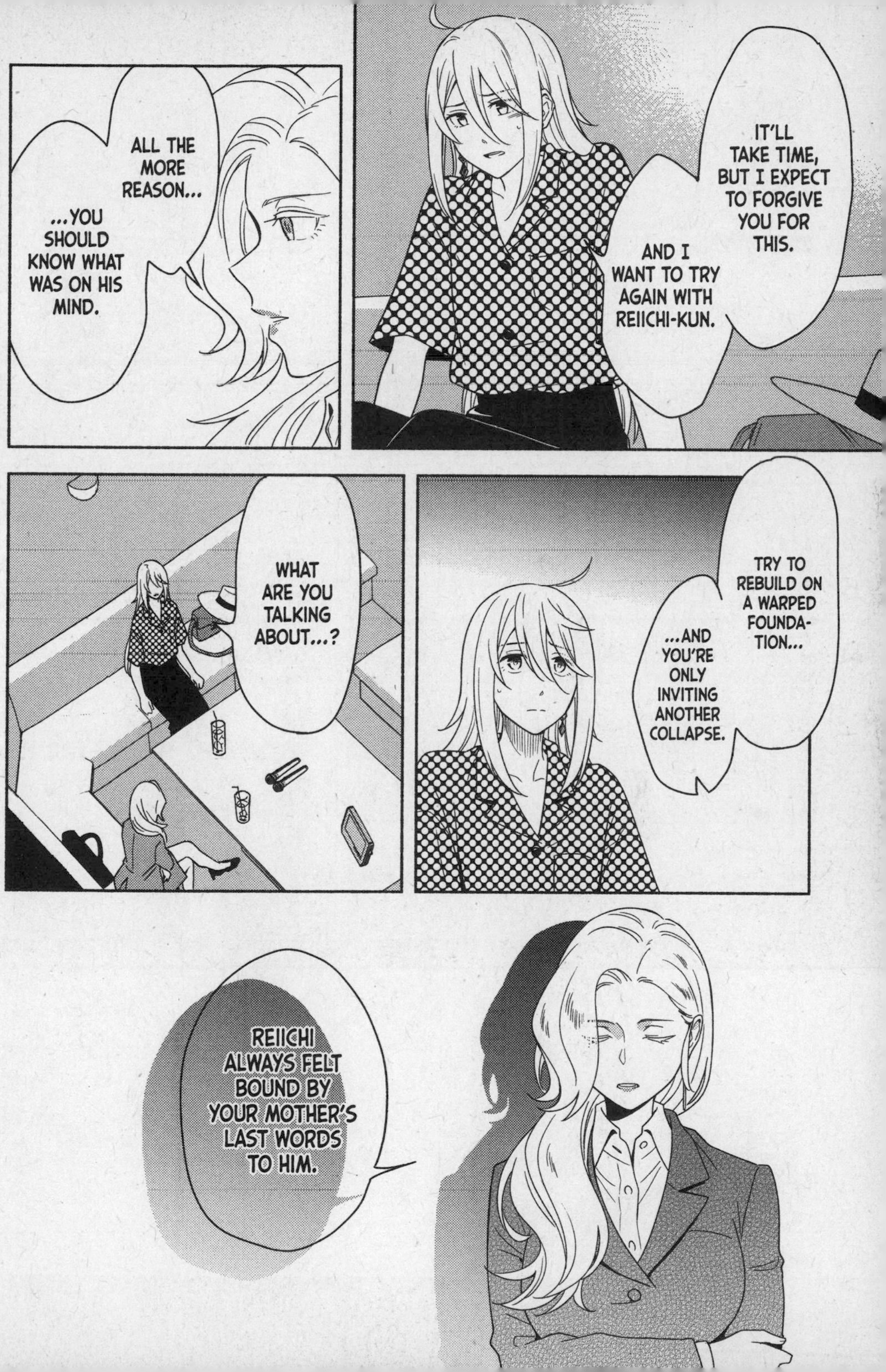
IT'LL TAKE TIME, BUT I EXPECT TO FORGIVE YOU FOR THIS.
AND I WANT TO TRY AGAIN WITH REIICHI-KUN.
ALL THE MORE REASON...
...YOU SHOULD KNOW WHAT WAS ON HIS MIND.
TRY TO REBUILD ON A WARPED FOUNDA-TION...
...AND YOU'RE ONLY INVITING ANOTHER COLLAPSE.
WHAT ARE YOU TALKING ABOUT...?
REIICHI ALWAYS FELT BOUND BY YOUR MOTHER'S LAST WORDS TO HIM.

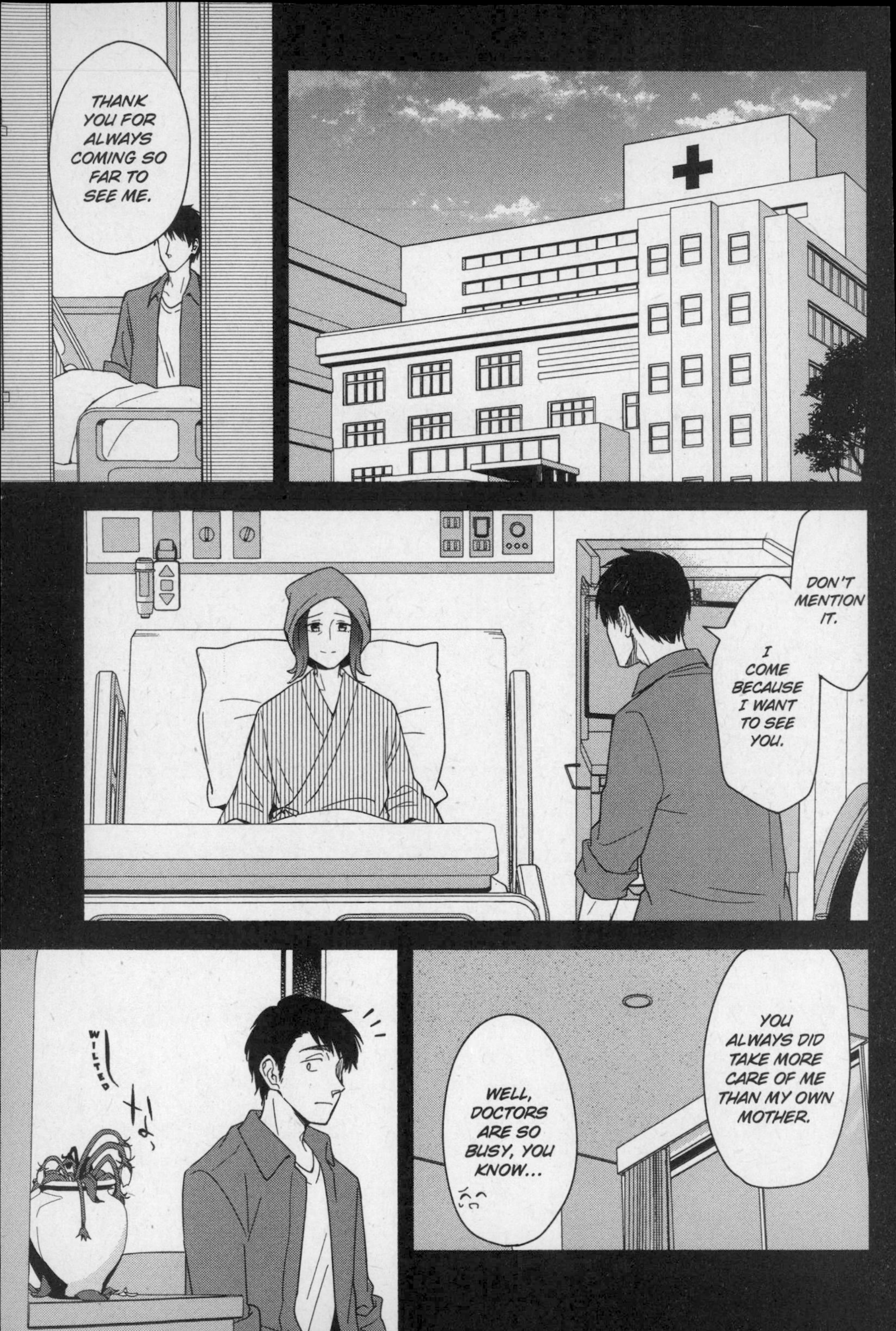
THANK YOU FOR ALWAYS COMING SO FAR TO SEE ME.
DON'T MENTION IT.
I COME BECAUSE I WANT TO SEE YOU.
YOU ALWAYS DID TAKE MORE CARE OF ME THAN MY OWN MOTHER.
WELL, DOCTORS ARE SO BUSY, YOU KNOW...
WILTED

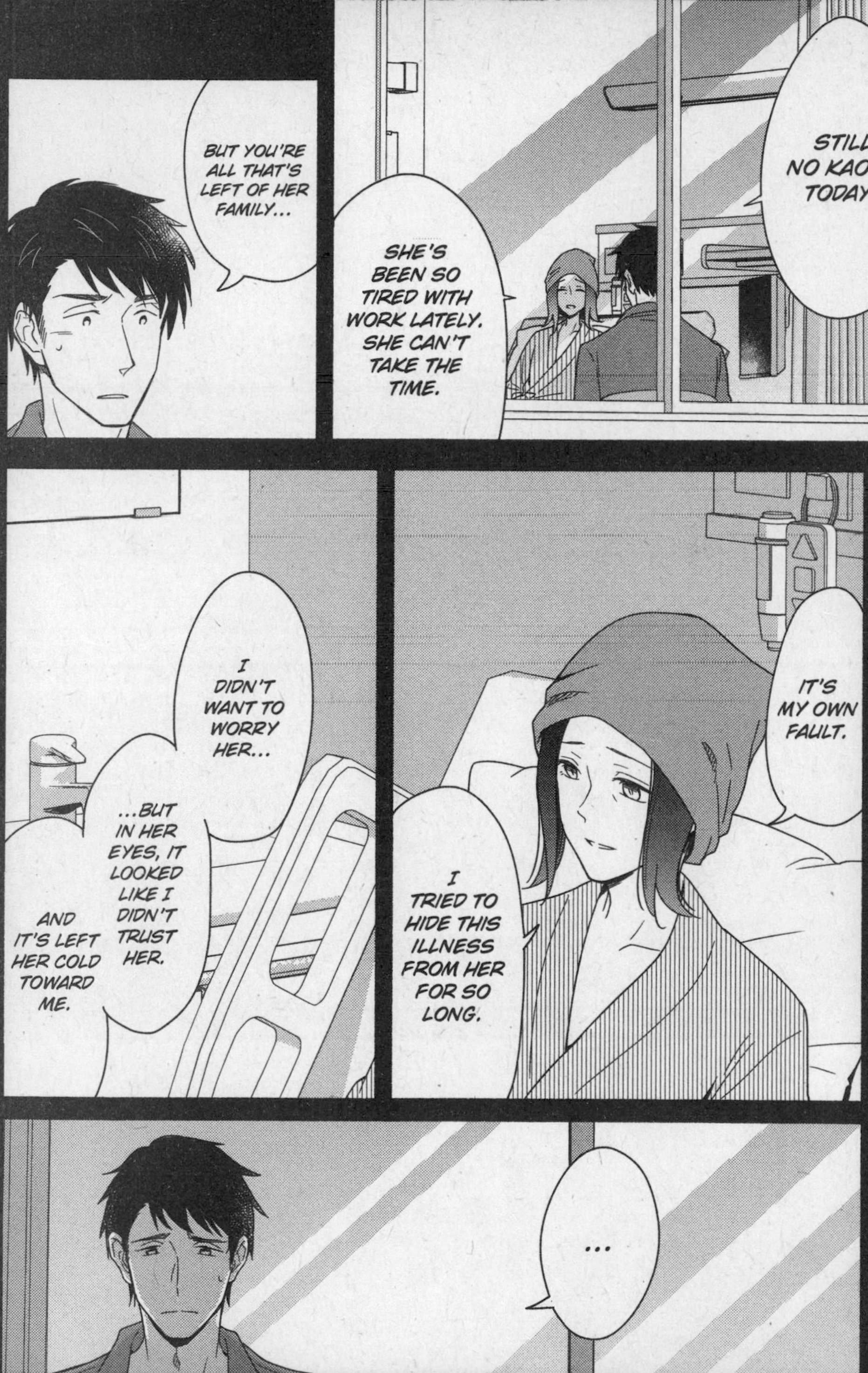
STILL NO KAORU TODAY?
SHE'S BEEN SO TIRED WITH WORK LATELY. SHE CAN'T TAKE THE TIME.
BUT YOU'RE ALL THAT'S LEFT OF HER FAMILY...
IT'S MY OWN FAULT.
I TRIED TO HIDE THIS ILLNESS FROM HER FOR SO LONG.
I DIDN'T WANT TO WORRY HER...
...BUT IN HER EYES, IT LOOKED LIKE I DIDN'T TRUST HER.
AND IT'S LEFT HER COLD TOWARD ME.
...

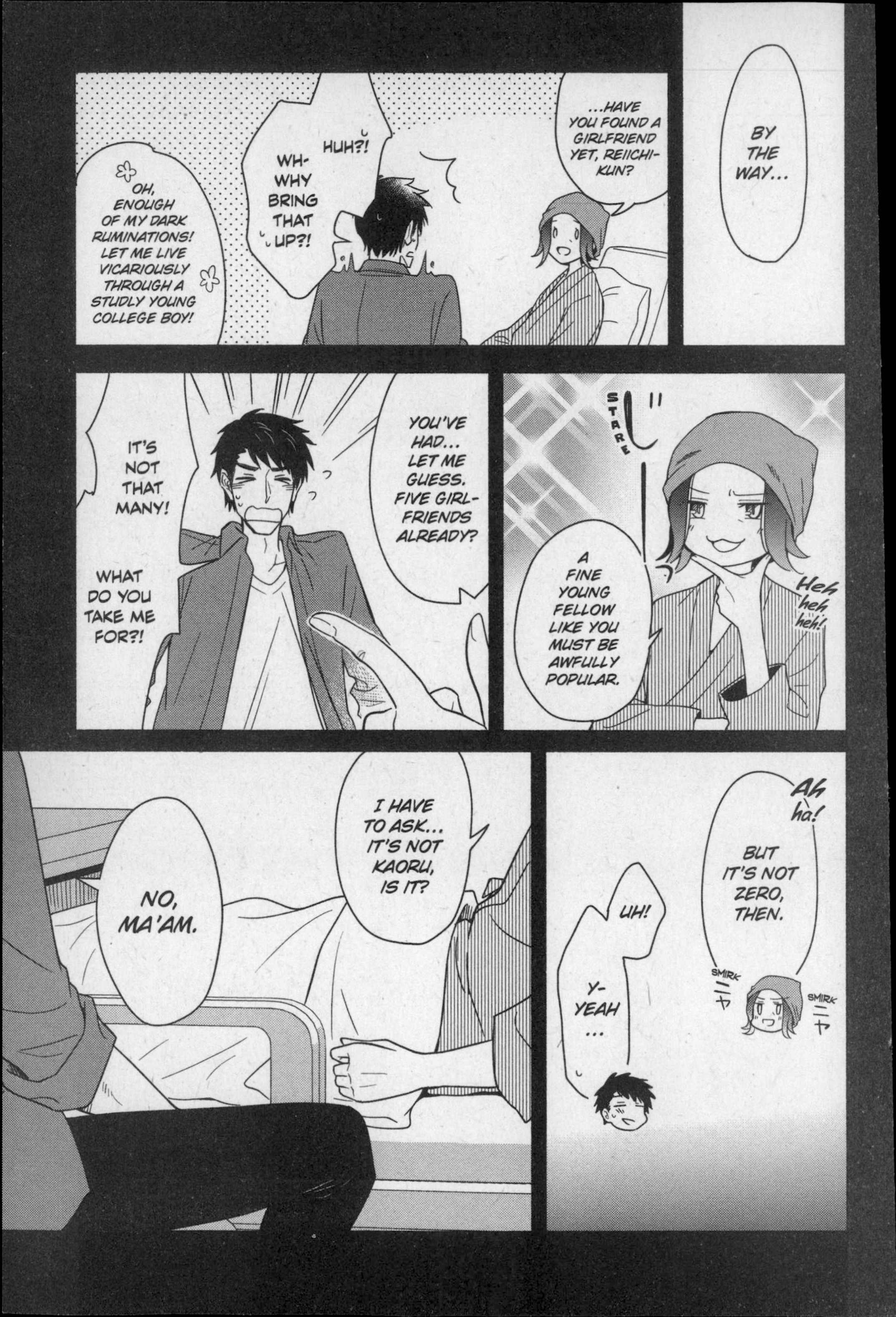
BY THE WAY...
...HAVE YOU FOUND A GIRLFRIEND YET, REIICHI-KUN?
HUH?!
WH-WHY BRING THAT UP?!
OH, ENOUGH OF MY DARK RUMINATIONS! LET ME LIVE VICARIOUSLY THROUGH A STUDLY YOUNG COLLEGE BOY!
STARE
A FINE YOUNG FELLOW LIKE YOU MUST BE AWFULLY POPULAR.
Heh heh heh!
YOU'VE HAD... LET ME GUESS. FIVE GIRLFRIENDS ALREADY?
IT'S NOT THAT MANY!
WHAT DO YOU TAKE ME FOR?!
Ah ha!
BUT IT'S NOT ZERO, THEN.
SMIRK
SMIRK
UH!
Y-YEAH...
I HAVE TO ASK... IT'S NOT KAORU, IS IT?
NO, MA'AM.

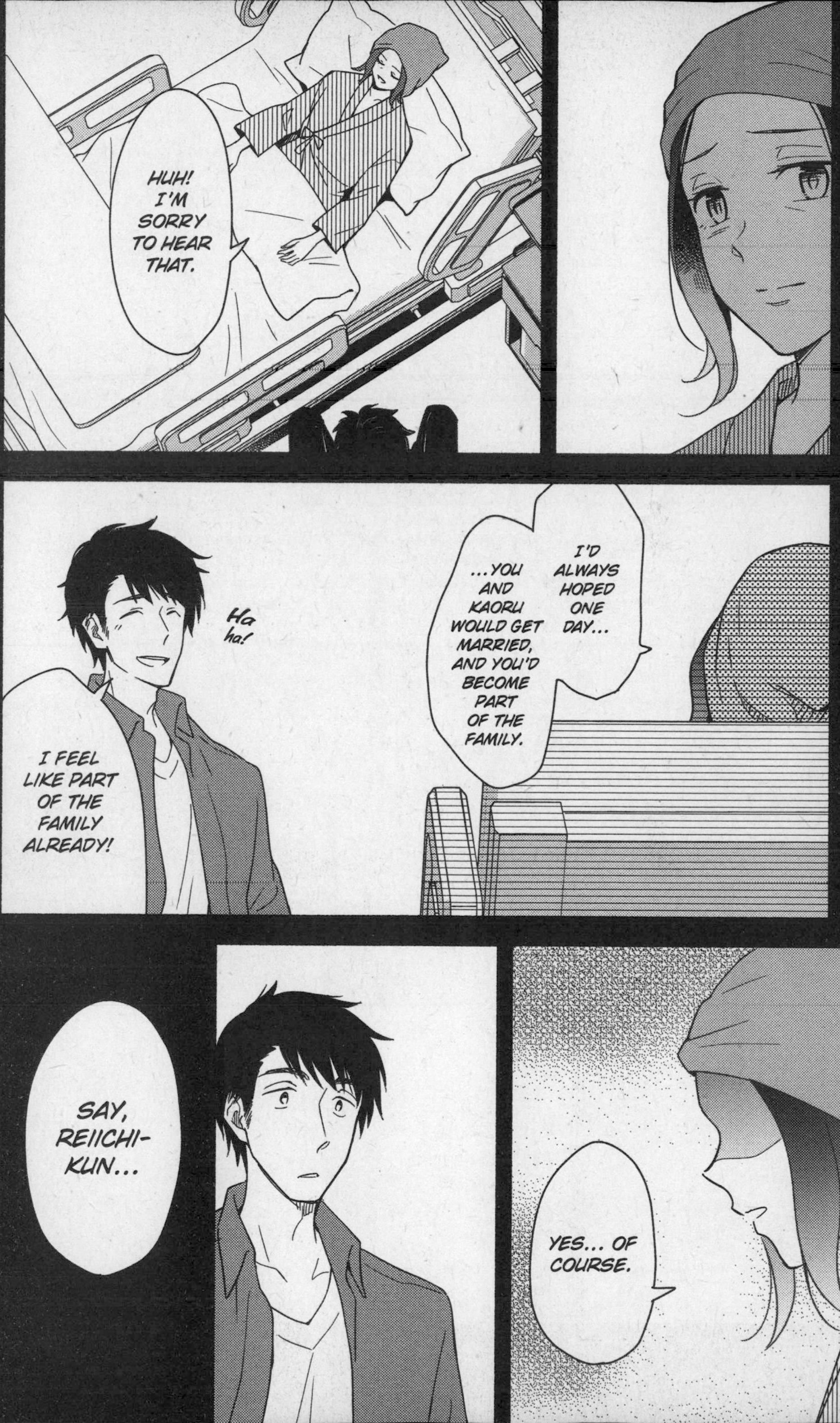
HUH! I'M SORRY TO HEAR THAT.
I'D ALWAYS HOPED ONE DAY...
...YOU AND KAORU WOULD GET MARRIED, AND YOU'D BECOME PART OF THE FAMILY.
Ha ha!
I FEEL LIKE PART OF THE FAMILY ALREADY!
YES... OF COURSE.
SAY, REIICHI-KUN...

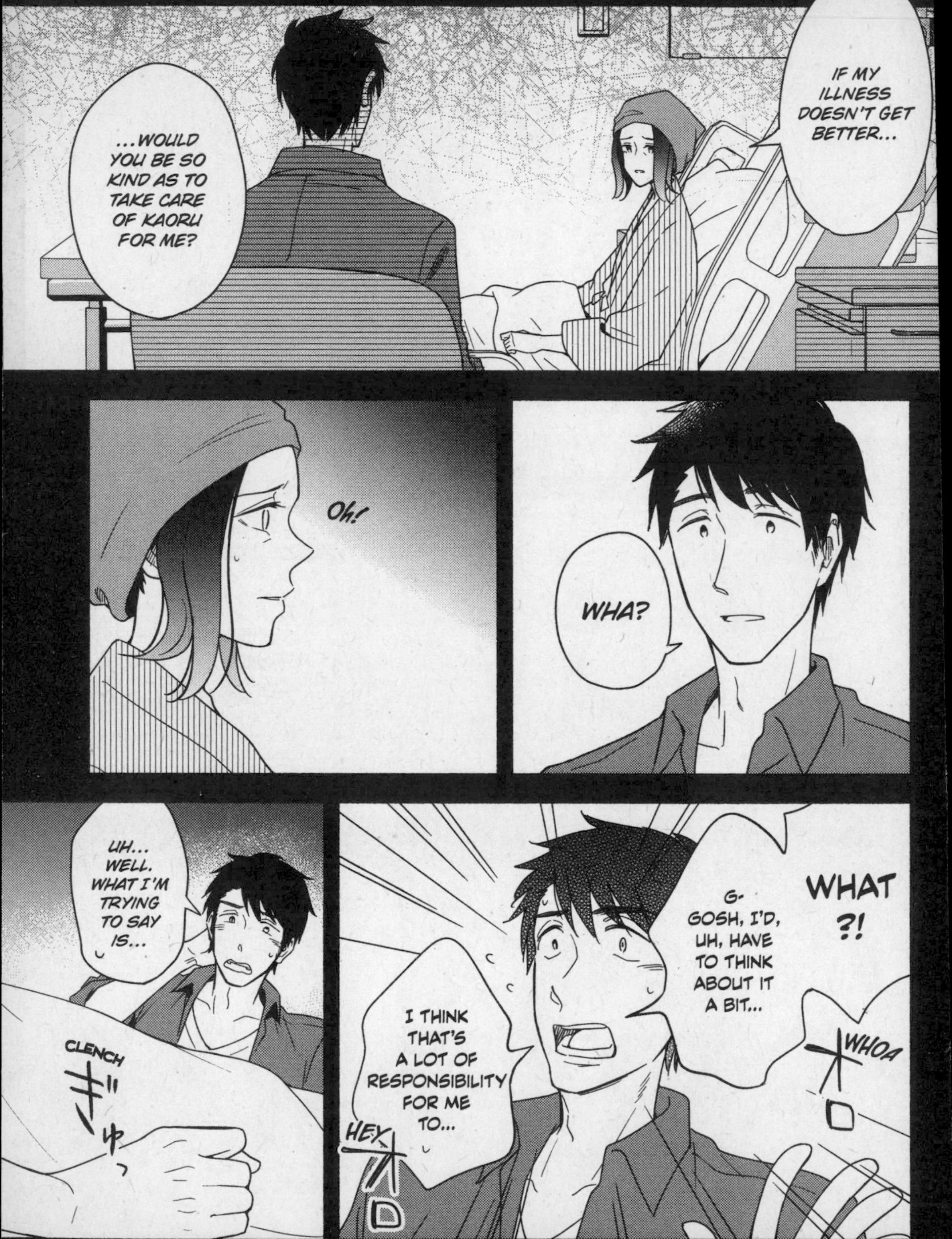
IF MY ILLNESS DOESN'T GET BETTER...
...WOULD YOU BE SO KIND AS TO TAKE CARE OF KAORU FOR ME?
WHA?
Oh!
WHAT ?!
WHOA
G-GOSH, I'D, UH, HAVE TO THINK ABOUT IT A BIT...
I THINK THAT'S A LOT OF RESPONSIBILITY FOR ME TO...
HEY
UH... WELL. WHAT I'M TRYING TO SAY IS...
CLENCH

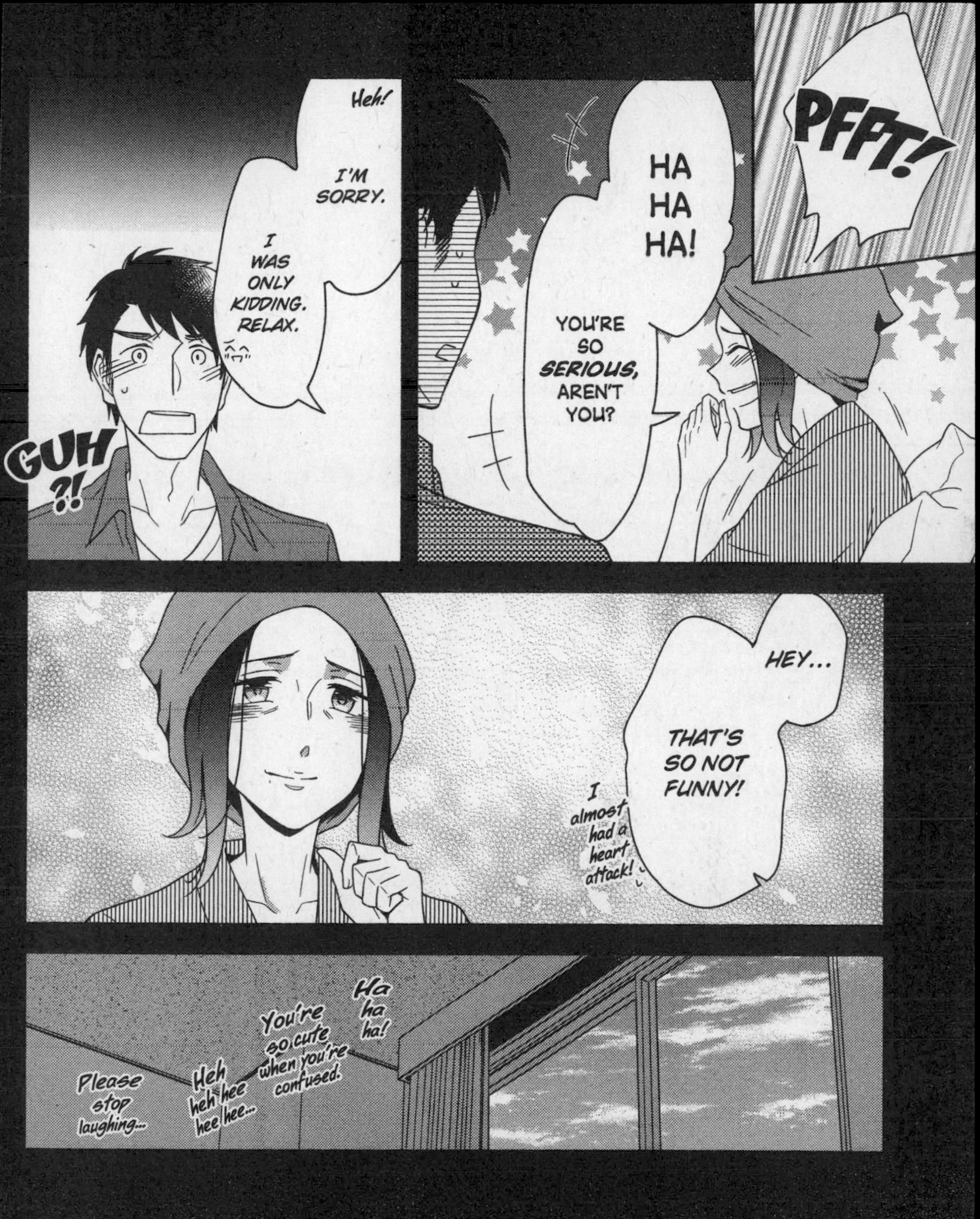
PFFT!
HA HA HA!
YOU'RE SO SERIOUS, AREN'T YOU?
Heh! I'M SORRY. I WAS ONLY KIDDING. RELAX.
GUH ?!
HEY... THAT'S SO NOT FUNNY!
I almost had a heart attack!
Ha ha ha!
You're so cute when you're confused.
Heh heh hee hee...
Please stop laughing...

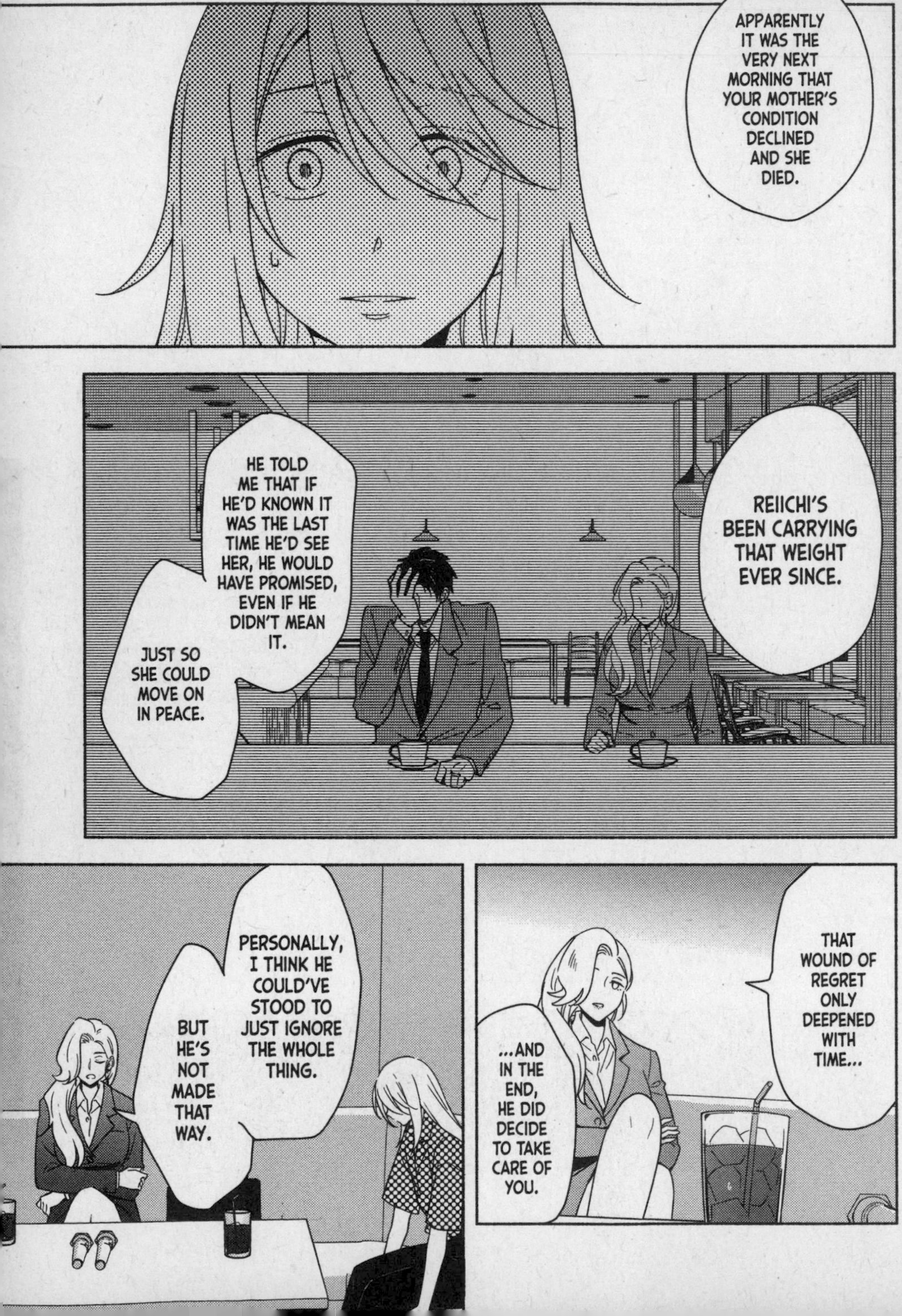
APPARENTLY IT WAS THE VERY NEXT MORNING THAT YOUR MOTHER'S CONDITION DECLINED AND SHE DIED.
REIICHI'S BEEN CARRYING THAT WEIGHT EVER SINCE.
HE TOLD ME THAT IF HE'D KNOWN IT WAS THE LAST TIME HE'D SEE HER, HE WOULD HAVE PROMISED, EVEN IF HE DIDN'T MEAN IT.
JUST SO SHE COULD MOVE ON IN PEACE.
THAT WOUND OF REGRET ONLY DEEPENED WITH TIME...
...AND IN THE END, HE DID DECIDE TO TAKE CARE OF YOU.
PERSONALLY, I THINK HE COULD'VE STOOD TO JUST IGNORE THE WHOLE THING.
BUT HE'S NOT MADE THAT WAY.

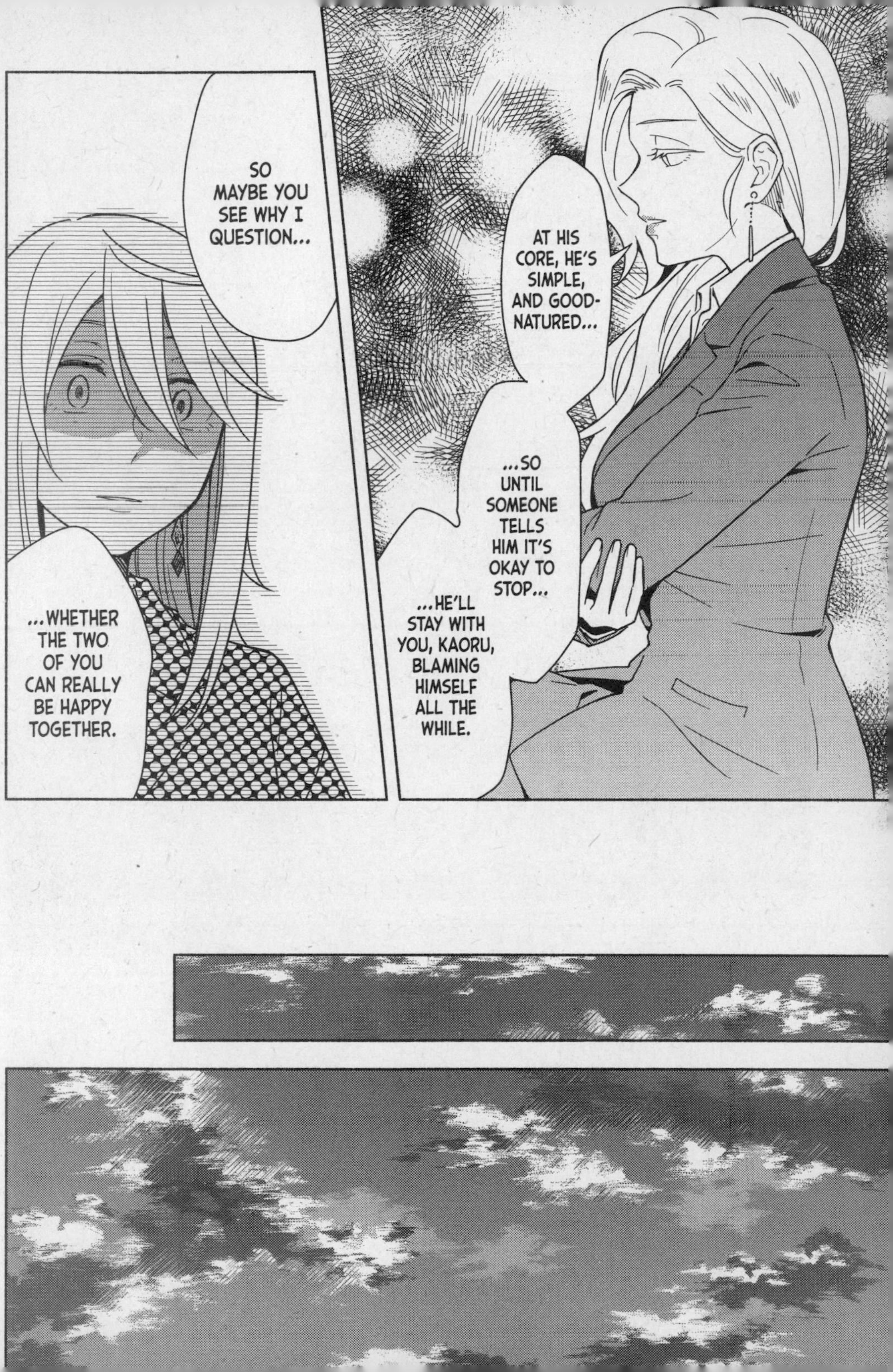
AT HIS CORE, HE'S SIMPLE, AND GOOD-NATURED...
...SO UNTIL SOMEONE TELLS HIM IT'S OKAY TO STOP...
...HE'LL STAY WITH YOU, KAORU, BLAMING HIMSELF ALL THE WHILE.
SO MAYBE YOU SEE WHY I QUESTION...
...WHETHER THE TWO OF YOU CAN REALLY BE HAPPY TOGETHER.

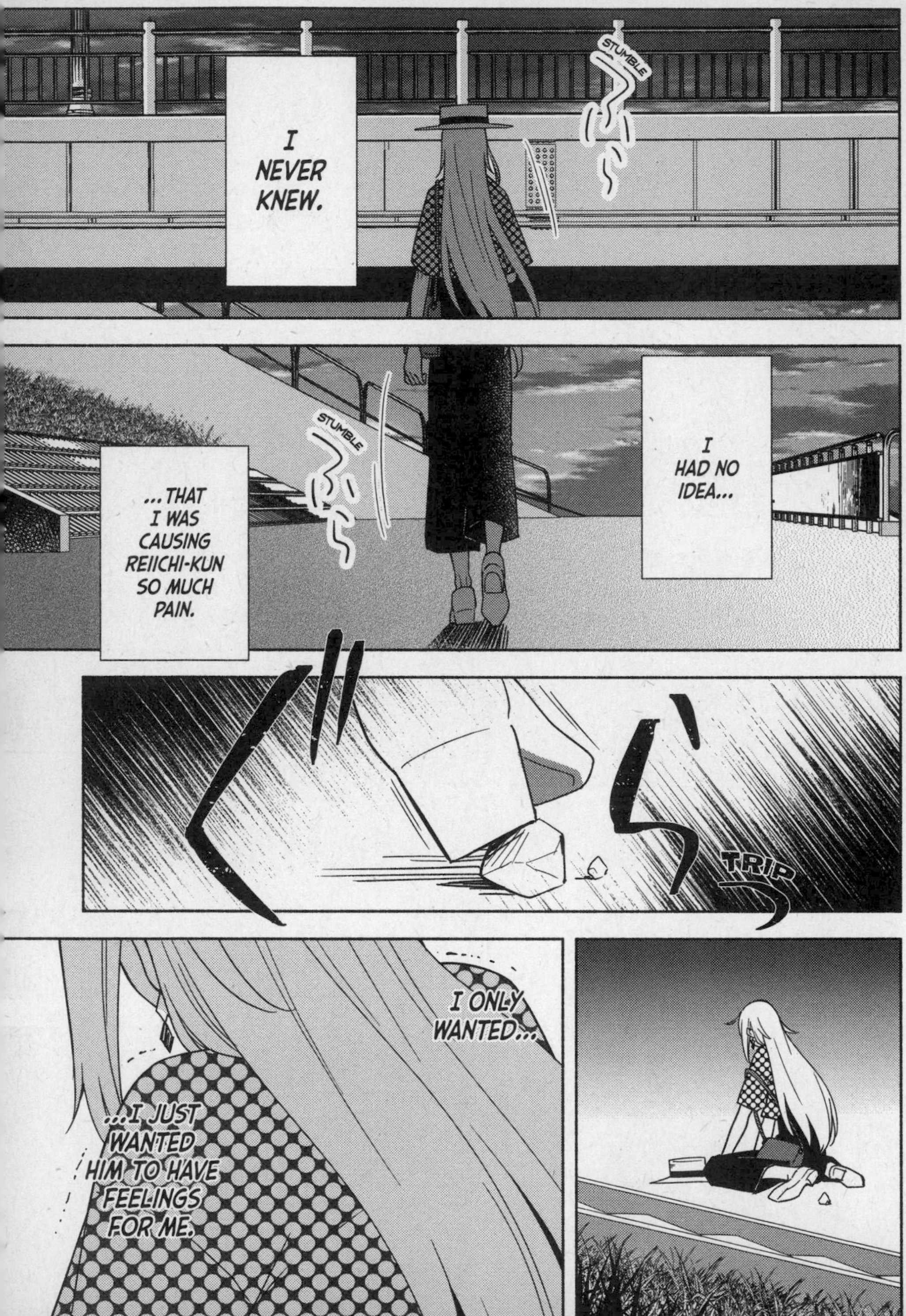
STUMBLE
I NEVER KNEW.
I HAD NO IDEA...
STUMBLE
...THAT I WAS CAUSING REIICHI-KUN SO MUCH PAIN.
TRIP
I ONLY WANTED...
...I JUST WANTED HIM TO HAVE FEELINGS FOR ME.

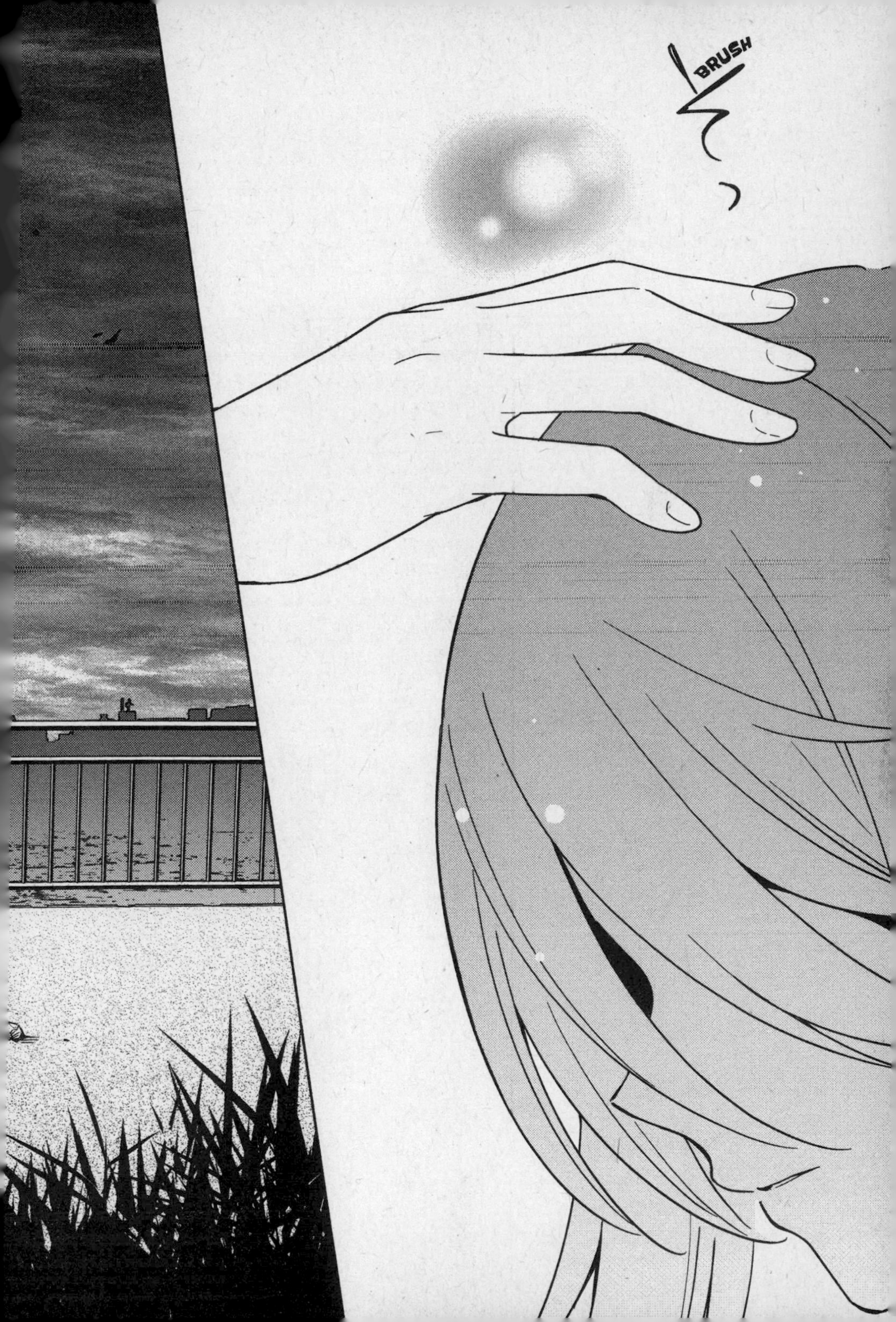
BRUSH

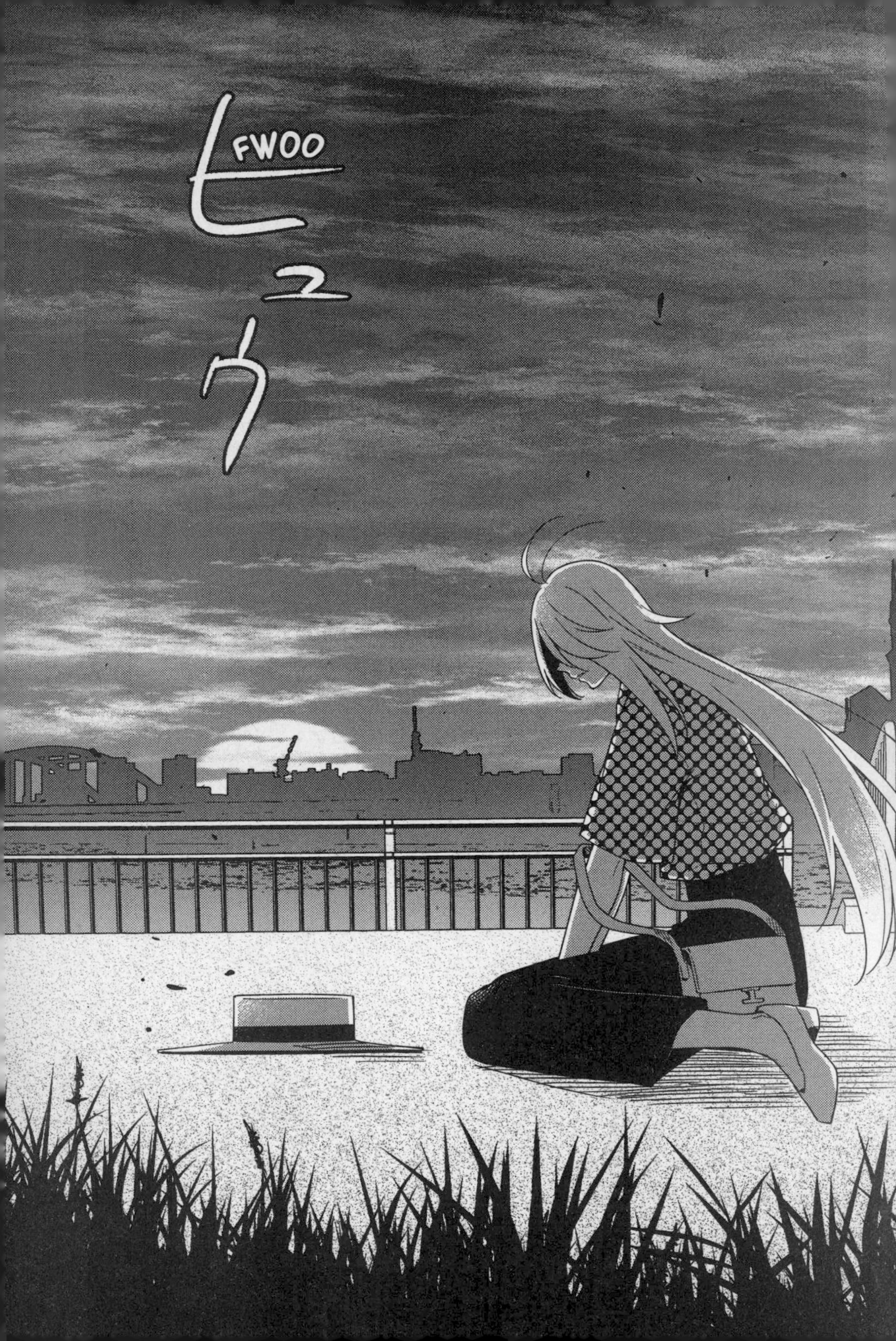
ヒュウ
FWOO

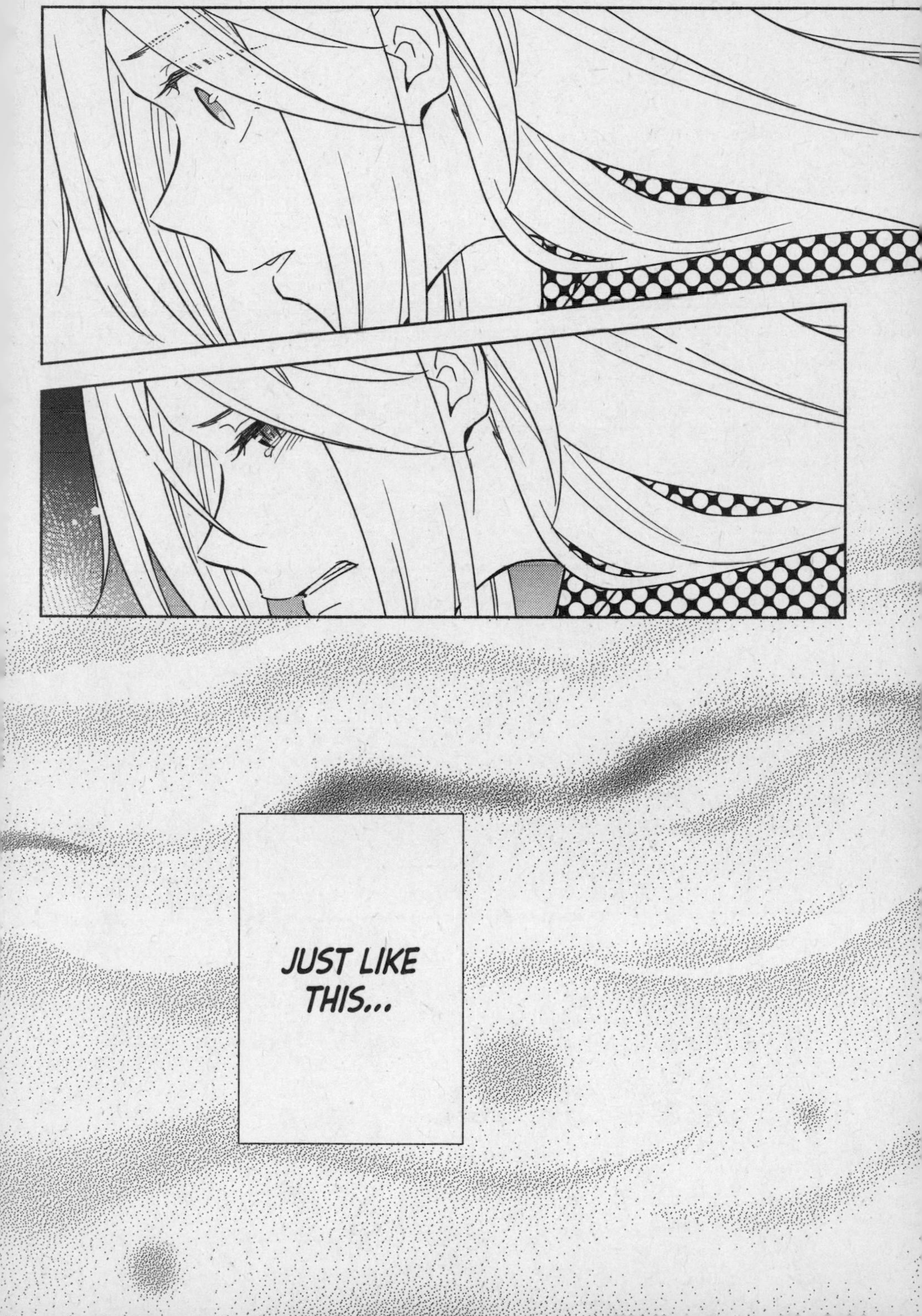
JUST LIKE THIS...

If I Could
Reach You

If I Could
Reach You

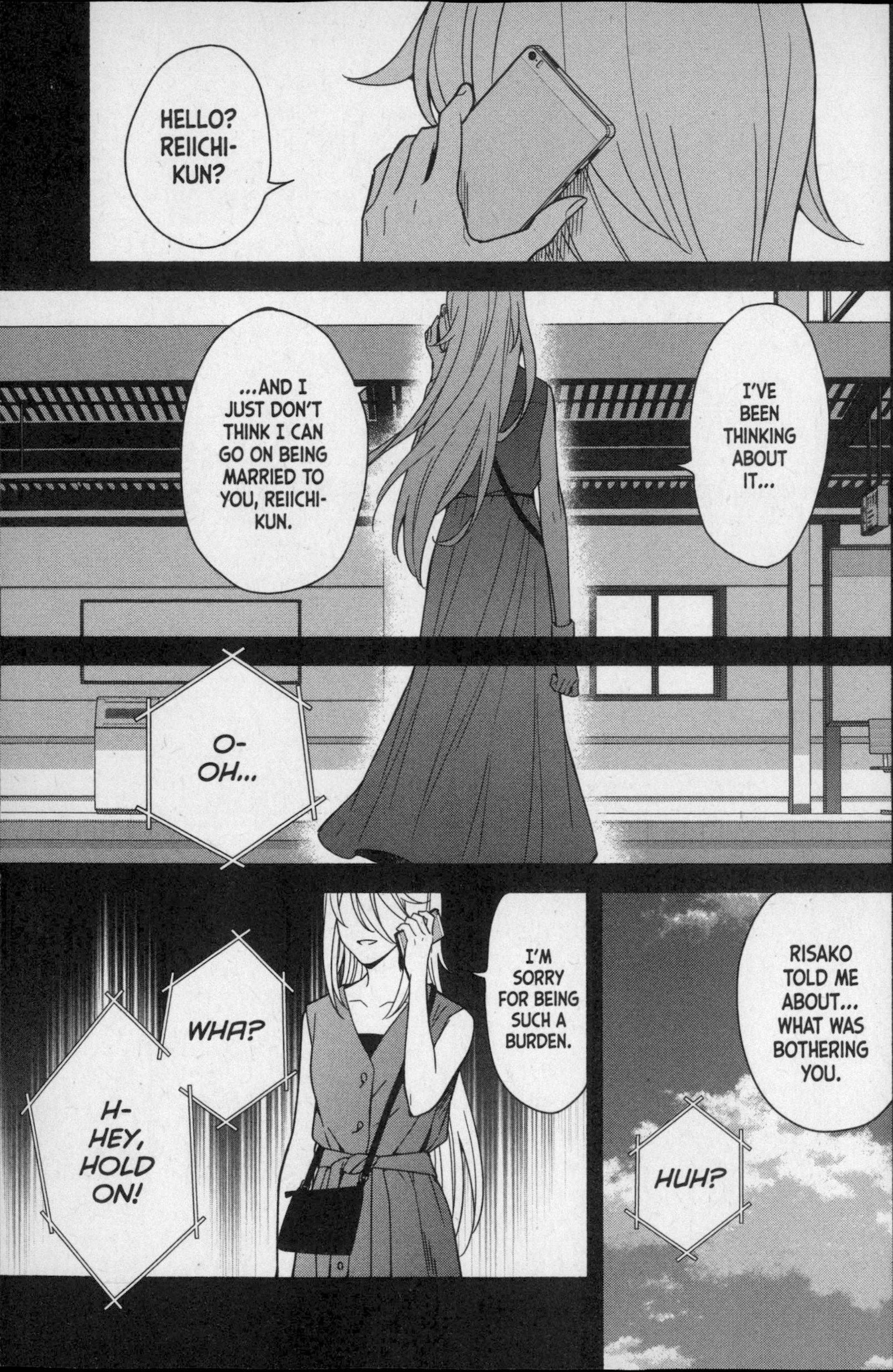
HELLO? REIICHI-KUN?
I'VE BEEN THINKING ABOUT IT...
...AND I JUST DON'T THINK I CAN GO ON BEING MARRIED TO YOU, REIICHI-KUN.
O-OH...
RISAKO TOLD ME ABOUT... WHAT WAS BOTHERING YOU.
HUH?
I'M SORRY FOR BEING SUCH A BURDEN.
WHA?
H-HEY, HOLD ON!

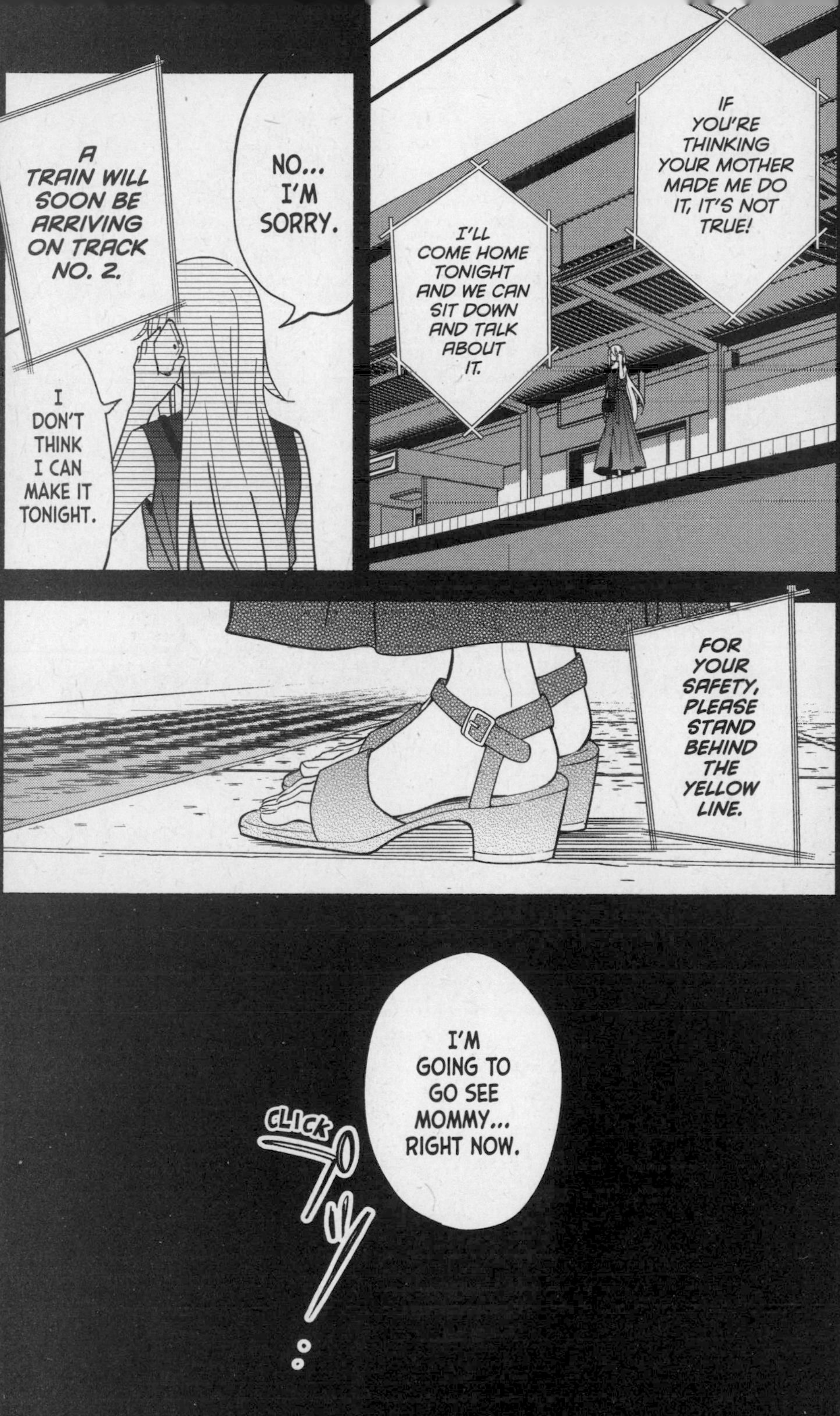
IF YOU'RE THINKING YOUR MOTHER MADE ME DO IT, IT'S NOT TRUE!
I'LL COME HOME TONIGHT AND WE CAN SIT DOWN AND TALK ABOUT IT.
NO... I'M SORRY.
A TRAIN WILL SOON BE ARRIVING ON TRACK NO. 2.
I DON'T THINK I CAN MAKE IT TONIGHT.
FOR YOUR SAFETY, PLEASE STAND BEHIND THE YELLOW LINE.
I'M GOING TO GO SEE MOMMY... RIGHT NOW.
CLICK

Chapter 36

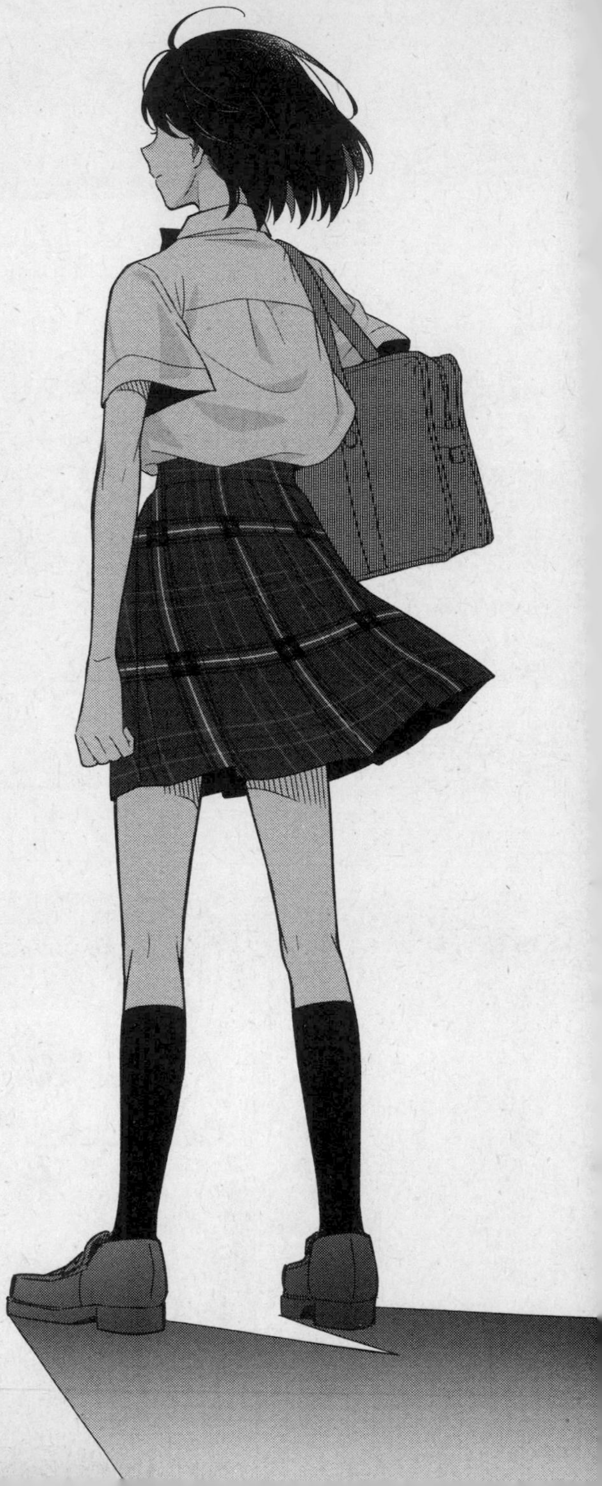

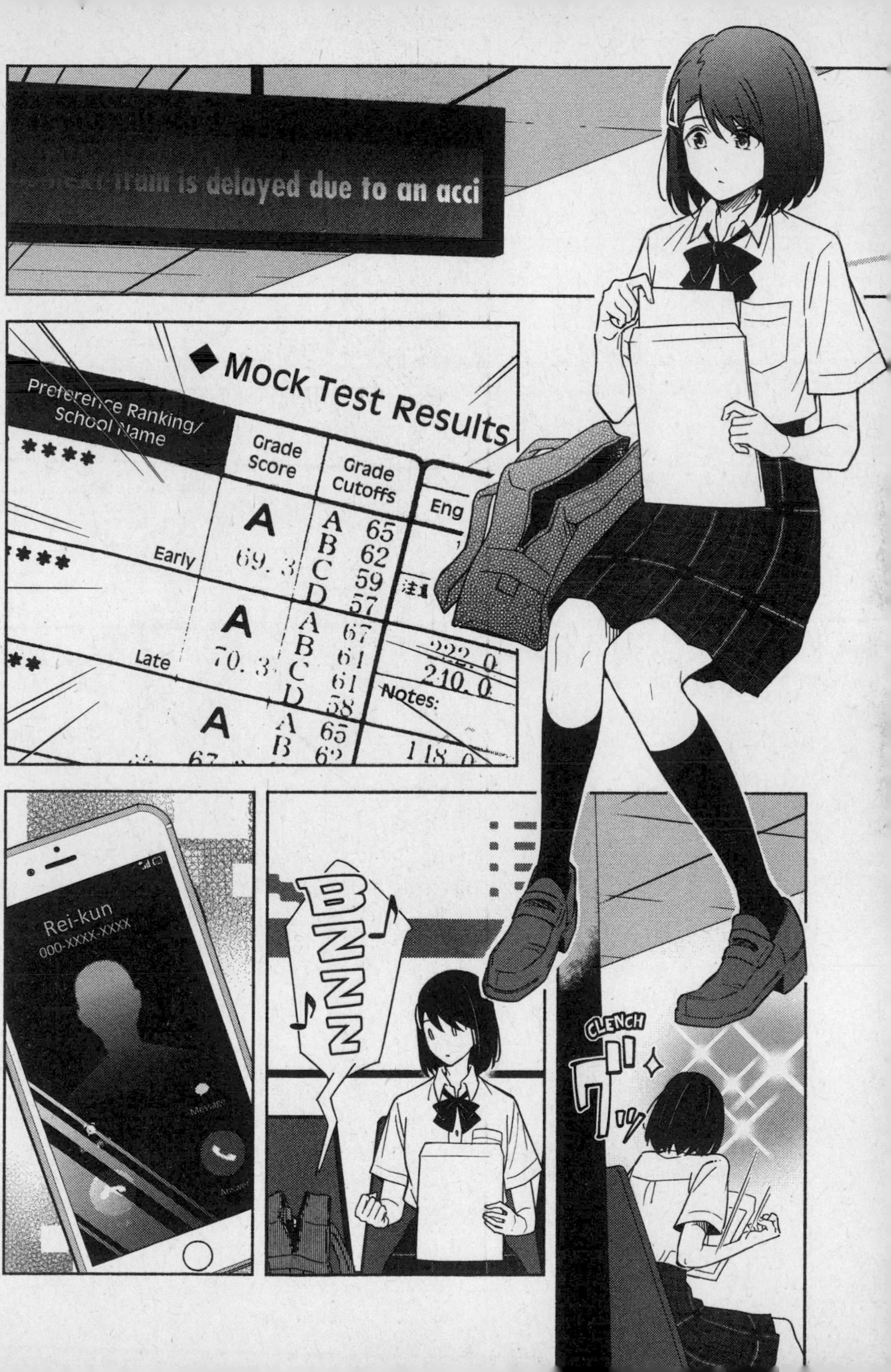
train is delayed due to an acci
◆Mock Test Results
Preference Ranking/ School Name
Grade Score
Grade Cutoffs
Eng
A
Early
69. 3
A 65
B 62
C 59
D 57
A
Late
70. 3
A 67
B 61
C 61
D 58
222. 0
210. 0
Notes:
A
A 65
118. 0
CLENCH
BZZZ
Rei-kun
000-XXXX-XXXX
Message
Answer

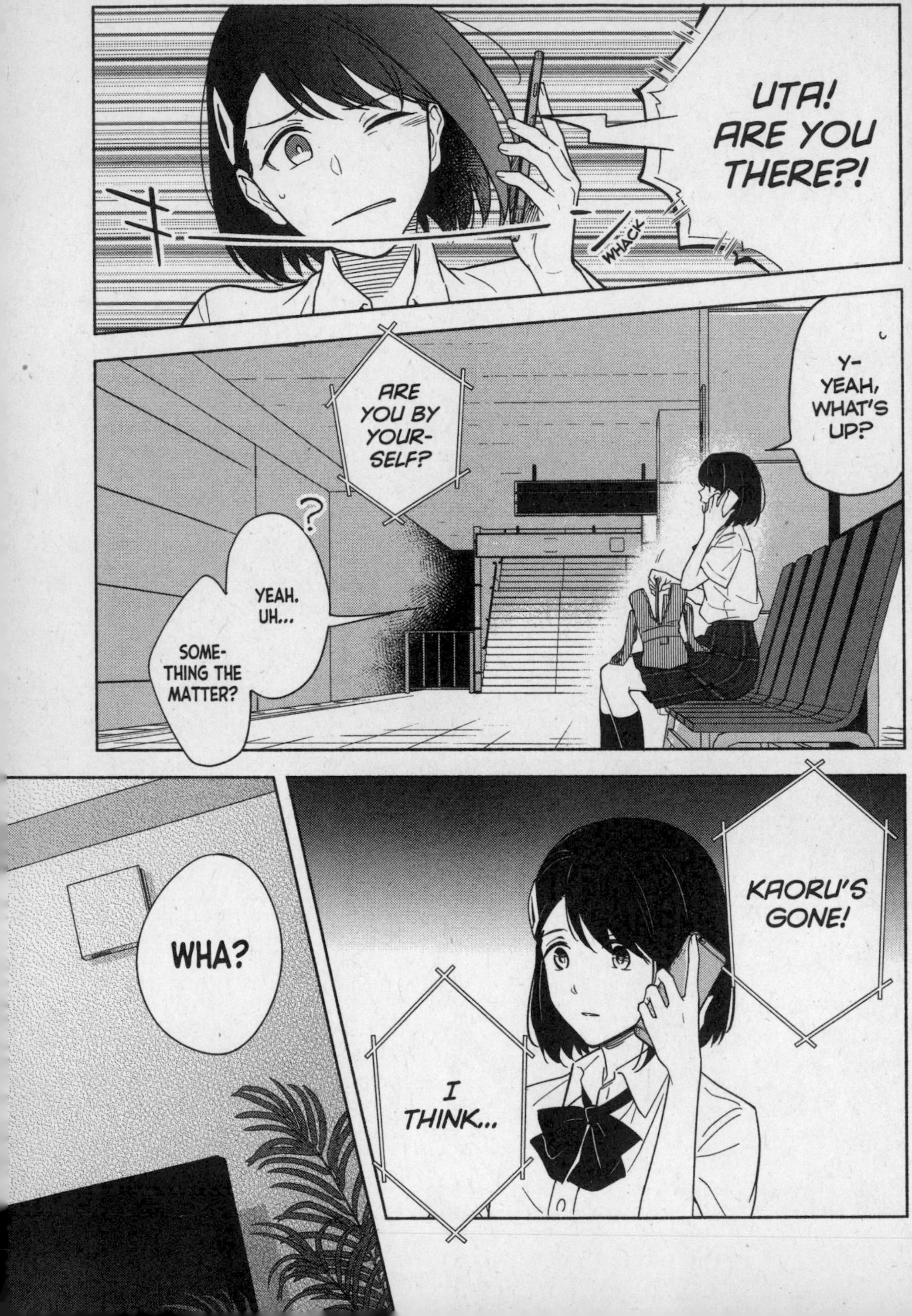
UTA! ARE YOU THERE?!
WHACK
Y- YEAH, WHAT'S UP?
ARE YOU BY YOUR-SELF?
YEAH. UH...
SOME-THING THE MATTER?
KAORU'S GONE!
I THINK...
WHA?

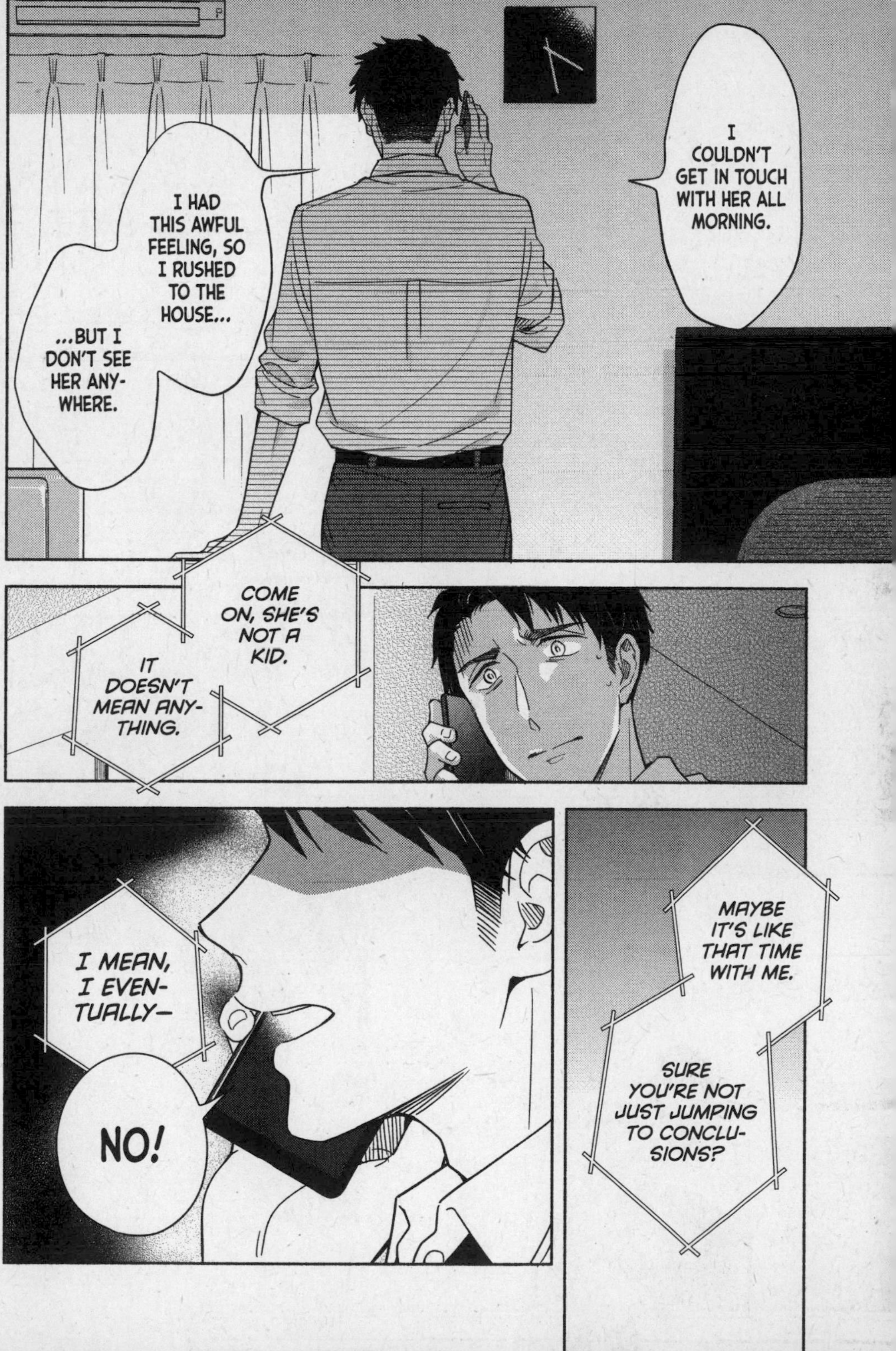
I COULDN'T GET IN TOUCH WITH HER ALL MORNING.
I HAD THIS AWFUL FEELING, SO I RUSHED TO THE HOUSE...
...BUT I DON'T SEE HER ANYWHERE.
COME ON, SHE'S NOT A KID.
IT DOESN'T MEAN ANYTHING.
MAYBE IT'S LIKE THAT TIME WITH ME.
SURE YOU'RE NOT JUST JUMPING TO CONCLUSIONS?
I MEAN, I EVENTUALLY—
NO!

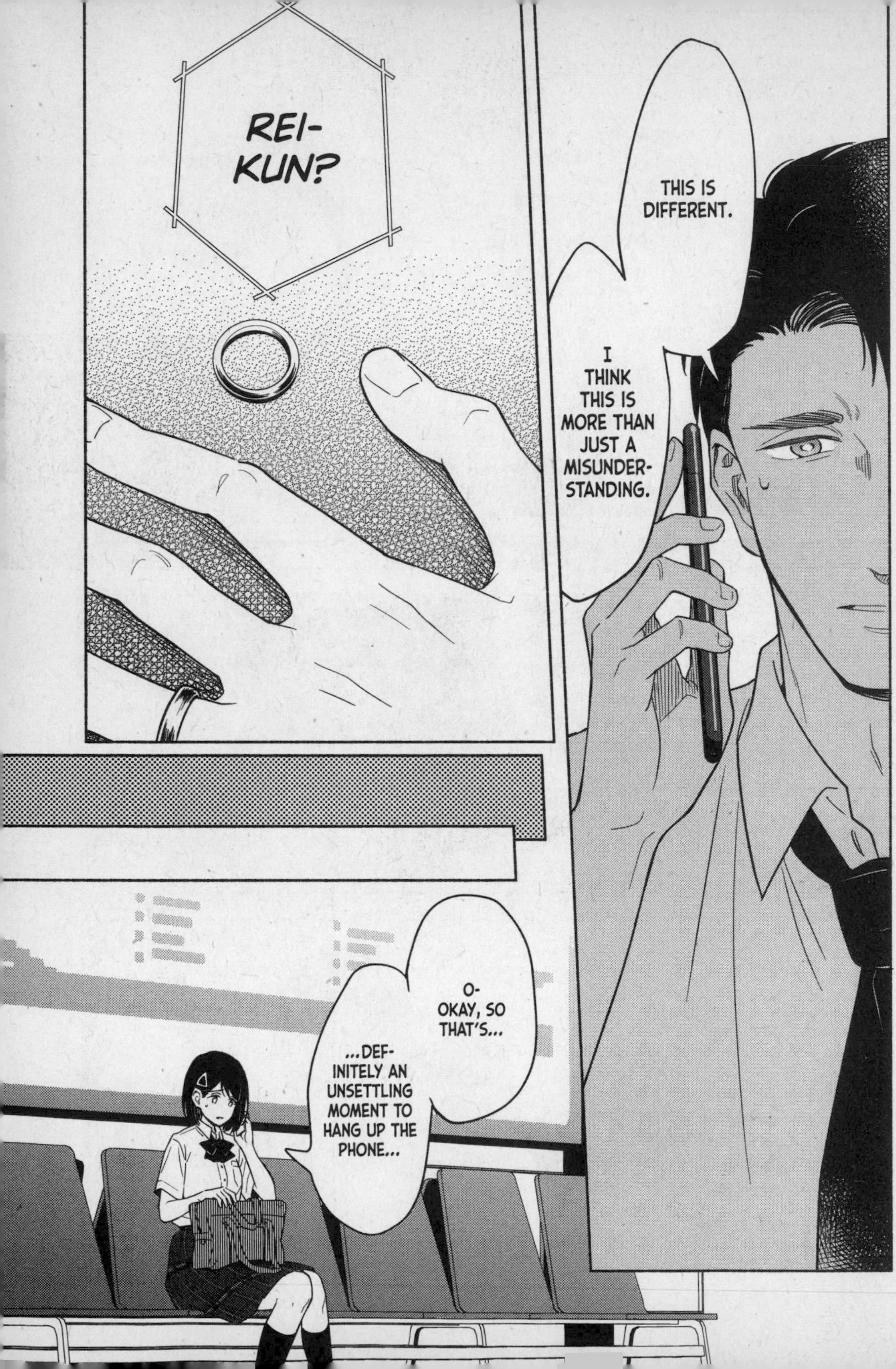
THIS IS DIFFERENT.
I THINK THIS IS MORE THAN JUST A MISUNDER-STANDING.
REI-KUN?
O-OKAY, SO THAT'S...
...DEF-INITELY AN UNSETTLING MOMENT TO HANG UP THE PHONE...

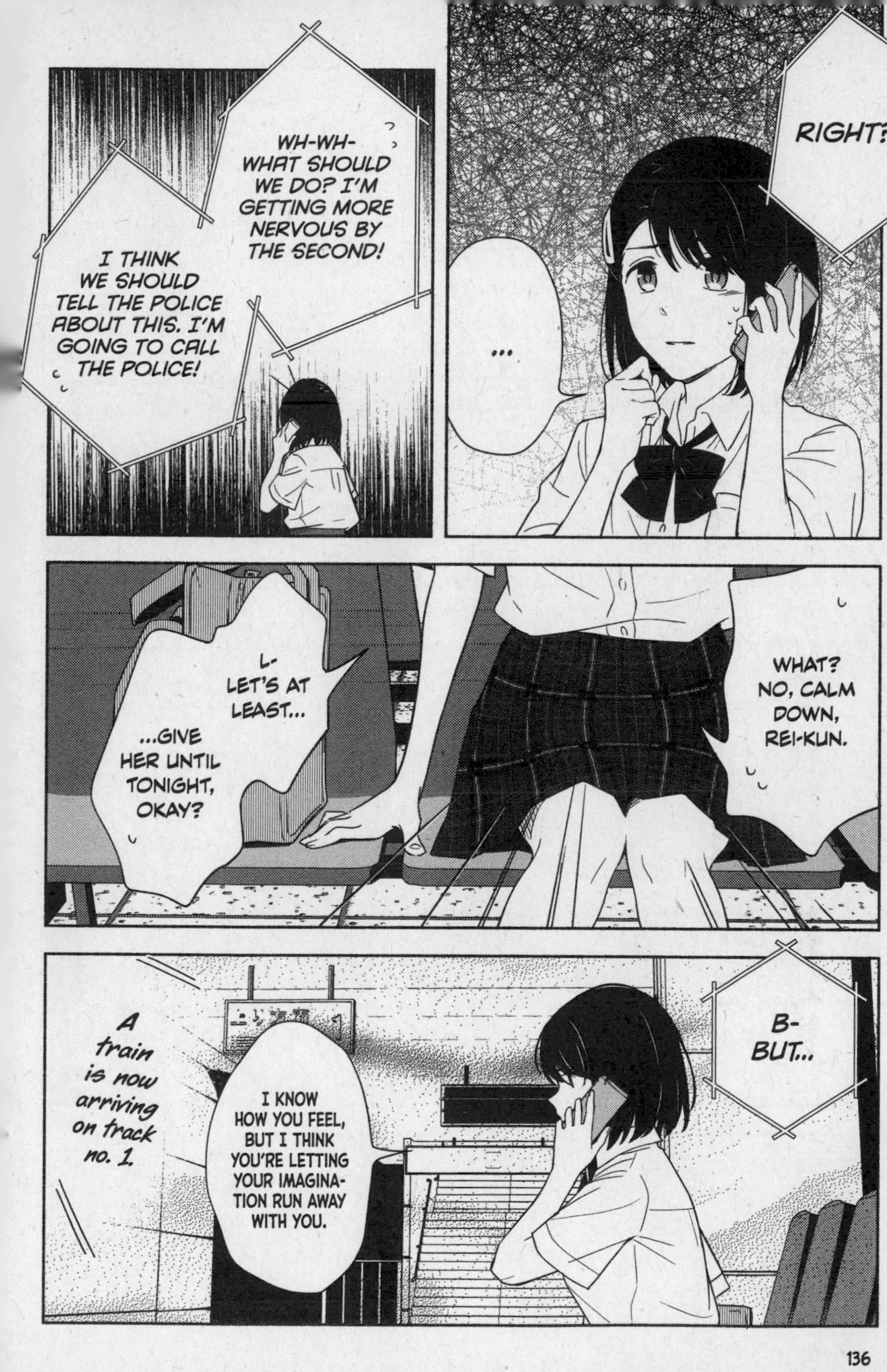
RIGHT?
...
WH-WH- WHAT SHOULD WE DO? I'M GETTING MORE NERVOUS BY THE SECOND!
I THINK WE SHOULD TELL THE POLICE ABOUT THIS. I'M GOING TO CALL THE POLICE!
WHAT? NO, CALM DOWN, REI-KUN.
L- LET'S AT LEAST...
...GIVE HER UNTIL TONIGHT, OKAY?
B- BUT...
I KNOW HOW YOU FEEL, BUT I THINK YOU'RE LETTING YOUR IMAGINA- TION RUN AWAY WITH YOU.
A train is now arriving on track no. 1.

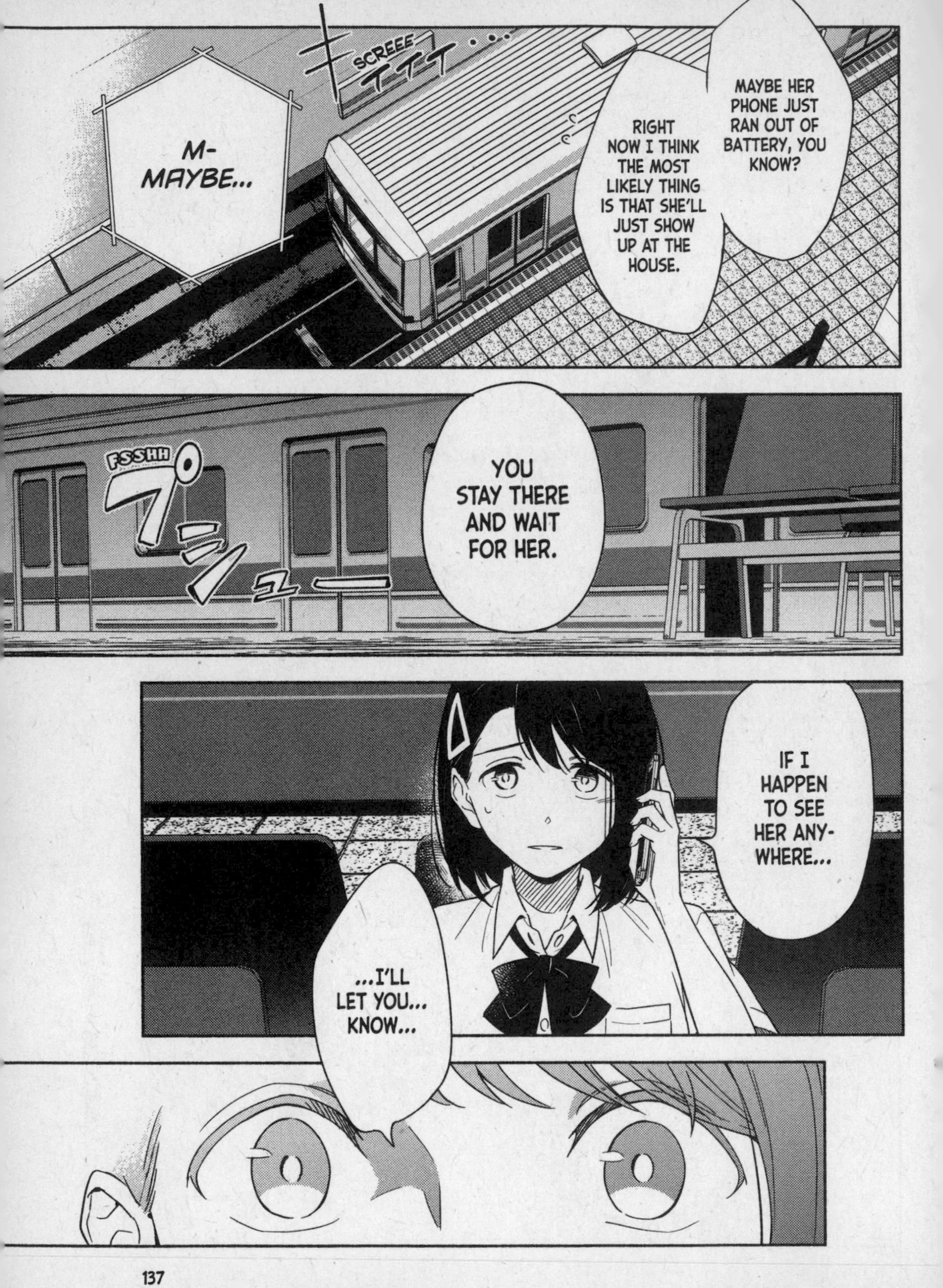
MAYBE HER PHONE JUST RAN OUT OF BATTERY, YOU KNOW?
RIGHT NOW I THINK THE MOST LIKELY THING IS THAT SHE'LL JUST SHOW UP AT THE HOUSE.
SCREEE
M-MAYBE...
YOU STAY THERE AND WAIT FOR HER.
FSSHH
IF I HAPPEN TO SEE HER ANY-WHERE...
...I'LL LET YOU... KNOW...

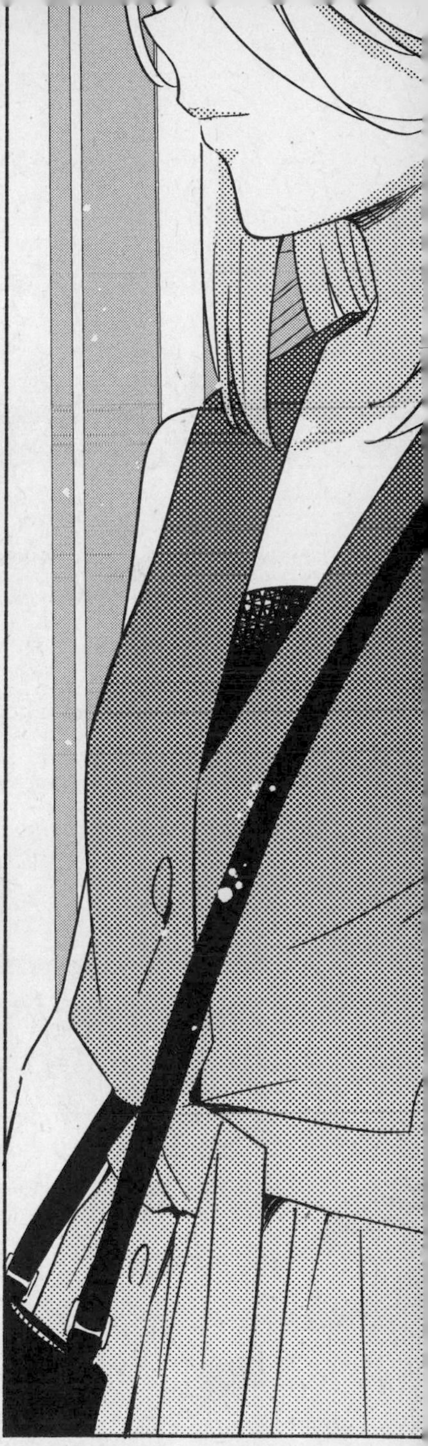
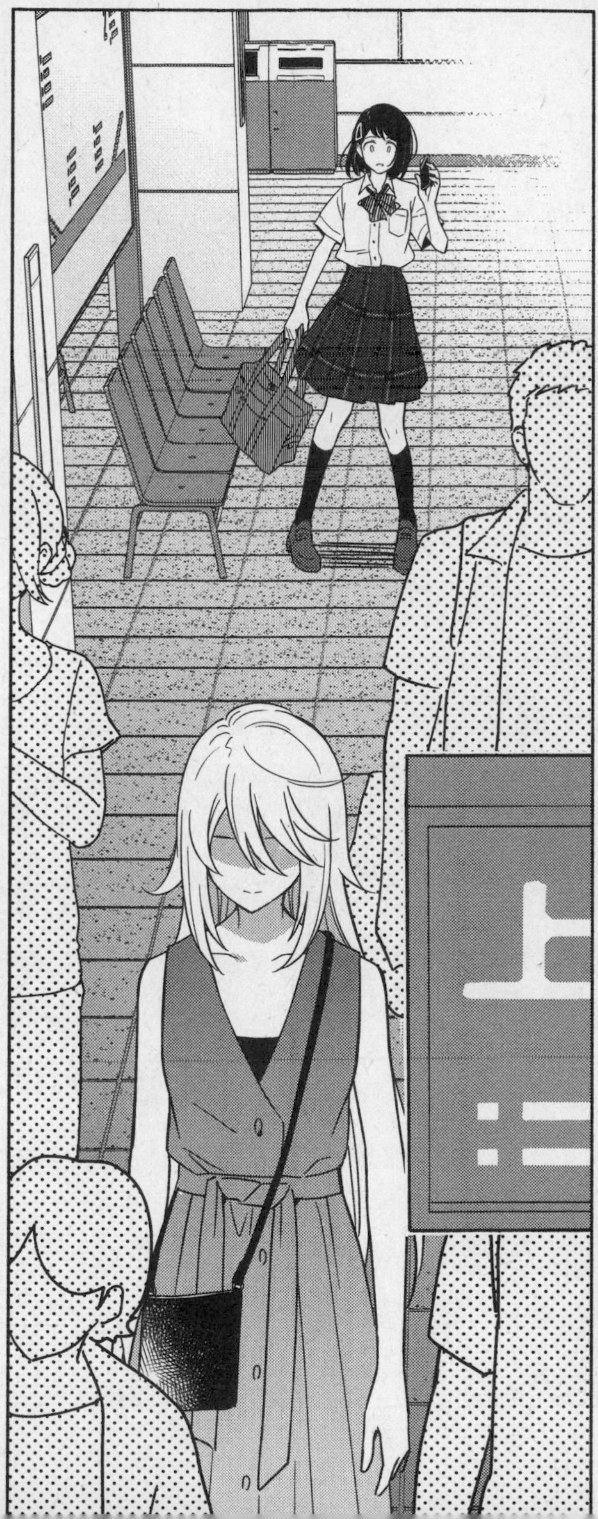
上

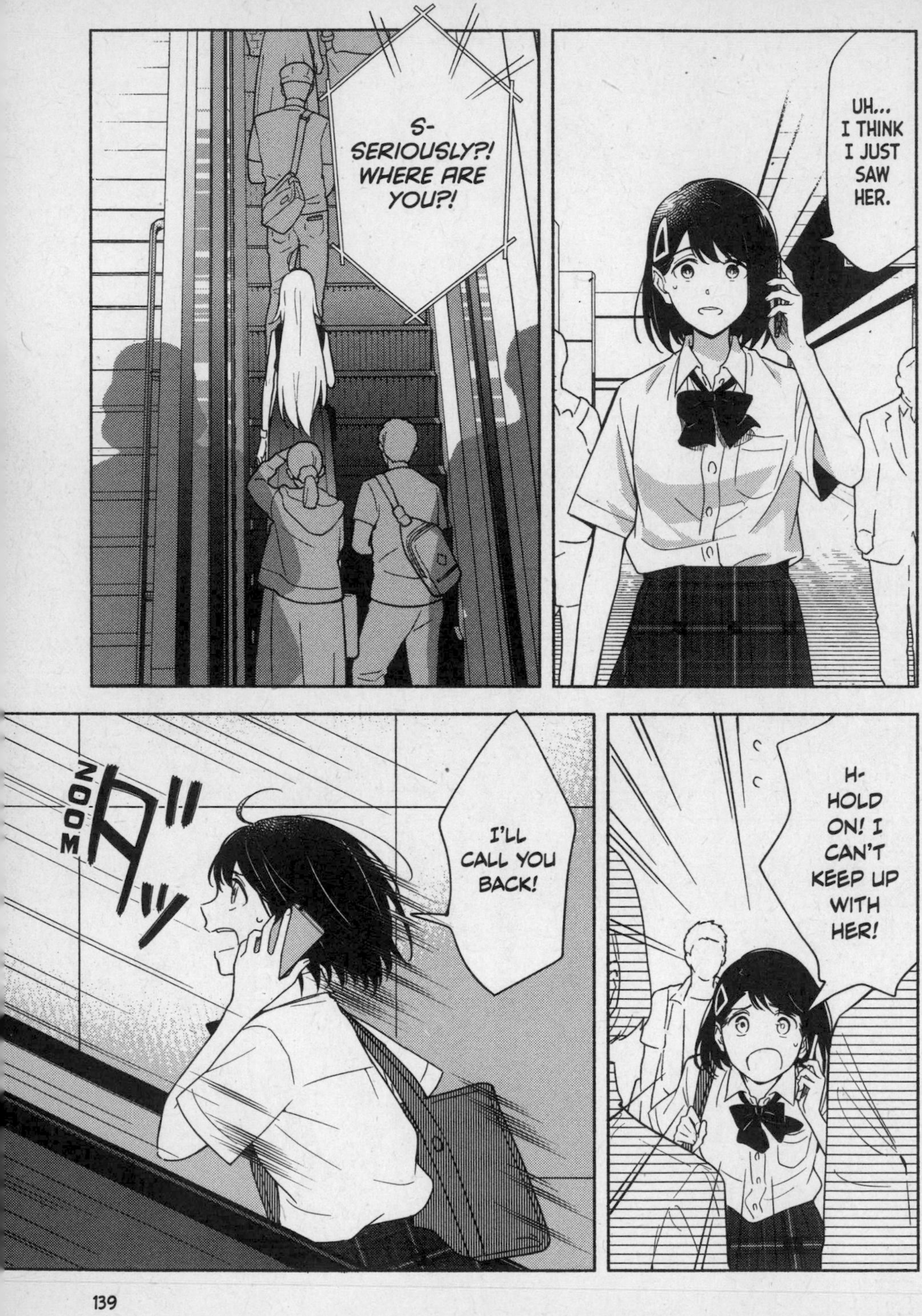
UH... I THINK I JUST SAW HER.
S-SERIOUSLY?! WHERE ARE YOU?!
H-HOLD ON! I CAN'T KEEP UP WITH HER!
ZOOM
I'LL CALL YOU BACK!

Puff

Puff

LOOK

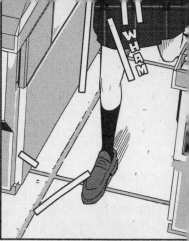

WHAM

VRMM

Tao...

AH!

Oh!

WHERE DOES THAT BUS GO?

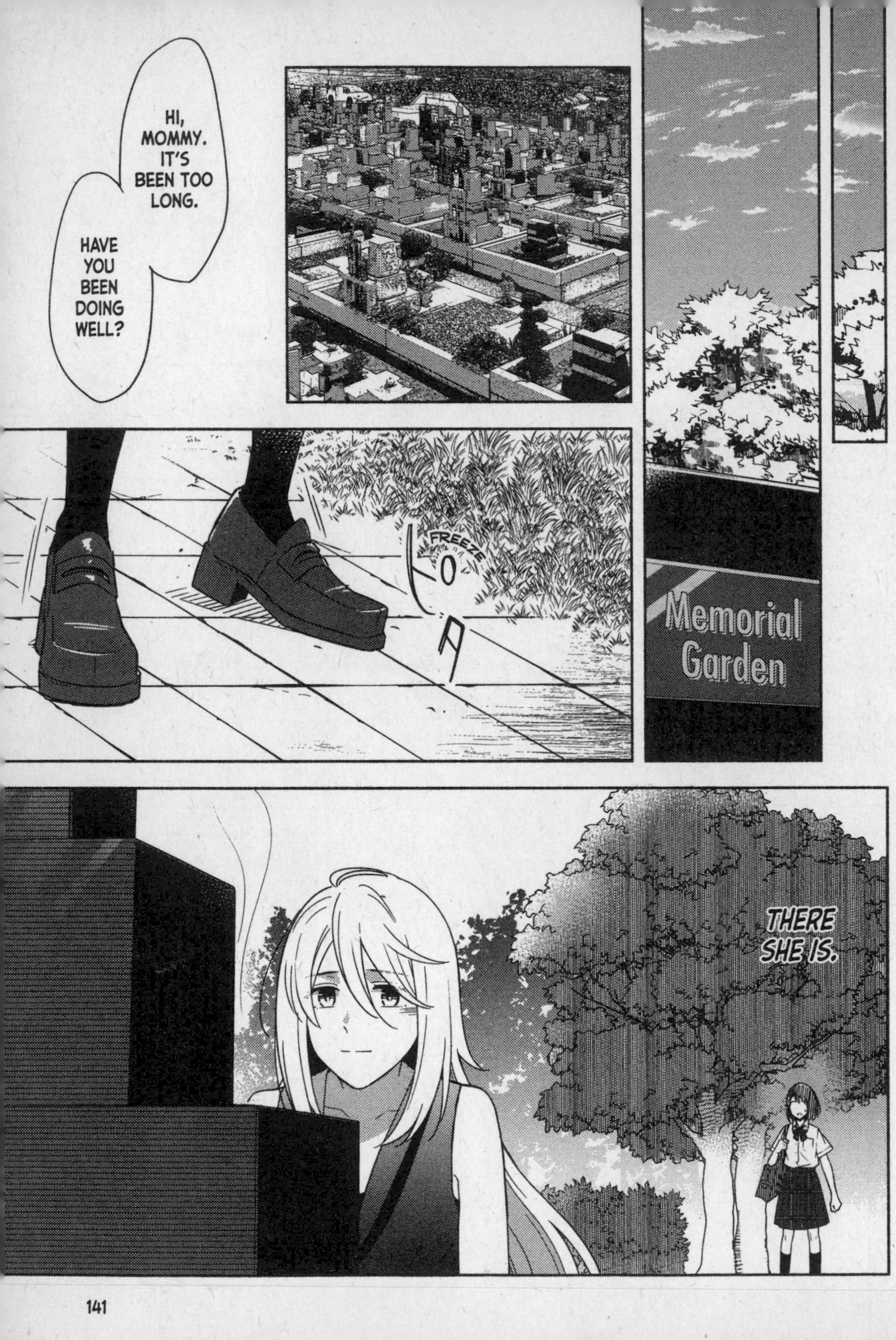
Memorial Garden
HI, MOMMY. IT'S BEEN TOO LONG.
HAVE YOU BEEN DOING WELL?
FREEZE
THERE SHE IS.

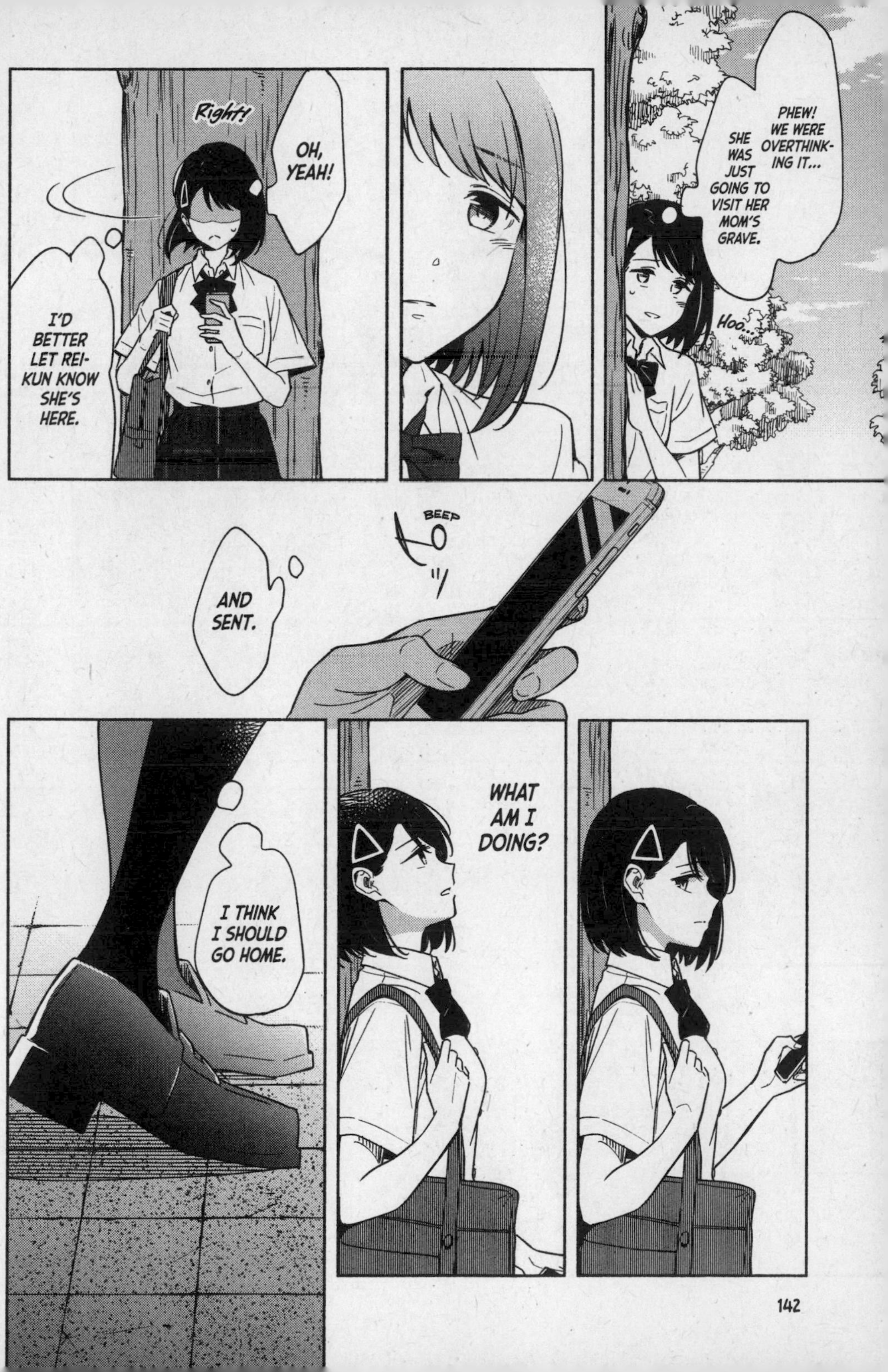
PHEW! WE WERE OVERTHINKING IT... SHE WAS JUST GOING TO VISIT HER MOM'S GRAVE.
Hoo...
OH, YEAH!
Right!
I'D BETTER LET REI-KUN KNOW SHE'S HERE.
BEEP
AND SENT.
WHAT AM I DOING?
I THINK I SHOULD GO HOME.

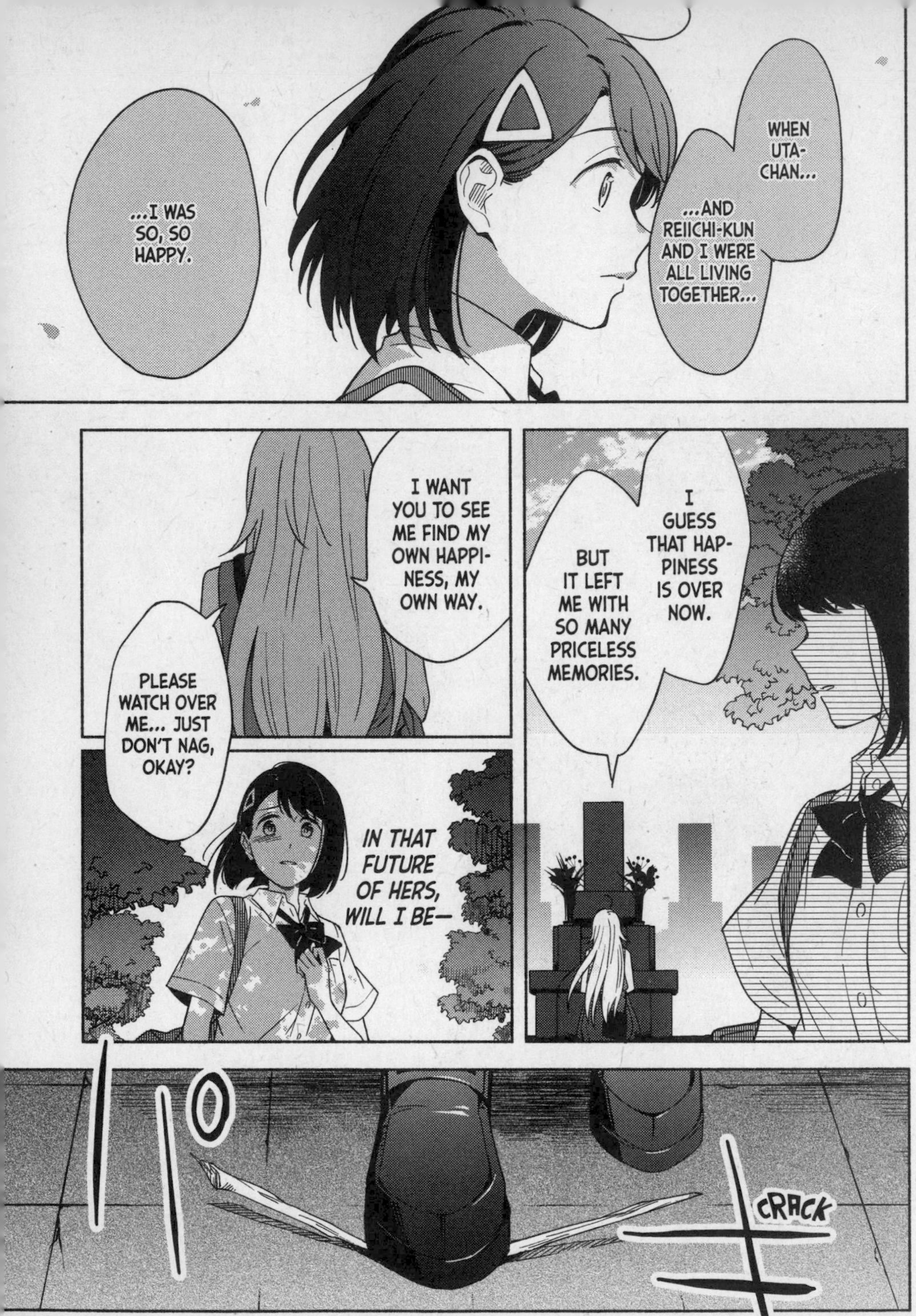
WHEN UTA-CHAN...
...AND REIICHI-KUN AND I WERE ALL LIVING TOGETHER...
...I WAS SO, SO HAPPY.
I GUESS THAT HAPPINESS IS OVER NOW.
BUT IT LEFT ME WITH SO MANY PRICELESS MEMORIES.
I WANT YOU TO SEE ME FIND MY OWN HAPPINESS, MY OWN WAY.
PLEASE WATCH OVER ME... JUST DON'T NAG, OKAY?
IN THAT FUTURE OF HERS, WILL I BE—
CRACK

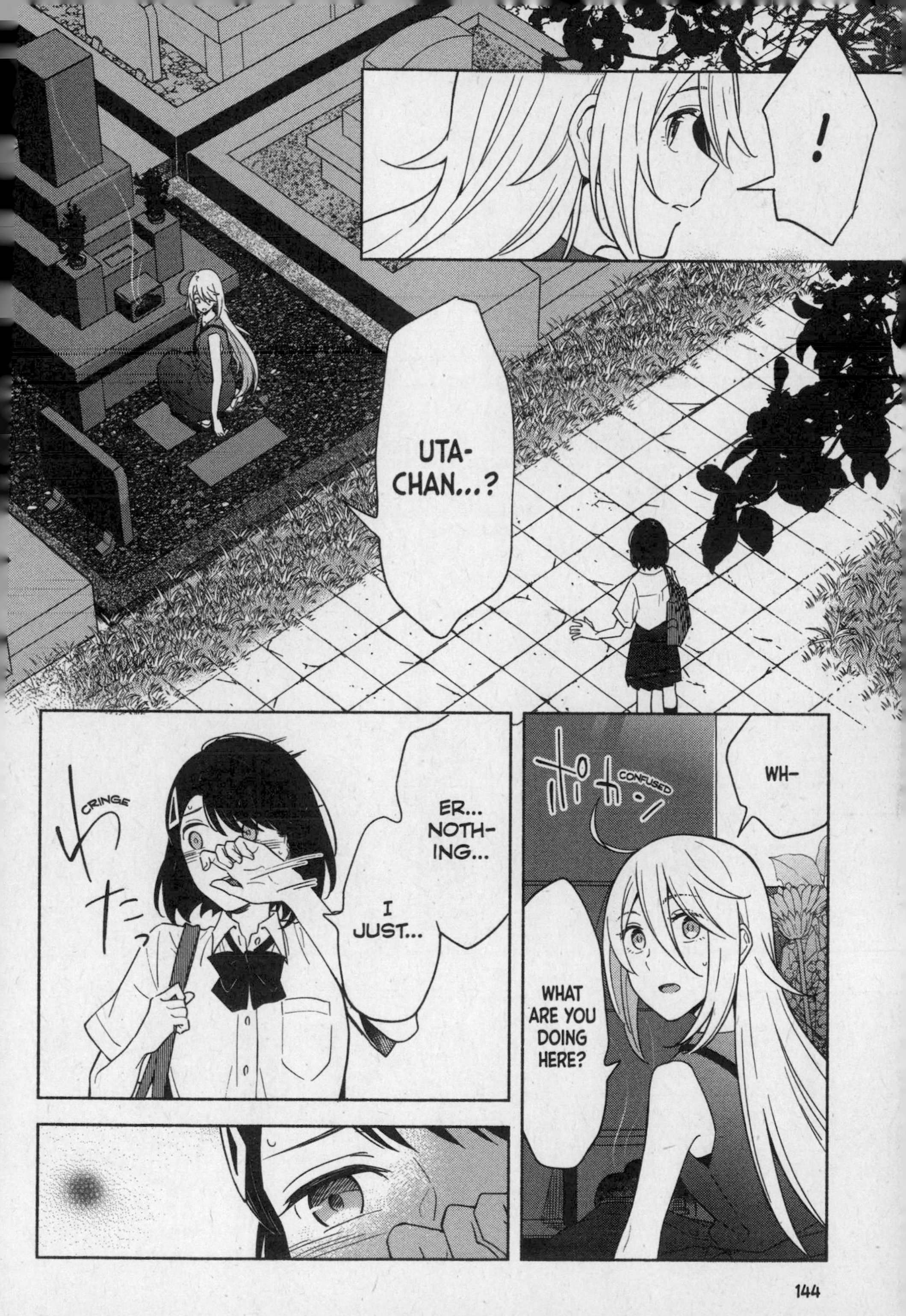
!
UTA-CHAN...?
WH-
CONFUSED
WHAT ARE YOU DOING HERE?
CRINGE
ER... NOTHING...
I JUST...

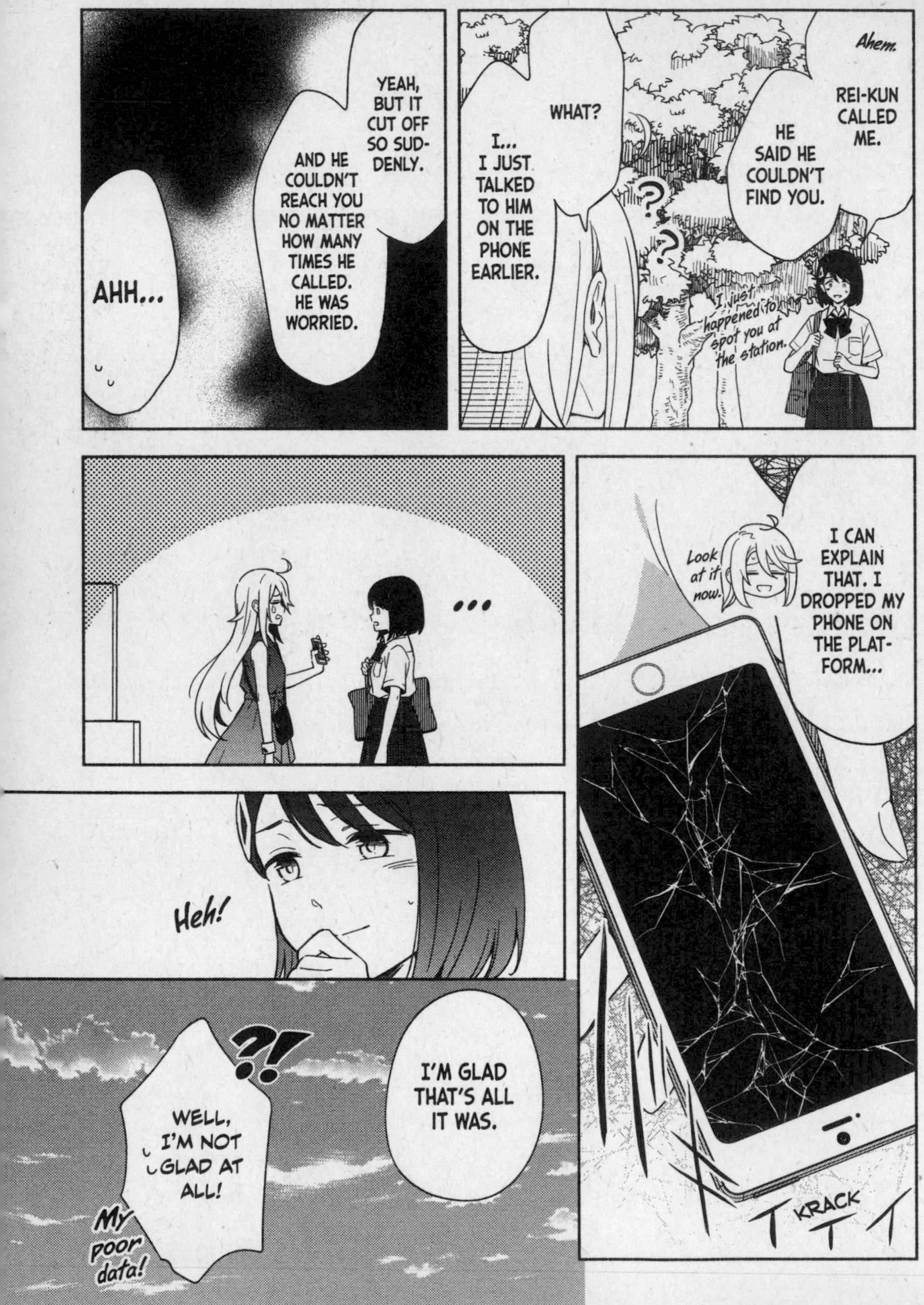
Ahem.
REI-KUN CALLED ME.
HE SAID HE COULDN'T FIND YOU.
I just happened to spot you at the station.
WHAT?
I... I JUST TALKED TO HIM ON THE PHONE EARLIER.
YEAH, BUT IT CUT OFF SO SUD-DENLY.
AND HE COULDN'T REACH YOU NO MATTER HOW MANY TIMES HE CALLED. HE WAS WORRIED.
AHH...
I CAN EXPLAIN THAT. I DROPPED MY PHONE ON THE PLAT-FORM...
Look at it now.
KRACK
...
Heh!
I'M GLAD THAT'S ALL IT WAS.
?!
WELL, I'M NOT GLAD AT ALL!
My poor data!

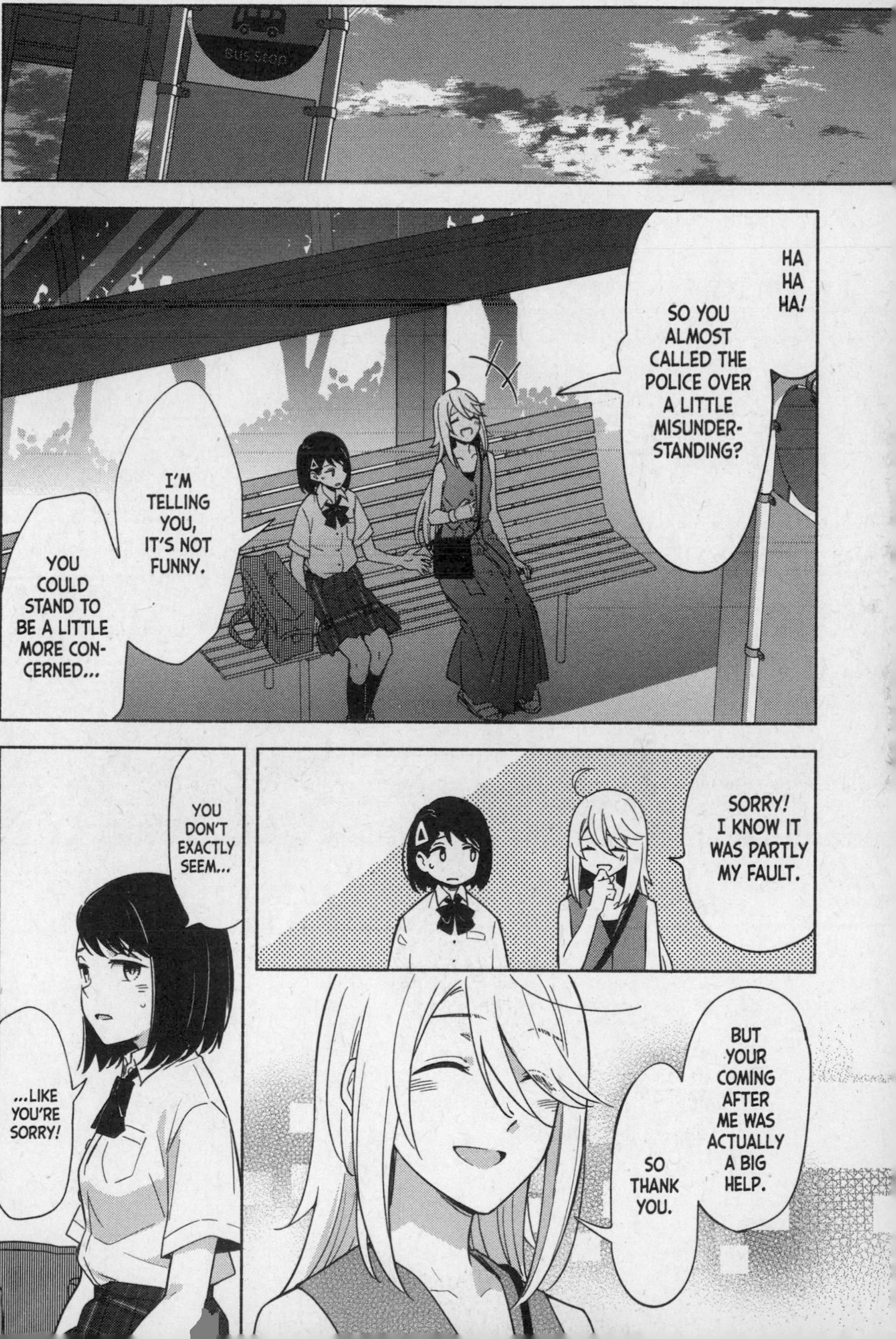
BUS STOP
HA HA HA!
SO YOU ALMOST CALLED THE POLICE OVER A LITTLE MISUNDERSTANDING?
I'M TELLING YOU, IT'S NOT FUNNY.
YOU COULD STAND TO BE A LITTLE MORE CONCERNED...
SORRY! I KNOW IT WAS PARTLY MY FAULT.
YOU DON'T EXACTLY SEEM...
...LIKE YOU'RE SORRY!
BUT YOUR COMING AFTER ME WAS ACTUALLY A BIG HELP.
SO THANK YOU.

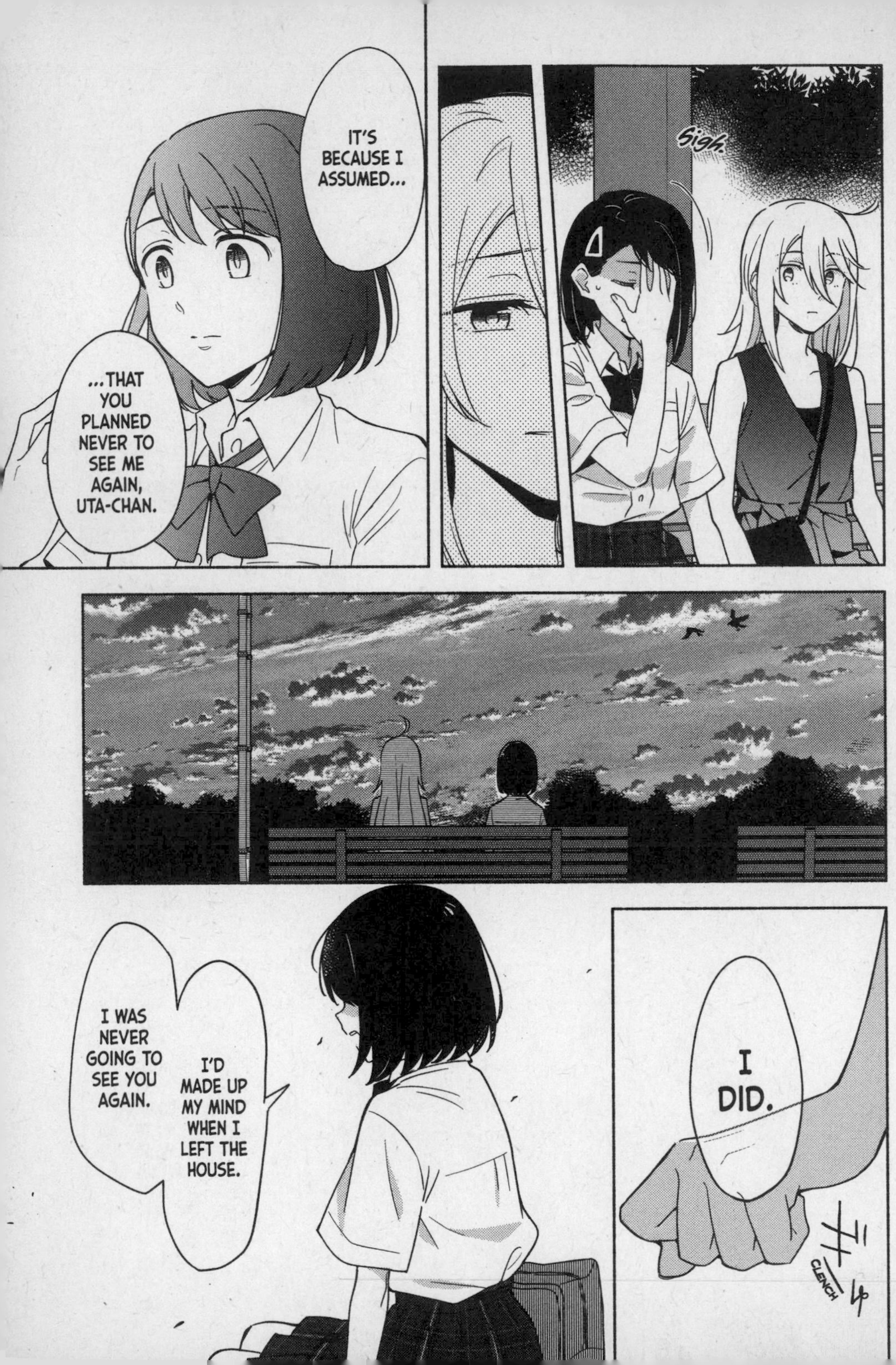
Sigh.
IT'S BECAUSE I ASSUMED...
...THAT YOU PLANNED NEVER TO SEE ME AGAIN, UTA-CHAN.
I DID.
CLENCH
I WAS NEVER GOING TO SEE YOU AGAIN.
I'D MADE UP MY MIND WHEN I LEFT THE HOUSE.

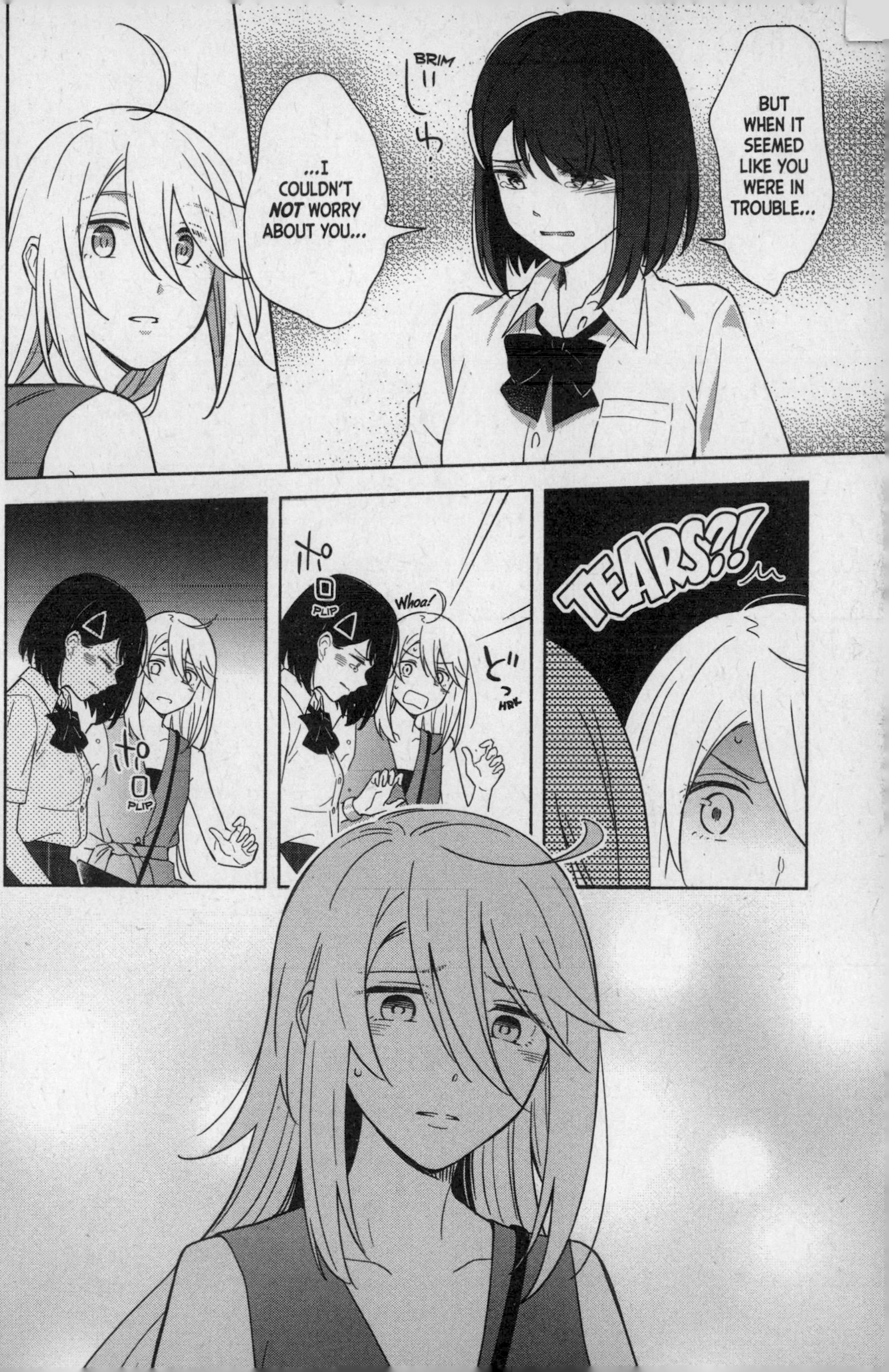
BUT WHEN IT SEEMED LIKE YOU WERE IN TROUBLE...
じわ…
BRIM
...I COULDN'T *NOT* WORRY ABOUT YOU...
TEARS?!
どっ
HRK
Whoa!
ポロ
PLIP
ポロ
PLIP

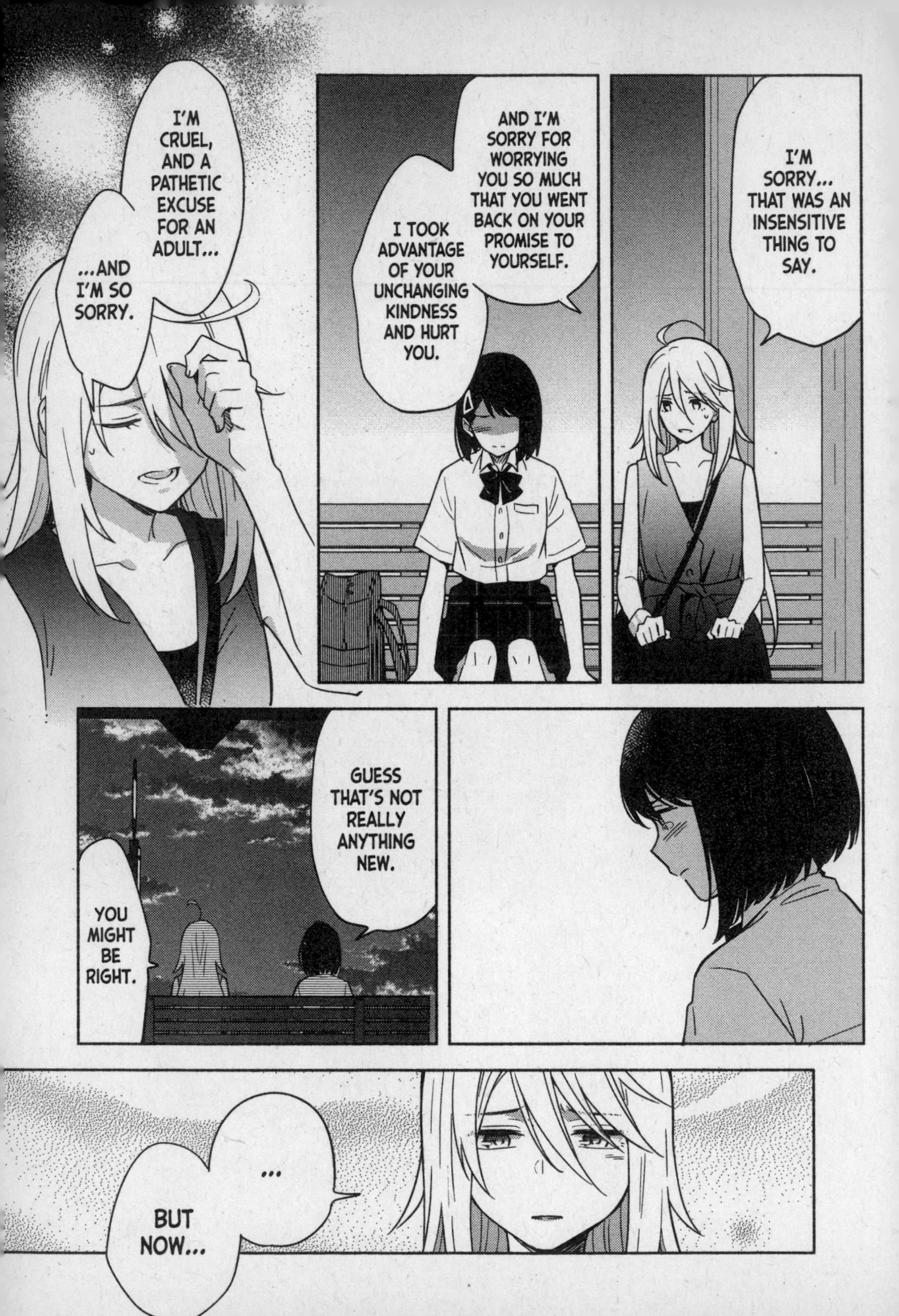
I'M SORRY... THAT WAS AN INSENSITIVE THING TO SAY.
I TOOK ADVANTAGE OF YOUR UNCHANGING KINDNESS AND HURT YOU.
AND I'M SORRY FOR WORRYING YOU SO MUCH THAT YOU WENT BACK ON YOUR PROMISE TO YOURSELF.
I'M CRUEL, AND A PATHETIC EXCUSE FOR AN ADULT...
...AND I'M SO SORRY.
GUESS THAT'S NOT REALLY ANYTHING NEW.
YOU MIGHT BE RIGHT.
...
BUT NOW...

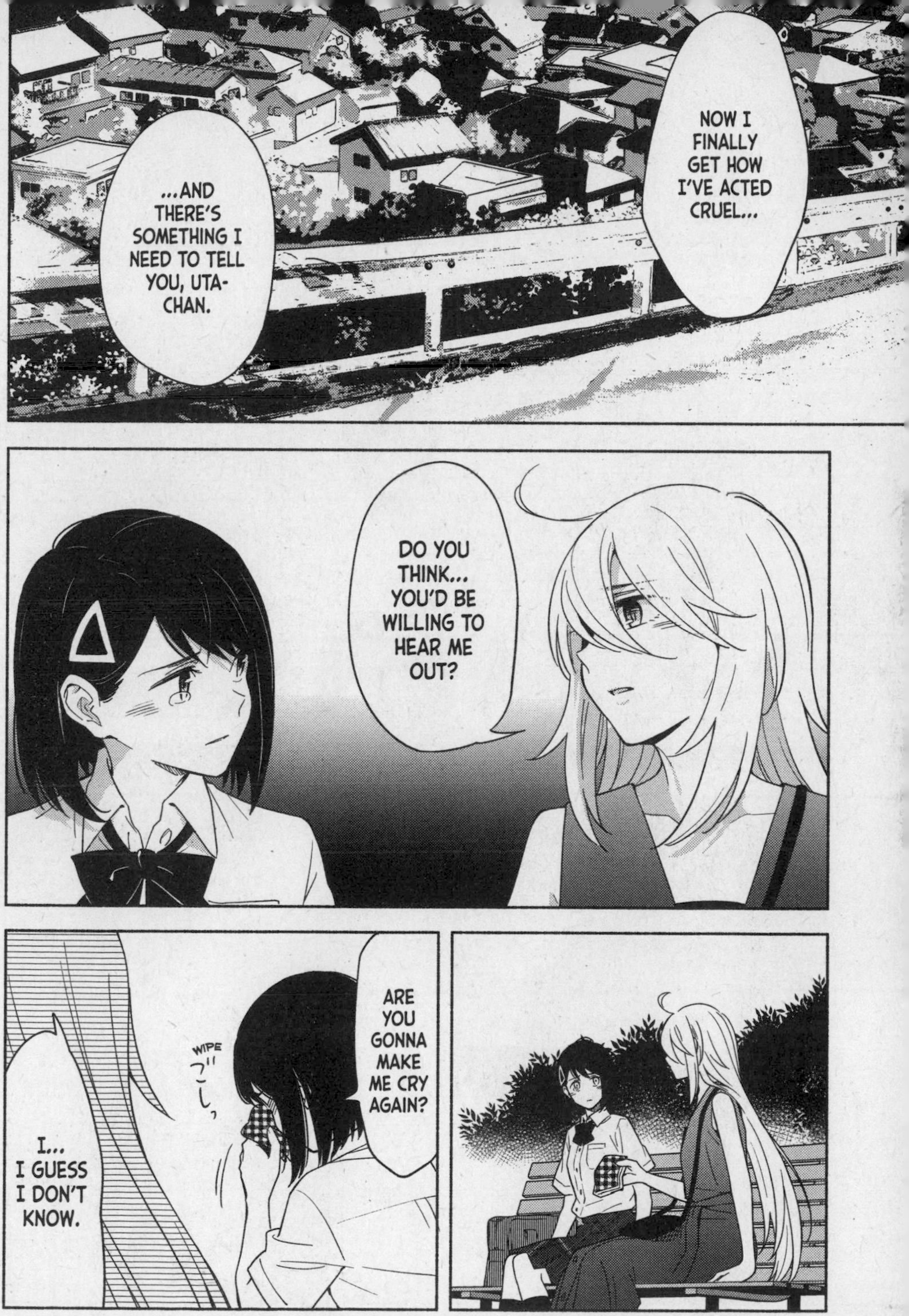
NOW I FINALLY GET HOW I'VE ACTED CRUEL...
...AND THERE'S SOMETHING I NEED TO TELL YOU, UTA-CHAN.
DO YOU THINK... YOU'D BE WILLING TO HEAR ME OUT?
ARE YOU GONNA MAKE ME CRY AGAIN?
WIPE
ゴシ
I... I GUESS I DON'T KNOW.

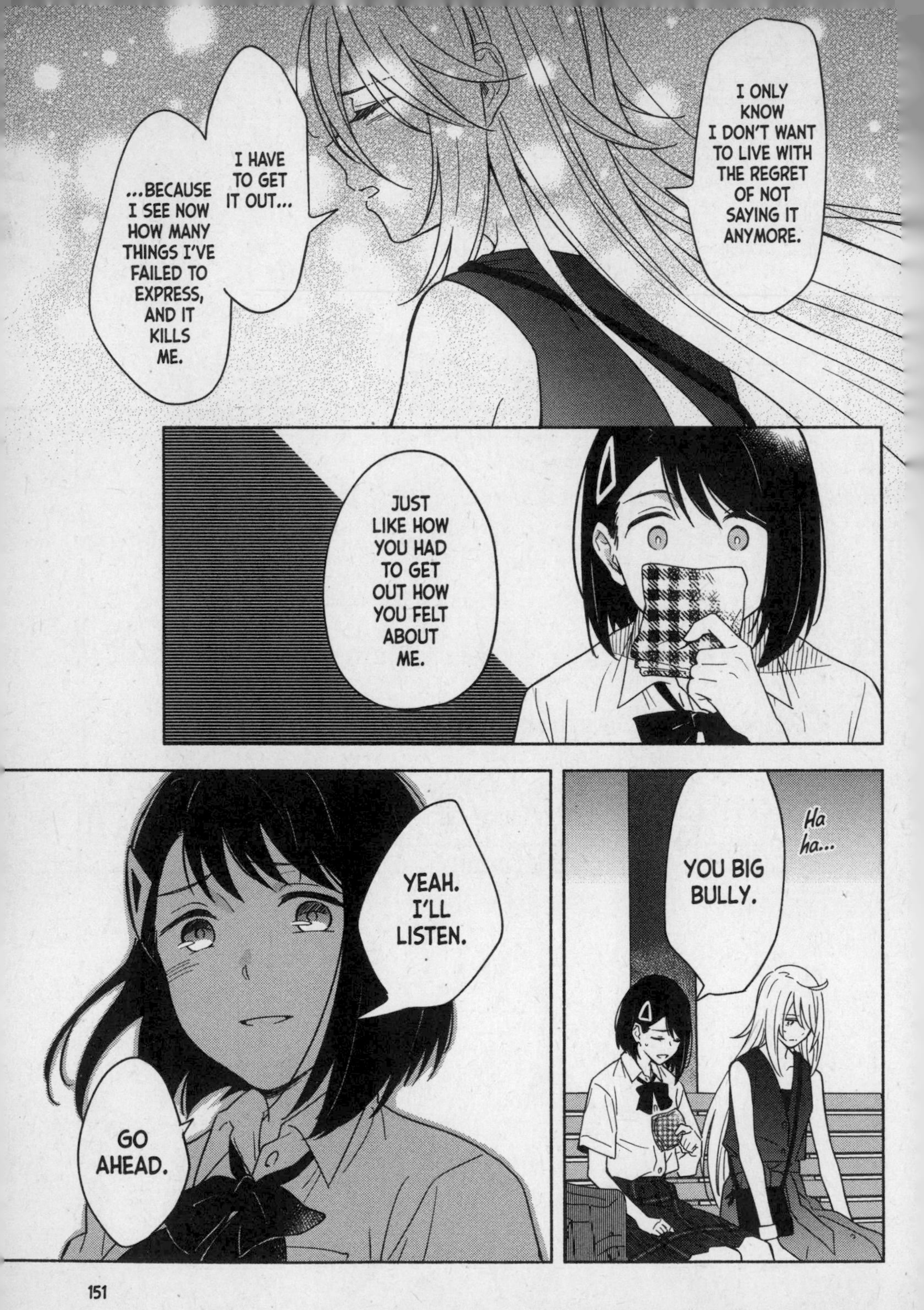
I ONLY KNOW I DON'T WANT TO LIVE WITH THE REGRET OF NOT SAYING IT ANYMORE.
I HAVE TO GET IT OUT...
...BECAUSE I SEE NOW HOW MANY THINGS I'VE FAILED TO EXPRESS, AND IT KILLS ME.
JUST LIKE HOW YOU HAD TO GET OUT HOW YOU FELT ABOUT ME.
Ha ha...
YOU BIG BULLY.
YEAH. I'LL LISTEN.
GO AHEAD.

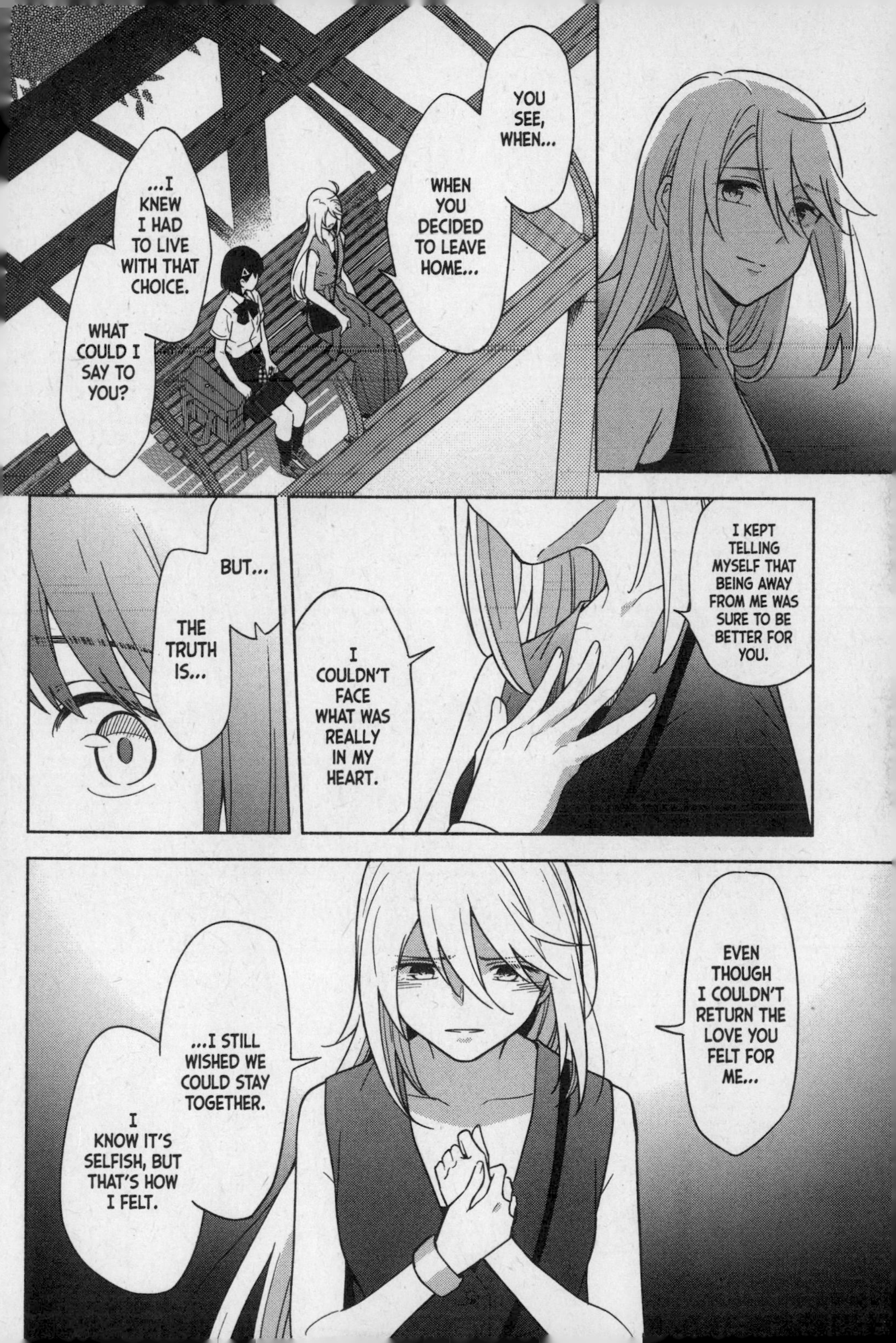
YOU SEE, WHEN...
WHEN YOU DECIDED TO LEAVE HOME...
...I KNEW I HAD TO LIVE WITH THAT CHOICE.
WHAT COULD I SAY TO YOU?
I KEPT TELLING MYSELF THAT BEING AWAY FROM ME WAS SURE TO BE BETTER FOR YOU.
I COULDN'T FACE WHAT WAS REALLY IN MY HEART.
BUT...
THE TRUTH IS...
EVEN THOUGH I COULDN'T RETURN THE LOVE YOU FELT FOR ME...
...I STILL WISHED WE COULD STAY TOGETHER.
I KNOW IT'S SELFISH, BUT THAT'S HOW I FELT.

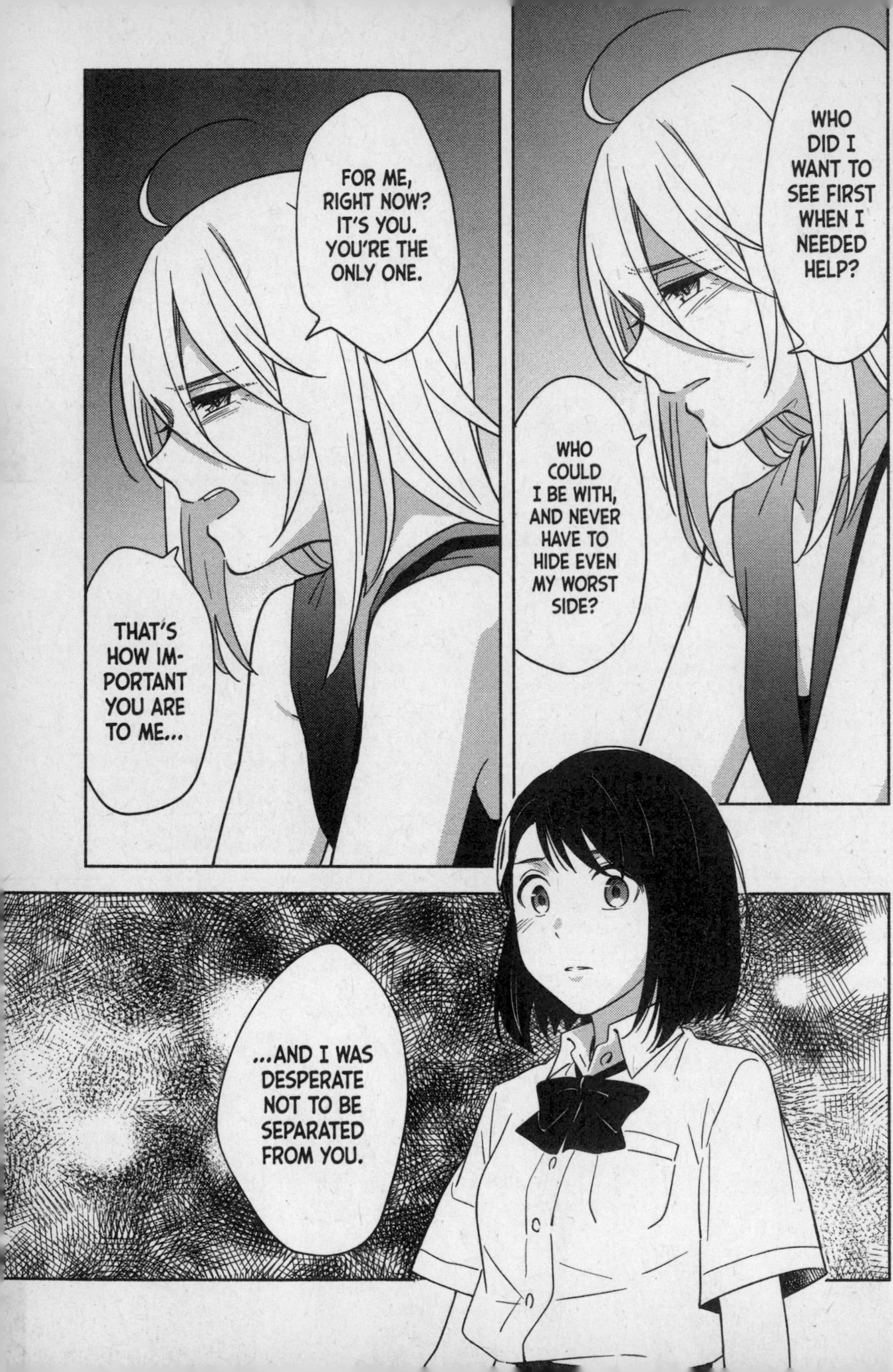
WHO DID I WANT TO SEE FIRST WHEN I NEEDED HELP?
WHO COULD I BE WITH, AND NEVER HAVE TO HIDE EVEN MY WORST SIDE?
FOR ME, RIGHT NOW? IT'S YOU. YOU'RE THE ONLY ONE.
THAT'S HOW IMPORTANT YOU ARE TO ME...
...AND I WAS DESPERATE NOT TO BE SEPARATED FROM YOU.

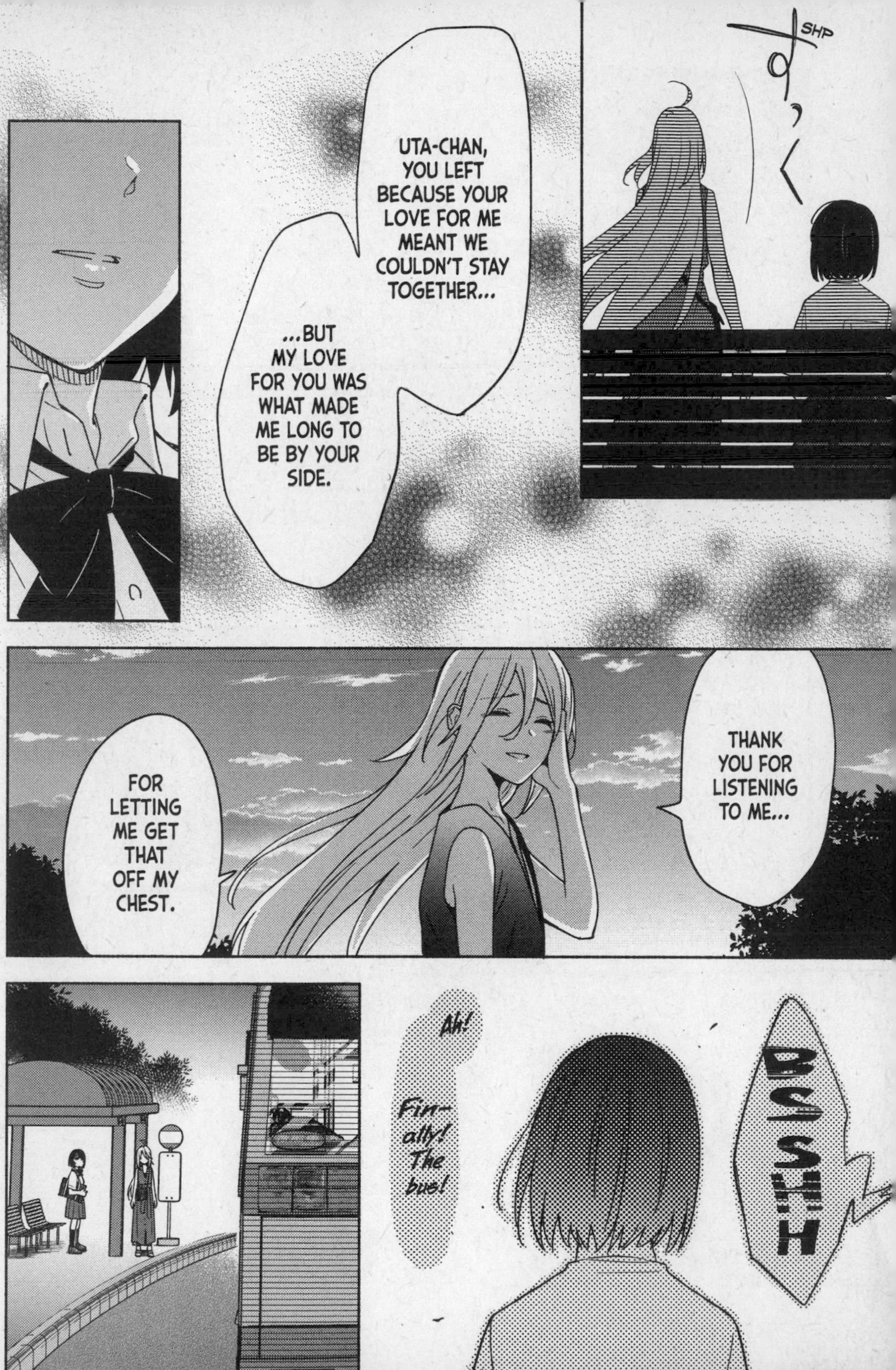
SHP
UTA-CHAN, YOU LEFT BECAUSE YOUR LOVE FOR ME MEANT WE COULDN'T STAY TOGETHER...
...BUT MY LOVE FOR YOU WAS WHAT MADE ME LONG TO BE BY YOUR SIDE.
THANK YOU FOR LISTENING TO ME...
FOR LETTING ME GET THAT OFF MY CHEST.
BSSHH
Ah!
Fin-ally! The bus!

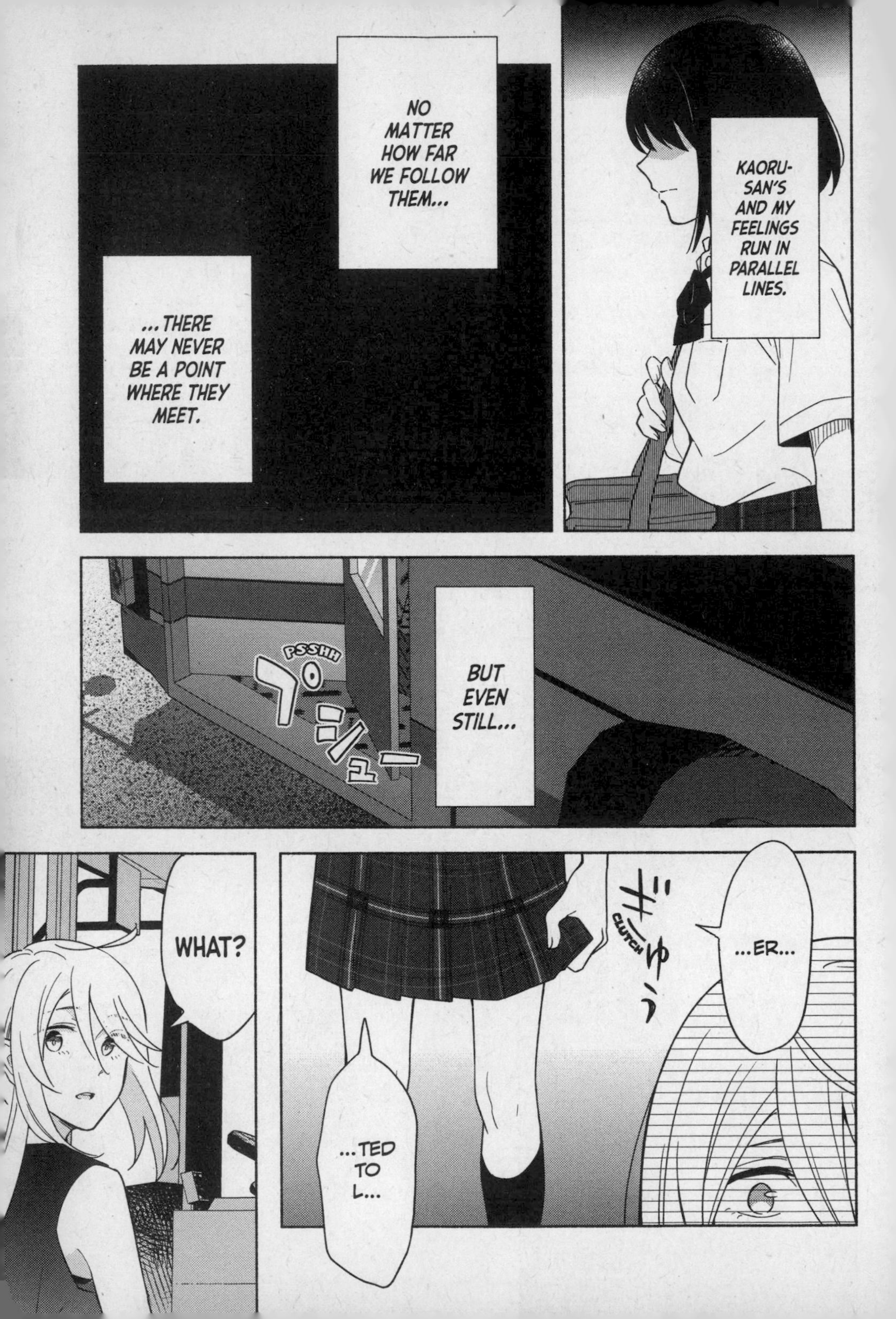
KAORU-SAN'S AND MY FEELINGS RUN IN PARALLEL LINES.
NO MATTER HOW FAR WE FOLLOW THEM...
...THERE MAY NEVER BE A POINT WHERE THEY MEET.
BUT EVEN STILL...
PSSHH
プシュー
...ER...
CLUTCH
...TED TO L...
WHAT?

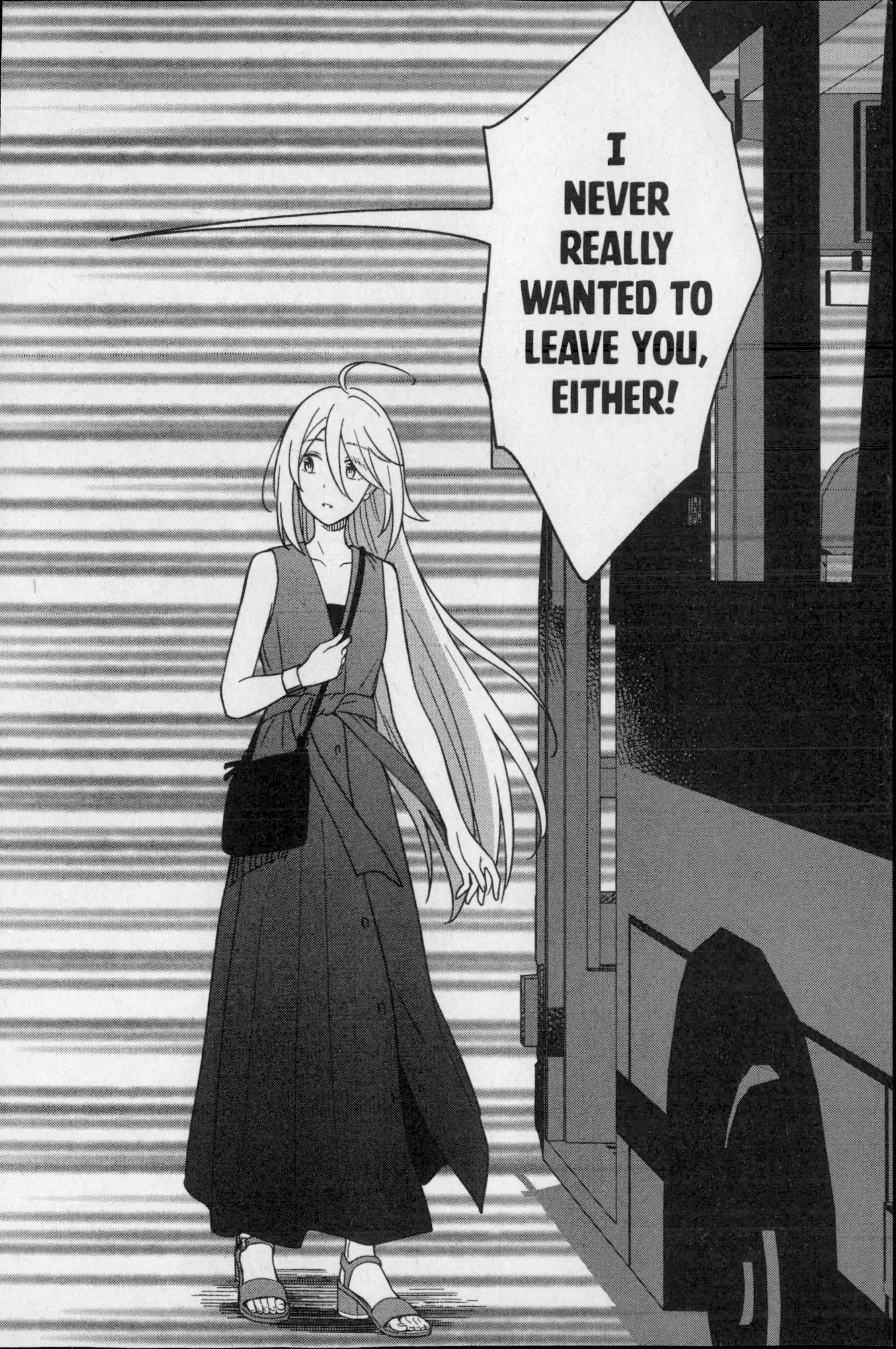
I NEVER REALLY WANTED TO LEAVE YOU, EITHER!

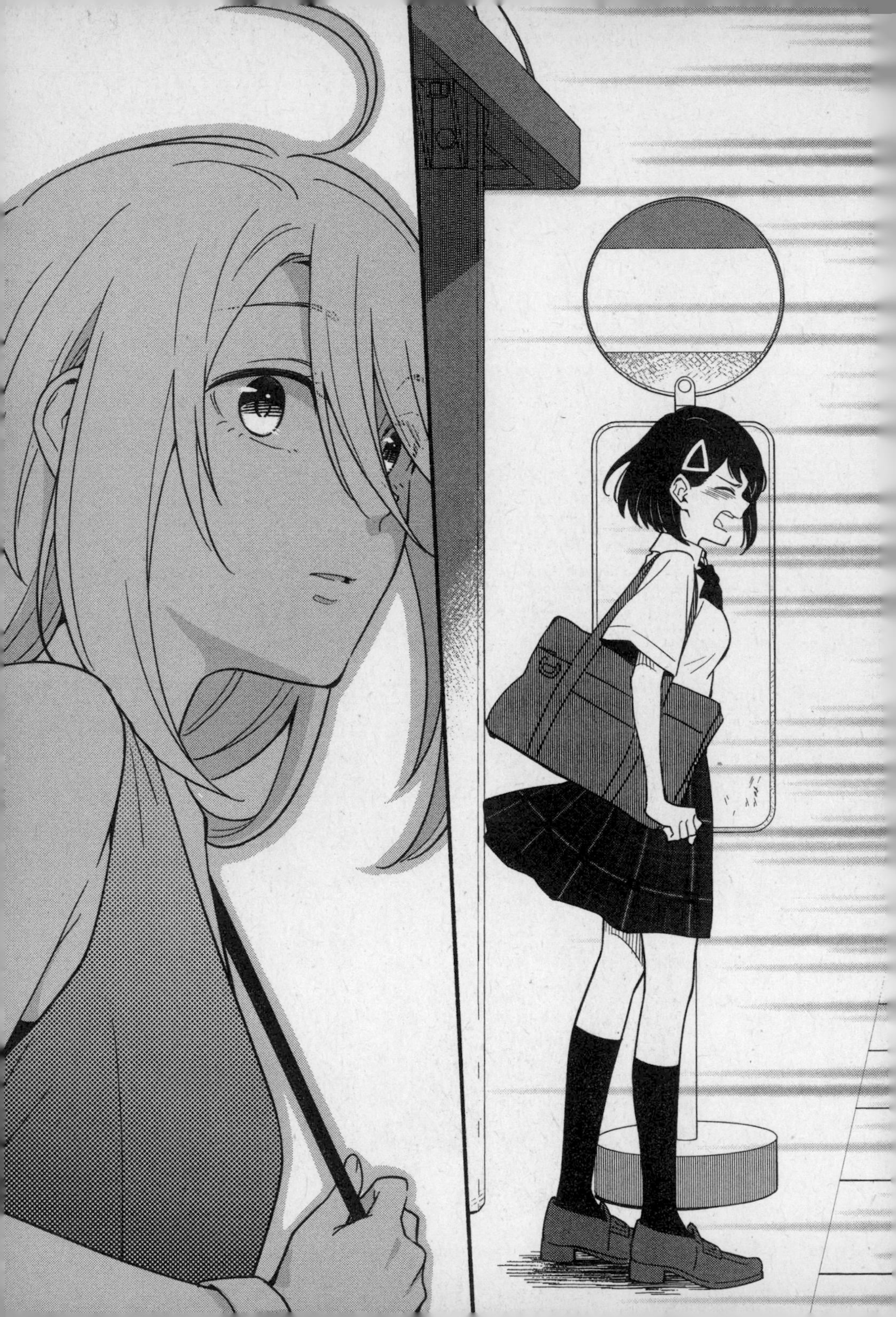

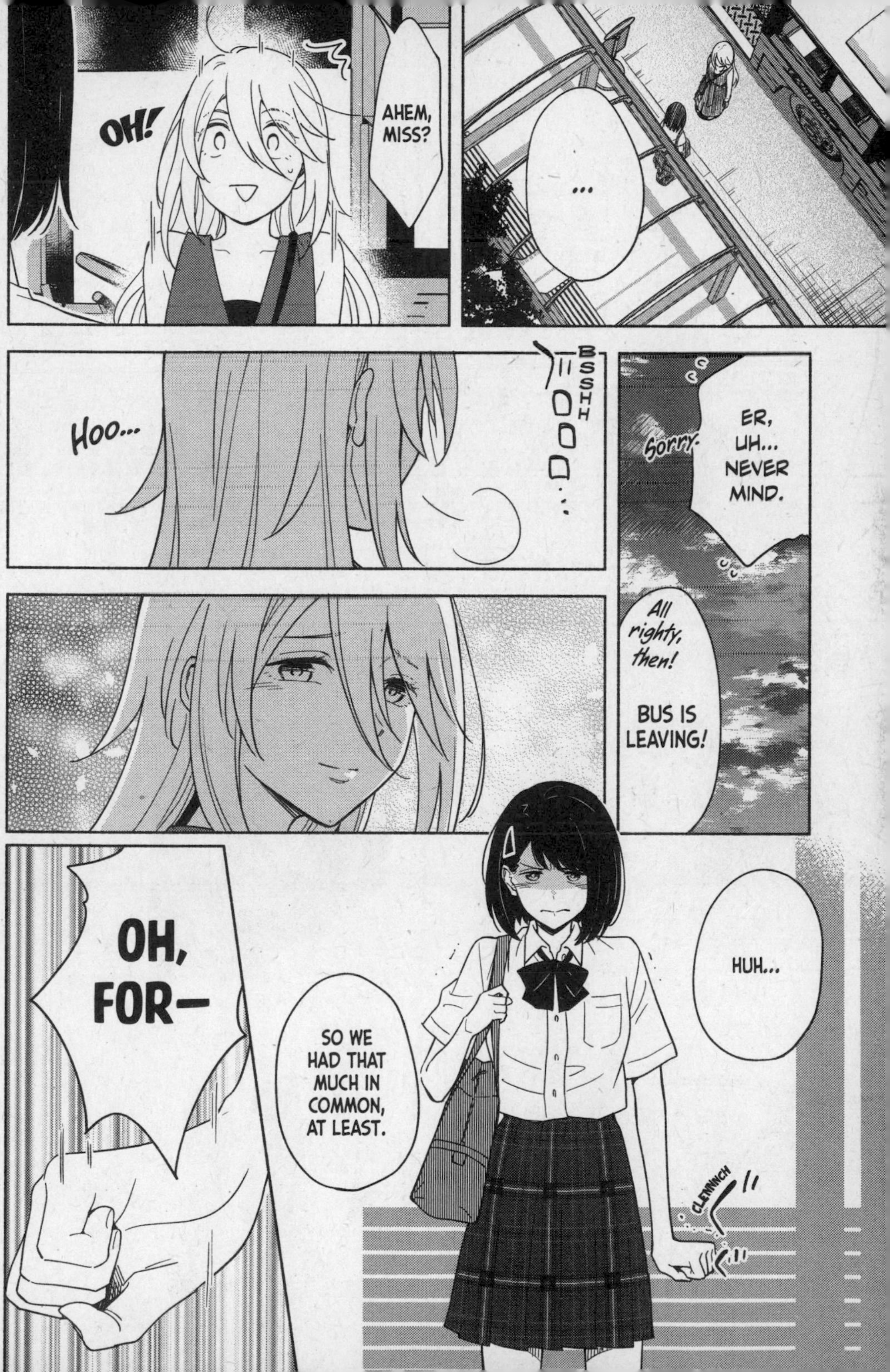
...
AHEM, MISS?
OH!
ER, UH... NEVER MIND.
Sorry.
All righty, then!
BUS IS LEAVING!
BSSHH
Hoo...
HUH...
SO WE HAD THAT MUCH IN COMMON, AT LEAST.
CLENNNCH
OH, FOR—

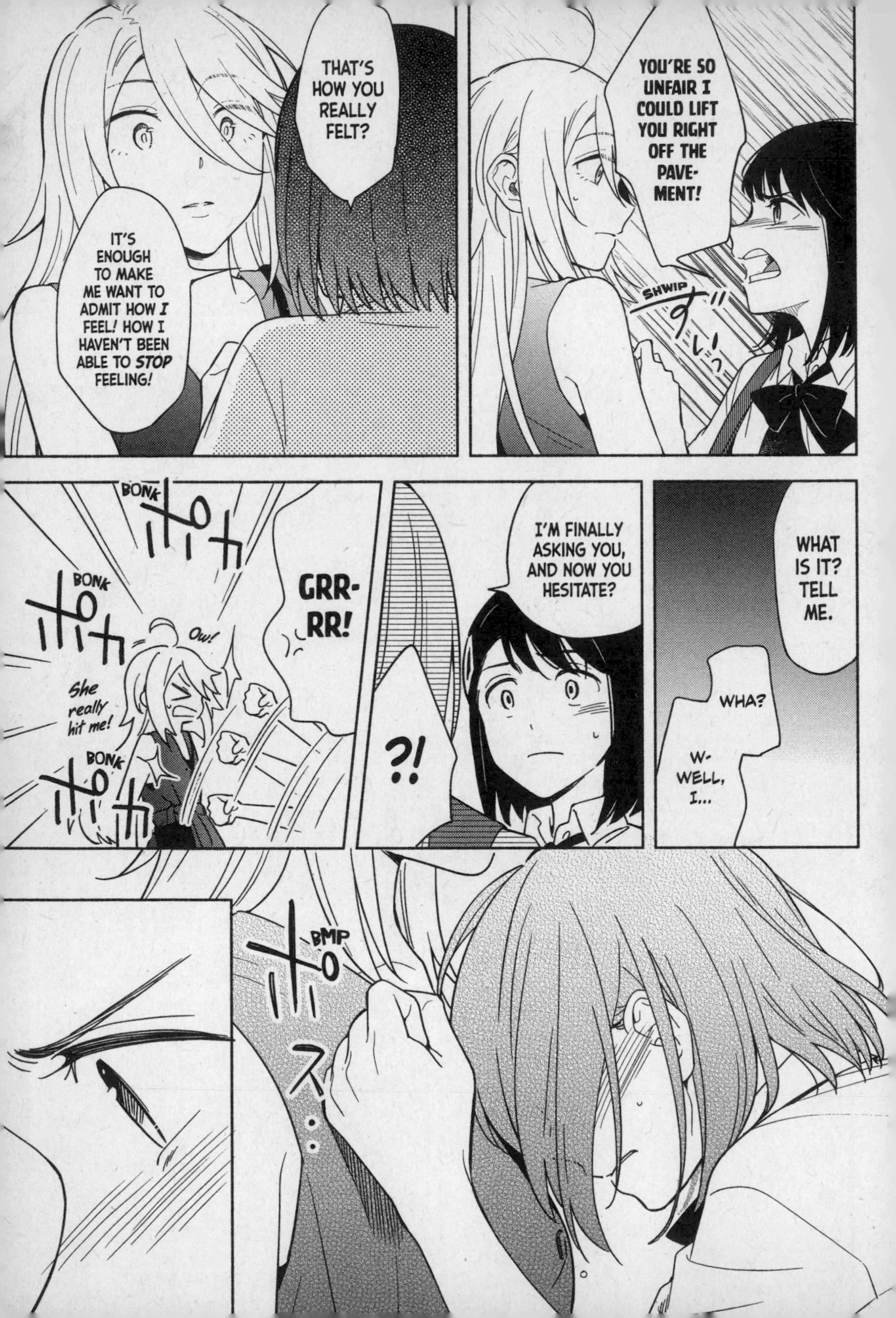
YOU'RE SO UNFAIR I COULD LIFT YOU RIGHT OFF THE PAVE-MENT!
SHWIP
THAT'S HOW YOU REALLY FELT?
IT'S ENOUGH TO MAKE ME WANT TO ADMIT HOW *I* FEEL! HOW I HAVEN'T BEEN ABLE TO *STOP* FEELING!
WHAT IS IT? TELL ME.
WHA?
W-WELL, I...
I'M FINALLY ASKING YOU, AND NOW YOU HESITATE?
?!
GRR-RR!
BONK
BONK
Ow!
She really hit me!
BONK
BMP

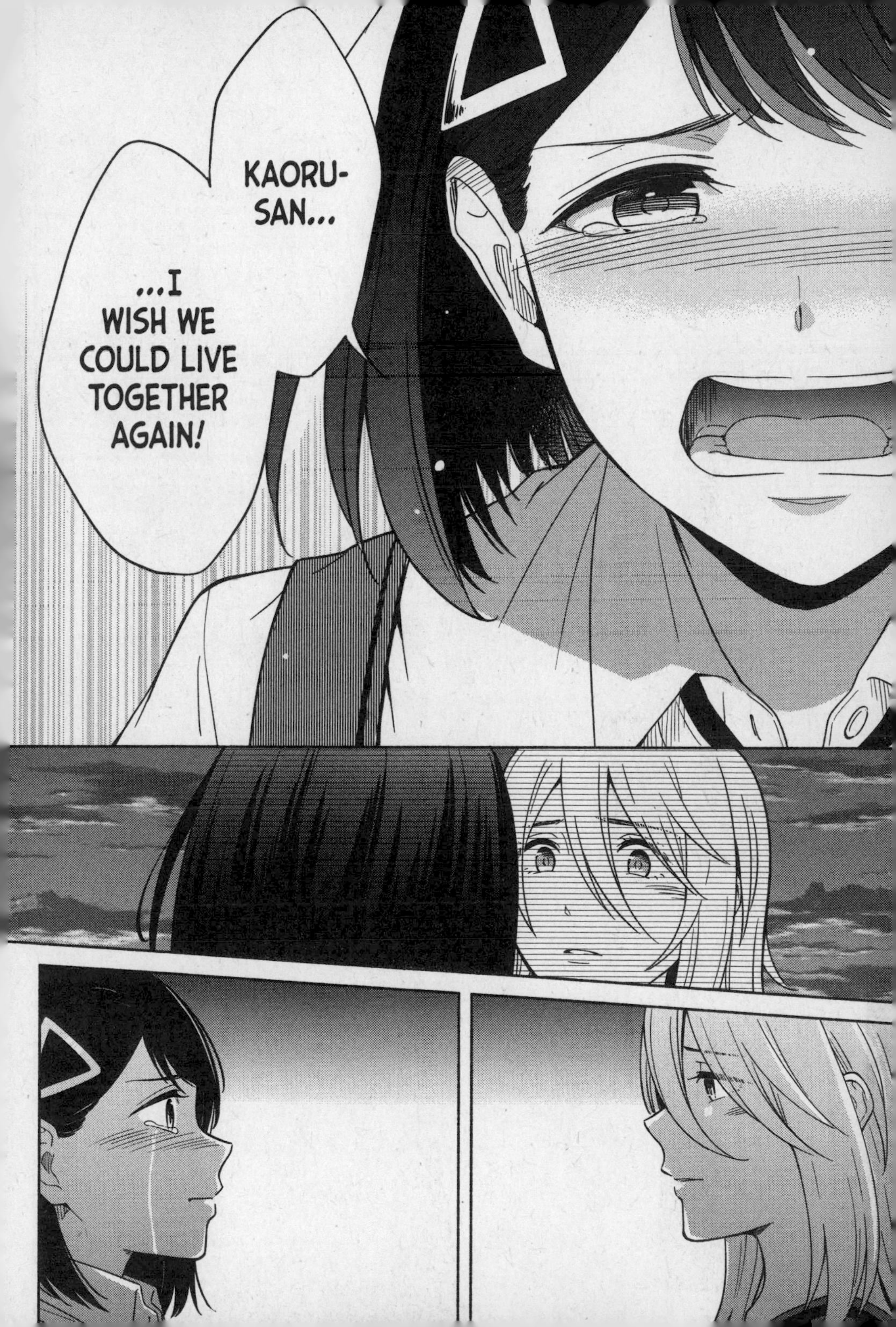
KAORU-SAN...
...I WISH WE COULD LIVE TOGETHER AGAIN!

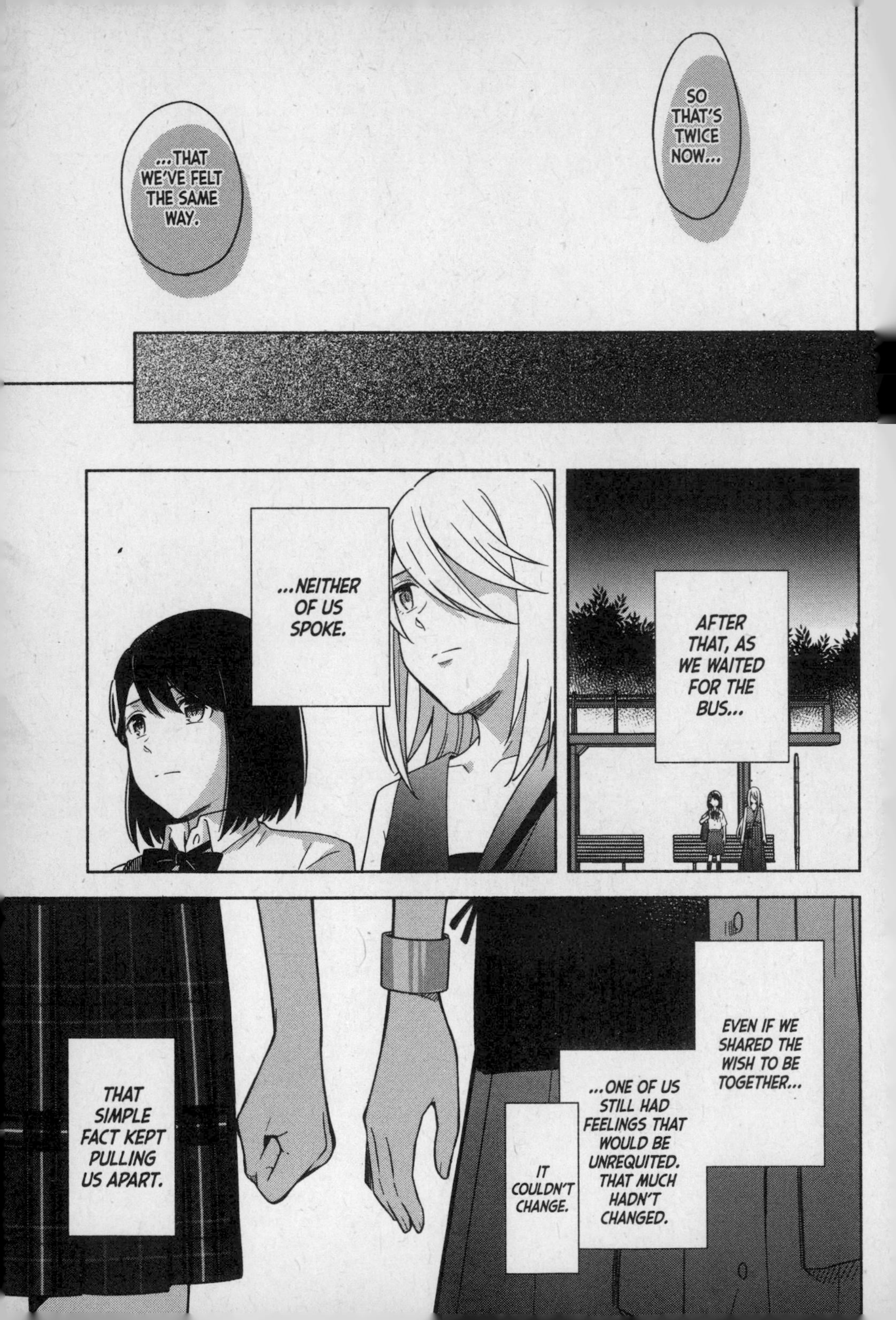
SO THAT'S TWICE NOW...
...THAT WE'VE FELT THE SAME WAY.
AFTER THAT, AS WE WAITED FOR THE BUS...
...NEITHER OF US SPOKE.
EVEN IF WE SHARED THE WISH TO BE TOGETHER...
...ONE OF US STILL HAD FEELINGS THAT WOULD BE UNREQUITED. THAT MUCH HADN'T CHANGED.
IT COULDN'T CHANGE.
THAT SIMPLE FACT KEPT PULLING US APART.

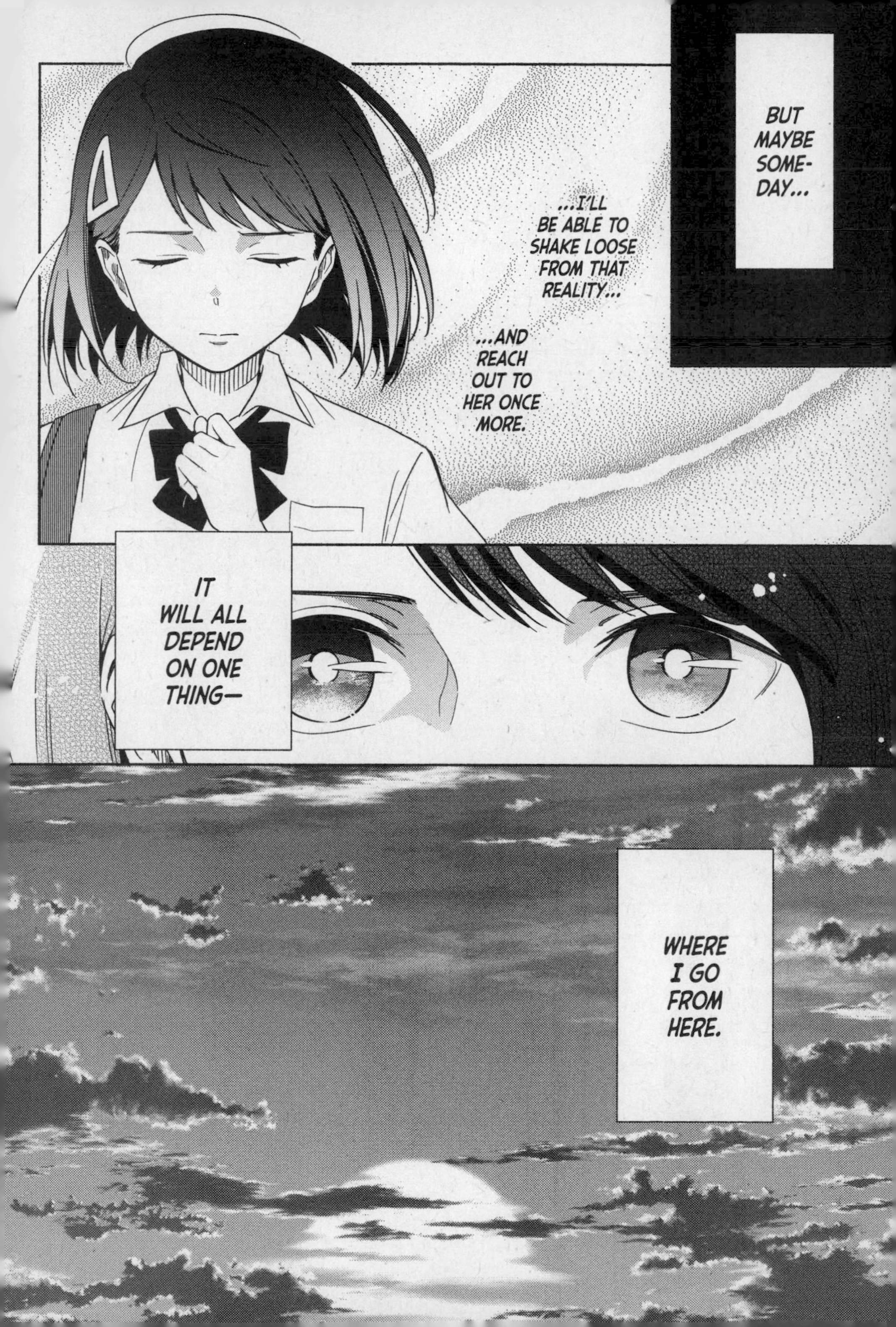
BUT MAYBE SOME-DAY...
...I'LL BE ABLE TO SHAKE LOOSE FROM THAT REALITY...
...AND REACH OUT TO HER ONCE MORE.
IT WILL ALL DEPEND ON ONE THING—
WHERE I GO FROM HERE.

If I Could
Reach You

If I Could Reach You

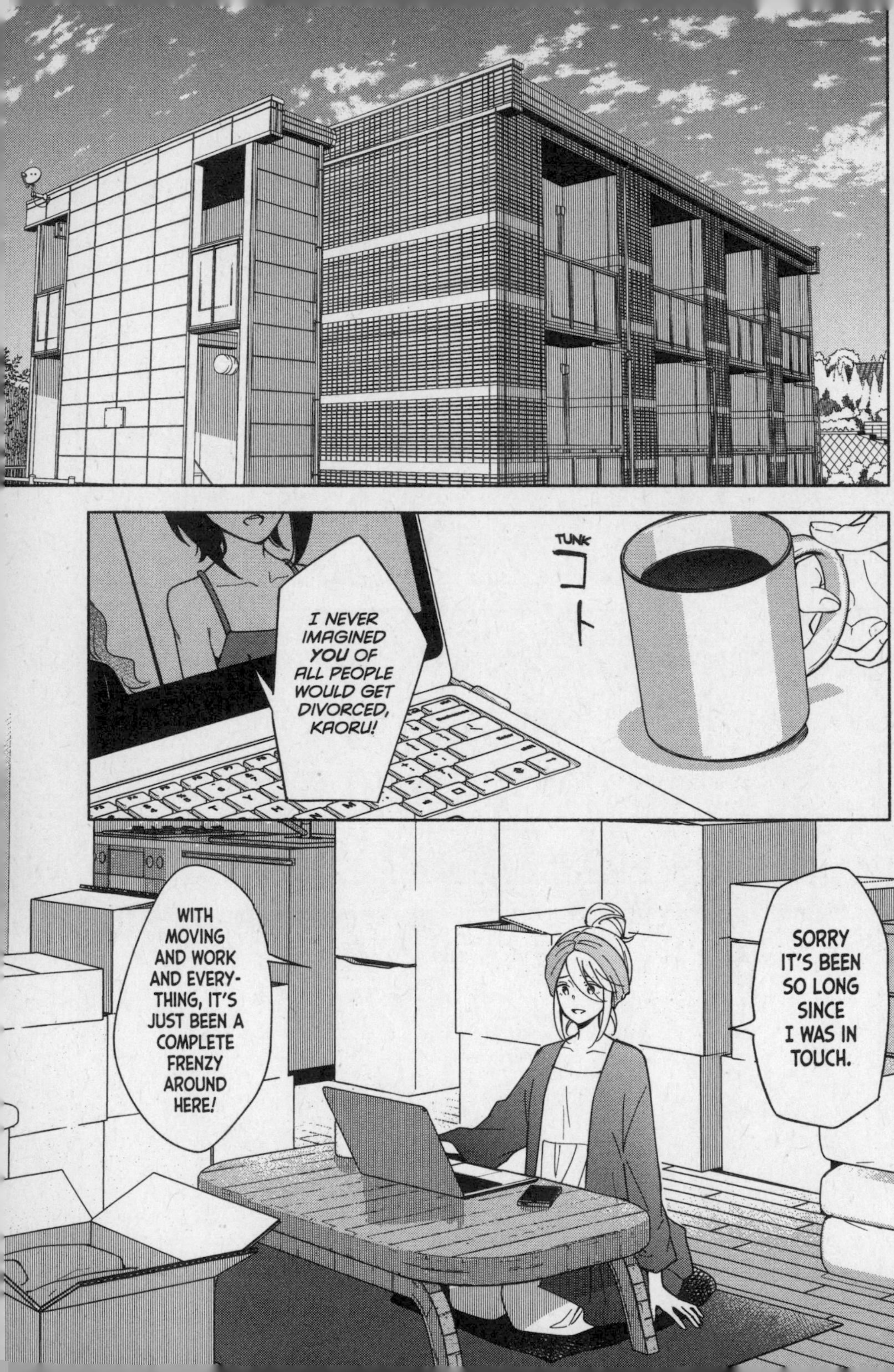
TUNK
コト
I NEVER IMAGINED YOU OF ALL PEOPLE WOULD GET DIVORCED, KAORU!
SORRY IT'S BEEN SO LONG SINCE I WAS IN TOUCH.
WITH MOVING AND WORK AND EVERY-THING, IT'S JUST BEEN A COMPLETE FRENZY AROUND HERE!

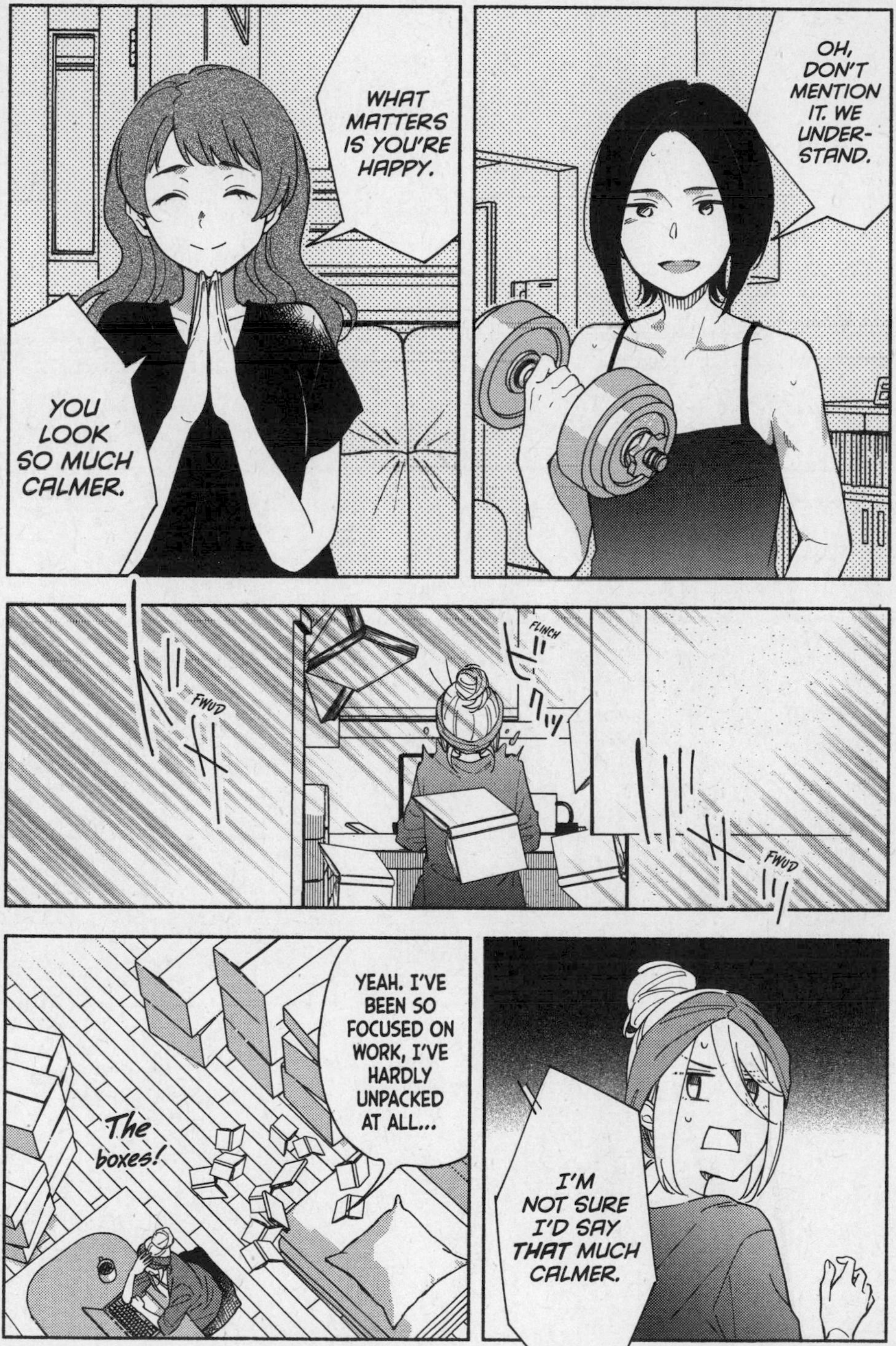
OH, DON'T MENTION IT. WE UNDER-STAND.
WHAT MATTERS IS YOU'RE HAPPY.
YOU LOOK SO MUCH CALMER.
FLINCH
FWUD
FWUD
I'M NOT SURE I'D SAY THAT MUCH CALMER.
YEAH. I'VE BEEN SO FOCUSED ON WORK, I'VE HARDLY UNPACKED AT ALL...
The boxes!

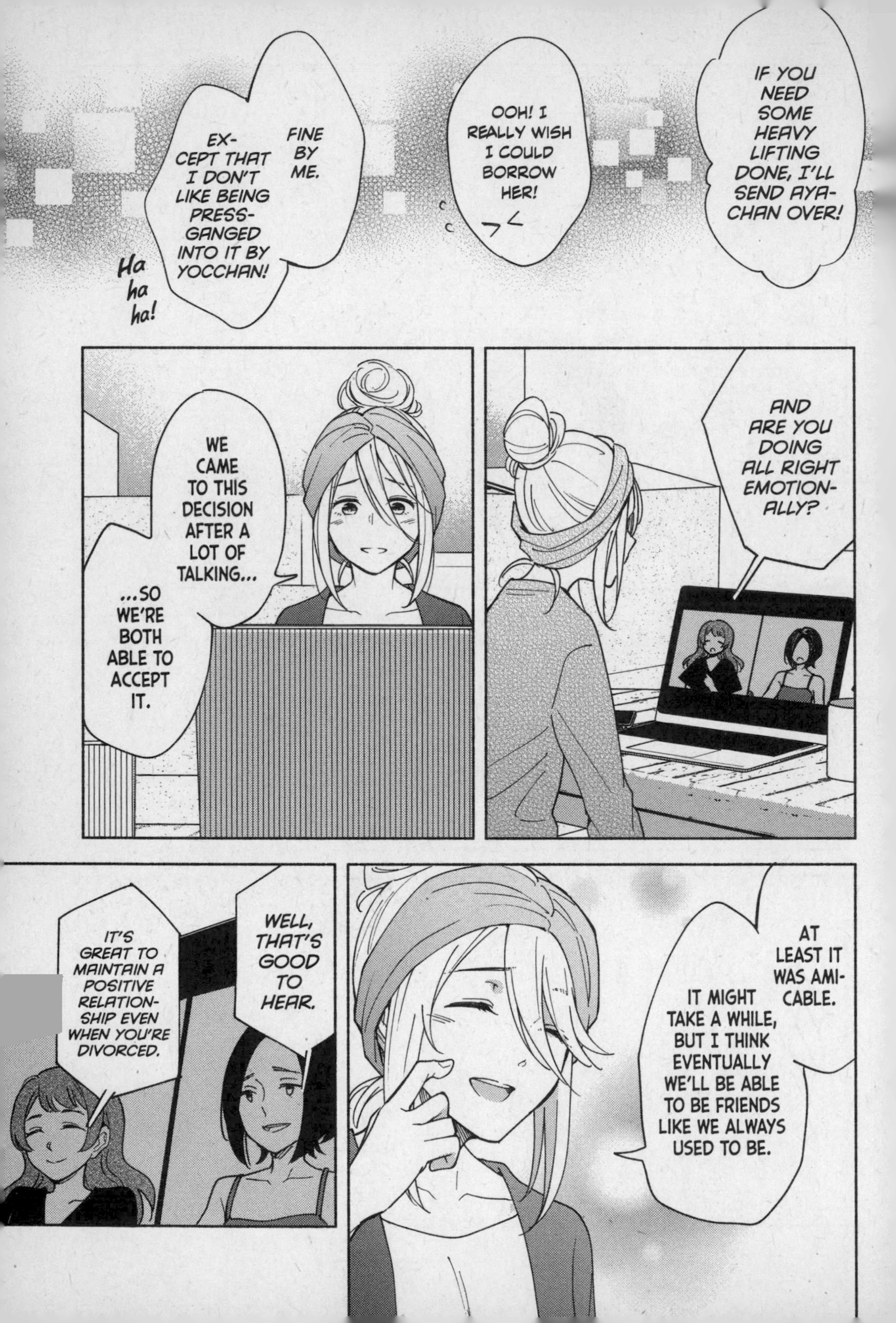
IF YOU NEED SOME HEAVY LIFTING DONE, I'LL SEND AYA-CHAN OVER!
OOH! I REALLY WISH I COULD BORROW HER!
FINE BY ME.
EX-CEPT THAT I DON'T LIKE BEING PRESS-GANGED INTO IT BY YOCCHAN!
Ha ha ha!
AND ARE YOU DOING ALL RIGHT EMOTION-ALLY?
WE CAME TO THIS DECISION AFTER A LOT OF TALKING...
...SO WE'RE BOTH ABLE TO ACCEPT IT.
AT LEAST IT WAS AMI-CABLE.
IT MIGHT TAKE A WHILE, BUT I THINK EVENTUALLY WE'LL BE ABLE TO BE FRIENDS LIKE WE ALWAYS USED TO BE.
WELL, THAT'S GOOD TO HEAR.
IT'S GREAT TO MAINTAIN A POSITIVE RELATION-SHIP EVEN WHEN YOU'RE DIVORCED.

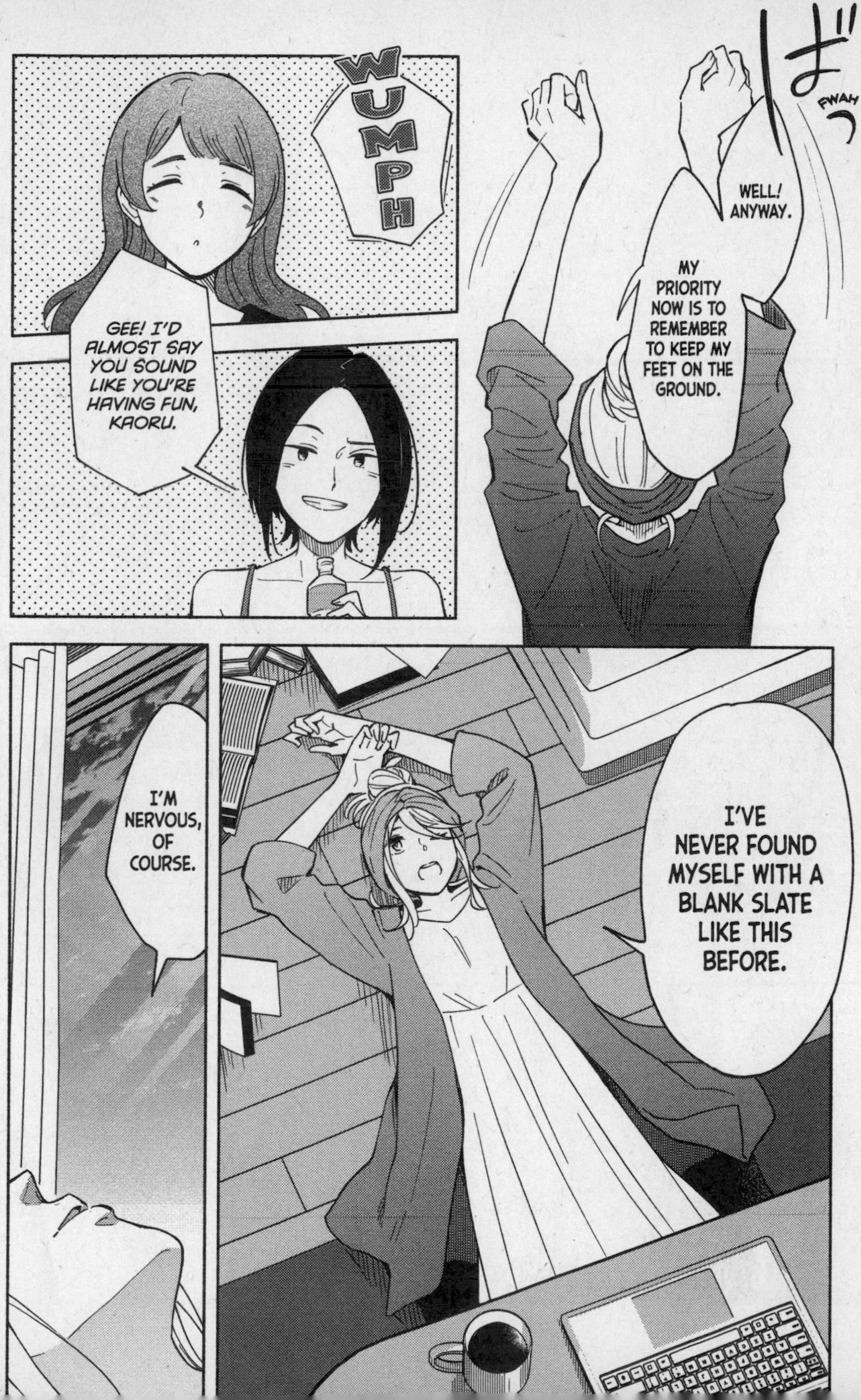
ばっ
FWAH
WELL! ANYWAY.
MY PRIORITY NOW IS TO REMEMBER TO KEEP MY FEET ON THE GROUND.
WUMPH
GEE! I'D ALMOST SAY YOU SOUND LIKE YOU'RE HAVING FUN, KAORU.
I'VE NEVER FOUND MYSELF WITH A BLANK SLATE LIKE THIS BEFORE.
I'M NERVOUS, OF COURSE.

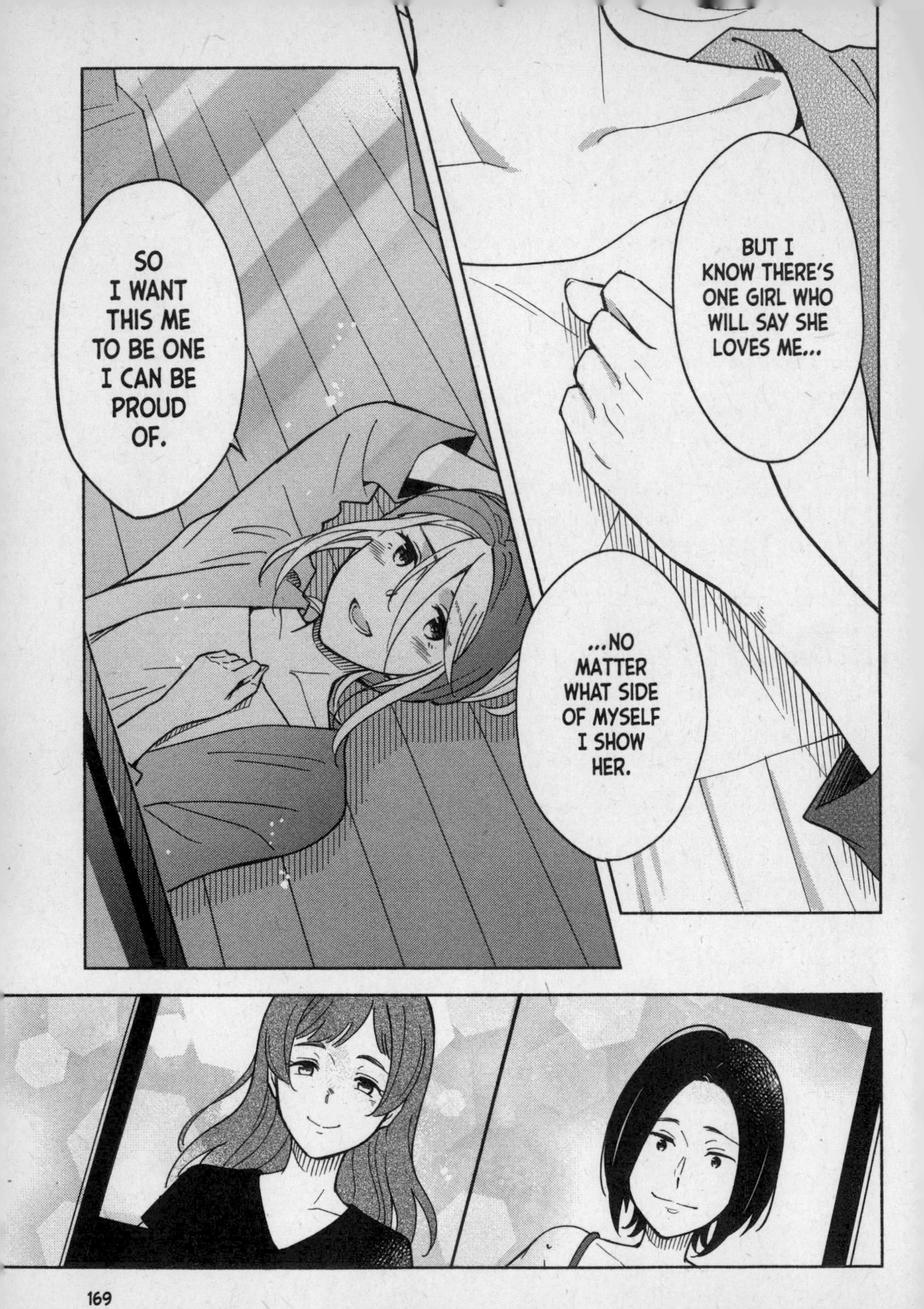
BUT I KNOW THERE'S ONE GIRL WHO WILL SAY SHE LOVES ME...
...NO MATTER WHAT SIDE OF MYSELF I SHOW HER.
SO I WANT THIS ME TO BE ONE I CAN BE PROUD OF.

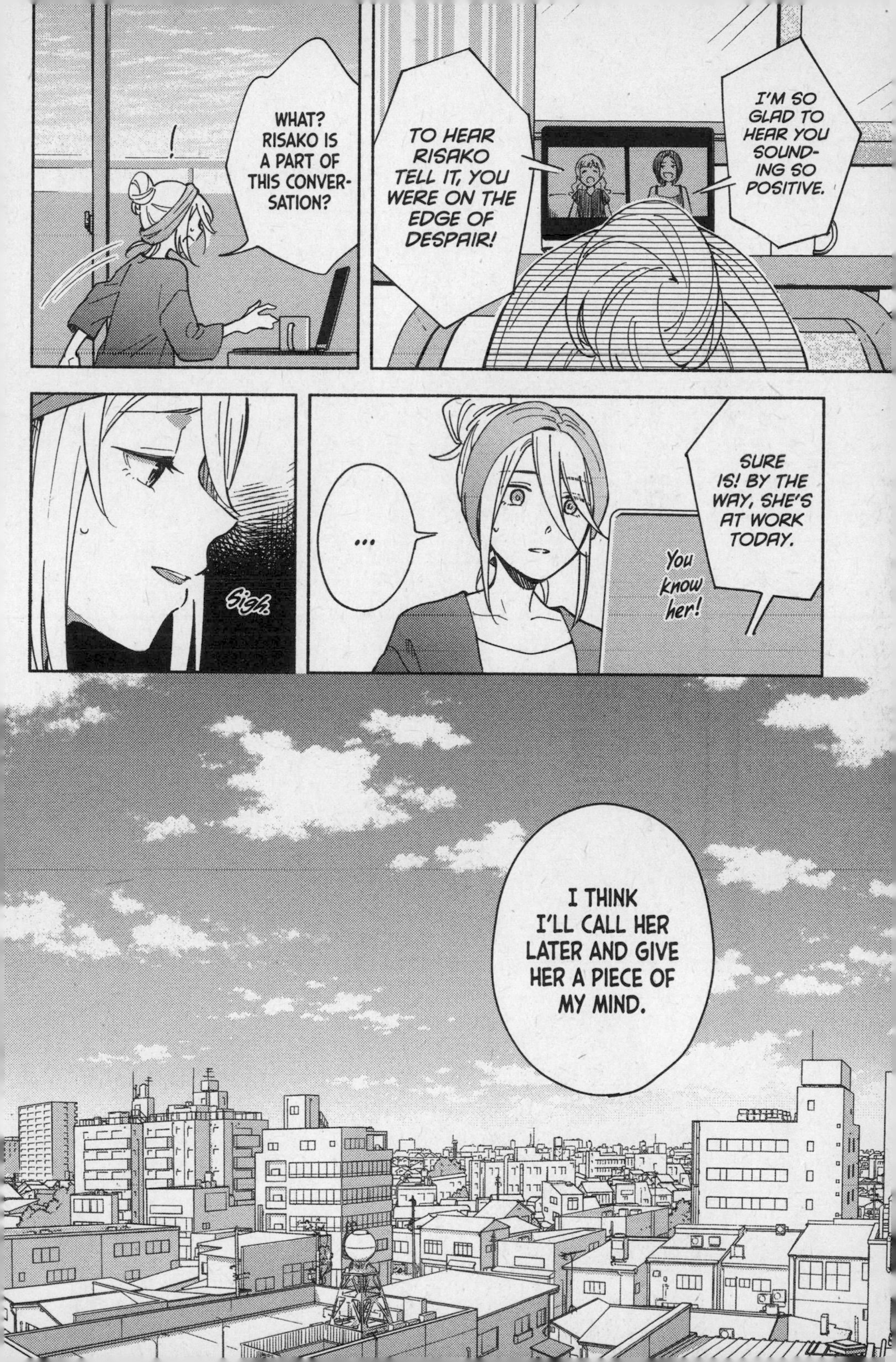
I'M SO GLAD TO HEAR YOU SOUNDING SO POSITIVE.
TO HEAR RISAKO TELL IT, YOU WERE ON THE EDGE OF DESPAIR!
!
WHAT? RISAKO IS A PART OF THIS CONVERSATION?
SURE IS! BY THE WAY, SHE'S AT WORK TODAY.
You know her!
...
Sigh.
I THINK I'LL CALL HER LATER AND GIVE HER A PIECE OF MY MIND.

Final Chapter

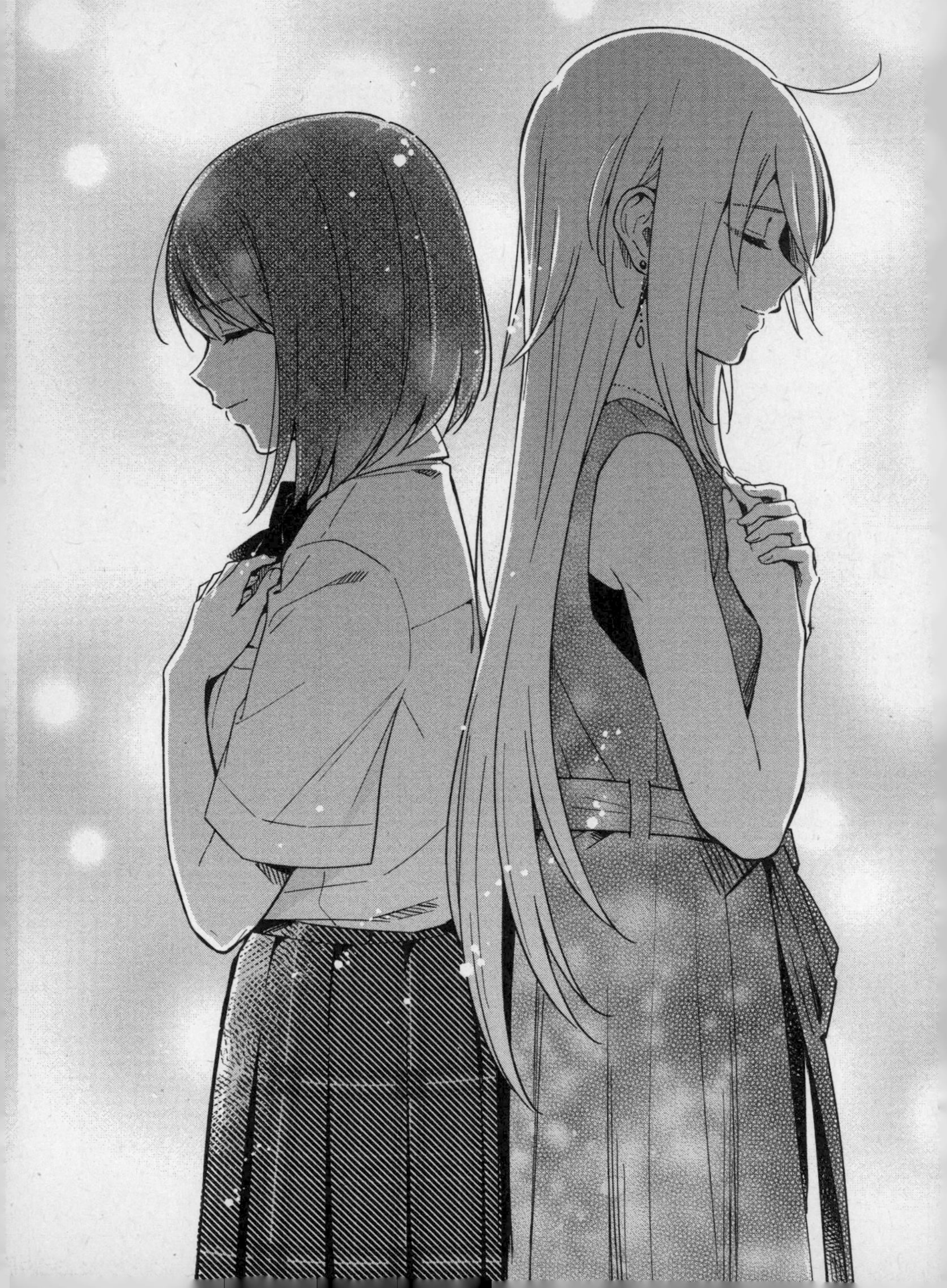

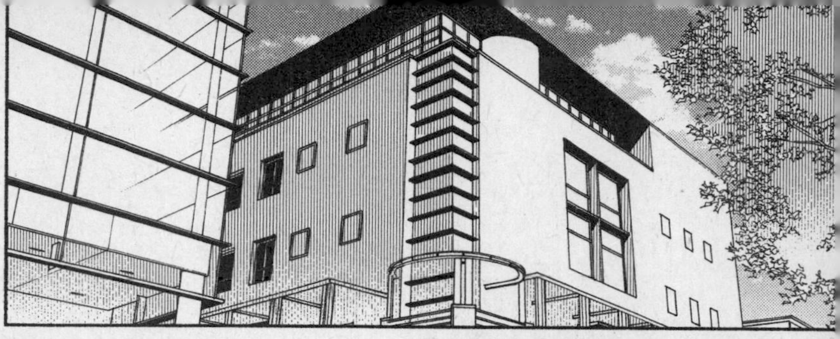
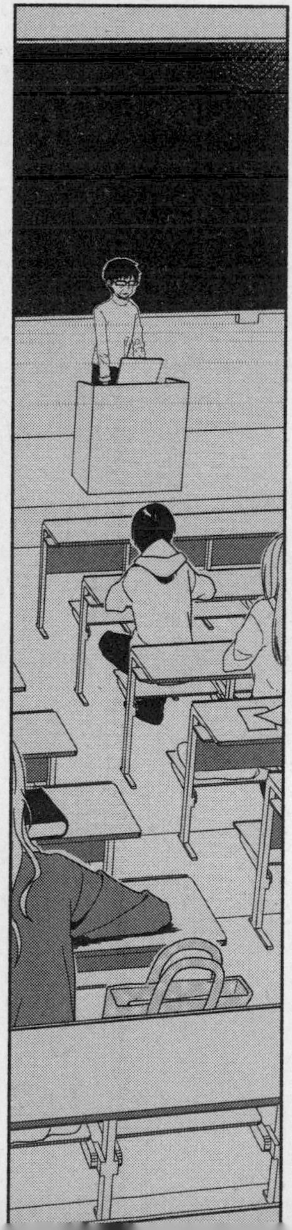
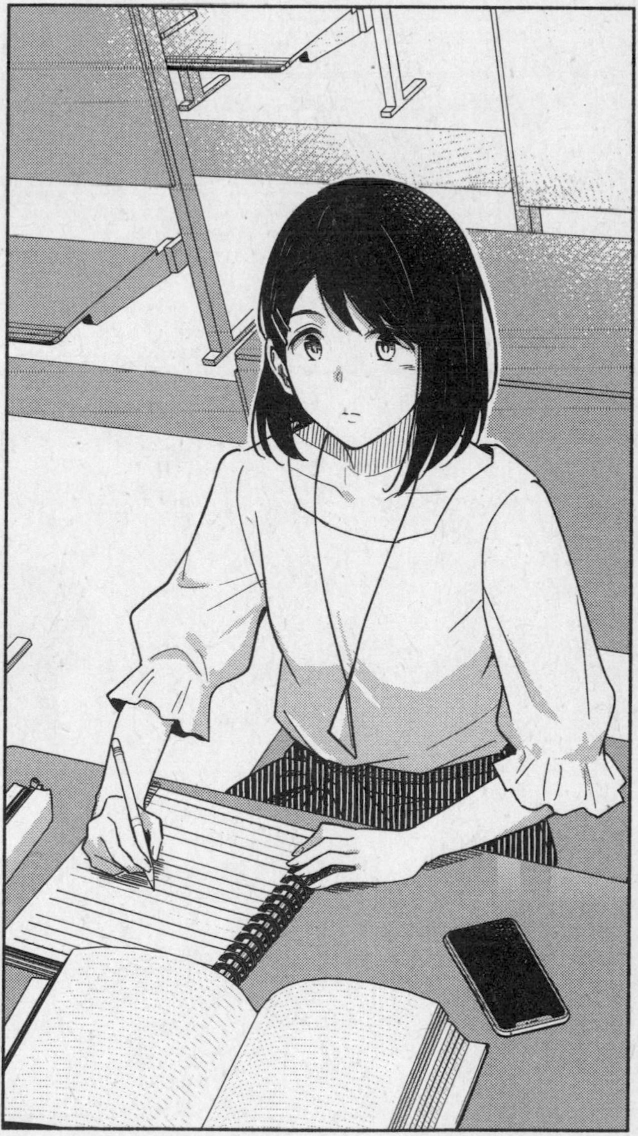

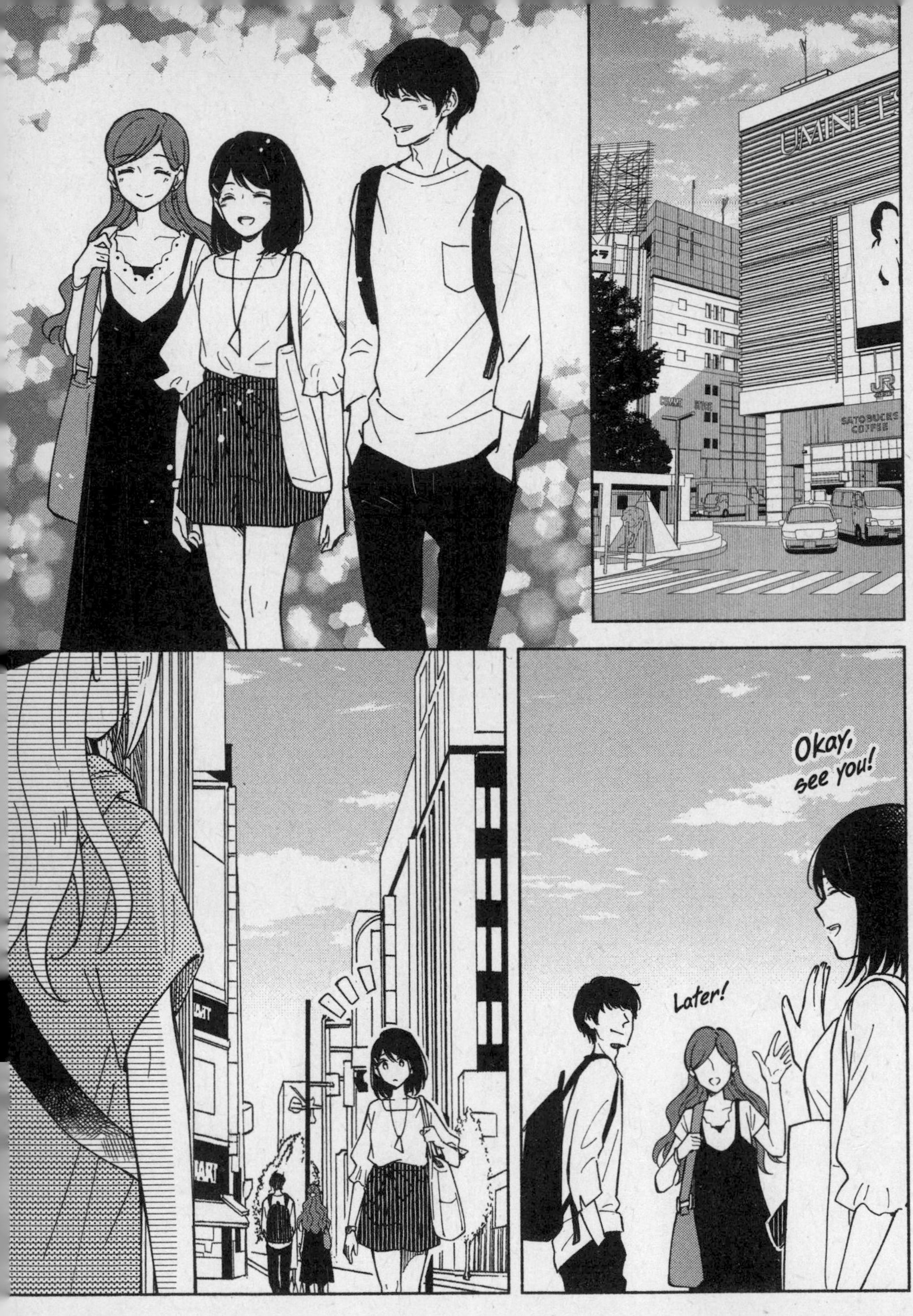
SATOBUCKS COFFEE
Okay, see you!
Later!

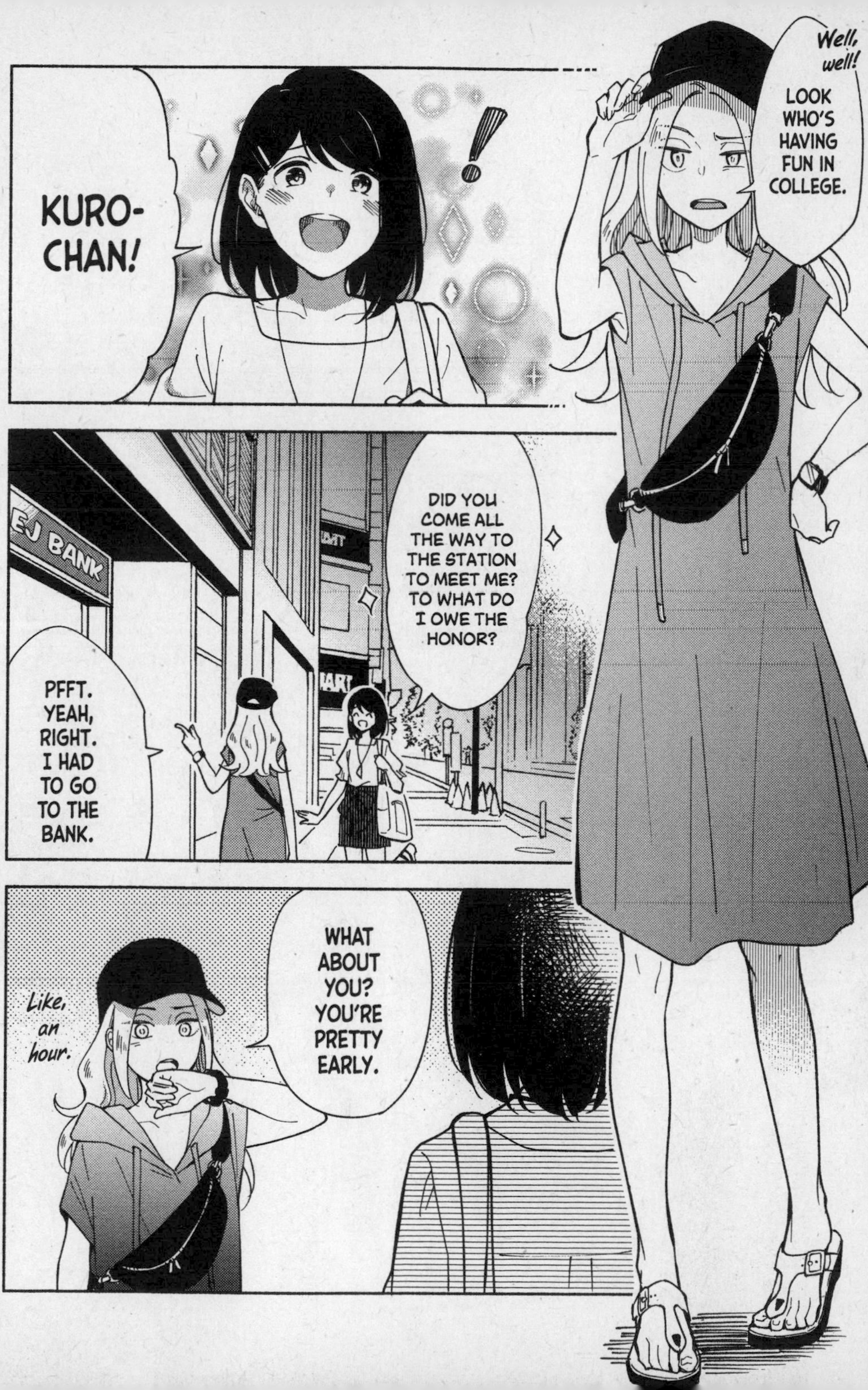
Well, well!
LOOK WHO'S HAVING FUN IN COLLEGE.
KURO-CHAN!
DID YOU COME ALL THE WAY TO THE STATION TO MEET ME? TO WHAT DO I OWE THE HONOR?
EJ BANK
PFFT. YEAH, RIGHT. I HAD TO GO TO THE BANK.
WHAT ABOUT YOU? YOU'RE PRETTY EARLY.
Like, an hour.

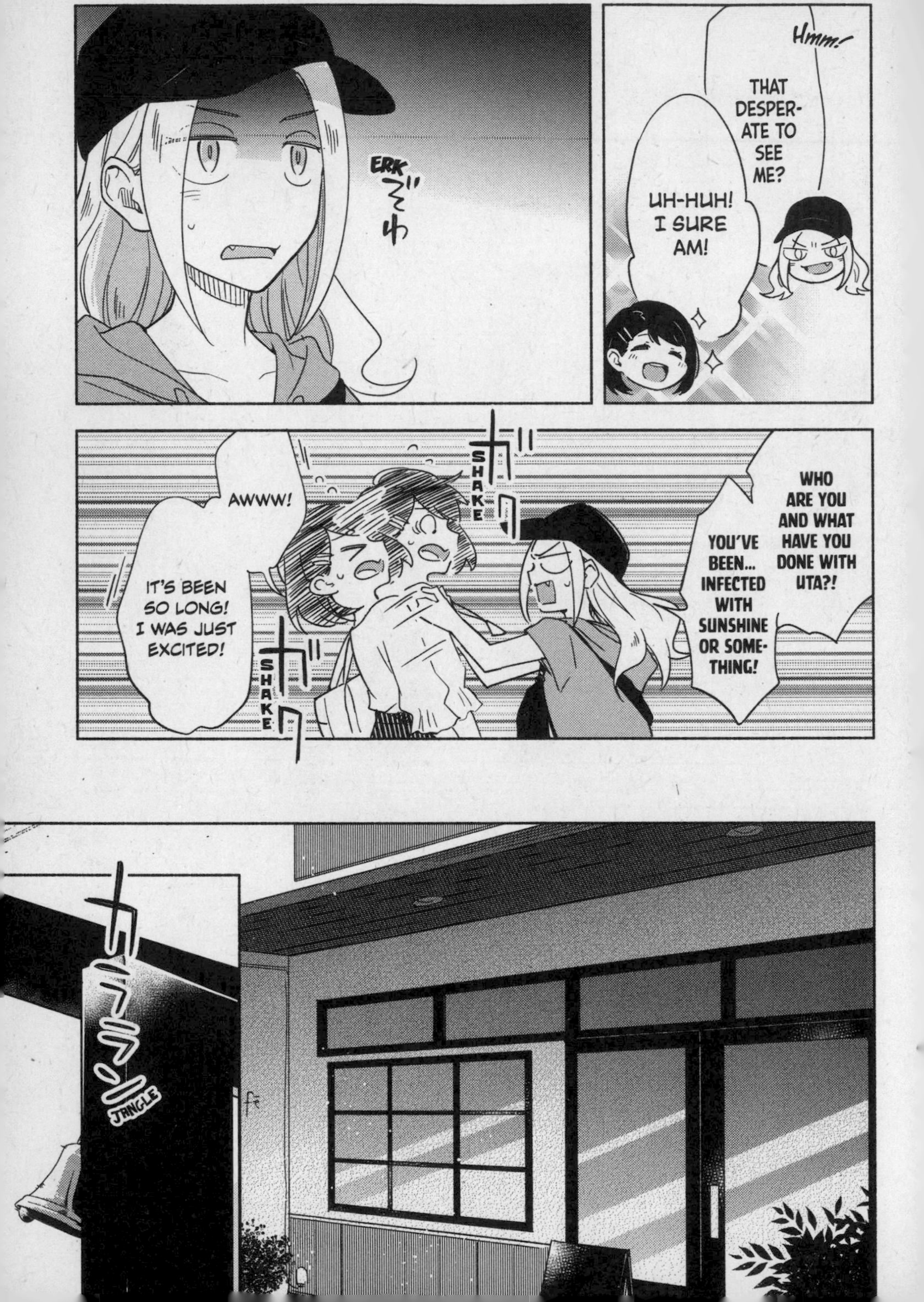
Hmm!
THAT DESPERATE TO SEE ME?
UH-HUH! I SURE AM!
ERK
WHO ARE YOU AND WHAT HAVE YOU DONE WITH UTA?!
YOU'VE BEEN... INFECTED WITH SUNSHINE OR SOMETHING!
SHAKE
AWWW!
IT'S BEEN SO LONG! I WAS JUST EXCITED!
SHAKE
JANGLE

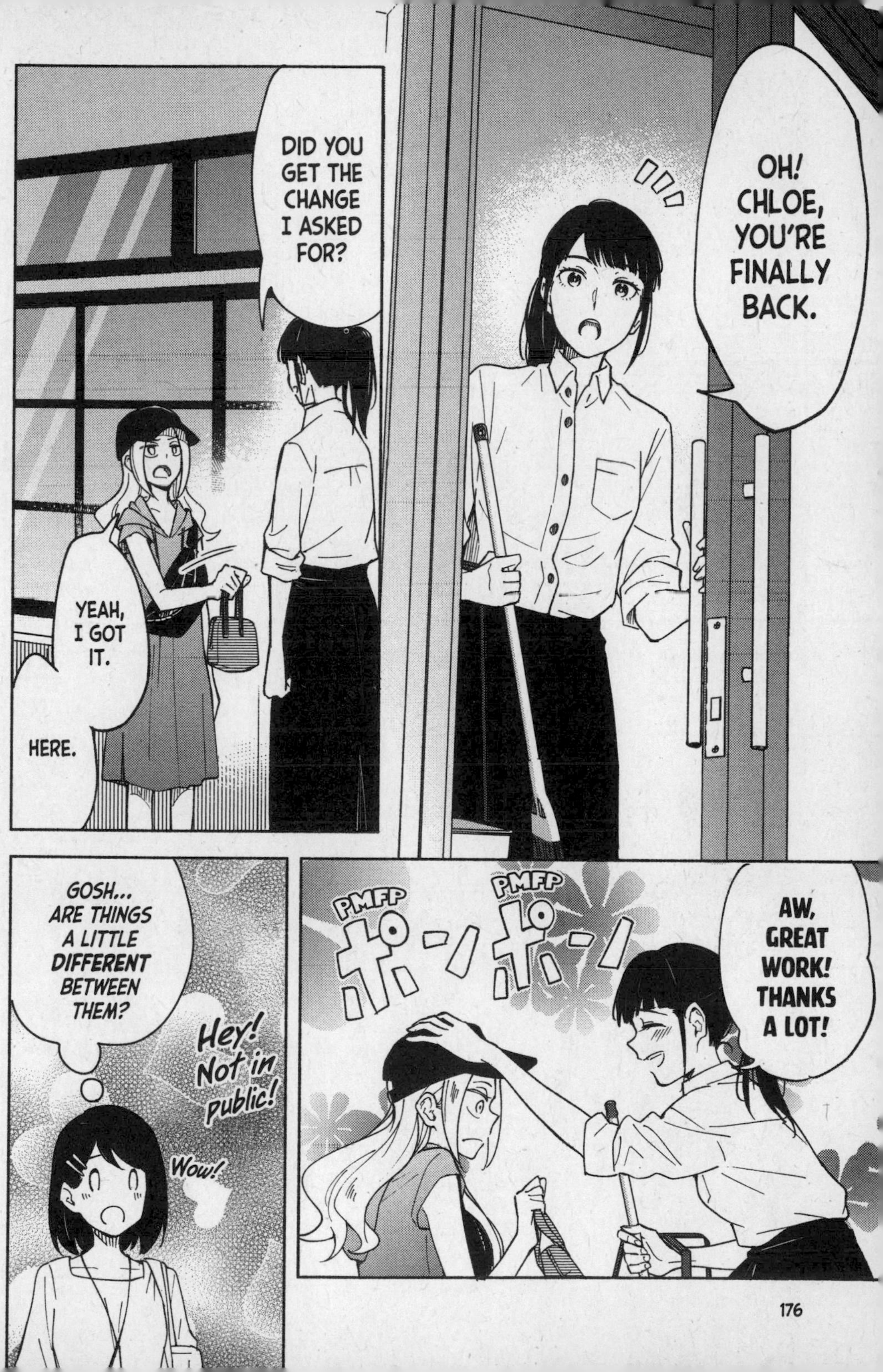

OH! CHLOE, YOU'RE FINALLY BACK.
DID YOU GET THE CHANGE I ASKED FOR?
YEAH, I GOT IT.
HERE.
AW, GREAT WORK! THANKS A LOT!
PMFP
PMFP
GOSH... ARE THINGS A LITTLE **DIFFERENT** BETWEEN THEM?
Hey! Not in public!
Wow!

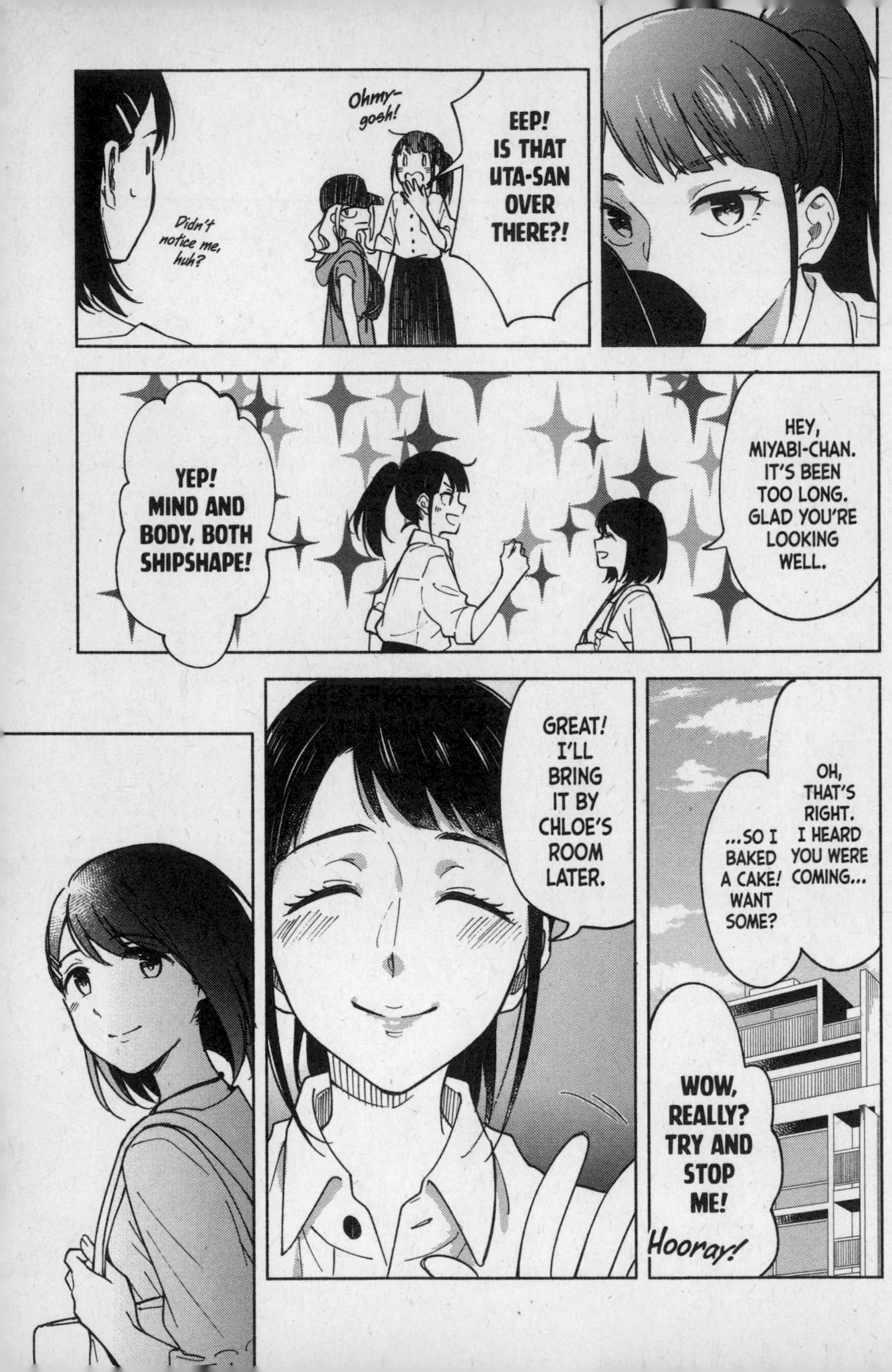
Ohmy-gosh!
EEP! IS THAT UTA-SAN OVER THERE?!
Didn't notice me, huh?
HEY, MIYABI-CHAN. IT'S BEEN TOO LONG. GLAD YOU'RE LOOKING WELL.
YEP! MIND AND BODY, BOTH SHIPSHAPE!
OH, THAT'S RIGHT. I HEARD YOU WERE COMING...
...SO I BAKED A CAKE! WANT SOME?
WOW, REALLY? TRY AND STOP ME!
Hooray!
GREAT! I'LL BRING IT BY CHLOE'S ROOM LATER.

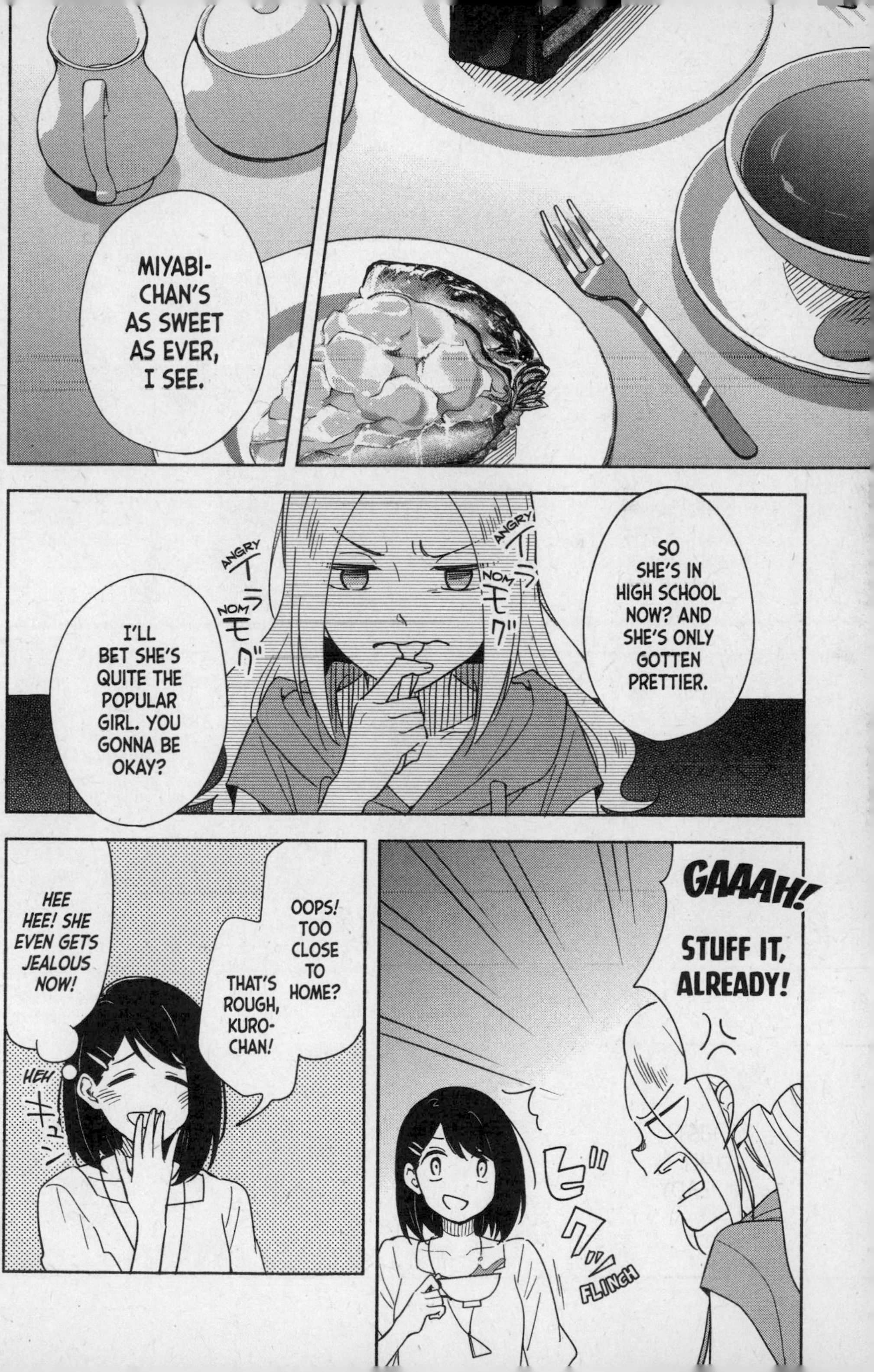
MIYABI-CHAN'S AS SWEET AS EVER, I SEE.
SO SHE'S IN HIGH SCHOOL NOW? AND SHE'S ONLY GOTTEN PRETTIER.
ANGRY
NOM
ANGRY
NOM
I'LL BET SHE'S QUITE THE POPULAR GIRL. YOU GONNA BE OKAY?
GAAAH!
STUFF IT, ALREADY!
FLINCH
OOPS! TOO CLOSE TO HOME?
THAT'S ROUGH, KURO-CHAN!
HEE HEE! SHE EVEN GETS JEALOUS NOW!
HEH

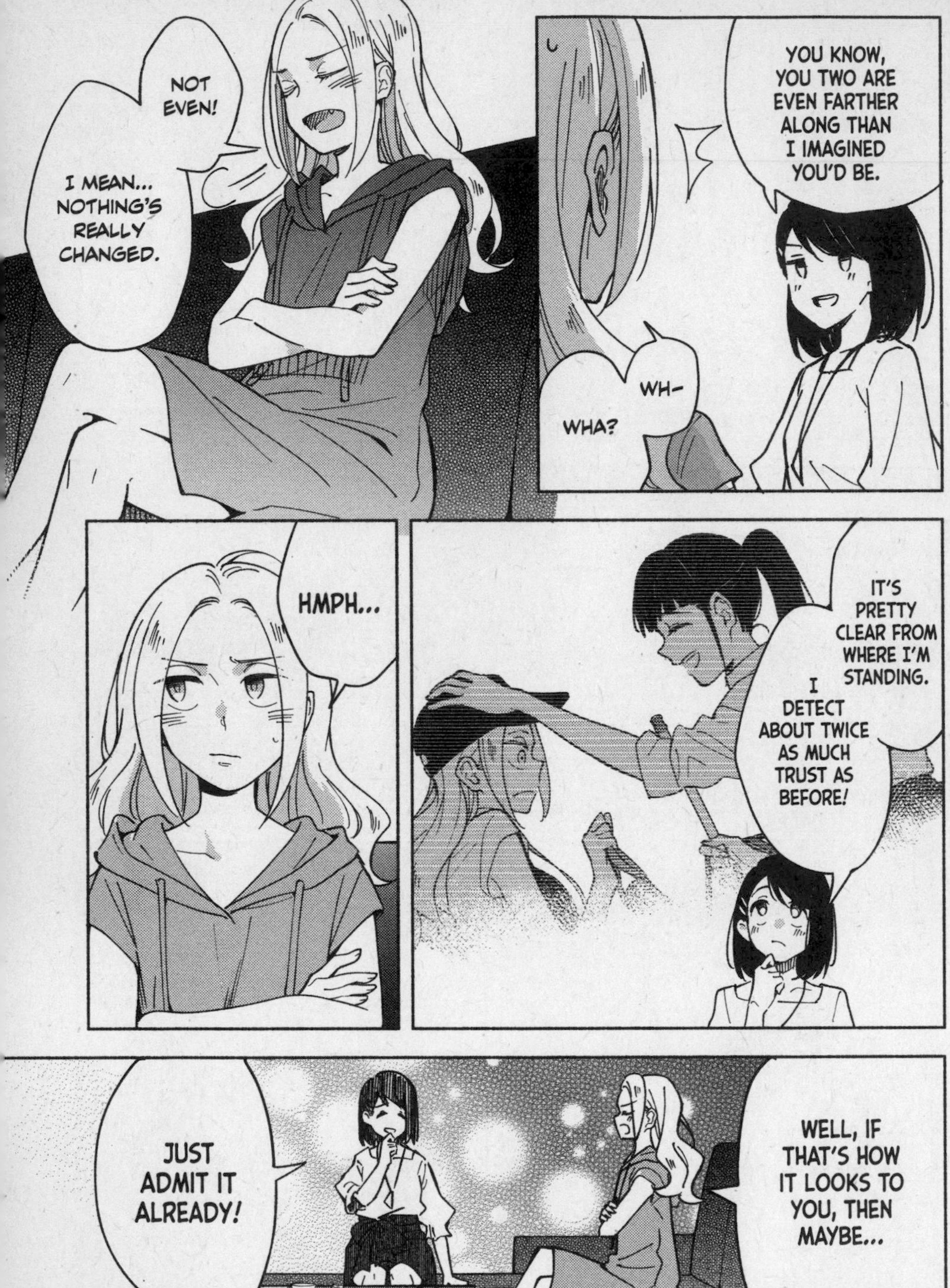
YOU KNOW, YOU TWO ARE EVEN FARTHER ALONG THAN I IMAGINED YOU'D BE.
WH- WHA?
NOT EVEN!
I MEAN... NOTHING'S REALLY CHANGED.
IT'S PRETTY CLEAR FROM WHERE I'M STANDING.
I DETECT ABOUT TWICE AS MUCH TRUST AS BEFORE!
HMPH...
WELL, IF THAT'S HOW IT LOOKS TO YOU, THEN MAYBE...
JUST ADMIT IT ALREADY!

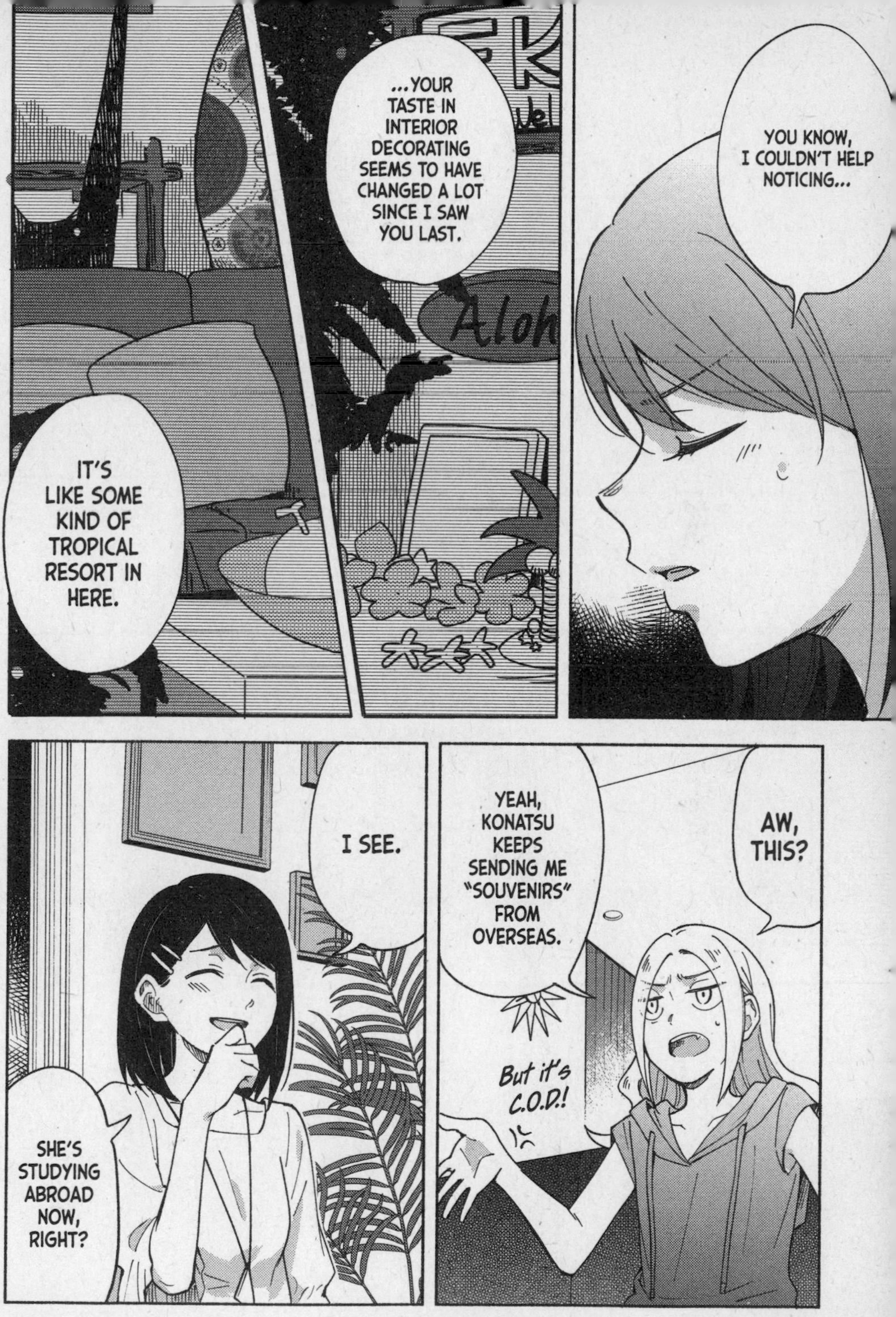
YOU KNOW, I COULDN'T HELP NOTICING...
...YOUR TASTE IN INTERIOR DECORATING SEEMS TO HAVE CHANGED A LOT SINCE I SAW YOU LAST.
Aloh
IT'S LIKE SOME KIND OF TROPICAL RESORT IN HERE.
AW, THIS?
YEAH, KONATSU KEEPS SENDING ME "SOUVENIRS" FROM OVERSEAS.
But it's C.O.D.!
I SEE.
SHE'S STUDYING ABROAD NOW, RIGHT?

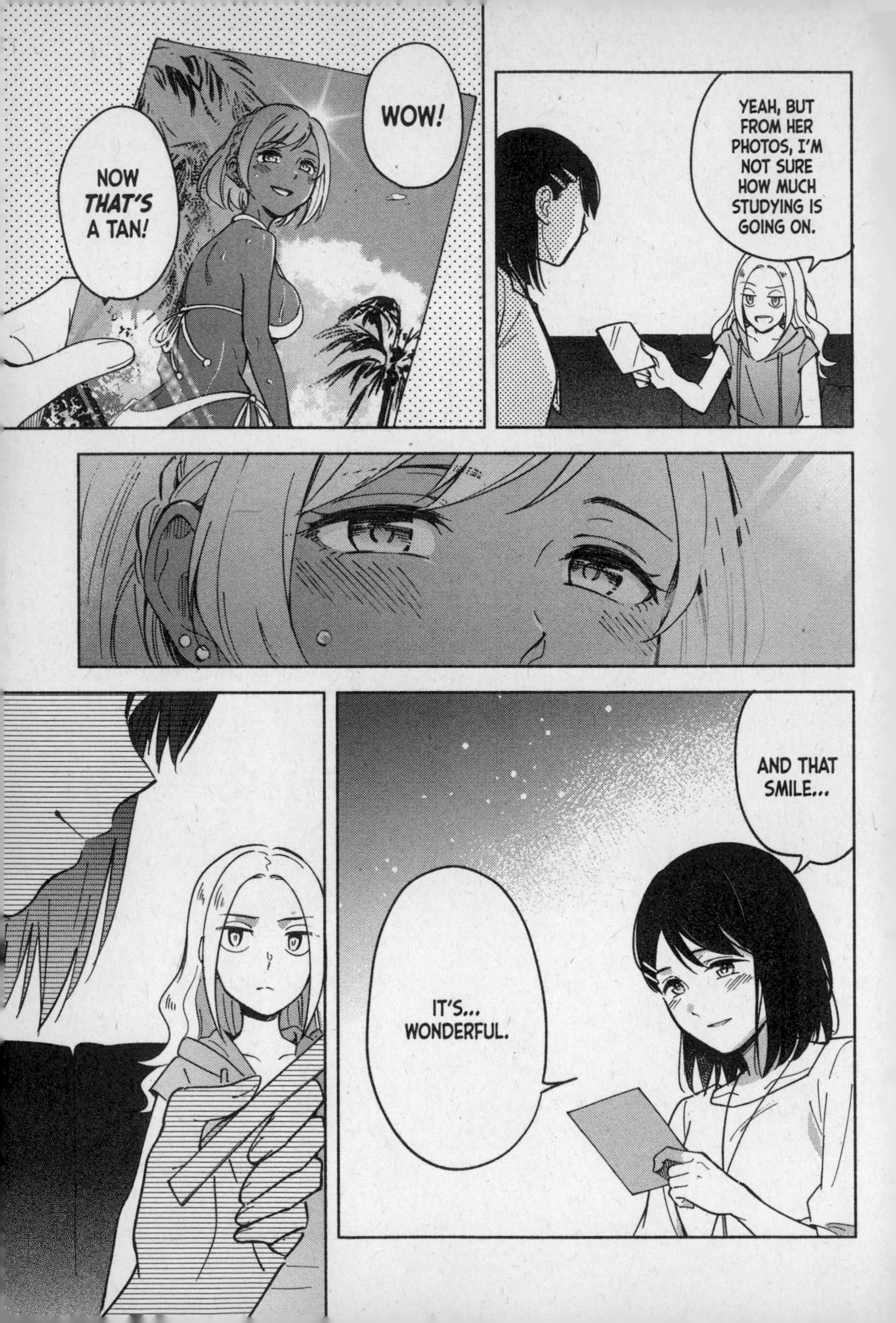
YEAH, BUT FROM HER PHOTOS, I'M NOT SURE HOW MUCH STUDYING IS GOING ON.
WOW!
NOW *THAT'S* A TAN!
AND THAT SMILE...
IT'S... WONDERFUL.

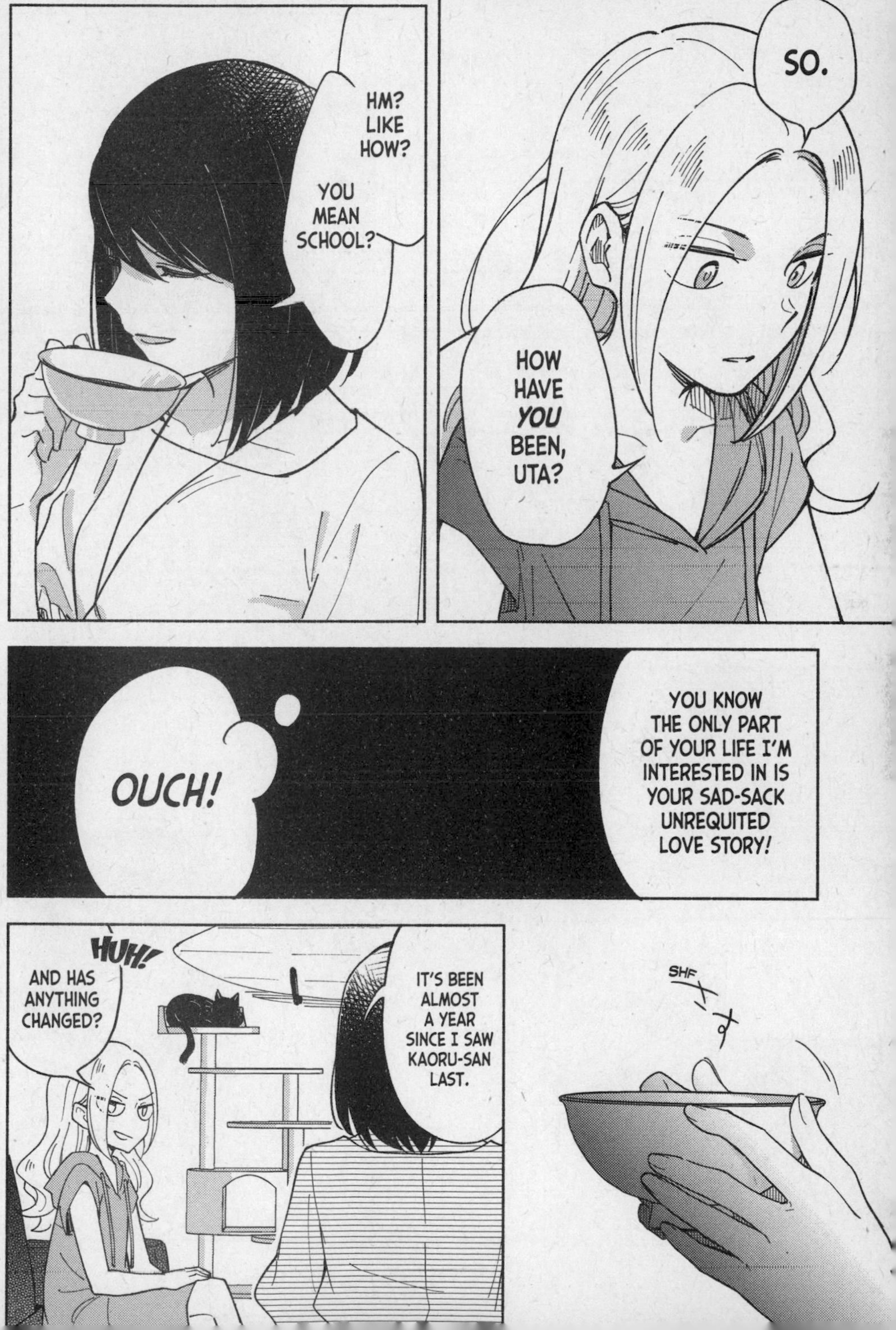
SO.
HOW HAVE *YOU* BEEN, UTA?
HM? LIKE HOW?
YOU MEAN SCHOOL?
YOU KNOW THE ONLY PART OF YOUR LIFE I'M INTERESTED IN IS YOUR SAD-SACK UNREQUITED LOVE STORY!
OUCH!
SHF
IT'S BEEN ALMOST A YEAR SINCE I SAW KAORU-SAN LAST.
HUH!
AND HAS ANYTHING CHANGED?

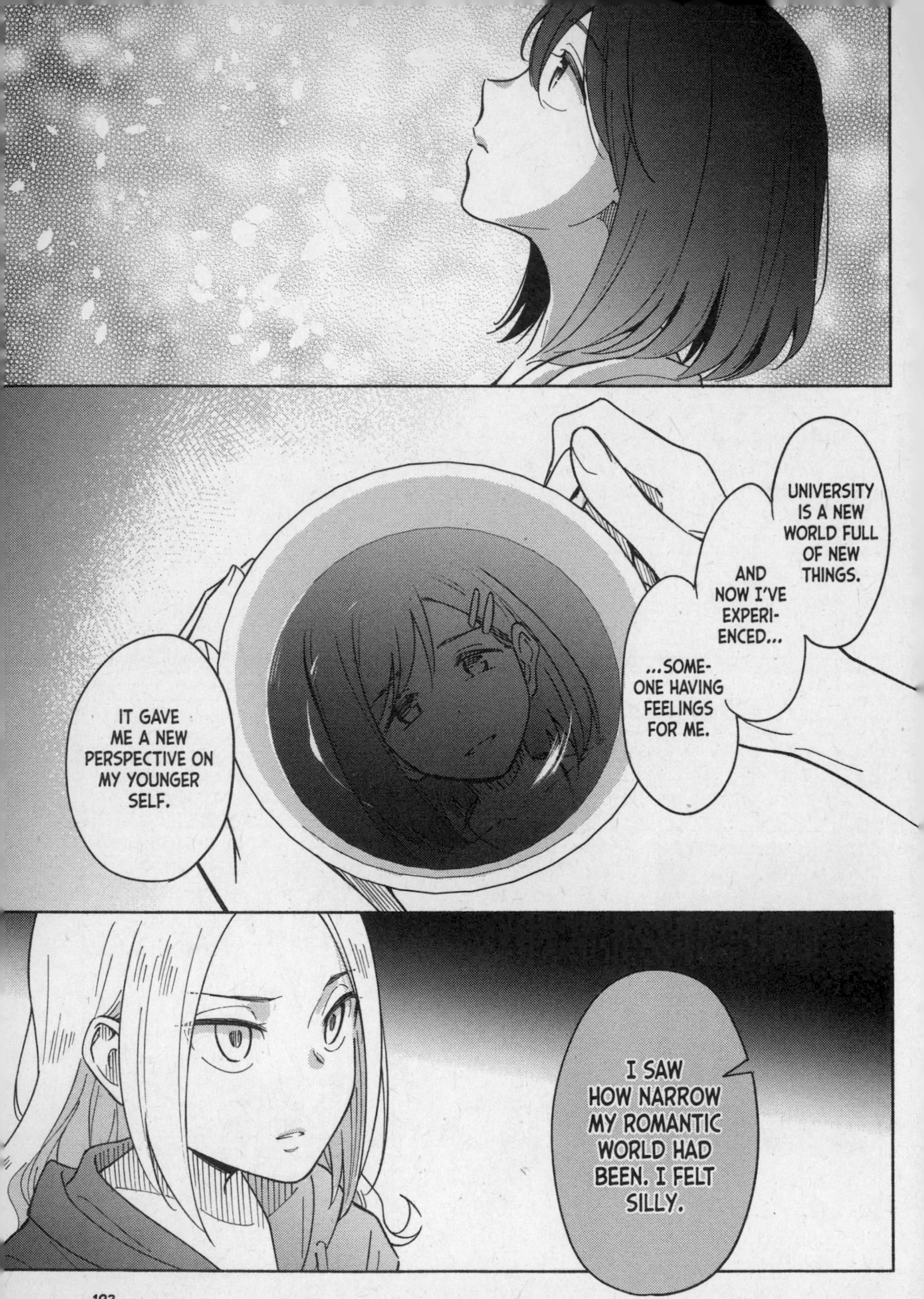
UNIVERSITY IS A NEW WORLD FULL OF NEW THINGS.
AND NOW I'VE EXPERIENCED...
...SOMEONE HAVING FEELINGS FOR ME.
IT GAVE ME A NEW PERSPECTIVE ON MY YOUNGER SELF.
I SAW HOW NARROW MY ROMANTIC WORLD HAD BEEN. I FELT SILLY.

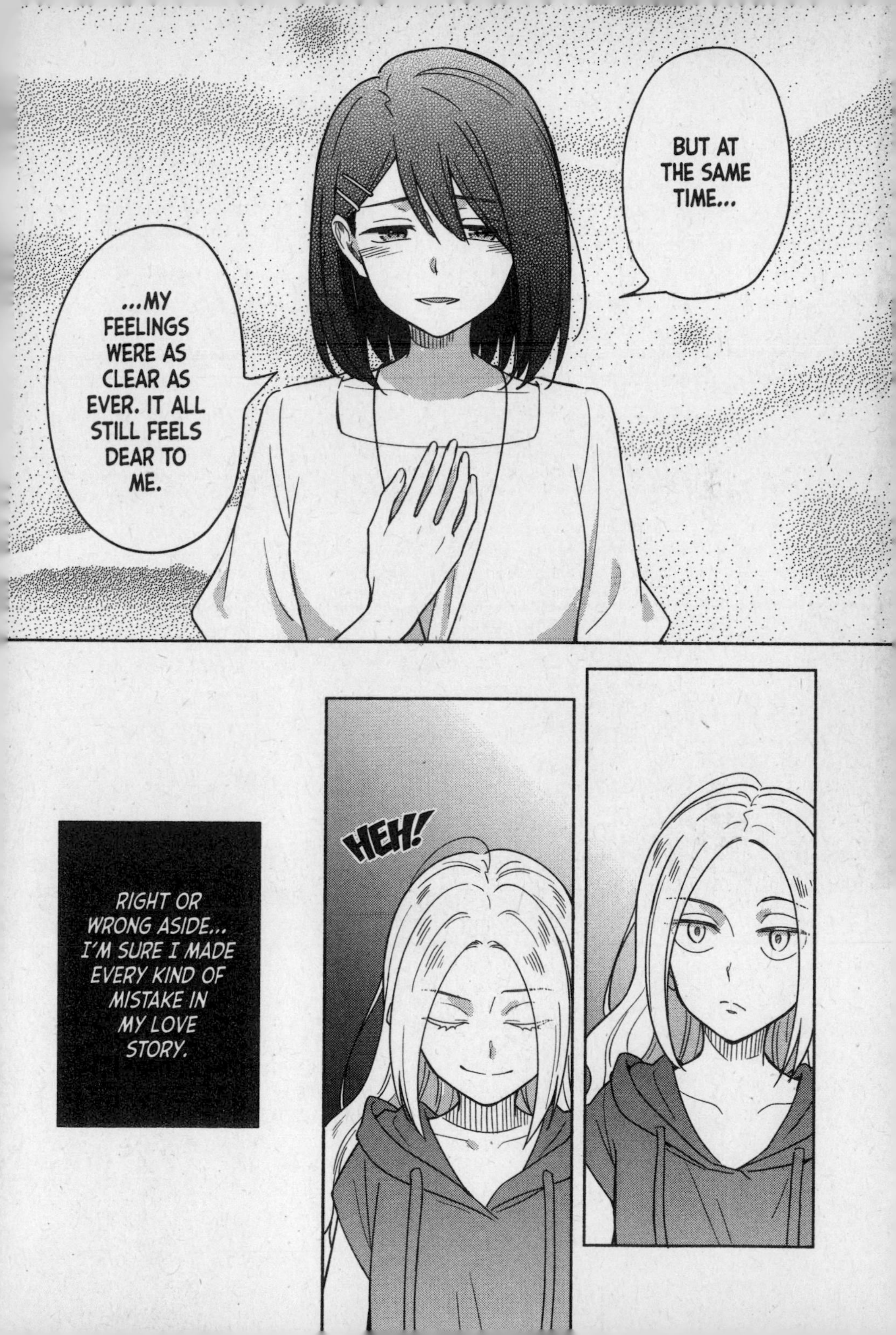
BUT AT THE SAME TIME...
...MY FEELINGS WERE AS CLEAR AS EVER. IT ALL STILL FEELS DEAR TO ME.
HEH!
RIGHT OR WRONG ASIDE... I'M SURE I MADE EVERY KIND OF MISTAKE IN MY LOVE STORY.

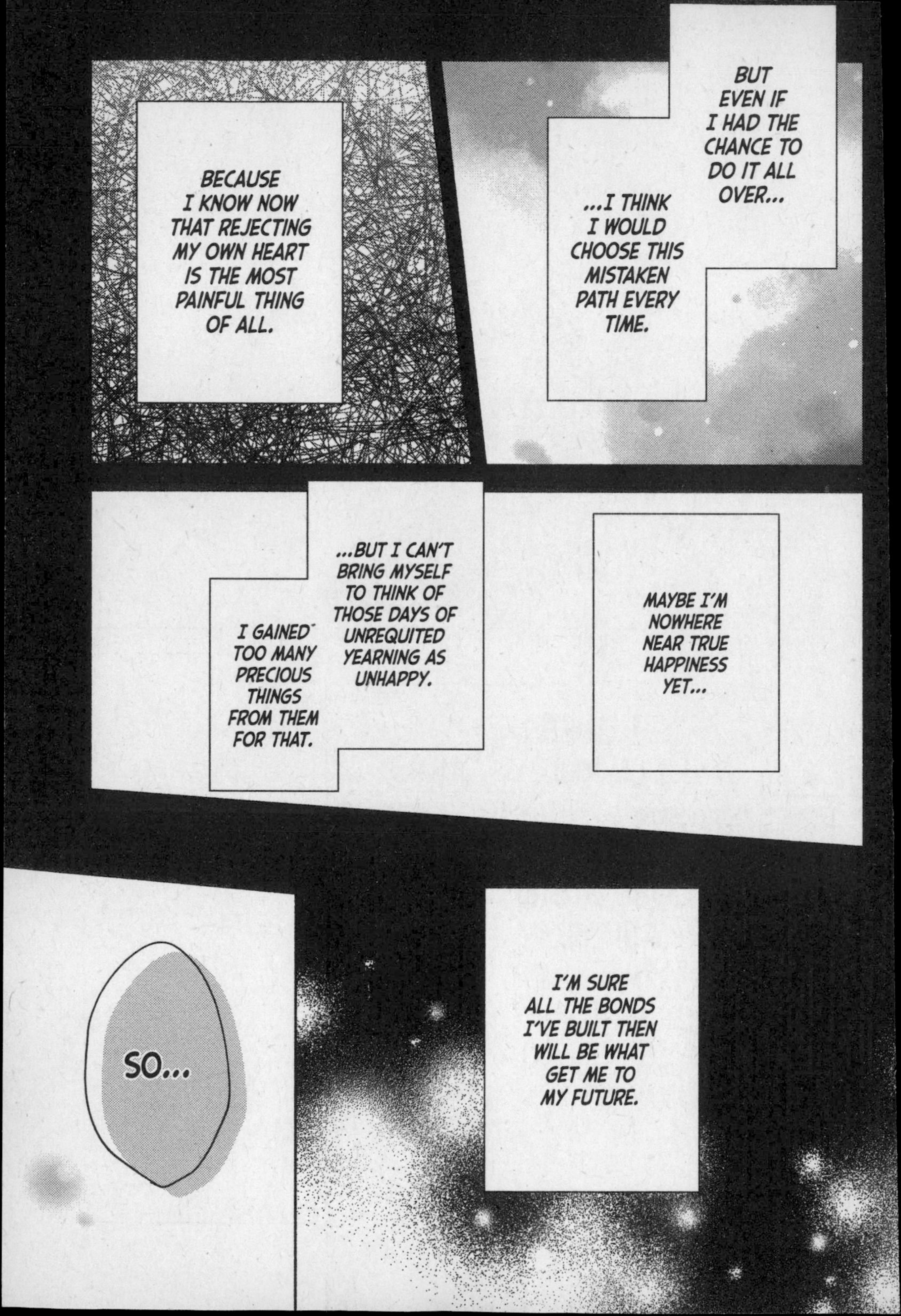
BUT EVEN IF I HAD THE CHANCE TO DO IT ALL OVER...
...I THINK I WOULD CHOOSE THIS MISTAKEN PATH EVERY TIME.
BECAUSE I KNOW NOW THAT REJECTING MY OWN HEART IS THE MOST PAINFUL THING OF ALL.
MAYBE I'M NOWHERE NEAR TRUE HAPPINESS YET...
...BUT I CAN'T BRING MYSELF TO THINK OF THOSE DAYS OF UNREQUITED YEARNING AS UNHAPPY.
I GAINED TOO MANY PRECIOUS THINGS FROM THEM FOR THAT.
I'M SURE ALL THE BONDS I'VE BUILT THEN WILL BE WHAT GET ME TO MY FUTURE.
SO...

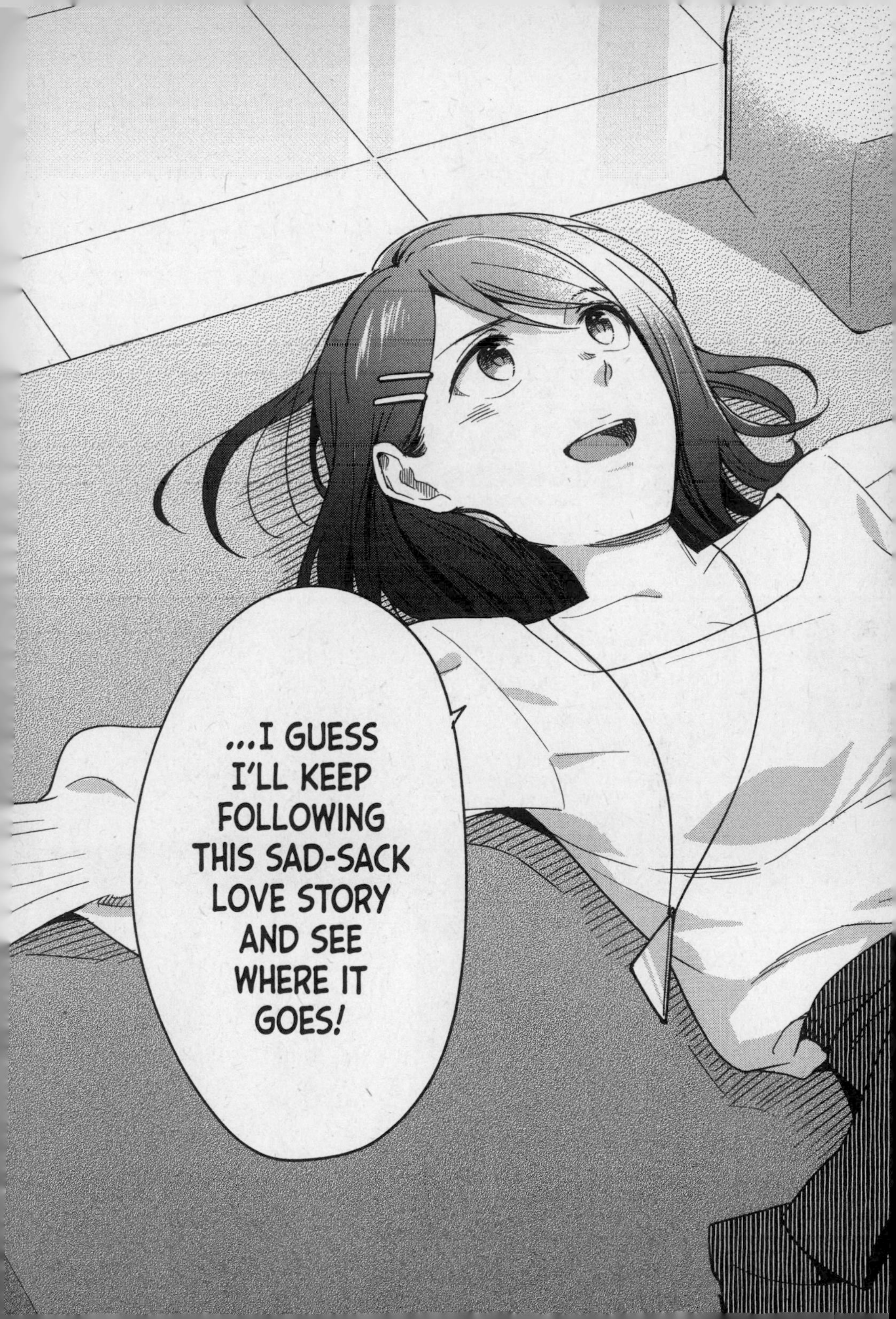
...I GUESS I'LL KEEP FOLLOWING THIS SAD-SACK LOVE STORY AND SEE WHERE IT GOES!

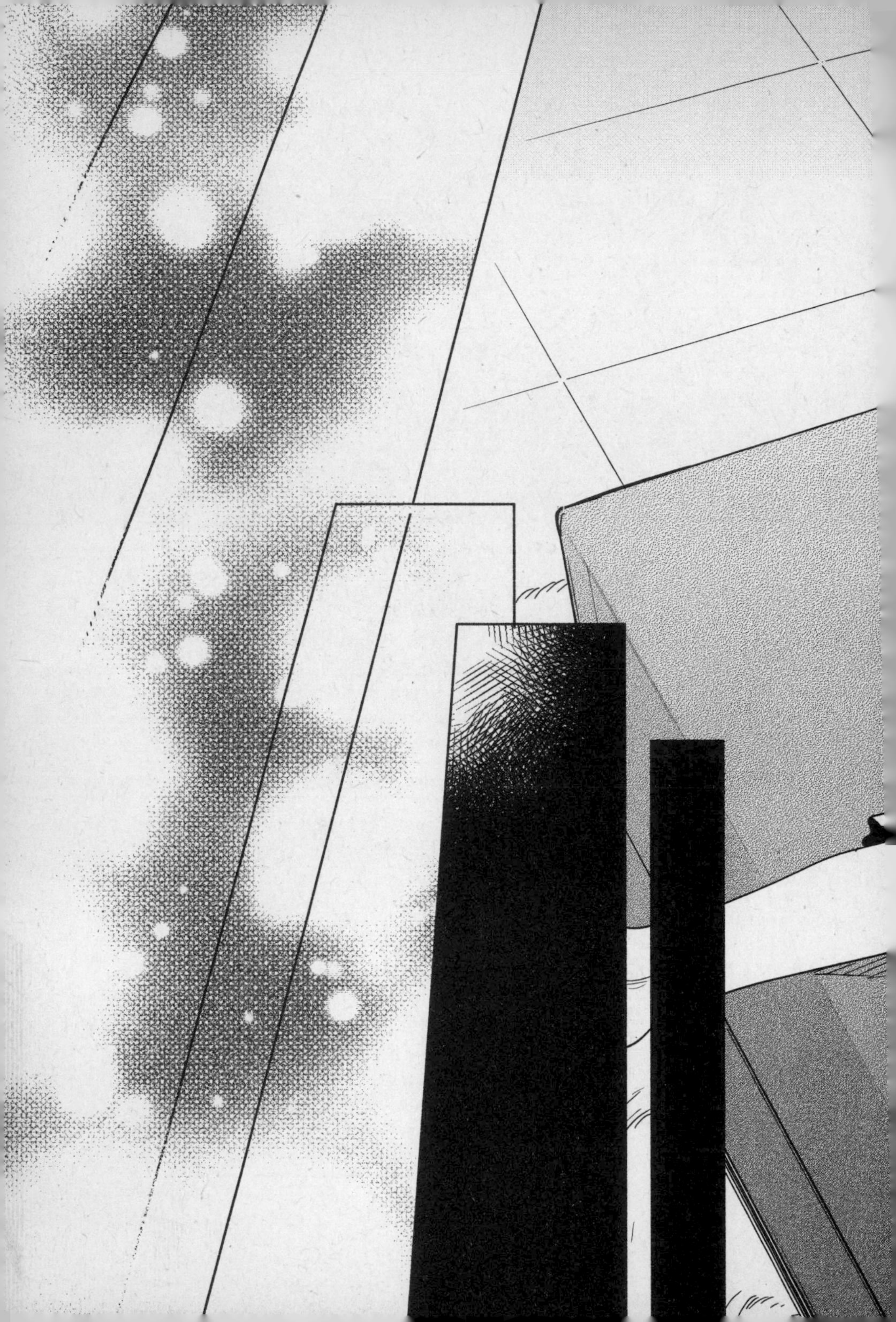

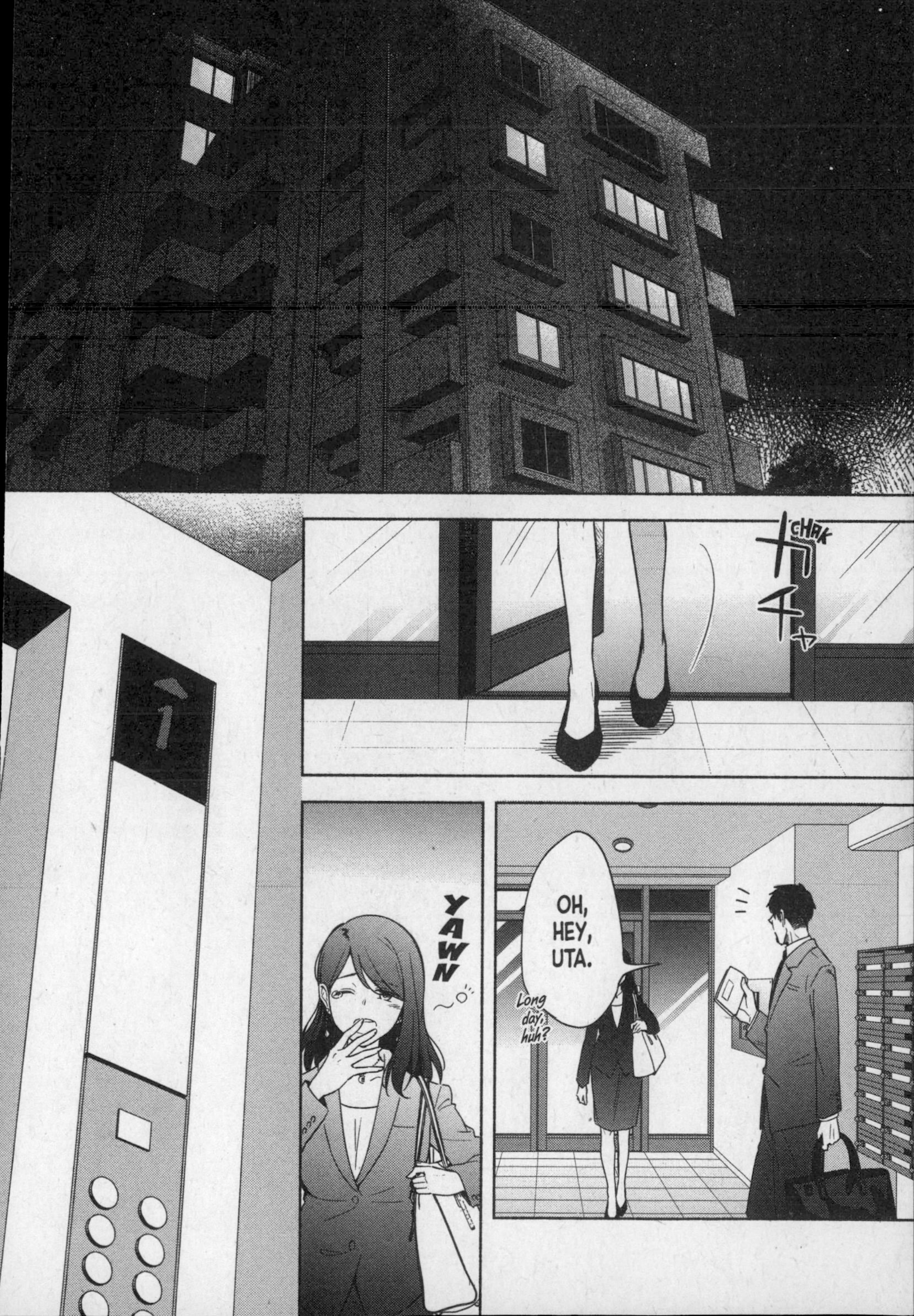
カチャ
CHAK
OH, HEY, UTA.
Long day, huh?
YAWN

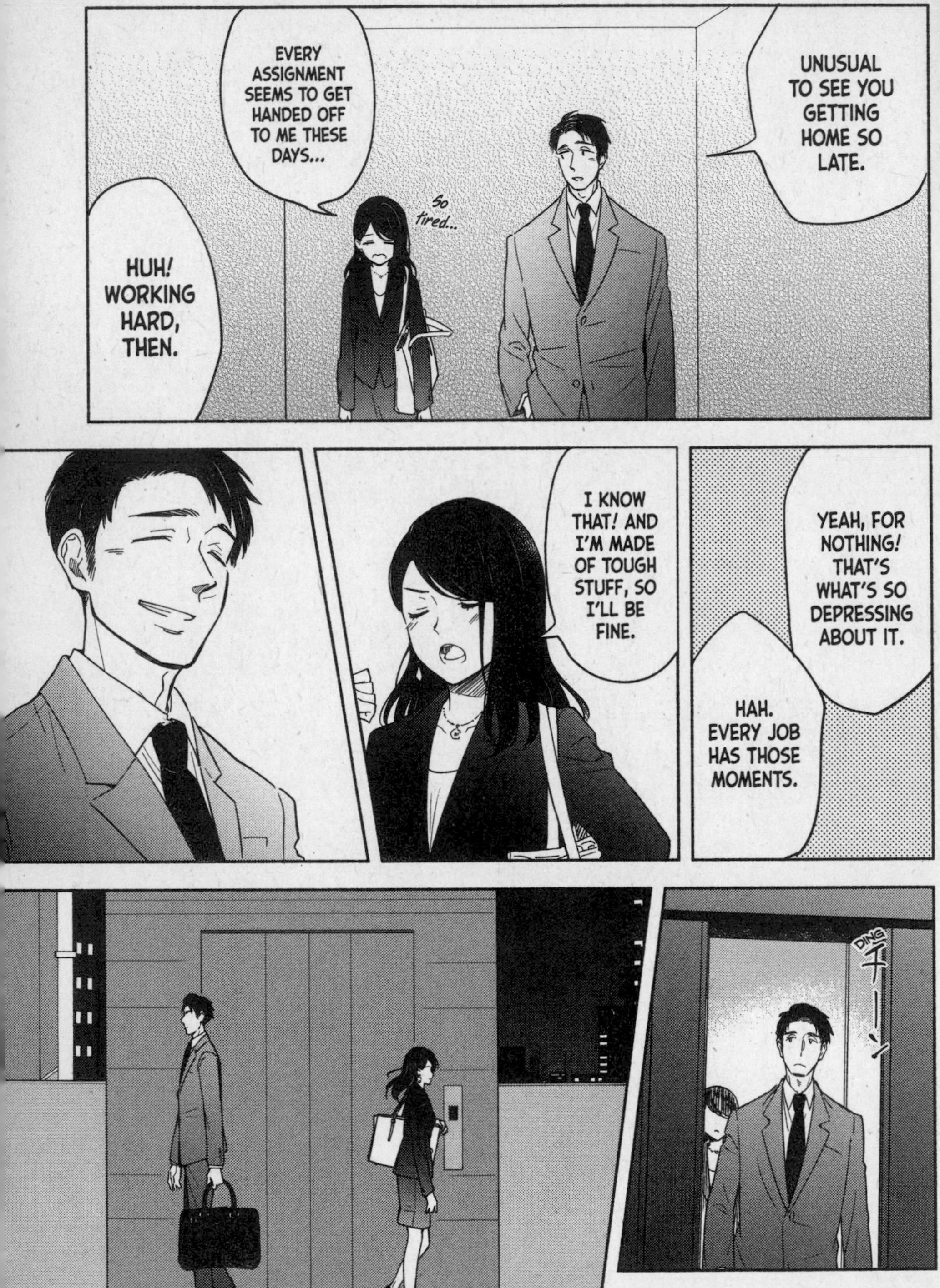
UNUSUAL TO SEE YOU GETTING HOME SO LATE.
EVERY ASSIGNMENT SEEMS TO GET HANDED OFF TO ME THESE DAYS...
So tired...
HUH! WORKING HARD, THEN.
YEAH, FOR NOTHING! THAT'S WHAT'S SO DEPRESSING ABOUT IT.
HAH. EVERY JOB HAS THOSE MOMENTS.
I KNOW THAT! AND I'M MADE OF TOUGH STUFF, SO I'LL BE FINE.
DING

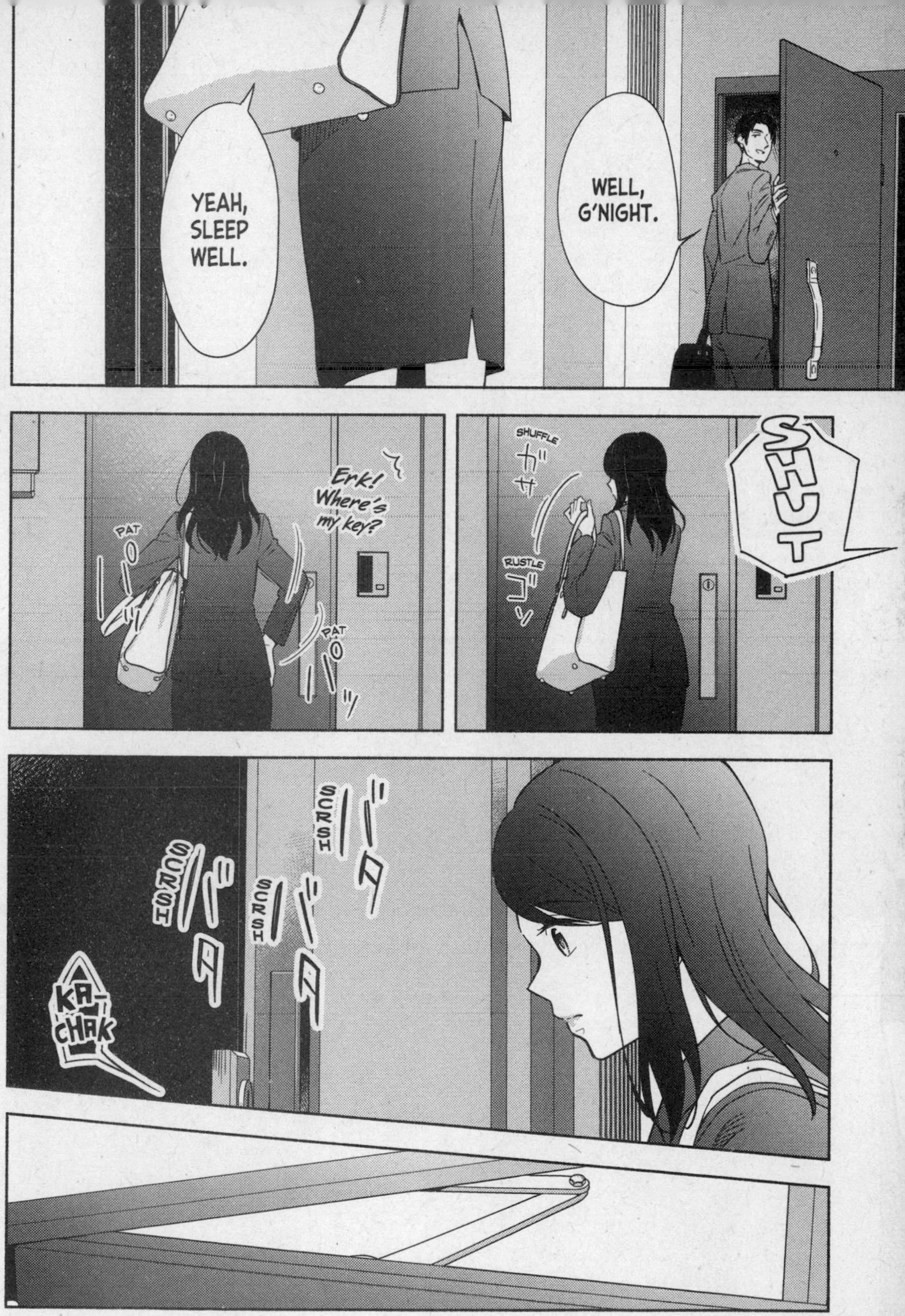
WELL, G'NIGHT.
YEAH, SLEEP WELL.
SHUT
SHUFFLE
RUSTLE
Erk! Where's my key?
PAT
PAT
SCRSH
SCRSH
SCRSH
KA-CHAK

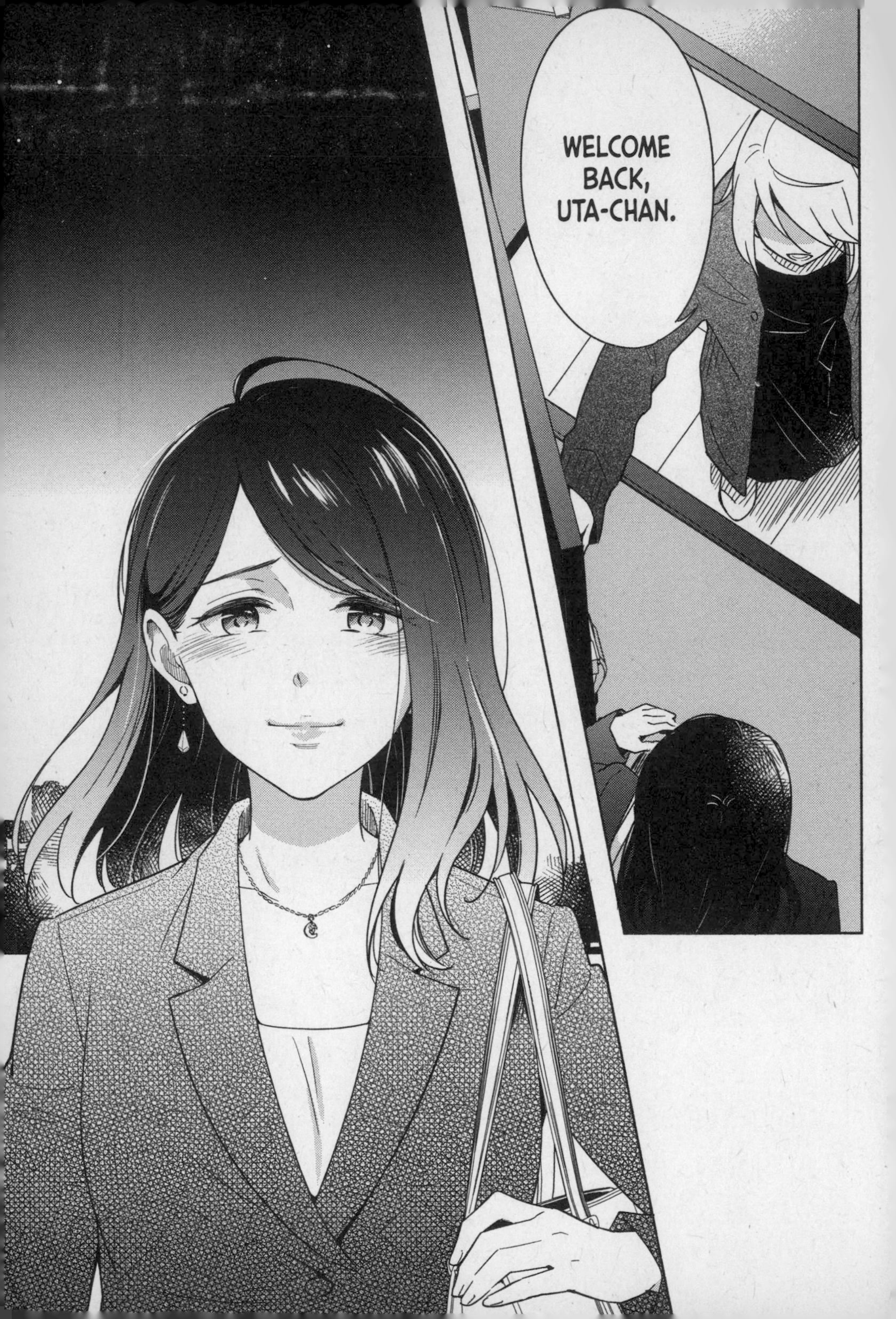
WELCOME BACK, UTA-CHAN.

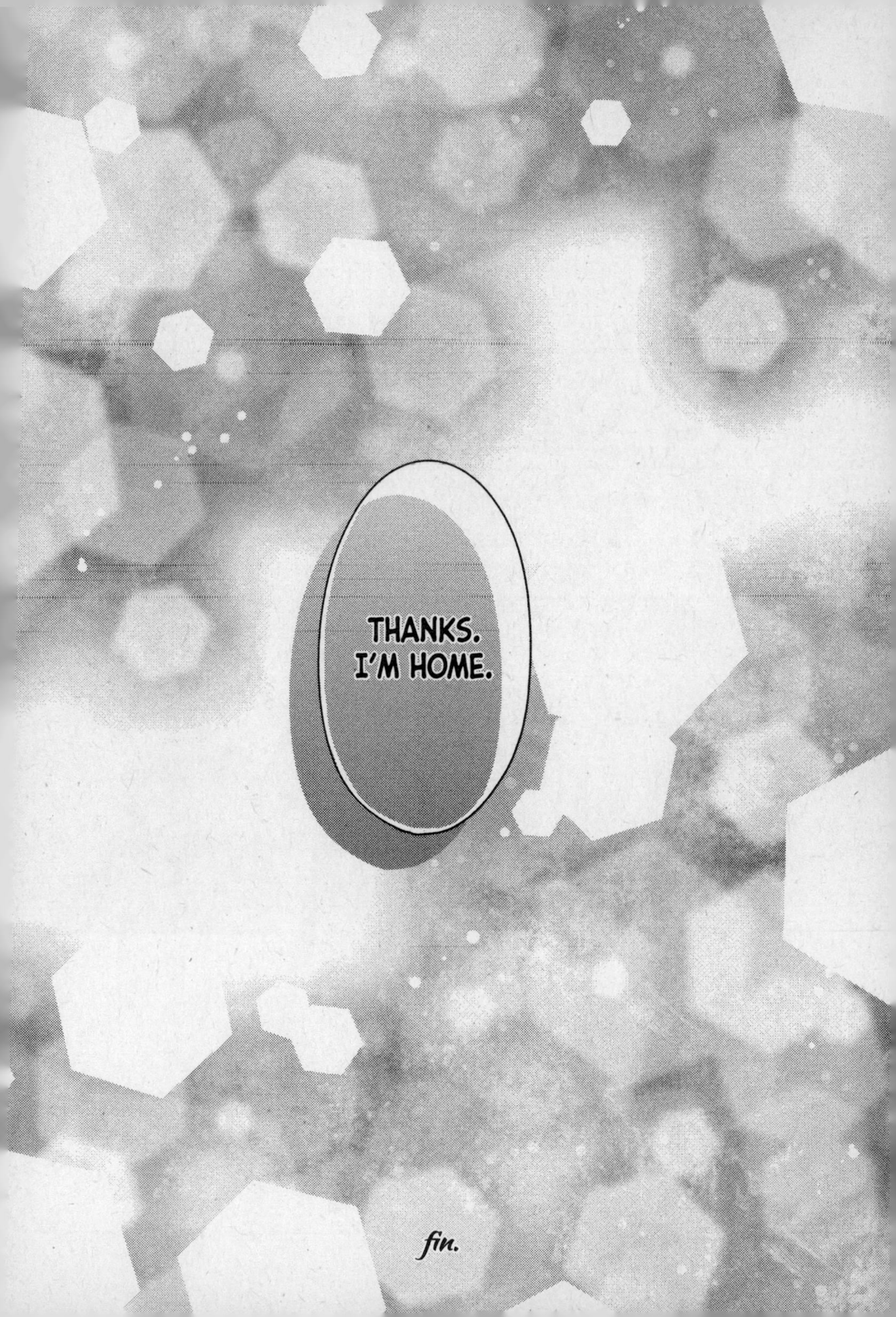
THANKS. I'M HOME.
fin.

If I Could
Reach You

Afterword

tMnR

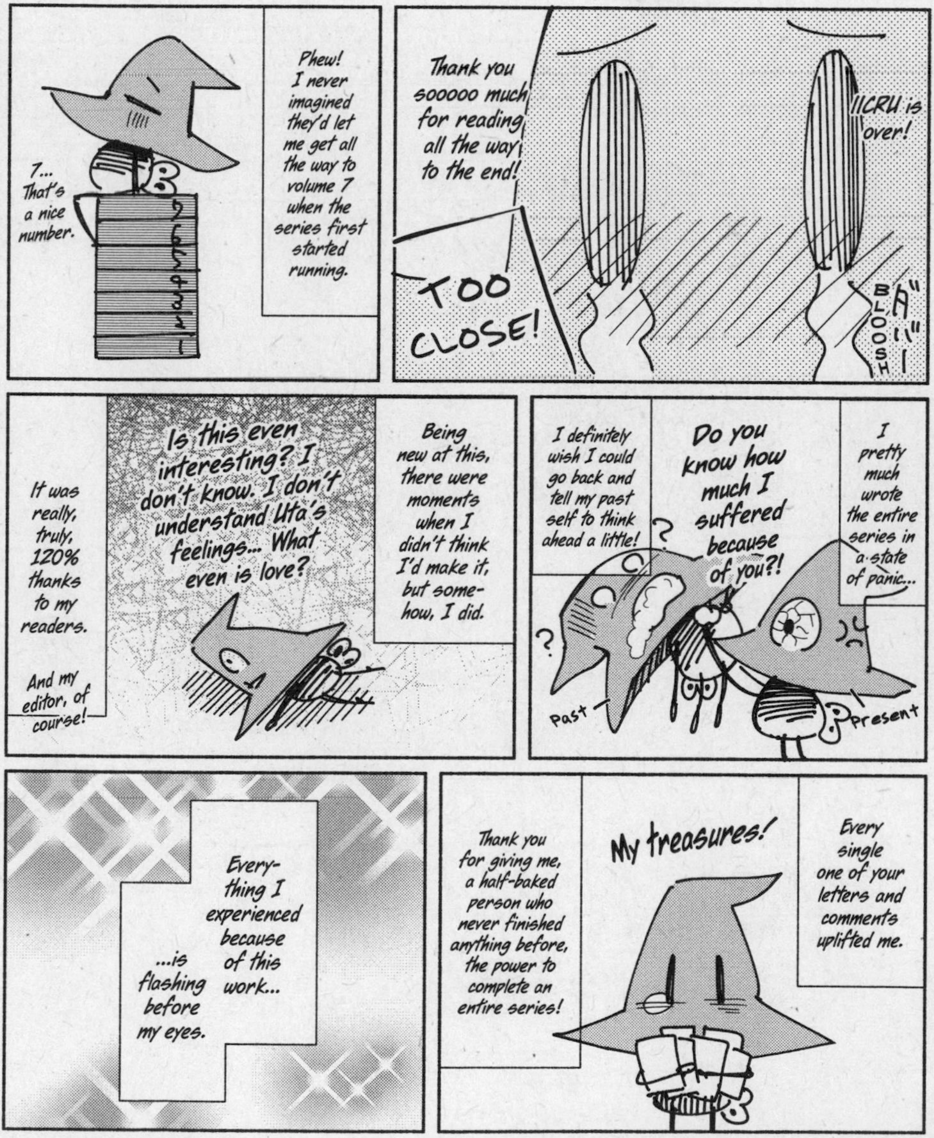

Thank you sooooo much for reading all the way to the end!
IICRU is over!
BLOOSH
TOO CLOSE!
Phew! I never imagined they'd let me get all the way to volume 7 when the series first started running.
7... That's a nice number.
I pretty much wrote the entire series in a state of panic...
Do you know how much I suffered because of you?!
I definitely wish I could go back and tell my past self to think ahead a little!
Past
Present
Being new at this, there were moments when I didn't think I'd make it, but somehow, I did.
Is this even interesting? I don't know. I don't understand Uta's feelings... What even is love?
It was really, truly, 120% thanks to my readers.
And my editor, of course!
Every single one of your letters and comments uplifted me.
My treasures!
Thank you for giving me, a half-baked person who never finished anything before, the power to complete an entire series!
Everything I experienced because of this work...
...is flashing before my eyes.

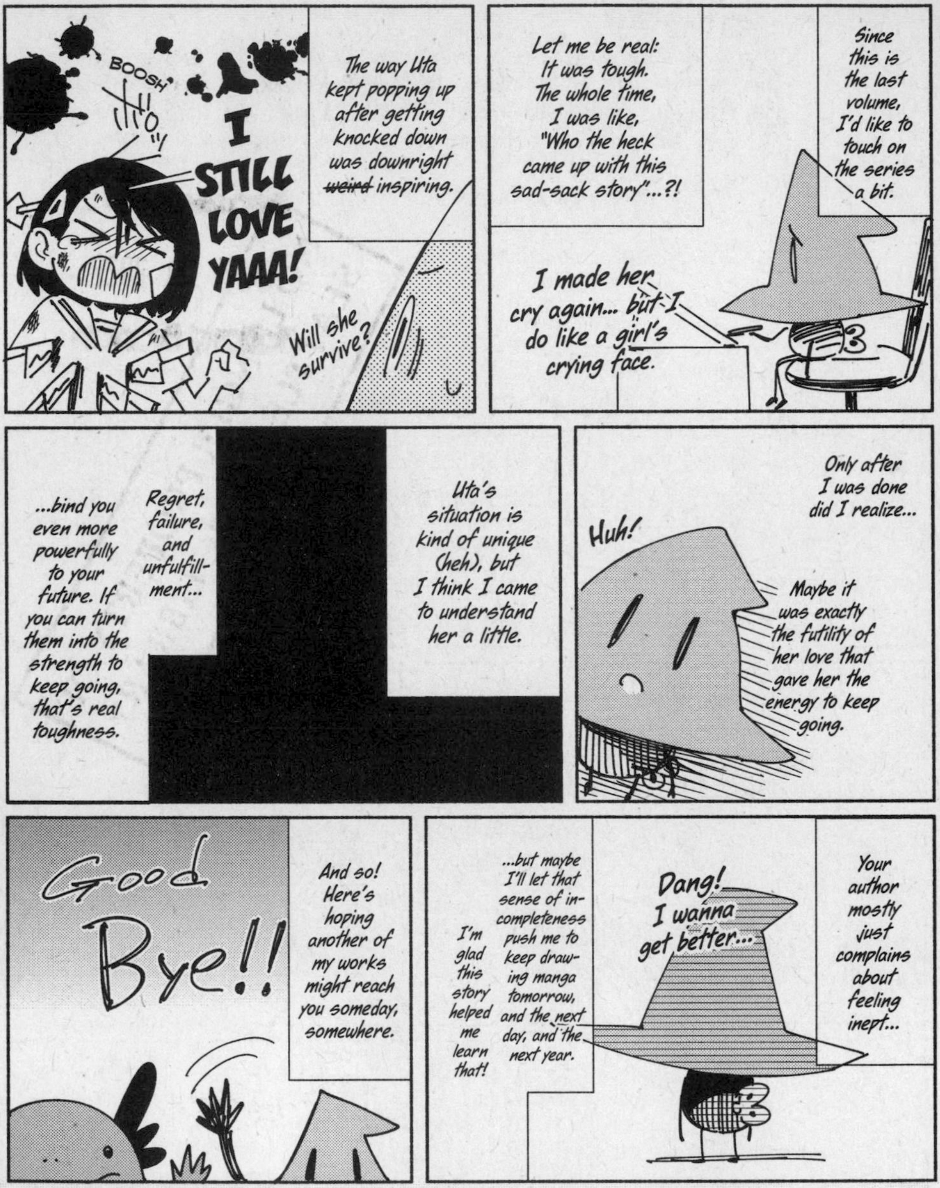
Since this is the last volume, I'd like to touch on the series a bit.
Let me be real: It was tough. The whole time, I was like, "Who the heck came up with this sad-sack story"...?!
I made her cry again... but I do like a girl's crying face.
The way Uta kept popping up after getting knocked down was downright ~~weird~~ inspiring.
BOOSH
I STILL LOVE YAAA!
Will she survive?
Only after I was done did I realize...
Huh!
Maybe it was exactly the futility of her love that gave her the energy to keep going.
Uta's situation is kind of unique (heh), but I think I came to understand her a little.
Regret, failure, and unfulfillment...
...bind you even more powerfully to your future. If you can turn them into the strength to keep going, that's real toughness.
Your author mostly just complains about feeling inept...
Dang! I wanna get better...
...but maybe I'll let that sense of incompleteness push me to keep drawing manga tomorrow, and the next day, and the next year.
I'm glad this story helped me learn that!
And so! Here's hoping another of my works might reach you someday, somewhere.
Good Bye!!

Special Thanks

Acha
Upa's

Designer-sama
My editor, Saito-san
Everyone involved with IICRU
and My Dear Readers!

If I Could Reach You 7 is a work of fiction. Names, characters, places, and incidents are the products of the author's imagination or are used fictitiously. Any resemblance to actual events, locales, or persons, living or dead, is entirely coincidental.

Published in the United States by Kodansha Comics, an imprint of
Kodansha USA Publishing, LLC, New York.

Publication rights for this English edition arranged through
Kodansha Ltd., Tokyo.

First published in Japan in 2021 by Ichijinsha, Inc., in Tokyo
as *Tatoe Todokanu Itodatoshitemo*, volume 7.

ISBN 978-1-64651-275-1

Printed in the United States of America.

www.kodansha.us

1st Printing
Translation: Kevin Steinbach
Lettering: Jennifer Skarupa
Editing: Haruko Hashimoto
Kodansha Comics edition cover design by Phil Balsman

Publisher: Kiichiro Sugawara

Director of publishing services: Ben Applegate
Director of publishing operations: Dave Barrett
Associate director, publishing operations: Stephen Pakula
Publishing services managing editors: Madison Salters, Alanna Ruse
Production managers: Emi Lotto, Angela Zurlo